Human–Computer Interaction Series

Editors-in-Chief

Desney Tan
Microsoft Research, Redmond, WA, USA

Jean Vanderdonckt
Louvain School of Management, Université catholique de Louvain,
Louvain-La-Neuve, Belgium

The Human–Computer Interaction Series, launched in 2004, publishes books that advance the science and technology of developing systems which are effective and satisfying for people in a wide variety of contexts. Titles focus on theoretical perspectives (such as formal approaches drawn from a variety of behavioural sciences), practical approaches (such as techniques for effectively integrating user needs in system development), and social issues (such as the determinants of utility, usability and acceptability).

HCI is a multidisciplinary field and focuses on the human aspects in the development of computer technology. As technology becomes increasingly more pervasive the need to take a human-centred approach in the design and development of computer-based systems becomes ever more important.

Titles published within the Human–Computer Interaction Series are included in Thomson Reuters' Book Citation Index, The DBLP Computer Science Bibliography and The HCI Bibliography.

More information about this series at http://www.springer.com/series/6033

Nadia Magnenat Thalmann · Jian Jun Zhang ·
Manoj Ramanathan · Daniel Thalmann
Editors

Intelligent Scene Modeling and Human-Computer Interaction

 Springer

Editors
Nadia Magnenat Thalmann 🆔
Institute for Media Innovation
Nanyang Technological University
Singapore, Singapore

Manoj Ramanathan
Institute for Media Innovation
Nanyang Technological University
Singapore, Singapore

Jian Jun Zhang
Bournemouth University
Poole, UK

Daniel Thalmann
School of Computer and Communication
Sciences
École Polytechnique Fédérale de Lausa
Lausanne, Switzerland

ISSN 1571-5035   ISSN 2524-4477 (electronic)
Human–Computer Interaction Series
ISBN 978-3-030-71004-0   ISBN 978-3-030-71002-6   (eBook)
https://doi.org/10.1007/978-3-030-71002-6

This Springer imprint is published by the registered company Springer Nature Switzerland AG
The registered company address is: Gewerbestrasse 11, 6330 Cham, Switzerland

Preface

Over the years, computers have revolutionised our work, our communication with people, and even our daily life. Recent development of machine learning and deep learning has provided an impetus in all fields. Technological advancements in computer vision, natural language processing and understanding, computer graphics, perception and understanding of environments have invigorated the overall innovation. In this process of technological changes, computers have themselves undergone a significant transformation. At the initial stages, computers were so big in size that they were occupying almost entire rooms, which is in constrast to what they are today—some are as tiny as a watch. Apart from the conventional laptops or PCs, computers have taken several other forms such as visualization tools, phones, watches, robots, and virtual humans. These new developments have an great impact into two major complementary fields: Intelligent Scene Modeling (ISM) and Human Computer Interaction (HCI). This unique book presents fundamentals and applications in these two fields and their mutual links.

The Part I of this book presents the latest research in Intelligent Scene Modeling (ISM). This part provides several chapters focusing on topics such as perception of 3D scenes, semantic scene modeling, 3D reconstruction of scenes. Starting from indoor environments, which is itself a challenging topic, each chapter increases in complexity with complete 3D building models being semantically modelled. By reading these chapters, one can understand the latest state of the technology, the limitations and how they can be overcome. The book begins with chapters on fundamentals of computer vision methods such as object detection, human action recognition that form blocks for computers and robots. For instance, 3D modeling of a navigation environment is essential for mobile robots. The Intelligent Scene Modeling part is a first prior knowledge for the Human Computer Interaction.

The Part II of this book is focused on Human Computer Interaction (HCI). The new devices have completely transformed the field of HCI. HCI involves three components: perception, processing and inference from any kind of data, whose scope evolves with the advances of the computer technology. Traditionally, the human-computer relationship was simple and basic whereby the user provides data and the computer produces results or new information. Today, the computer not only can take data from the user but can also take them from the environment, the context, and the behavior of the user. The contemporary HCI framework relies on a robust and accurate perception of the environment from the users. Different types of data and signals are used by a computer to analyze the underline contextual significance, such as visual and audio cues, which are essential for reliable perception and understanding of the environment and the tasks to be performed. Millions of people have benefited of face recognition for private and confidential transactions in place of typing passwords. With such a rapid development, it is important for people to understand these methods and the state of the art in HCI.

This book with its two parts offers a comprehensive insight into the 3D modeling and reconstruction and the three components of HCI, perception, processing, and inference of multimodal data such as audio, visual, and none verbal interactions. It provides a closer look at how visual cues are processed. Computer vision and machine learning are vast topics permanent all along the book. They are essential for several applications such as face recognition, emotion recognition and motion detection. They have also transformed other fields including computer graphics and computer animation where huge amounts of images and motion data are analyzed and understood.

As mentioned earlier, computers have come in different forms and are used for various applications. With the expansion of ISM and HCI, computers can process different types of data and the interaction experience can be improved based on the applications. The book also looks at several different applications of ISM and HCI such as GUI based assistant for visual analytics, social robotics, virtual humans, and how different data are being perceived, processed, or inferred. Apart from the conventional visual, audio interaction methods, these chapters investigate other forms of interaction methods. They also highlight the cutting-edge technology in the interaction with robots and virtual humans.

Overall, this book tries to provide an insight into the various components and procedures involved in ISM and HCI. The chapters on computer vision and 3D modeling form the backbone of how computers can understand the visual data they receive. The chapters on applications of computers, such as robotics and virtual humans show how HCI has evolved in the use of other modalities including haptics, gestures, reading documents. The way how visual cues and these modalities are interlinked is essential for the development of robust ISM and HCI.

The co-editors of this book would like to thank all contributors for their great collaboration as well as our editor at Springer, Helen Desmond.

Singapore, Singapore   Prof. Nadia Magnenat Thalmann
Poole, UK   Prof. Jian Jun Zhang
Singapore, Singapore   Dr. Manoj Ramanathan
Lausanne, Switzerland   Prof. Daniel Thalmann

Contents

Contributors

Evangelia Baka MIRALab, University of Geneva, Geneva, Switzerland

Selim Balcisoy Sabanci University, Istanbul, Turkey

Hasan Alp Boz Sabanci University, Istanbul, Turkey

Abdullah Bulbul Computer Engineering Department, Ankara Yildirim Beyazit University, Etlik/Ankara, Turkey

Tolga Capin Computer Engineering Department, TED University, Ankara, Turkey

Jian Chang Bournemouth University, Poole, UK

Yihao Chen School of Computer Science and Engineering, Nanyang Technological University, Singapore, Singapore

J. Divya Udayan Computer Science and Engineering, GITAM Institute of Technology, Visakhapatnam, India

Yasin Findik Sabanci University, Istanbul, Turkey

Pradeep Kumar Jayaraman School of Computer Science and Engineering, Nanyang Technological University, Singapore, Singapore

Xudong Jiang School of Electrical & Electronics Engineering, Nanyang Technological University, Singapore, Singapore

Hoijoon Jung Biomedical & Multimedia Information Technology (BMIT) Research Group, School of Computer Science, The University of Sydney, Sydney, Australia

Younhyun Jung Biomedical & Multimedia Information Technology (BMIT) Research Group, School of Computer Science, The University of Sydney, Sydney, Australia;
School of Computing, Gachon University, Seongnam-si, Republic of Korea

HyungSeok Kim Department of Computer Engineering, Konkuk University, Seoul, South Korea

Jinman Kim Biomedical & Multimedia Information Technology (BMIT) Research Group, School of Computer Science, The University of Sydney, Sydney, Australia; Nepean Telehealth Technology Center, Nepean Hospital, Kingswood, Australia

Hanhui Li Nanyang Technological University, Singapore, Singapore

Hui Liang Amazon, Seattle, USA

Guoliang Luo East China Jiaotong University, Nanchang, China

Nadia Magnenat Thalmann MIRALab, University of Geneva, Geneva, Switzerland;
Institute of Media Innovation, Nanyang Technological University, Singapore, Singapore

Nidhi Mishra Institute of Media Innovation, Nanyang Technological University, Singapore, Singapore

Yinyu Nie Bournemouth University, Poole, UK

George Papagiannakis Institute of Computer Science, Foundation for Research and Technology—Hellas (FORTH), Heraklion, Greece;
Department of Computer Science, University of Crete, Heraklion, Greece

Nikolaos Partarakis Institute of Computer Science, Foundation for Research and Technology—Hellas (FORTH), Heraklion, Greece

Manoj Ramanathan Institute for Media Innovation, Nanyang Technological University, Singapore, Singapore

Ranjan Satapathy School of Computer Science and Engineering, Nanyang Technological University, Singapore, Singapore

Hyewon Seo CNRS-University of Strasbourg, Strasbourg, France

Evropi Stefanidi University of Bremen, Bremen, Germany;
Institute of Computer Science, Foundation for Research and Technology—Hellas (FORTH), Heraklion, Greece;
MIRALab, University of Geneva, Geneva, Switzerland

Chee Boon Tan Government Technology Agency of Singapore, Singapore, Singapore

Daniel Thalmann EPFL, Lausanne, Switzerland

Junwu Weng School of Electrical & Electronics Engineering, Nanyang Technological University, Singapore, Singapore

Yuhao Wu Biomedical & Multimedia Information Technology (BMIT) Research Group, School of Computer Science, The University of Sydney, Sydney, Australia

Zeynep Cipiloglu Yildiz Computer Engineering Department, Manisa Celal Bayar University, Yunusemre/Manisa, Turkey

Junsong Yuan Department of Computer Science and Engineering, University at Buffalo, The State University of New York, Buffalo, NY, USA

Xenophon Zabulis Institute of Computer Science, Foundation for Research and Technology—Hellas (FORTH), Heraklion, Greece

Jian Jun Zhang Bournemouth University, Poole, UK

Jianmin Zheng School of Computer Science and Engineering, Nanyang Technological University, Singapore, Singapore

Paul Zikas Institute of Computer Science, Foundation for Research and Technology—Hellas (FORTH), Heraklion, Greece

Part I
Intelligent Scene Modeling (ISM)

Chapter 1
Introduction

Nadia Magnenat Thalmann, Jian Jun Zhang, Manoj Ramanathan,
and Daniel Thalmann

Technological advances have a tremendous impact on everyone's life and are inter-woven into everything we do. The computer was a significant invention in the last century, which has quietly transformed and morphed into many devices that have rapidly become indispensable to our daily life, such as phones, cameras, TVs, and autonomous vehicles. Many such devices and equipment have a computer engine embedded: cars, washing machines, ovens, microwaves, and digital books. Even lights and coffee machines can be operated from a smartphone with a Home Facili-ties app. There has been a tremendous increase in their capabilities due to the inbuilt computer systems. For instance, digital cameras can now recognize faces, perform auto focus, and enact numerous different functions, allowing us to capture the details of our lives with very realistic photos. However, the development of such functions relies more and more on the recognition and the creation of 3D scenes, making Intelligent Scene Modeling (ISM) a key field of research and development.

The smartphone is a key example of the fast development of the technology in recent years. The phone is now an essential device for everyone as it is able to perform

N. Magnenat Thalmann (✉) · M. Ramanathan
Nanyang Technological University, Singapore, Singapore
e-mail: thalmann@miralab.ch

M. Ramanathan
e-mail: ramanthan.manoj@gmail.com

N. Magnenat Thalmann
University of Geneva, Geneva, Switzerland

J. J. Zhang
Bournemouth University, Poole, UK
e-mail: Jzhang@bournemouth.ac.uk

D. Thalmann
EPFL, Lausanne, Switzerland
e-mail: Daniel.Thalmann@epfl.ch

many tasks a person chooses. There is no longer a need to use a specific device such as a camera to take photos or a receptor to listen to the radio. The phone is no longer just used for voice communications. In fact, the smartphone is rather like a pocket-sized computer with inbuilt devices allowing us to communicate with our family and friends, to pay for our cup of coffee, or even to board a plane. It is now possible for any of these devices to recognize faces and objects through computer vision, to understand speech through natural language processing to name just a few. Recent progress on machine learning and deep learning methods has enabled the devices to operate not only more intelligently, but with less power and memory consumption.

The development of AI and deep learning methods has made these devices understand more about the 3D environment and the users involved. This has also led to the substantial advances in graphics (to show/render any output), virtual reality (to create immersive and interactive virtual environments) and augmented reality (to combine virtual entities with real-life scenes). These devices are now starting to emulate human behaviors and actions in many possible scenarios leading to the creation of Artificial Intelligence (AI)-based robots and virtual humans. AI has helped reduce the size of the devices and transform them into different products in addition to the significant elevation of the machine intelligence. AI-based technology, machine learning, and deep learning-based technology are becoming increasingly viable to every device. For instance, smart voice assistants such as Alexa from Amazon, Google Assistant, and Apple Siri have the ability to understand and respond to user speech and commands. Most of these devices allow interconnections, meaning that phones can be connected to voice assistants, and videos can be cast from phones or computers on to the TV screen making the user experience smooth and easy. The field of Human–Computer Interaction (HCI) has indeed dramatically changed and will continue these very fast transformations. As mentioned above, computers and phones can now interact in different ways to support our daily needs. Apart from the conventional methods of interaction such as keyboards and mouse, computers and devices can now interact through touch screens, voices and gestures, etc. For instance, face recognition or fingerprint recognition are more and more used to unlock computers and phones instead of keying in passwords. HCI is an ever-expanding research field with different modalities of interaction and different ways of understanding the various environments and user-related cues. With such a broad scope, this book aims to highlight the state of the art in HCI and its future. Specifically, we will look at different modalities of interaction and different algorithms in understanding the cues, and how they are applied in several devices ranging from PC, phones to robots, and virtual humans.

An easy and natural way of interaction with a computer is through a digital camera. It serves as an eye and provides visual cues to understand the environment and people within. The rise of computer vision (CV) algorithms has made the camera an integral part of any computer or smartphone. CV algorithms form the backend or backbone for several tasks performed by the devices. Object detection, action recognition, face recognition, emotion recognition, etc. are considered today as basic and core modules for any computer vision related interactions. Despite the wide use of CV techniques, computer vision itself as a fast-growing research discipline has seen a number of open research challenges facing the research community implying a pressing need for intensive research efforts.

The book is organized into two sections: Intelligent Scene Modeling (ISM) and Human–Computer Interaction (HCI).

In the first section on ISM, after the introduction Chap. 1 of this book, for an optimum visual content understanding, we begin with simple 2D retrieval and recognition. In Chap. 2, Hanhui Li et al. present a comprehensive study on available object detection methods based on the recent development in deep learning. They introduce a general framework of utilizing deep learning techniques to detect object, which becomes a de facto solution for object detection, In Chap. 3, Weng Junwu et al. describe a non-parametric model for skeleton-based action/gesture recognition. In Chap. 4, Hui Liang et al. discuss about random forest-based Hough-voting techniques that form the basis of several computer vision algorithms such as pose estimation and gesture recognition. They propose further improvements to the algorithms and conduct experiments in several vision-related applications. This chapter is at the forefront of AI-based learning techniques as it combines two advanced methods: Random Forests and Hough Voting.

For a comprehensive understanding of environment, simple 2D recognition and retrieval are not sufficient. Understanding the 3D arrangement of a scene is essential for the computer or the device to conduct the tasks. Depth cameras or RGBD cameras such as Kinect, HoloLens devices have become increasingly important as they help perceive and understand 3D objects and environments. 3D scene modeling and 3D reconstruction of scenes are important research fields in computer vision.

In Chap. 5, Zeynep, Cipiloglu, Yildiz et al. present a survey of AI-based solutions for modeling human perception of 3D scenes which includes topics such as modeling human visual attention, 3D object shape and quality perception, and material recognition. The authors emphasize the impact of deep learning methods in several aspects of human perception, in particular for visual attention, visual quality perception, and visual material recognition.

In Chaps. 6, 7, 8, and 9, semantic scene modeling and rendering are being described. To understand a scene, it is necessary for the computer to analyze the 3D scene layout, the spatial functional and semantic relationship between the various 3D objects detected. Semantic modeling and rendering allow computers to recreate and render immersive graphics outputs for the end user. The ability to reconstruct scenes and render them plays an important role in virtual reality and augmented reality applications. It also opens a new way of interaction with the objects represented in the virtual world. To explain 3D scene modeling and reconstruction, several chapters in this book are dedicated to these topics. In particular, in Chap. 6, Yonghyun Jung et al. describe the reconstruction of 3D real-world objects using Microsoft HoloLens. The next three chapters specifically focus on semantic scene modeling and rendering starting from indoor environments to complete 3D semantics-based building models. In Chap. 7, Divya Udayan et al. provide examples of segmentation on façade components using deep learning methods. In Chap. 8, Yinyu Nie et al. describe a method for automatic indoor scene modeling based on deep convolutional features, In Chap. 9,

Pradeep Kumar Jayaraman et al. introduce a method for interactively grouping and labeling the faces of building models.

Three-dimensional reconstruction is not only essential for semantic scene understanding and modeling, it also opens research avenues and applications in various areas presented in Chaps. 10 and 11. In Chap. 10, Evropi Stefanidi et al. discuss a new tool called "TooltY", a 3D authoring platform to demonstrate simple operations of tools such as hammer, scissors, screwdriver, which are direct products of 3D reconstruction. The 3D reconstructed tools can be immersively experienced in Virtual environments. Additionally, they can be used to recreate 3D faces, their emotions, the expressions, and the subtleties involved. This ability to recreate faces has been a key aspect for many new applications. For instance, 3D Animoji in phones can representatively replicate facial expressions and voice messages of the user. In Chap. 11, Hyewon Seo et al. propose a recurrent neural network with a marker-based shape representation as the base to generate 3D facial expressions. The authors explain how the fast development of deep learning started to replace linear function approximators with deep neural networks to achieve drastically improved performance. In the complementary area of Big Data, visualization tools and user interfaces have become essential to analyze massive amounts of information and make data-driven decisions.

In the second section of the book, chapters deal with HCI-related topics. In Chap. 12, Yasin Findik et al. introduce an assistive analytical agent that can help with decision-making in exploratory and collaborative visual analytics sessions.

One of the newest and fast-developing topics is the embodiment of the computer through virtual humans or social robots. In order to create realistic and reliable human–computer interactions, virtual humans or humanoid robots can understand and mimic possible human behaviors in many situations. It opens different ways of communication including, for example, non-verbal interactions. They are an integral part of high-level Human–Computer Interaction.

A good example of new Human–Computer Interface can be found in Chap. 13. Evangelia Baka et al. review the currently available technologies in HCI with a focus on virtual humans and robots. In Chap. 14, Manoj Ramanathan et al. provide an insight into currently available non-verbal interaction methods with social robots. In Chap. 15, Nidhi Mishra et al. explore the possibility of using social robots in different roles such as customer guide, teacher, and companion, and study user acceptance of social robots in these roles using Human–Robot Interaction experiments.

Over the years, HCI has undergone a massive transformation with changes in hardware and software possibilities. The ability to shrink computing engines has led to the development of numerous devices that can be interconnected to each other. The development of machine learning and deep learning algorithms has contributed to a boom in artificial intelligence. Combining these developments has broadened the horizon of ISM and HCI, as there is a necessity to build complex scenes and to perceive, process, and interpret data from various sources such as cameras, microphones, and wearable sensors. Due to the fast and ever-changing nature of ISM and HCI, it is essential to understand and update the latest research methods available.

To summarize, this book aims to provide an insight into the most recent developments in ISM and HCI with new machine and deep learning methods, how these two complementary fields have expanded in modeling, perception, processing, and inference of multimodal data such as audio, video, speechless cues, and sensor data.

This book is specially dedicated to researchers and Masters/Ph.D. students who will enjoy a comprehensive overview of ISM and HCI methods, containing surveys, state-of-the-art reviews, novel research, and concrete results. In addition, the book provides new research methods in various global fields linked to both ISM and HCI and their integration including computer vision, 3D scene modeling, virtual humans, and social robots.

The contributors of this book are international researchers from diversified research backgrounds and universities working under the broad umbrellas of ISM and HCI or both. This allows the readers to understand the evolution of ISM and HCI over time and the current limitations.

Acknowledgements Part of the research described in this book is supported by the BeingTogether Centre, a collaboration between Nanyang Technological University (NTU) Singapore and University of North Carolina (UNC) at Chapel Hill. The BeingTogether Centre is supported by the National Research Foundation, Prime Minister's Office, Singapore under its International Research Centres in Singapore Funding Initiative.

Chapter 2
Object Detection: State of the Art and Beyond

Hanhui Li, Xudong Jiang, and Nadia Magnenat Thalmann

Abstract As one of the fundamental problems of scene understanding and modeling, object detection has attracted extensive attention in the research communities of computer vision and artificial intelligence. Recently, inspired by the success of deep learning, various deep neural network-based models have been proposed and become the de facto solution for object detection. Therefore, in this chapter, we propose to present an overview of object detection techniques in the era of deep learning. We will first formulate the problem of object detection in the framework of deep learning, and then present two mainstream architectures, i.e., the one-stage model and the two-stage model, with the widely used detectors such as Fast R-CNN, YOLO, and their variants. Lastly, we will also discuss the potential and possible improvements on current methods and outline trends for further study.

2.1 Introduction

Object detection is important for scene recognition and modeling, since it can detect and recognize targets of interest among various complex scenes, such as humans, vehicles, and any other objects. Its related techniques serve as one of the building stones in many applications, such as face recognition in Yang et al. (2016), automated driving, and robotics systems in Geiger et al. (2013).

Traditional object detectors mainly consist of a hand-crafted feature extraction module and a classification/regression model, which require elaborating design and

H. Li (✉) · X. Jiang · N. Magnenat Thalmann
Nanyang Technological University, Singapore, Singapore
e-mail: hanhui.li@ntu.edu.sg

X. Jiang
e-mail: xdjiang@ntu.edu.sg

N. Magnenat Thalmann
e-mail: nadiathalmann@ntu.edu.sg

optimization. However, a recent breakthrough in artificial intelligence, particularly in deep learning that utilizes Deep Neural Network (DNN), has changed this situation. Since a network can be trained in an end-to-end learning scheme, the previous cumbersome process of designing complicated features and models can be discarded. More importantly, the feature extraction and object localization processes are implicitly incorporated in the network architecture, and can be jointly optimized to obtain the performance superior to that of traditional methods. Therefore, DNN-based object detectors are the current de facto solution, and we believe it is necessary to provide an overview focusing on them.

We notice that there are several comprehensive surveys on object detection with deep learning, as summarized in Table 2.1. The major difference between this chapter and other surveys is that we aim at providing practical and detailed guidelines for beginners. Specifically, we will present a general framework of DNN-based object

Table 2.1 Recent surveys on object detection with deep learning

Latest version	Title	Description
Jan 2018	Han et al. (2018) Advanced deep-learning techniques for salient and category-specific object detection: a survey	Review and categorize related techniques into (1) objectness detection, (2) salient object detection, and (3) category-specific object detection
Sep 2018	Agarwal et al. (2018) Recent advances in object detection in the age of deep convolutional neural networks	Besides generic object detection, this article also summarizes specialized datasets, including aerial imagery, text/face/pedestrian/logo/traffic sign detection, as well as 3D datasets and video datasets
Apr 2019	Zhao et al. (2019b) Object detection with deep learning: a review	Focus on generic object detection, include detailed descriptions of several milestone networks before 2018, such as Mask R-CNN and YOLO
May 2019	Zou et al. (2019) Object detection in 20 years: a survey	Comprehensive review of related techniques published from 1998 to 2018, providing a clear road map of the development of object detection
Jun 2019	Liu et al. (2018) Deep learning for generic object detection: a survey	Cover several aspects of generic object detection, such as object feature representation, object proposal generation, and context modeling
Jul 2019	Jiao et al. (2019) A survey of deep learning-based object detection	Specific description of typical baselines, branches, and applications of object detection
Aug 2019	Wu et al. (2019) Recent advances in deep learning for object detection	Analyze object detection methods on the aspects of (1) detection components, (2) learning strategies, and (3) applications and benchmarks

detection to help readers better grasp the gist, and then explain every component of the framework in detail, with canonical detectors as examples. Useful resources for implementing object detectors, such as publicly available datasets and tools, will be introduced as well. In a word, we hope this chapter could be a solid starting point for beginners interested in this topic.

2.2   Preliminary

2.2.1   Definition

In this chapter, we focus on the problem of generic object detection, which means we are interested in detecting objects of various categories. To define the location of a target, we can use either a bounding box or a segmentation mask, as demonstrated in Fig. 2.1. Most conventional methods adopt the bounding box annotation, while the segmentation mask is widely used in the segmentation problem. Specifically, given an input image I, our task is to predict a set of bounding boxes $\mathcal{B} = \{b_1, b_2, ..., b_N\}$, where N denotes the number of target objects in the input image. We assume that the bounding boxes $b_n, n = 1, ..., N$ are unrotated, so that b_n can be represented as $b_n = (x, y, w, h)$, where x and y represent the horizontal and vertical coordinates of the center of b_n, and w and h denote the width and height of b_n, respectively. Furthermore, we need to predict the specific category of each object enclosed by the corresponding bounding box, i.e., given a pre-defined set of C classes, we also predict a class label $l_n \in \{1, ..., C\}$ for b_n.

Fig. 2.1 Examples of images (left), bounding boxes (middle), and segmentation masks (right) from the COCO dataset by Lin et al. (2014)

2.2.2 General Framework of DNN-Based Object Detection

In this section, we introduce a general framework of utilizing deep learning techniques to detect objects. Our goal of introducing such a framework is to help readers grasp the gist of current methods, therefore the technical details are omitted here but will be explained in the later sections.

As demonstrated in Fig. 2.2, a DNN-based object detector can be divided into the following components:

backbone: a backbone network is firstly adopted to generate the abstract and high-level feature maps of the input image. Usually, the backbone is a Convolutional Neural Network (CNN) composed of multiple convolutional layers, pooling layers, and activation layers. The convolutional layer is the core of CNN, which is a group of filters with learnable parameters to capture significant information with respect to a certain task. The pooling layer is used to aggregate features in a small region (local) or of the whole image (global), simply with the max or mean operation. With the pooling layer, we could reduce the computational cost, as well as increase the network's robustness to spatial translation and rotation. The activation layer transforms the

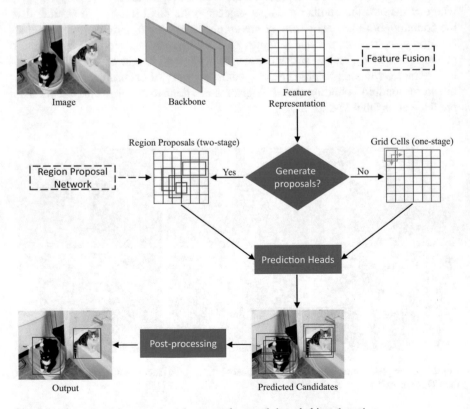

Fig. 2.2 The general framework of deep neural network-based object detection

value of feature into a desirable range and non-linear activation functions are the common choice, such as sigmoid $f(x) = (1 + e^{-x})^{-1}$ and ReLU $f(x) = max(0, x)$. Most current DNN-based detectors pre-train their backbone module on a large-scale image dataset, e.g., on ImageNet proposed by Russakovsky et al. (2015), to speed up convergence in the training process.

Feature Fusion: feature fusion is optional, yet it is a considerable module to refine features and improve the performance of the detector. This is mainly because features extracted by the backbone might lose the important details of targets. Zeiler and Fergus (2014) demonstrate that such features have a strong hierarchical characteristic such that features near the input end of the backbone are closely related to low-level patterns like edges, corners, and textures, while those near the output end have high responses to high-level, semantic, class-specific patterns like objects. Consequently, it is hard to distinguish objects of small inter-class variances merely based on the high-level output of the backbone. Moreover, pooling layers and convolutional layers with large stride will significantly reduce the resolution of feature maps, e.g., the resolution of feature map extracted by the last convolutional layer (conv5_x) of the widely used backbone ResNet-50 proposed by He et al. (2016) is only $\frac{1}{32}$ of the size of the input image. With such down-sampled feature maps, small objects are likely to be omitted.

Next, depending on whether they generate region proposals for representing candidates, most current object detectors can be roughly divided into two groups, i.e., one-stage detectors and two-stage detectors.

One-stage detectors are those that skip the procedure of generating proposals and predict the locations of objects directly. A typical detector in this group will split the feature map into a grid of multiple cells and predict multiple bounding boxes on each cell, as in YOLO proposed by Redmon et al. (2016). This type of detectors are much faster than two-stage detectors, as reported by Huang et al. (2017), and are more suitable for real-time applications. However, their disadvantages are obvious as well: without proposals, it is harder to capture the holistic information of objects and hence the performance of one-stage detectors are generally worse than that of two-stage detectors. Besides, in earlier one-stage detectors, the maximum number of boxes and objects in each grid is empirically defined, so it might be ineffective to detect multiple small objects appearing in the same grid.

Two-stage detectors first generate hundreds of region proposals, and then predict the class label of each proposal. Region proposals can be extracted via traditional split-and-merge methods like Selective Search proposed by Girshick et al. (2014), Uijlings et al. (2013), but current methods prefer to adopt a proposal network, such as the Region Proposal Network (RPN proposed by Ren et al. (2015)), so that the proposal network could be jointly optimized with the detector. However, in order to ensure the recall rate of the detector, the number of proposals is usually much larger than that of objects, making two-stage detectors less efficient than one-stage detectors.

Despite the difference between the candidate sampling strategy of one-stage detectors (grid) and two-stage detectors (region proposals), similar *prediction heads* could be applied in both types of detectors. The prediction head is the module that actually accomplishes the task of detecting objects. It could be the combination of multiple heads, where each head could be a classifier, regressor, or ranking function, based on how we model the detection task. As we have defined in Sect. 2.2.1, our goal is to tell the position and the class of object, and accordingly, our task could be split into two subtasks: *localization* and *classification*. For the localization problem, Girshick (2015), He et al. (2015), Redmon et al. (2016) adopt a straightforward solution which is to learn a bounding box regressor directly. Liu et al. (2016), Ren et al. (2015) also define a set of reference boxes with various scales and aspect ratios, namely, *anchors*, to represent candidates. As to the classification problem, we can construct a classifier via a shallow network, to calculate the probability of a candidate belonging to each class. The class with the highest probability (confidence score) is considered as the predicted class of the candidate.

Post-processing: the last step in the detection framework is to perform post-processing to remove duplicate predictions. Note that we have over-sampled candidates to guarantee the recall: for one-stage detectors, each cell could have multiple boxes of different sizes, while for two-stage detectors, the proposals are densely located on image and overlap each other. Hence removing duplicate predictions is necessary to ensure each object is detected only once, and so to reduce the false positive rate of the detector. This can be achieved via the traditional Non-Maximum Suppression (NMS) method proposed by Felzenszwalb et al. (2009), which iteratively selects the candidate of the highest confidence while discarding others having an Intersection over Union (IoU) larger than a threshold.

2.2.3 Datasets

Training DNNs for object detection requires lots of images and annotations, which are tedious and time-consuming to collect. Also, it is important to compare various methods fairly with the same experimental setting. Thus, here we introduce 4 widely used benchmarks for generic object detection.

Pascal VOC: This dataset proposed by Everingham et al. (2015) stems from the PASCAL Visual Object Classes (VOC) challenge, which was held from 2005 to 2012. It consists of 5 tasks, including image classification, object detection, semantic segmentation, action classification, and person layout prediction. The most commonly used tracks of VOC are VOC 2007 and VOC 2012, mainly because VOC 2007 has established the 20 classes of objects in VOC, while VOC 2012 is the last update on this dataset. There are 9,963 images with 24,640 annotated objects in VOC 2007, and 11,530 images with 27,450 annotated objects in VOC 2012. Although the VOC dataset seems like it might not be large enough by today's standard, it does significantly boost the development of DNN-based object detectors.

ImageNet: The ImageNet Large-Scale Visual Recognition Challenge proposed by Russakovsky et al. (2015) (ILSVRC) is one of the most important benchmarks in the community of computer vision. This challenge focuses on image classification and object detection, and has been run annually from 2010 to 2017. ImageNet contains about 1.4 million images, and its object classes are organized according to the WordNet[1] hierarchy. For the image classification task, ImageNet has annotated 1,000 object classes, whereas 200 classes for the object detection task. Specifically, the training and validation data for the object detection task remains unchanged since ILSVRC 2014, i.e., 456,567 images and 478,807 annotated bounding boxes for training, and 21,121 images and 55,502 annotated bounding boxes for validation. The number of test images is 40,152 and gradually increases to 65,500 in ILSVRC 2017. ImageNet is of great importance not only because of its large-scale data, but also due to the fact that extensive networks use backbones trained on this dataset.

COCO: The Microsoft Common Objects in Context (COCO) proposed by Lin et al. (2014) is a large-scale object detection, segmentation, and captioning dataset. It contains more than 200,000 images of 80 object categories for the object detection task. Although the number of object classes in COCO is lesser than that of ImageNet, COCO has 2.5 million labeled objects in total and has more objects per class. This dataset is challenging because plenty of its images are objects in non-iconic (non-canonical) views and of various scales. Except for bounding boxes, this dataset also provides segmentation masks for objects and stuff, which makes it become a popular choice when investigating the problem of instance segmentation and panoptic segmentation, proposed by Kirillov et al. (2019).

Open Images: The Open Images dataset proposed by Kuznetsova et al. (2018) was introduced in 2016 and has been updated several times since then. To the best of our knowledge, it is the largest dataset on this topic now. Its latest version, Open Images V5, has annotated about 1.9 million images with 15 million boxes of objects across 600 classes. Besides, the bounding boxes in this dataset are labeled with 5 attributes, including *Occluded*, *Truncated*, *GroupOf*, *Depiction*, and *Inside*, which can be used for describing the property of the corresponding object, e.g., a box with the *Occluded* annotation indicates that its corresponding object is occluded by another object.

Except for the above benchmarks for generic object detection, there are various specialized datasets for specific targets, e.g., the Wider Face dataset proposed by Yang et al. (2016) for face detection, DOTA proposed by Xia et al. (2018) for object detection in aerial images, and the Falling Things dataset proposed by Tremblay et al. (2018) for 3D object detection. We found that Agarwal et al. (2018) have provided a comprehensive review of almost 60 datasets on this topic, and interested readers can refer to Sects. 5.2–5.4 of the review for more details.

2.2.4   Evaluation Metrics

To evaluate the performance of object detector, Average Precision (AP) is the most commonly used metric. The AP metric is based on the precision-recall curve calculated for each class separately. Let b and b_{gt} denote a predicted bounding box and the

---

[1] https://wordnet.princeton.edu/.

ground truth, respectively. To evaluate the quality of b, we calculate the Intersection over Union between b and b_{gt} as follows:

$$IoU(b, b_{gt}) = \frac{Area(b \cap b_{gt})}{Area(b \cup b_{gt})}. \tag{2.1}$$

The prediction b is considered as true positive (TP) and is matched with b_{gt} if (i) its confidence score is not smaller than a pre-defined confidence threshold τ_c and (ii) $IoU(b, b_{gt})$ is not smaller than a pre-defined IoU threshold τ_b (typically $\tau_b = 0.5$). Note that each ground truth can be matched only once. Predictions that fail to match any ground truth are considered as false positive (FP), and unmatched ground truths as false negative (FN). Precision (P) and Recall (R) then can be calculated as

$$P = \frac{TP}{TP + FP}, \quad R = \frac{TP}{TP + FN}. \tag{2.2}$$

By varying the value of τ_c, we can get different pairs of P and R, and then draw the precision-recall curve and calculate AP as the area under the curve. Yet each dataset might have its own way to do the calculation, e.g., the VOC dataset proposed by Everingham et al. (2015) before 2010 uses TREC-style sampling. The COCO dataset emphasizes the quality of predicted bounding boxes and uses the average on AP with IoU thresholds in the range from 0.50 to 0.95 at the interval of 0.05.

To compare the speed of different detectors, we can consider the Frames Per Second (FPS) metric. A real-time object detector usually runs on more than 20 FPS. However, in the age of deep learning, merely using FPS to evaluate the efficiency of DNN-based detectors is not enough, since these detectors could be implemented via different deep learning frameworks, and on different devices. Hence the number of float-point operations (FLOPs) is also utilized as an auxiliary measure of the computational complexity of DNNs, as suggested by Ma et al. (2018), Zhang et al. (2018).

2.2.5 Open-Source Libraries for Object Detection

Currently, there are several open-source deep learning frameworks that greatly accelerate the process of deploying DNNs, such as PyTorch,[2] TensorFlow,[3] Caffe2,[4] Keras,[5] and MXNet.[6] Yet it might still be difficult for beginners to build a satisfactory object detection system or to reproduce the state of the arts, considering the

---

[2] https://pytorch.org/.

[3] https://www.tensorflow.org/.

[4] https://github.com/facebookarchive/caffe2.

[5] https://keras.io/.

[6] https://mxnet.apache.org/.

elaborate preprocessing steps and tricks in training DNNs. Therefore, in this section, we will introduce a few open-source libraries for object detection.

Detectron proposed by Girshick et al. (2018) and **maskrcnn-benchmark** by Massa and Girshick (2018): These two libraries are both published by Facebook and implement several two-stage detectors like Faster R-CNN proposed by Ren et al. (2015) and Mask R-CNN by He et al. (2017). Detectron is powered by the Caffe2 framework while maskrcnn-benchmark is implemented in PyTorch. It is noted that maskrcnn-benchmark is published after Detectron, therefore it has been further optimized in both effectiveness and efficiency, e.g., the training speed of the same network via maskrcnn-benchmark can be almost two times faster than its implementation via Detectron.[7]

TensorFlow Object Detection API proposed by Huang et al. (2017): This library is supported by researchers from Google, and obviously it is built within the TensorFlow framework. Its baselines cover multiple one-stage and two-stage detectors, such as SSD by Liu et al. (2016) and Faster R-CNN by Ren et al. (2015). It also provides several demos closely related to researches and applications supported by Google, e.g., running object detection on Android devices with MobileNets proposed by Howard et al. (2017).

MMDetection proposed by Chen et al. (2019a): This toolbox is based on PyTorch, started by the winning team in the COCO Detection Challenge in 2018. Now it is maintained by researchers and engineers from multiple colleges and companies, and it supports various and even the latest network modules and features for object detection, such as Mask Scoring R-CNN proposed by Huang et al. (2019) and Guided Anchoring by Wang et al. (2019b).

SimpleDet proposed by Chen et al. (2019b) and **GluonCV**[8]: These two toolboxes are designed for users of the MXNet framework. SimpleDet was released in early 2019; it aims at providing out-of-the-box optimized engines and components for constructing DNN-based detectors, such as mixed precision training and in-place activated batch normalization proposed by Rota Bulò et al. (2018). GluonCV, on the other hand, is a more universal library that implements deep learning algorithms for several problems in computer vision, including image classification, object detection, semantic/instance segmentation, and pose estimation.

2.3   Exemplar Baselines

In this section, we propose to demonstrate the specific implementation of DNN-based object detectors, with examples of both two-stage detectors (Sect. 2.3.1) and one-stage detectors (Sect. 2.3.2).

---

[7] https://github.com/facebookresearch/maskrcnn-benchmark/blob/master/MODEL_ZOO.md.
[8] https://gluon-cv.mxnet.io/index.html.

2.3.1 Two-Stage Detectors

In this section, we introduce 6 exemplar two-stage detectors, including R-CNN from Girshick et al. (2014), SPP-net from He et al. (2015), Fast R-CNN from Girshick (2015), Faster R-CNN from Ren et al. (2015), R-FCN from Dai et al. (2016), and Mask R-CNN from He et al. (2017).

R-CNN proposed by Girshick et al. (2014) has established the pipeline of two-stage object detectors in the era of deep learning. It consists of 4 steps: (i) generate region proposals (about 2000 per image) via the selective search method; (ii) crop patches on image based on the proposals, and wrap them into a fixed size (227 × 227) for the convenience of feature extraction; (iii) use the AlexNet pre-trained on ImageNet (Krizhevsky et al. 2012) to extract a feature vector (4096D, outputted by the last fully connected layer before the classification layer) to represent each proposal, and write all features to disk (due to the limitation of GPU memory); (iv) train a Support Vector Machine (SVM) for each class, and use it to estimate the possibility of the proposal belonging to the corresponding class. Although R-CNN is not implemented within a unified framework of deep learning, it indeed exploits the power of feature extraction of DNNs and significantly outperforms traditional hand-crafted features.

However, the disadvantages of R-CNN are notable as well: (i) the network used in R-CNN has two fully connected layers, which requires inputs to have the same dimensions; (ii) its network is utilized on densely overlapped patches, which cannot reuse the extracted features and causes the unnecessary computational cost; (iii) several components in R-CNN are implemented outside the network, and hence cannot be optimized simultaneously. These disadvantages of R-CNN, on the other hand, can provide us with clues of where and how the successors improve R-CNN.

SPP-net proposed by He et al. (2015) aims at providing R-CNN with the ability to handle inputs of arbitrary sizes. Recall that R-CNN is composed of several convolutional layers, which can process inputs of arbitrary sizes. Therefore, the first disadvantage of R-CNN can be tackled if we can turn various sizes of feature maps generated by the convolutional layers into a fixed-length feature vector. To this end, SPP-net introduces a novel Spatial Pyramid Pooling (SPP) module as the intermediate layer between convolutional layers and fully connected layers. As demonstrated in Fig. 2.3, the SPP layer has employed three pooling modules to divide a feature map into three grids of fixed sizes (1×1, 2×2, and 4×4). For example, assume the dimensions of the output of the convolutional layers are $H \times W \times D$, then each cell in the three grids will cover an area of $H \times W$, $\frac{H}{2} \times \frac{W}{2}$, and $\frac{H}{4} \times \frac{W}{4}$, respectively. The pooled features will be concatenated together to generate the feature vector (of size $D \times (1 + 4 + 16)$ in our example) for subsequent processing. Also, since the process of feature extraction is performed only once for an image, SPP-net can run orders of magnitude faster than R-CNN.

The Region of Interest (RoI) pooling module in *Fast R-CNN* by Girshick (2015) in fact is a special case of SPP which adopts only one pooling module. Yet what makes Fast R-CNN significantly different from previous methods is that its classifier is

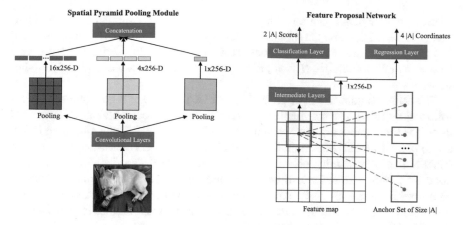

Fig. 2.3 Demonstration of the Spatial Pyramid Pooling layer by He et al. (2015) and the Region Propose Network with anchors by Ren et al. (2015)

implemented via a sequence of fully connected layers followed by softmax. In other words, except for the region proposal module, Fast R-CNN can be implemented completely in a single network. This property makes it to be able to update all network layers in a single forward-backward propagation scheme, without the need for caching features in a disk. But Fast R-CNN still uses the selective search for generating proposals, which not only slows down the speed (because its selective search tool is not implemented on GPUs), but also blocks the sharing of information (computation) across different components in the network.

Therefore, the last problem we need to consider is that, can we use a network to generate region proposals as well? The answer is definitely yes. In *Faster R-CNN*, a Region Proposal Network (RPN) is connected to the end of the backbone to predict object bounds and objectness scores. As demonstrated in Fig. 2.3, the RPN module works as a sliding window scanning over each position on the feature map generated by the backbone. To generate region proposals, RPN defines a set of anchors, which are reference boxes associated with empirical scales and aspect ratios. In this way, a region proposal can be represented as one of the anchors plus a small offset. Specifically, let A denote the anchor set and $|A|$ be its cardinality. At each position on the feature map, RPN adopts two sibling layers to simultaneously predict the probabilities of anchors being objects and the offsets relative to anchors. For the probability part, RPN generates $2|A|$ objectness scores to denote the probability of object and non-object (background), while the offsets are $4|A|$ coordinates parameterized as follows:

$$t_x = (x - x_a)/w_a, \quad t_y = (y - y_a)/h_a, \quad t_w = \log(w/w_a), \quad t_h = \log(h/h_a), \quad (2.3)$$

where x, y, h, w denote the bounding box of a proposal (or ground truth), as mentioned in Sect. 2.2.1, and the subscript a denotes the four variables of an anchor, and $\mathbf{t} = (t_x, t_y, t_w, t_h)$ denotes the parameterized coordinates. In all, for a feature map whose spatial resolution is $H \times W$, RPN generates $H \times W \times |A| \times (2 + 4)$ predictions.

The RPN module in Faster-RCNN is realized via a 3×3 convolutional layer followed by two 1×1 convolutional layers. The 3×3 convolutional layer is used to reduce the number of feature channels, while the two 1×1 convolutional layers are to predict probabilities and offsets. Such design of RPN has three advantages: (i) RPN and the remaining object classifier in the network can share the same backbone, so feature extraction can be performed only once; (ii) convolutional layer-based architecture makes RPN suitable for feature maps of various sizes and become translation-invariant; (iii) implementation inside the network ensures RPN to be optimized jointly and take advantage of GPUs.

In the above two-stage detectors, region proposals are fed into subsequent classifiers hundreds of times, which is too time-consuming to be applied to real-time applications. To tackle this problem, Dai et al. (2016) propose an alternative way of exploiting RoI pooling. Instead of using RoI pooling on the feature map, it first utilizes a fully convolutional network (FCN) to predict a score map representing the probability of the object of each class centered at each position. In other words, the number of channels of the score map is $C + 1$, where C is the number of classes and "1" indicates the background. Furthermore, the authors of R-FCN argue that localized representations could help to handle the object detection task. Therefore, it further splits the score map into $K \times K$ cells to encode spatial information. For example, setting $K \times K = 3 \times 3$ to encode class probabilities at the *top-left*, *top-center*, *top-right*,..., *bottom-right* positions. In this way, we get a position-sensitive score map whose number of channels is $(C + 1)K^2$. After that, given a region proposal predicted by RPN, we crop the corresponding patch from the score map, divide it into a grid of $K \times K$ cells, and perform average pooling for each class on each cell to get K^2 position-sensitive $(C + 1)$-dimensional score vectors. At last, the probabilities of the proposal belonging to each class are calculated simply by average voting.

The last two-stage detector we introduce here is *Mask R-CNN*. Technically speaking, the two modules proposed by Mask R-CNN to augment Faster R-CNN are quite intuitive. Firstly, it adds a branch for predicting an object mask parallel with the existing detection branches, namely, it predicts an extra $h \times w \times C$ segmentation mask for each proposal. Secondly, considering that the quantizations in previous RoI pooling will introduce misalignments and do harm to localization and mask prediction, RoI pooling is replaced with a new RoIAlign model, which avoids any quantization and uses bilinear interpolation to compute and aggregate features at sampled locations in each RoI cell. With these two modules, Mask R-CNN successfully outperforms previous methods. Yet the importance of Mask R-CNN comes from the fact that it has provided a unified architecture to combine the techniques of object detection and semantic segmentation (because of the predicted masks), and generated a direct solution to the so-called instance segmentation problem.

2.3.2   One-Stage Detectors

Detectors without proposal generation are considered as a one-stage model in this chapter, though such criterion might not be strict enough to categorize all detectors. For example, Najibi et al. (2016) propose to replace region proposal with a multi-scale grid of fixed bounding boxes, yet it still has a separate stage of refining these boxes iteratively, and uses RoI pooling to aggregate features. Therefore, here we focus on two networks that are widely recognized as one-stage detectors, including *YOLO* proposed by Redmon et al. (2016), *SSD* by Liu et al. (2016) and their variants from Fu et al. (2017), Jeong et al. (2017), and Redmon and Farhadi (2017, 2018).

YOLO is an excellent demonstration of the speed advantage of one-stage detectors. The base model of YOLO can process images at 45 FPS while its smaller version can achieve 155 FPS. The pipeline of YOLO is refreshingly simple as well. Firstly, YOLO splits the input image into $K \times K$ cells. And then, for each cell, it predicts B bounding boxes relative to the center of the cell. Each bounding box b is parameterized by 4 coordinated as defined in the previous section, and is also associated with a confidence score, which is defined as $P(o|b) \times IoU(b, b_{gt})$, i.e., the probability of the box containing an object multiplied by the IoU between the predicted b and the ground truth b_{gt}. For each cell, YOLO also predicts C class probabilities conditioned on the cell containing an object, that is, $P(c|o), c = 1, ..., C$. Putting the conditional class probability and confidence score together, we have

$$P(c|o) \times P(o|b) \times IoU(b, b_{gt}) = P(c) \times IoU(b, b_{gt}), \tag{2.4}$$

which can be interpreted as the probability of a predicted box containing an object from class c, and how well the box fits the object. In all, YOLO generates $K \times K \times (5 \times B + C)$ predictions for a given image. YOLO sets $K = 7$ and $B = 2$, thus its computational cost is far less than that of two-stage detectors with hundreds of proposals.

However, such settings of YOLO also imply a strong constraint that each cell could only contain two objects of the same class. Hence YOLO would struggle to detect small and grouped objects, or objects appearing in the same cell with different classes. Also, YOLO has adopted a network architecture stemming from GoogLeNet, which uses two fully connected layers to generate predictions. Compared with convolutional layers, these fully connected layers are not only less flexible, but also cannot enjoy the advantage of translation-invariance.

To remedy the above problems of YOLO, *Single Shot multi-box Detector* (SSD) proposes to conduct detection on multiple feature maps of different resolutions. It adds several convolutional layers to the end of the backbone network, to generate feature maps decreasing in size progressively. On each of these feature maps, SSD adopts an anchor set, similar to that used in RPN of Faster R-CNN, to predict the locations of objects. But unlike Faster R-CNN, SSD combines classification and localization into a single inference step carried by a convolutional layer, so that it generates $(C + 4) \times |A|$ predictions at each position of the feature map. Furthermore, SSD has delicately defined different anchor sets for its several feature maps. With the multiple feature maps, SSD could predict more than 8,000 bounding boxes given an input image of size 300×300. This allows SSD to better handle objects of various sizes, and predicting locations and classes simultaneously lets SSD run at a satisfactory speed (46 FPS, according to Liu et al. (2016)).

Lately, several variants of YOLO and SSD have been proposed by Bochkovskiy et al. (2020), Fu et al. (2017), Jeong et al. (2017), Redmon and Farhadi (2017, 2018), and achieved a better balance between speed and performance. For instance, the V2 version of YOLO proposed by Redmon and Farhadi (2017) introduces several improvements, such as the use of batch normalization, anchors, and high-resolution classifier. Currently, the latest variant of YOLO is V4 by Bochkovskiy et al. (2020), and it includes more bells and whistles. A famous improvement over SSD is the *Deconvolutional Single Shot Detection* (DSSD) model by Fu et al. (2017). The major contribution of DSSD is to use deconvolution to up-sample and integrate feature maps, so that more high-level context can be exploited for detection. Similar to SSD, DSSD extracts a sequence of feature maps. But it first generates predictions starting from the end of the sequence, of which the feature map has the lowest spatial resolution. A deconvolutional module proposed by Pinheiro et al. (2016) is adopted to up-sample the feature map, and then the feature map is combined with the next-to-last one in the sequence, so that the combined feature map has encoded more high-level information and DSSD conducts another detection on it. Such a process iterates throughout the whole sequence. Also, DSSD replaces the backbone network of SSD with ResNet-101 to obtain a performance gain.

2.4 Cutting-Edge Detectors and Trends

In this section, we introduce some cutting-edge detectors mostly proposed from 2018 to 2020. We roughly divide these detectors into two groups, on the aspects of feature fusion (Sect. 2.4.1) and anchor-free detection (Sect. 2.4.2). We believe each of them presents an important direction in the development of object detection technologies and has much room for improvement.

2.4.1 Feature Fusion

As we have emphasized, feature representation plays an important role in object detection. Feature maps generated by the network could encode information of various levels, areas, and modalities. To construct a reliable object detector, we need to sufficiently exploit the critical information across feature maps. To this end, feature fusion that combines features of multiple scales, locations, and levels is worth a try, as suggested by Cai and Vasconcelos (2018), Li et al. (2019), Lin et al. (2017), Pang et al. (2019), Singh and Davis (2018), Singh et al. (2018), Wang et al. (2018, 2019a), Zhao et al. (2019a), Zhou et al. (2018), and Zhu et al. (2017).

There are several paradigms to perform feature fusion, as demonstrated in Fig. 2.4. To distinguish these paradigms, we could mainly consider the following factors: First, the fusion step is performed on the images or on the feature maps, i.e., before or after feature extraction? Second, how do we define the connections between the feature maps for a combination? Third, do we perform detection only on the final output of the feature fusion module, or on every intermediate feature map generated by the network?

Different answers to the above questions yield plenty of implementations, and here we introduce a few examples. Featurized image pyramids are those that obtain a multi-scale feature representation of an image pyramid. For instance, Singh and Davis (2018), Singh et al. (2018) show that CNNs are not robust to scale variance. Hence they propose to back-propagate the gradients of object instances of different sizes selectively. In fact, an image pyramid is a simple yet effective strategy to

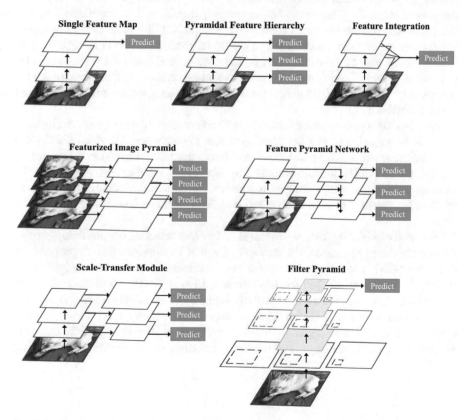

Fig. 2.4 Demonstration of various types of feature fusion

improve the performance of baselines. However, its computational cost is expensive, since we need to perform feature extraction and detection on each level of the image pyramid. Therefore, many methods choose to perform fusion on the feature maps directly. Pyramidal feature hierarchy and feature integration are two basic ways to do so. The former introduces several lateral prediction heads, which can be considered as adding constraints during the feature extraction process, e.g., the scale-transfer module by Zhou et al. (2018) combines and obtains features of various scales via pooling and up-sampling. The latter tries to combine features from different layers and generate a single prediction, e.g., Wang et al. (2018) propose to combine feature maps outputted by higher layers in VGG, and approximate the features with a location-aware polynomial kernel. Yet the information flow in these two strategies is unidirectional, such that only low-level features are used to refine those of high level.

To achieve a trade-off between featurized image pyramid and pyramidal feature hierarchy, Lin et al. (2017) propose the Feature Pyramid Network (FPN), which is a top-down architecture with lateral connections propagating high-level semantic feature maps across all levels. Pang et al. (2019) adopt lightweight modules to reduce the cost of extracting features from the image pyramid, and incorporate them into the pyramidal feature hierarchy framework. CoupleNet Zhu et al. (2017) proposes various strategies to combine local and global information. Zhao et al. (2019a) first fuse a feature map of the backbone, and then use several thinned U-shape modules to generate a multi-level feature pyramid. A feature selective anchor-free module is proposed by Zhu et al. (2019) to find the most suitable level from the feature pyramid for each instance.

An alternative way to perform feature fusion is combining multiple convolutional filters in a single layer, aka the filter pyramid. For instance, Yu et al. (2017) use groups of filters with different dilation rates to construct their residual learning blocks. Instead, the ELASTIC module proposed by Wang et al. (2019a) adds parallel down-sampling and up-sampling branches in each feature extraction module of the network, to allow the network to learn to choose the optimal branches based on the size of the object.

Except for the fusing feature, we can also consider selecting or combining predictions for better performance. For example, Cai and Vasconcelos (2018) propose the Cascade R-CNN consisting of a sequence of detectors with progressively increasing IoU thresholds to reduce the false positive rate. Li et al. (2019) adopt three branches for prediction, where each branch shares the same transformation parameters but with convolutional layers of different dilation rates. Most recently, Chen et al. (2019c), Ghiasi et al. (2019) have begun to develop automatic searching engines to find new architectures and modules, to replace the exhausting and elaborate manual trying process.

2.4.2   Anchor-Free Detectors

The introduction of anchors has successfully increased the performance of object detector, yet it requires a large set of anchors with careful settings to cover as many ground truths as possible. Such requirement is hard to satisfy when the scale variance among objects is large. Therefore, several anchor-free detectors, such as Dong et al. (2020), Duan et al. (2020), Lan et al. (2020), Law and Deng (2018), Law et al. (2019), Tian et al. (2019), Wang et al. (2019b), Yang et al. (2019), and Zhou et al. (2019a, b) are proposed to tackle this problem.

Law and Deng (2018) propose CornerNet to locate an object via detecting the top-left corner and bottom-right corner of the bounding box. It predicts the heat maps of these two corners for selecting corners, and learns an embedding function that the distance between the embedded features of two corners of the same box is small, and hence it can group corners and detect objects. Law et al. (2019) further improve the efficiency of CornerNet via selecting candidate regions governed by attention maps. Duan et al. (2019) then extends the embedding function in CornerNet to the triplet form (a pair of corners and a center), and provides two pooling layers to enrich the information encoded in centers and corners. Besides, Zhou et al. (2019b) notice that the four corners of a bounding box are not necessarily on the object, therefore they propose to replace them with extreme points that have the peak value along one of the four cardinal directions (top, bottom, left, right) among points in the same box. Yang et al. (2019) use a set of representative points to better bound an object. In summary, the core of these methods is to use key points to replace anchors.

Another way to construct an anchor-free detector is to directly predict bounding boxes and class probabilities through all locations on the feature map, similar to Huang et al. (2015) (and SSD without anchors). Previously, such a strategy is not suitable due to the complexity of generic object detection. However, with current strong baselines and other optimization techniques, it is possible to do so. Tian et al. (2019) propose an FCN-based object-stage object detector without anchors. For an arbitrary location, they directly regress the distances from the location to the four sides of the smallest bounding box which the location falls into. To improve the quality of predicted boxes, they adopt FPN and limit the range of box regression for each level. They also introduce the idea of "center-ness", which measures the normalized distance from a location to the center of an object. They predict the center-ness for each location, so that predictions far from the center of an object can be suppressed. A similar idea is employed in another CenterNet proposed by Zhou et al. (2019a). They also demonstrate that such a technique can be applied to applications like human pose estimation and 3D object detection. Wang et al. (2019b) propose guided anchoring, which aims at generating sparse, non-uniform distributed anchors for proposals. They model the distribution of anchors in a probabilistic framework factorized by two parts: one is the probability of an anchor centered at a location conditioned on the input image, and the other one is the probability of the box of certain shape given the input image and the center of the anchor. In other words, they believe that the shape of an anchor is closely related to its location. They further devise a feature adaption module to transform features with information of the anchor, which in fact performs deformable convolution with offsets governed by the anchor.

2.5　Conclusion

In this chapter, we have reviewed the state-of-the-art object detectors based on deep neural networks. We have summarized typical methods in the general framework, and introduced its core components in detail. We have also discussed cutting-edge technologies in several directions. We hope this chapter can present readers with the route map of object detection with deep neural networks and provide beginners with practical guideline.

References

Agarwal S, Terrail JOD, Jurie F (2018) Recent advances in object detection in the age of deep convolutional neural networks. arXiv:180903193

Bochkovskiy A, Wang CY, Liao HYM (2020) Yolov4: optimal speed and accuracy of object detection. arXiv:200410934

Cai Z, Vasconcelos N (2018) Cascade r-cnn: delving into high quality object detection. In: Proceedings of the international conference on computer vision and pattern recognition, pp 6154–6162

Chen K, Wang J, Pang J, Cao Y, Xiong Y, Li X, Sun S, Feng W, Liu Z, Xu J et al (2019a) Mmdetection: open mmlab detection toolbox and benchmark. arXiv:190607155

Chen Y, Han C, Li Y, Huang Z, Jiang Y, Wang N, Zhang Z (2019b) Simpledet: a simple and versatile distributed framework for object detection and instance recognition. arXiv:190305831

Chen Y, Yang T, Zhang X, Meng G, Pan C, Sun J (2019c) Detnas: neural architecture search on object detection. arXiv:190310979

Dai J, Li Y, He K, Sun J (2016) R-fcn: object detection via region-based fully convolutional networks. In: Advances in neural information processing systems, pp 379–387

Dong Z, Li G, Liao Y, Wang F, Ren P, Qian C (2020) Centripetalnet: pursuing high-quality keypoint pairs for object detection. In: Proceedings of the international conference on computer vision and pattern recognition, pp 10519–10528

Duan K, Bai S, Xie L, Qi H, Huang Q, Tian Q (2019) Centernet: keypoint triplets for object detection. arXiv:190408189

Duan K, Xie L, Qi H, Bai S, Huang Q, Tian Q (2020) Corner proposal network for anchor-free, two-stage object detection. In: Proceedings of the European conference on computer vision, pp 1–17

Everingham M, Eslami SA, Van Gool L, Williams CK, Winn J, Zisserman A (2015) The pascal visual object classes challenge: a retrospective. Int J Comput Vis 111(1):98–136

Felzenszwalb PF, Girshick RB, McAllester D, Ramanan D (2009) Object detection with discriminatively trained part-based models. IEEE Trans Pattern Anal Mach Intell 32(9):1627–1645

Fu CY, Liu W, Ranga A, Tyagi A, Berg aC (2017) Dssd: deconvolutional single shot detector. arXiv:170106659

Geiger A, Lenz P, Stiller C, Urtasun R (2013) Vision meets robotics: the kitti dataset. Int J Robot Res 32(11):1231–1237

Ghiasi G, Lin TY, Le QV (2019) Nas-fpn: Learning scalable feature pyramid architecture for object detection. In: Proceedings of the international conference on computer vision and pattern recognition, pp 7036–7045

Girshick R (2015) Fast r-cnn. In: Proceedings of the international conference on computer vision, pp 1440–1448

Girshick R, Donahue J, Darrell T, Malik J (2014) Rich feature hierarchies for accurate object detection and semantic segmentation. In: Proceedings of the international conference on computer vision and pattern recognition, pp 580–587

Girshick R, Radosavovic I, Gkioxari G, Dollár P, He K (2018) Detectron. https://github.com/facebookresearch/detectron

Han J, Zhang D, Cheng G, Liu N, Xu D (2018) Advanced deep-learning techniques for salient and category-specific object detection: a survey. IEEE Signal Process Mag 35(1):84–100

He K, Zhang X, Ren S, Sun J (2015) Spatial pyramid pooling in deep convolutional networks for visual recognition. IEEE Trans Pattern Anal Mach Intell 37(9):1904–1916

He K, Zhang X, Ren S, Sun J (2016) Deep residual learning for image recognition. In: Proceedings of the international conference on computer vision and pattern recognition, pp 770–778

He K, Gkioxari G, Dollár P, Girshick R (2017) Mask r-cnn. In: Proceedings of the IEEE international conference on computer vision, pp 2961–2969

Howard AG, Zhu M, Chen B, Kalenichenko D, Wang W, Weyand T, Andreetto M, Adam H (2017) Mobilenets: efficient convolutional neural networks for mobile vision applications. arXiv:170404861

Huang J, Rathod V, Sun C, Zhu M, Korattikara A, Fathi A, Fischer I, Wojna Z, Song Y, Guadarrama S, et al (2017) Speed/accuracy trade-offs for modern convolutional object detectors. In: Proceedings of the international conference on computer vision and pattern recognition, pp 7310–7311

Huang L, Yang Y, Deng Y, Yu Y (2015) Densebox: unifying landmark localization with end to end object detection. arXiv:150904874

Huang Z, Huang L, Gong Y, Huang C, Wang X (2019) Mask scoring r-cnn. In: Proceedings of the international conference on computer vision and pattern recognition, pp 6409–6418

Jeong J, Park H, Kwak N (2017) Enhancement of ssd by concatenating feature maps for object detection. arXiv:170509587

Jiao L, Zhang F, Liu F, Yang S, Li L, Feng Z, Qu R (2019) A survey of deep learning-based object detection. arXiv:190709408

Kirillov A, He K, Girshick R, Rother C, Dollár P (2019) Panoptic segmentation. In: Proceedings of the international conference on computer vision and pattern recognition, pp 9404–9413

Krizhevsky A, Sutskever I, Hinton GE (2012) Imagenet classification with deep convolutional neural networks. Adv Neural Inf Process Syst 25:1097–1105

Kuznetsova A, Rom H, Alldrin N, Uijlings J, Krasin I, Pont-Tuset J, Kamali S, Popov S, Malloci M, Duerig T, et al (2018) The open images dataset v4: unified image classification, object detection, and visual relationship detection at scale. arXiv:181100982

Lan S, Ren Z, Wu Y, Davis LS, Hua G (2020) Saccadenet: a fast and accurate object detector. In: Proceedings of the international conference on computer vision and pattern recognition, pp 10397–10406

Law H, Deng J (2018) Cornernet: detecting objects as paired keypoints. In: Proceedings of the European conference on computer vision, pp 734–750

Law H, Teng Y, Russakovsky O, Deng J (2019) Cornernet-lite: efficient keypoint based object detection. arXiv:190408900

Li Y, Chen Y, Wang N, Zhang Z (2019) Scale-aware trident networks for object detection. arXiv:190101892

Lin TY, Maire M, Belongie S, Hays J, Perona P, Ramanan D, Dollár P, Zitnick CL (2014) Microsoft coco: common objects in context. In: Proceedings of the European conference on computer vision. Springer, pp 740–755

Lin TY, Dollár P, Girshick R, He K, Hariharan B, Belongie S (2017) Feature pyramid networks for object detection. In: Proceedings of the international conference on computer vision and pattern recognition, pp 2117–2125

Liu L, Ouyang W, Wang X, Fieguth P, Chen J, Liu X, Pietikäinen M (2018) Deep learning for generic object detection: a survey. arXiv:180902165

Liu W, Anguelov D, Erhan D, Szegedy C, Reed S, Fu CY, Berg AC (2016) Ssd: single shot multibox detector. In: Proceedings of the European conference on computer vision. Springer, pp 21–37

Ma N, Zhang X, Zheng HT, Sun J (2018) Shufflenet v2: practical guidelines for efficient cnn architecture design. In: Proceedings of the European conference on computer vision, pp 116–131

Massa F, Girshick R (2018) Maskrcnn-benchmark: fast, modular reference implementation of instance segmentation and object detection algorithms in PyTorch. https://github.com/facebookresearch/maskrcnn-benchmark

Najibi M, Rastegari M, Davis LS (2016) G-cnn: an iterative grid based object detector. In: Proceedings of the international conference on computer vision and pattern recognition, pp 2369–2377

Pang Y, Wang T, Anwer RM, Khan FS, Shao L (2019) Efficient featurized image pyramid network for single shot detector. In: Proceedings of the international conference on computer vision and pattern recognition, pp 7336–7344

Pinheiro PO, Lin TY, Collobert R, Dollár P (2016) Learning to refine object segments. In: Proceedings of the European conference on computer vision. Springer, pp 75–91

Redmon J, Farhadi A (2017) Yolo9000: better, faster, stronger. In: Proceedings of the international conference on computer vision and pattern recognition, pp 7263–7271

Redmon J, Farhadi A (2018) Yolov3: an incremental improvement. arXiv:180402767

Redmon J, Divvala S, Girshick R, Farhadi A (2016) You only look once: unified, real-time object detection. In: Proceedings of the international conference on computer vision and pattern recognition, pp 779–788

Ren S, He K, Girshick R, Sun J (2015) Faster r-cnn: towards real-time object detection with region proposal networks. In: Advances in neural information processing systems, pp 91–99

Rota Bulò S, Porzi L, Kontschieder P (2018) In-place activated batchnorm for memory-optimized training of dnns. In: Proceedings of the international conference on computer vision and pattern recognition, pp 5639–5647

Russakovsky O, Deng J, Su H, Krause J, Satheesh S, Ma S, Huang Z, Karpathy A, Khosla A, Bernstein M et al (2015) Imagenet large scale visual recognition challenge. Int J Comput Vis 115(3):211–252

Singh B, Davis LS (2018) An analysis of scale invariance in object detection snip. In: Proceedings of the international conference on computer vision and pattern recognition, pp 3578–3587

Singh B, Najibi M, Davis LS (2018) Sniper: efficient multi-scale training. In: Advances in neural information processing systems, pp 9310–9320

Tian Z, Shen C, Chen H, He T (2019) Fcos: Fully convolutional one-stage object detection. arXiv:190401355

Tremblay J, To T, Birchfield S (2018) Falling things: a synthetic dataset for 3d object detection and pose estimation. In: International conference on computer vision and pattern recognition (workshop), pp 2038–2041

Uijlings JR, Van De Sande KE, Gevers T, Smeulders AW (2013) Selective search for object recognition. Int J Comput Vis 104(2):154–171

Wang H, Wang Q, Gao M, Li P, Zuo W (2018) Multi-scale location-aware kernel representation for object detection. In: Proceedings of the international conference on computer vision and pattern recognition, pp 1248–1257

Wang H, Kembhavi A, Farhadi A, Yuille AL, Rastegari M (2019a) Elastic: improving cnns with dynamic scaling policies. In: Proceedings of the international conference on computer vision and pattern recognition, pp 2258–2267

Wang J, Chen K, Yang S, Loy CC, Lin D (2019b) Region proposal by guided anchoring. In: Proceedings of the international conference on computer vision and pattern recognition, pp 2965–2974

Wu X, Sahoo D, Hoi SC (2019) Recent advances in deep learning for object detection. arXiv:190803673

Xia GS, Bai X, Ding J, Zhu Z, Belongie S, Luo J, Datcu M, Pelillo M, Zhang L (2018) Dota: a large-scale dataset for object detection in aerial images. In: Proceedings of the international conference on computer vision and pattern recognition, pp 3974–3983

Yang S, Luo P, Loy CC, Tang X (2016) Wider face: a face detection benchmark. In: Proceedings of the international conference on computer vision and pattern recognition, pp 5525–5533

Yang Z, Liu S, Hu H, Wang L, Lin S (2019) Reppoints: point set representation for object detection. arXiv:190411490

Yu F, Koltun V, Funkhouser T (2017) Dilated residual networks. In: Proceedings of the international conference on computer vision and pattern recognition, pp 472–480

Zeiler MD, Fergus R (2014) Visualizing and understanding convolutional networks. In: Proceedings of the European conference on computer vision. Springer, pp 818–833

Zhang X, Zhou X, Lin M, Sun J (2018) Shufflenet: an extremely efficient convolutional neural network for mobile devices. In: Proceedings of the international conference on computer vision and pattern recognition, pp 6848–6856

Zhao Q, Sheng T, Wang Y, Tang Z, Chen Y, Cai L, Ling H (2019a) M2det: a single-shot object detector based on multi-level feature pyramid network. Proc AAAI Conf Artif Intell 33:9259–9266

Zhao ZQ, Zheng P, Xu St, Wu X (2019b) Object detection with deep learning: a review. IEEE Trans Neural Netw Learn Syst

Zhou P, Ni B, Geng C, Hu J, Xu Y (2018) Scale-transferrable object detection. In: Proceedings of the international conference on computer vision and pattern recognition, pp 528–537

Zhou X, Wang D, Krähenbühl P (2019a) Objects as points. arXiv:190407850

Zhou X, Zhuo J, Krahenbuhl P (2019b) Bottom-up object detection by grouping extreme and center points. In: Proceedings of the international conference on computer vision and pattern recognition, pp 850–859

Zhu C, He Y, Savvides M (2019) Feature selective anchor-free module for single-shot object detection. arXiv:190300621

Zhu Y, Zhao C, Wang J, Zhao X, Wu Y, Lu H (2017) Couplenet: coupling global structure with local parts for object detection. In: Proceedings of the international conference on computer vision, pp 4126–4134

Zou Z, Shi Z, Guo Y, Ye J (2019) Object detection in 20 years: a survey. arXiv:190505055

Chapter 3
NBNN-Based Discriminative 3D Action and Gesture Recognition

Junwu Weng, Xudong Jiang, and Junsong Yuan

Abstract The non-parametric models, e.g., Naive Bayes Nearest Neighbor (NBNN) Boiman et al. (Proceedings of the IEEE conference on Computer Vision and Pattern Recognition (CVPR). IEEE, pp 1–8, 2008), have achieved great success in object recognition problem. This success in object recognition motivates us to develop non-parametric model to recognize skeleton-based action and gesture sequences. In our proposed method, each action/gesture instance is represented by a set of temporal stage descriptors composed of features from spatial joints in a 3D pose. Considering the sparsity of involved joints in certain actions/gestures and the redundancy of stage descriptors, we choose Principal Component Analysis (PCA) as a pattern mining tool to pick out informative joints with high variance. To further boost the discriminative ability of the low-dimensional stage descriptor, we introduce the idea proposed in Yuan et al. (2009) to help discriminative variation patterns learnt by PCA to emerge. Experiments on two benchmark datasets, MSR-Action 3D dataset and SBU Interaction dataset, show the efficiency of the proposed method. Evaluation on the SBU Interaction dataset shows that our method can achieve better performance than state-of-the-art results using sophisticated models such as deep learning.

J. Weng (✉) · X. Jiang
School of Electrical & Electronics Engineering, Nanyang Technological University,
50 Nanyang Avenue, Singapore 639798, Singapore
e-mail: WE0001WU@e.ntu.edu.sg

X. Jiang
e-mail: exdjiang@ntu.edu.sg

J. Yuan
Department of Computer Science and Engineering, The State University of New York,
Buffalo, NY 14260-2500, USA
e-mail: jsyuan@buffalo.edu

© The Author(s), under exclusive license to Springer Nature Switzerland AG 2021
N. Magnenat Thalmann et al. (eds.), *Intelligent Scene Modeling and Human-Computer Interaction*, Human–Computer Interaction Series,
https://doi.org/10.1007/978-3-030-71002-6_3

31

3.1   Introduction

In this decade, due to the availability of commodity depth cameras and the contribution of pose extraction method Shotton et al. (2013), skeleton-based action and gesture recognition has drawn considerable attention in computer vision community. The leading methods for 3D action/gesture recognition so far are learning-based classifiers including deep learning-based method Du et al. (2015), Veeriah et al. (2015), Zhu et al. (2016), Shahroudy et al. (2016), Liu et al. (2016), Li et al. (2016), and these methods have shown promising results in benchmark datasets.

While learning-based methods have made great progress in 3D action and gesture recognition problems, non-parametric models, which do not involve training or learning for parameters, have not been well explored. Meanwhile, we have already witnessed the success of the non-parametric model Naive-Bayes Nearest-Neighbor (NBNN) being applied in the image recognition problem. Motivated by the success of NBNN in image recognition, we develop it to recognize 3D actions. As 3D action and 3D hand gesture are both sequences of 3D poses, we use 3D action to represent the 3D action and the 3D hand gesture in this paper.

The motivation for applying NBNN in the 3D action recognition problem comes from two observations. (1) Compared with RGB-based image or video analysis problem which always faces millions or billions of pixels, skeletal data only consists of tens of joints. We believe that compared with the sophisticated end-to-end model, a simple non-parametric model can still well handle such a lightweight problem. (2) Similar to images that are the composition of local visual primitives, actions can be represented as a set of temporal primitives, as the temporal stage descriptor we defined in Sect. 3.2.1. We can generalized NBNN in 3D action problems by applying the *primitive-to-class* distance to recognized actions.

In our proposed method, each 3D action instance is represented by a collection of temporal stages composed of 3D poses, and each pose in stages is presented by a set of spatial joints. In each temporal stage, due to the combination of several pose features from consecutive frames, the stage representation will be redundant and the high dimension of it will slow down the search progress of the nearest neighbor. Meanwhile, a widely accepted idea is that the recognition of a certain action is only related to the movement of a subset of joints. Therefore we can reduce the dimension of temporal stage representation by picking out the set of informative joints. In Ofli et al. (2014), the most informative joints are selected simply based on measures such as mean or variance of joint angle trajectories, which inspires us to focus on those joints that have high variance during action performance. Interestingly, Principal Component Analysis (PCA) is able to project a high-dimensional signal into a low-dimensional subspace, and at the same time maintain the energy (variance) of the signal in the subspace by picking out elements of high variance in high-dimensional signal via principal components Jiang (2011). Based on this consideration, we introduce PCA in the proposed method to help select informative joints. Each element of the low-dimensional signal can be regarded as a representation of a variation pattern of actions. As the dimension of each sequence representation is highly reduced, the whole algorithm can be highly effective, and it is able to well satisfy the efficiency requirement of an embedded system, which is widely utilized in human-computer interaction.

Another aspect we should pay attention to is that actions may share several variation patterns, and these patterns do not help distinguish actions. We follow the idea proposed in Yuan et al. (2009) and introduce it on the dimension level of a low-dimensional descriptor. Those dimensions that are similar to each other in both positive descriptor and negative descriptor will be suppressed and those that are discriminative will be augmented.

By involving the selection of informative joints and discriminative matching, our proposed NBNN-based model can recognize 3D action in an effective way. Experiments on two benchmark datasets show that the PCA can effectively pick out informative joints and boost or maintain the recognition performance. Meanwhile, discriminative matching can further boost the performance by emphasizing discriminative variation patterns in low-dimensional stage descriptors.

3.1.1 Related Work

In action recognition, the data to be analyzed is a fully observed segmented video. Each video includes only one action instance. The goal of action recognition is to take a segmented video as input and output a corresponding category label. This task has been widely explored in the community. Considering the different data types of action sequences, the existing methods can be roughly categorized into two groups, the group of RGB-based methods and the group of skeleton-based methods. The RGB-based approaches take the RGB action sequence as input, while the skeleton-based approaches take the 3D pose sequence as input. Due to the different data structures, the methods to process them are quite different.

With the development of deep learning techniques, various deep learning-based models are proposed for action recognition. Given the great success in image analysis, the Convolutional Neural Network (CNN) becomes a very popular tool for video analysis. One intuitive idea is to utilize CNN directly for frame-level feature extraction, and then fuse the features or classification score from each frame for action classification. For example, in Karpathy et al. (2014), different fusion techniques are explored to be applied in video recognition, which initially verifies the feasibility of the usage of CNN on video analysis. In Temporal Segment Network (TSN, Wang et al. 2016b), Temporal Shift Module (TSM, Lin et al. 2019), the strategy of 2D CNN combined with simple temporal fusions is applied, and in TDRL Weng et al. (2020b), the temporal dynamic of human motion is further enhanced. A popular track of applying the CNN model on video analysis is the Two-Stream Model Simonyan and Zisserman (2014). Two CNNs are involved to extract the appearance and motion features of action sequences, respectively. Another direction of CNN feature fusion is to involve the Recurrent Neural Network (RNN) Donahue et al. (2015) in which the extracted CNN feature from each frame is further fed into an RNN for temporal modeling. Different from the traditional simple fusion strategy, RNN is able to well model the long-term motion dynamics of human motion. However, as for the high complexity of the model, it is easy to overfit on the training data. The 3D convolution neural network (3D CNN) Hara et al. (2018) is another representative model. In 3D CNN, the 2D convolution operator in 2D CNN is extended to fully utilize the spatio-temporal information of action sequence, which achieves satisfactory recognition performance. However, one drawback of the 3D CNN model is that it bears many parameters to be learned. During training, a large number of training samples are required to feed the model to achieve good performance.

In recent years, the skeleton-based action recognition problem attracts considerable attention, and many learning-based methods, especially deep learning-based methods Du et al. (2015), Veeriah et al. (2015), Zhu et al. (2016), Shahroudy et al. (2016), Liu et al. (2016), Li et al. (2016), and Song et al. (2017), have been proposed. In HBRNN Du et al. (2015), skeletal joints of 3D pose are partitioned into five parts: two arms, two legs and one torso. Then a hierarchical recurrent neural network is designed to model the relationship between different body parts. A similar idea is proposed in Shahroudy et al. (2016). A part-aware LSTM is designed to construct relationship among the body parts. In Liu et al. (2016), the LSTM model is extended to a spatio-temporal domain to analyze skeletons. An LSTM-based spatio-temporal attention model is proposed in Song et al. (2017) to recognize 3D actions. This model is able to discover key frames and key joints during action recognition.

Compared with the considerable amount of learning-based method, the number of non-parametric models is limited Ofli et al. (2014), Yang and Tian (2012). In SMIJ Ofli et al. (2014), the most informative joints are selected simply based on measures such as mean or variance of joint angle trajectories. Compared with this method, our proposed model can select a different group of informative joints by using PCA. Besides, the proposed method involves discriminative matching to improve action recognition performance. In EigenJoint Yang and Tian (2012), relative joint positions in spatial and temporal dimensions are involved, and PCA is also applied to reduce the dimension of descriptors. Compared with EigenJoint, our proposed method directly extracts features from raw skeletal data and there is no relative position information involved. In this way, the principal components learnt by PCA are more physically interpretable in our method, and we can utilize to analyze human behavior.

We can also witness the application of NBNN in the video analysis field. In Yuan et al. (2009), NBNN is re-designed as *Naive-Bayes-based Mutual Information Maximization* (NBMIM) to solve the action detection problem. The involvement of negative samples in nearest neighbor matching can help improve the discriminative ability of descriptors, and therefore further improve the recognition accuracy. Recently, the combination of NBNN and CNN Kuzborskij et al. (2016) as well as the effort to speeding up NN search Kusner et al. (2014); Muja and Lowe (2014) revive the possibility of NBNN's return in the computer vision community.

3.2 Proposed Method

In this section, we first introduce the representation for 3D action recognition in Sect. 3.2.1, which includes the representation for single-person action, Sect. 3.2.1.1, and two-persons interaction, Sect. 3.2.1.2. Our NBNN-based method for 3D action recognition is introduced in Sect. 3.2.2. The overview of our proposed method is shown in Fig. 3.1. We extract descriptors from each temporal stage first. Then informative pattern selection is performed by PCA, and the dimension of the original feature is thereby reduced. The action label of the action instance is then determined by the proposed discriminative matching method.

3.2.1 3D Action Representation

In this section, we introduce two different action representations for both the Single-Person Action (Sect. 3.2.1.1) and the Two-Persons Interaction (Sect. 3.2.1.2).

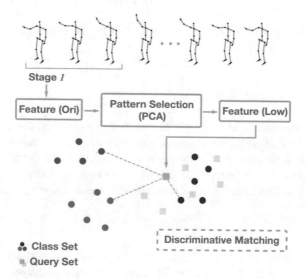

Fig. 3.1 The overview of the proposed method. Each action instance includes the same number of temporal stages, and there is equal number of poses included in each stage. Here, we only show the processing path of one stage. The orange squares are query sets from the action instance, and other colored dots are class sets for the nearest neighbor search

3.2.1.1 Single-Person Action

3D action is a sequence of 3D poses in skeleton-based action recognition, and different actions performed by different subjects may have different action durations. In our proposed method, to provide a unified presentation, we partition each action into N temporal windows of equal length. Each temporal window is called a *temporal stage*, and it is represented by the 3D poses in its corresponding window. Assuming each 3D pose has J joints for its skeleton, for a temporal stage descriptor x, the 3D pose in its jth frame is denoted as $p_j \in \mathbb{R}^{3J}$, and the related velocity of that pose is denoted as $v_j \in \mathbb{R}^{3J}$. Then the pose part x_p and velocity part x_v of x are defined as follows:

$$x_p = [(p_1)^{\mathsf{T}}, \ \ldots, (p_l)^{\mathsf{T}}]^{\mathsf{T}}$$
$$x_v = [(v_1)^{\mathsf{T}}, \ \ldots, (v_l)^{\mathsf{T}}]^{\mathsf{T}} \tag{3.1}$$

We follow the idea in Wang et al. (2016a) to also normalize x_p and x_v. As we use both original 3D pose and its velocity to represent 3D actions, a temporal stage descriptor x of l frames is presented as

$$x = [(x_p)^{\mathsf{T}}, (x_v)^{\mathsf{T}}]^{\mathsf{T}} \tag{3.2}$$

Based on the above notation, a 3D action video is described by its N stages-descriptors $V = \{x^i\}_{i=1}^N$.

3.2.1.2 Two-Persons Interaction

Inspired by the work in Yun et al. (2012), we notice that the relative position between joints from two different persons is much more informative in interaction recognition than the individual position. On the basis of this idea, we use the difference between stage descriptors of person A and person B, namely x_a and x_b, as the interaction representation. Therefore the jth element of ith stage descriptor for interactive action is defined as

$$x_\delta^{ij} = |x_a^{ij} - x_b^{ij}| \tag{3.3}$$

where x_a^{ij} and x_b^{ij} denote the jth element of ith stage descriptor x_a and x_b, and $|x|$ returns the absolute value of x. Based on this representation, a 3D interaction video is represented by its N stage descriptors $V = \{x_\delta^i\}_{i=1}^N$. For simplicity, we use $V = \{x^i\}_{i=1}^N$ to represent both the single-person action and two-persons interaction.

Considering that the stage descriptor includes several poses and velocity features in consecutive frames, the involved information in this representation is redundant, and the long dimension will slow down the nearest neighbor searching. Hence, we involve Principal Component Analysis (PCA) to help reduce the dimension of the stage descriptor. The involvement of PCA is a process of pattern mining. Different principal components learnt from PCA focus on a different aspect of each temporal stage descriptor. Due to using the raw skeleton features as action representation, each element of the feature bears explicitly intuitive insight, and principal components can help select informative aspects of actions. These principal components can be regarded as different variation patterns of actions.

The dimension of the temporal stage descriptor is reduced by linear projection. We denote the principal components as $u \in \mathbb{R}^{d_o}$, where d_o is the dimension of the original temporal stage descriptor. By principal component analysis, we can have M principal components $\{u_m\}_{m=1}^{M}$, and $m < d_o$. This set of principal components constructs the project matrix $U = [u_1^T, \dots, u_M^T]$, $U \in \mathbb{R}^{d_o \times M}$. Therefore, the dimension reduction is achieved by

$$\bar{x} = x \cdot U \tag{3.4}$$

where $\bar{x}$ is the low-dimensional stage descriptor. The reduced dimension is determined by the number of the principal components M. When M equals d_o, all the information in the original stage descriptor is kept, while when M is small, much information is lost but the principal ones are kept for temporal stage representation. Considering the notation simplicity, we keep the symbol x for each stage descriptor.

3.2.2 Classification

In this section, we introduce how the proposed approach recognizes human actions. We first introduce the original Naive-Bayes Nearest-Neighbor (NBNN) with PCA dimension reduction in Sect. 3.2.2.1. In Sect. 3.2.2.2, we introduce the proposed discriminative matching method.

3.2.2.1 NBNN

When given a query action video $V_q = \{x^i\}_{i=1}^{N}$, the goal of our action recognition task is to find which class $c \in \{1, 2, \dots, C\}$ the video V_q belongs to. NBNN follows the maximum a posteriori (MAP) rule for classification. With the assumption of equal prior $p(c) = \frac{1}{C}$, the predicted class is

$$c^* = \arg\max_c p(c|V_q) = \arg\max_c p(V_q|c) \tag{3.5}$$

Assuming that the stage descriptors are independent of each other, Eq. 3.5 can be written as

$$c^* = \arg\max_c p(V_q|c)$$
$$= \arg\max_c p(x^1, \dots, x^N|c)$$
$$= \arg\max_c \prod_{i=1}^{N} p(x^i|c) \tag{3.6}$$

In Boiman et al. (2008), the probability density of each primitive x in a class c, namely $p(x|c)$, is estimated according to the distance between x and the nearest neighbor of x in class c, and Eq. 3.6 is then re-written as

$$c^* = \arg\min_c \sum_{i=1}^{N} \|x^i - NN_c(x^i)\|^2 \tag{3.7}$$

where $NN_c(x^i)$ denotes the nearest neighbor of x^i in class c.

3.2.2.2 Discriminative Matching

For each stage descriptor x from $V = \{x^i\}_{i=1}^{N}$, we define its distance vector to class c as

$$x_c = (x - NN_c(x)) \odot (x - NN_c(x)) \tag{3.8}$$

where $\odot$ is the element-wise product.

In Yuan et al. (2009), negative samples are involved in nearest distance calculation to improve the discriminative ability of descriptors. In our proposed method, we introduce this idea in dimension level of the descriptor. As mentioned in the previous section, each element of low-dimensional stage descriptor can be regarded as a representation of an aspect of actions. For positive stage descriptor x_c and negative stage descriptor $x_{\bar{c}}$, they may have several similar elements, and these elements do not help distinguish the positive descriptor from the negative descriptor, while those dimensions that have much variation among positive and negative descriptors are more informative for action recognition. On the basis of this motivation, each element of positive distance vector x_c is subtracted by the distance of nearest related element in negative distance vector $x_{\bar{c}}$. The jth element of the ith new distance vector to class c, $\hat{x}_c^i$, is then defined as

$$\hat{x}_c^{ij} = x_{c^*}^{ij} - x_c^{ij} \tag{3.9}$$

where $x_{c^*}^{ij}$ is defined as $x_{c^*}^{ij} = \min_{\bar{c} \neq c} x_{\bar{c}}^{ij}$. $x_{\bar{c}}^{ij}$ and x_c^{ij} are the jth element of ith distance vector in class $\bar{c}$ and class c, respectively. Therefore, the action classification is then determined by

$$c^* = \arg\max_c \sum_{i=1}^{N} \|\hat{x}_c^i\|_1 \tag{3.10}$$

where $\| \cdot \|_1$ is l_1-norm.

3.3 Experiments

In this section, we test the proposed method on two benchmark datasets, and provide the comparison with state of the arts. Details of our implementation are provided in Sect. 3.3.1. Comparison results on the MSR-Action3D dataset Li et al. (2010) and the SBU interaction dataset Yun et al. (2012) are provided and discussed in Sect. 3.3.2. Experiment results show the efficiency of the proposed non-parametric method in 3D action recognition.

3.3.1 Implementation Details

3D Action Representation. In single-person action recognition, to ensure that the representation is location-invariant, the whole pose is shifted so that the hip joint is located at the coordinate origin. That is to say, all the locations of the pose joint are subtracted by the location of the hip joint. Similarly, for the two-persons interactive action, each joint of two poses is centralized by subtracting coordinates of the mean hip joint, namely the mid-point of hip joints of two involved poses.

Nearest Neighbor Search. To speed up the nearest neighbor searching process, KD-tree implementation Mount and Arya (1998) is used in our implementation, indexing the data point in tree structures to speed up the search process.

Principal Component Analysis. We obtain the principal components u by utilizing the PCA toolbox in MATLAB on the training data, and reduce the dimension of the temporal stage descriptor x by using the obtained principal components for both the training and testing data.

3.3.2 Results and Analysis

We compare the classification performance of the proposed method with the baselines and the state of the arts in this section on two benchmark datasets. Besides, a detailed analysis of the proposed NBNN-based method is also provided to check the abilities of it from different perspectives.

3.3.2.1 SBU Interaction

This dataset contains eight classes of two-person interactive actions. 282 skeleton sequences are captured by the Kinect depth sensor. For each skeleton, there are 15 joints in total. We follow the protocol proposed in Yun et al. (2012) to evaluate our method. There are fivefold cross validations. The number of stages is 15, and there

Table 3.1 Comparison of results on SBU interaction (%)

Method	Accuracy
NBNN-∞	91.1
NBNN-15	92.8
NBNN+PCA-∞	92.9
NBNN+PCA-15	93.6
HBRNN Du et al. (2015)	80.4
CHARM Li et al. (2015)	83.9
Deep LSTM Vemulapalli et al. (2014)	86.0
Co-occurrence Wang et al. (2016c)	90.4
ST-LSTM Liu et al. (2016)	93.3
Discr. NBNN+PCA-∞	94.0
Discr. NBNN+PCA-15	**94.2**

are five poses in each stage. The dimension of the subspace is set to 128, which is around 30% of the original dimension. The selected principal components can cover 95% of the energy. In this comparison, there are four baseline methods and five state of the arts included. The results are shown in Table 3.1.

Four baseline methods included in the comparison are (1) NBNN with video-length-related stage setting (NBNN-∞), (2) NBNN with 15 stages (NBNN-15), (3) NBNN-∞ with PCA dimension reduction (NBNN+PCA-∞), and (4) NBNN-15 with PCA dimension reduction (NBNN+PCA-15). In NBNN-∞ and NBNN+PCA-∞, the number of stages N is determined by $N = P - l + 1$, and P is the length of an action sequence. Table 3.1 shows that after dimension reduction, there are 1.8% improvement from NBNN-∞ and 0.8% improvement from NBNN-15, respectively. The improvement indicates that PCA can help select informative elements of the original stage descriptor and improve the performance.

In Fig. 3.3, we select the first six principal components to illustrate. The principal bases learnt by PCA can be regarded as weights for element selection. As we can see from Fig. 3.3, there is an explicit periodicity of the learnt components. There are five poses involved in each stage descriptor, and meanwhile, we can see five explicit peaks in the pose-related and velocity-related parts of the selected principal components. The peaks of each principal component are related to the active joints of skeletal poses, such as left and right hands as well as left and right feet. The selected principal components highlight different aspects of actions that are to be recognized. With our discriminative setting in decision function Eq. 3.10, we can see 1.1% improvement from NBNN-∞ and 0.6% improvement from NBNN-15. The discriminative matching can help the informative elements of distance vector x_c to emerge and suppress those elements that are not discriminative. Comparisons with state-of-the-art methods show that the proposed method outperforms the deep learning-based method on the SBU dataset, which proves our motivation that the non-parametric method is also suitable for the skeleton-based action recognition problem. The confusion matrix of the SBU Interaction Dataset is shown in Fig. 3.2.

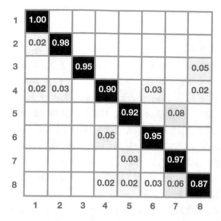

Fig. 3.2 Confusion Matrix of SBU Interaction Dataset. There are eight different indoor two-persons interactions in this dataset. The eight interactions are *1. Approaching*, *2. Departing*, *3. Pushing*, *4. Kicking*, *5. Punching*, *6. Exchanging Objects*, *7. Hugging*, and *8. Shaking Hands*

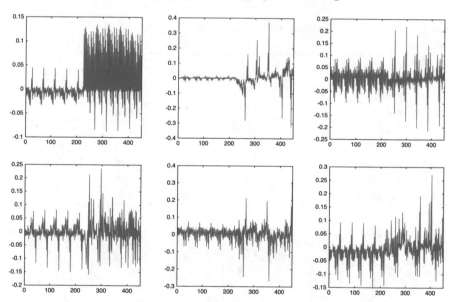

Fig. 3.3 First six principal components learnt from the SBU interaction dataset. The x- and y-axes are the dimension index and the related value of principal components, respectively. The dimension of each principal component is 450. The first half dimensions (0–224) of the principal component are related to the pose feature and the second half dimensions (225–449) are related to the velocity feature

3.3.2.2   MSR-Action 3D

There are 557 skeletal action sequences included in this dataset, and 20 human actions are involved. Each action is performed by 10 subjects twice or three times. The evaluation protocol we use is described in Li et al. (2010). In this protocol, the 20 actions are grouped into three subsets AS1, AS2, and AS3, in each of which there are eight actions included. In this dataset, the number of poses in the local window is 10, and the number of stages N is set to 15. The dimension of the stage descriptor in the low-dimensional subspace is set to 200, which is around 20% of the original dimension. This comparison experiment includes four baseline methods and three state of the arts. The results are shown in Table 3.2. The confusion matrix of AS1, AS2, and AS3 are shown in Fig. 3.4.

As we can see from Table 3.2, although we reduce the dimension of the stage descriptor, NBNN+PCA still can maintain the performance. Meanwhile in AS1, there is a slight improvement by adding the PCA. This means that PCA does help

Table 3.2 Comparison of results on MSR-Action3D (%)

Method	AS1	AS2	AS3	Ave.
NBNN-∞	85.8	92.0	96.4	91.4
NBNN-15	86.8	92.0	96.4	91.7
NBNN+PCA-∞	87.7	92.0	96.4	92.0
NBNN+PCA-15	87.7	92.0	96.4	92.0
Skeletal Quads Evangelidis et al. (2014)	88.4	86.6	94.6	89.9
Hussein et al. (2013)	88.0	89.3	94.5	90.5
Lie Group Vemulapalli et al. (2014)	**95.4**	83.9	**98.2**	**92.5**
Discr. NBNN+PCA-∞	86.8	**92.9**	96.4	92.0
Discr. NBNN+PCA-15	87.7	**92.9**	96.4	92.3

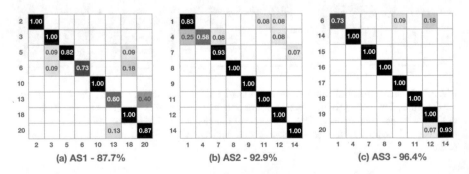

Fig. 3.4 Confusion Matrix of MSR-Action 3D Dataset. The action indexes are 1. *High Arm Wave*, 2. *Horizontal Arm Wave*, 3. *Hammer*, 4. *Hand Catch*, 5. *Forward Punch*, 6. *High Throw*, 7. *Draw X*, 8. *Draw Tick*, 9. *Draw Circle*, 10. *Hand Clap*, 11. *Two Hand Wave*, 12. *Side Boxing*, 13. *Bend*, 14. *Forward Kick*, 15. *Side Kick*, 16. *Jogging*, 17. *Tennis Swing*, 18. *Tennis Serve*, 19. *Golf Swing*, and 20. *Pick Up & Throw*

Table 3.3 Time comparison of proposed method with and without PCA on MSR-Action 3D (*ms*)

Method	AS1	AS2	AS3	Ave.
Without PCA	5.5	04.7	05.4	05.2
With PCA	0.44	00.35	00.45	00.41
Δ (%)	−92	−92.6	−91.7	−92.1

pick out the informative elements. Furthermore, the proposed method with a discriminative setting can achieve slight improvement. Comparisons with state of the arts show that our proposed method outperforms these methods on AS2, and the average performance is comparable with the state-of-the-art methods.

The time comparison of the proposed method is shown in Table 3.3. The table records the average searching time of each stage descriptor in all action class sets. The experiment is conducted on a computer with 8 GB memory and a 2.6 GHz i7 CPU. As we can see, our NBNN-based 3D action recognition method is around 13 times faster with PCA pattern selection than the one without PCA. Our proposed method can achieve better performance with faster speed than NBNN.

As the scale of the dataset increases, the relatively increasing number of samples and dimension of descriptors will slow down the nearest neighbor search. Our proposed method can well handle the increasing scale of the dataset, maintain or improve the performance at a fast speed with the help of PCA pattern selection.

We further range the number of stages N from 1 to 21 to evaluate the proposed model on the MSR-Action 3D dataset. As Fig. 3.5 shows, as the number of stages N increases, the accuracy will increase relatively. The proposed method can achieve good performance with only 5 stages, and further increasing N will not improve the accuracy. Besides, we can see that the proposed method can achieve better or the same accuracy than NBNN under a different setting of N. This phenomenon shows that our proposed method can well discover the informative joints and help maintain recognition accuracy with high efficiency.

3.4 Conclusions

In this work, we develop a non-parametric model NBNN for 3D action recognition. The proposed method is able to select informative joints by PCA, which can help speed up the nearest neighbor search process and at the same time maintain or improve action recognition performance. Besides, the introduction of discriminative matching in the nearest neighbor search part can help achieve better recognition accuracy by suppressing similar variation patterns and emphasizing discriminative patterns. Evaluation on two benchmark datasets shows the efficiency of the proposed method and demonstrates the potential of using the non-parametric method for 3D action recognition.

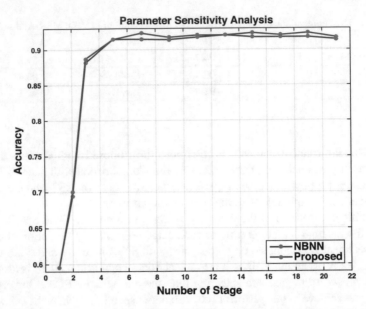

Fig. 3.5 Parameter analysis of the proposed method. The range of the stage is set from 1 to 21. When the number of stages is large enough, the recognition performance tend to be stable

3.5 Future Work

The objective of the Principal Component Analysis (PCA) is to maximize the data reconstruction capability of the features Jiang (2008). The PCA is a learning method for dimension reduction without considering the class-related label supervision. Therefore, although PCA is a great tool for pattern selection, it is not optimized for pattern classification. Meanwhile, in the real-world application, sample unbalance is always the problem that needs to be faced. Hence, we consider how to introduce the label information, and meanwhile solving the problem of unbalanced training data can be the next directions to focus on. The Asymmetric Principal Component and Discriminant Analyses proposed in Jiang (2008) provide a good attempt for these two problems, and future work can focus on it.

The discovery of informative joints is quite important in skeleton-based action and gesture recognition. The action labels are closely related to the movement of a certain subset of a human pose. In this chapter, we propose to use an unsupervised learning method, Principal Component Analysis (PCA), to discover informative joints, which shows the effectiveness of involving informative joint discovery. In Weng et al. (2017, 2018b), the informative joints selection is driven by action labels, and it is designed in a non-parametric model. The deformable pose model Weng et al. (2018a) further involves the key joint selection in the deep learning model and achieves good performance in skeleton-based action recognition. We believe this sub-topic can be further explored in the future.

Another direction is the online action recognition, which is of great significance in human-computer interaction applications. The method proposed in this chapter is for offline action recognition tasks, in which the whole action sequence is observed by the model in inference. In this way, the quick response of the machine to human behavior cannot be well guaranteed. Compared with offline action recognition, the online task is to recognize the action in a video stream where the human behavior is temporally partially observed, and the goal is to predict the action label when the human action is done. Orderlet Yu et al. (2014) is proposed to recognize 3D human action in a video stream. Orderlet is a mid-level pose representation, and its lightweight design makes it quite suitable for real-time online recognition. In Weng et al. (2020a), a policy-based reinforcement strategy is proposed to solve the online action recognition task. In this method, the negative categories are excluded during action performing, and the precision of action recognition in the late stages can be higher. As the action sequence is partially observed, this task is very challenging. There will be much space to explore in the future.

References

Boiman O, Shechtman E, Irani M (2008) In defense of nearest-neighbor based image classification. In: Proceedings of the IEEE conference on Computer Vision and Pattern Recognition (CVPR). IEEE, pp 1–8

Donahue J, Anne Hendricks L, Guadarrama S, Rohrbach M, Venugopalan S, Saenko K, Darrell T (2015) Long-term recurrent convolutional networks for visual recognition and description. In: Proceedings of the IEEE conference on Computer Vision and Pattern Recognition (CVPR), pp 2625–2634

Du Y, Wang W, Wang L (2015) Hierarchical recurrent neural network for skeleton based action recognition. In: Proceedings of the IEEE conference on computer vision and pattern recognition (CVPR), pp 1110–1118

Evangelidis G, Singh G, Horaud R (2014) Skeletal quads: human action recognition using joint quadruples. In: International conference on pattern recognition (ICPR), pp 4513–4518

Hara K, Kataoka H, Satoh Y (2018) Can spatiotemporal 3D CNNS retrace the history of 2D CNNS and imagenet? In: Proceedings of the IEEE conference on Computer Vision and Pattern Recognition (CVPR), pp 6546–6555

Hussein ME, Torki M, Gowayyed MA, El-Saban M (2013) Human action recognition using a temporal hierarchy of covariance descriptors on 3D joint locations. IJCAI 13:2466–2472

Jiang X (2008) Asymmetric principal component and discriminant analyses for pattern classification. IEEE Trans Pattern Anal Mach Intell (T-PAMI) (5):931–937

Jiang X (2011) Linear subspace learning-based dimensionality reduction. IEEE Signal Process Mag 28(2):16–26

Karpathy A, Toderici G, Shetty S, Leung T, Sukthankar R, Fei-Fei L (2014) Large-scale video classification with convolutional neural networks. In: Proceedings of the IEEE conference on Computer Vision and Pattern Recognition (CVPR), pp 1725–1732

Kusner M, Tyree S, Weinberger KQ, Agrawal K (2014) Stochastic neighbor compression. In: Proceedings of the 31st International Conference on Machine Learning (ICML), pp 622–630

Kuzborskij I, Carlucci FM, Caputo B (2016) When Naive Bayes nearest neighbours meet convolutional neural networks. In: Proceedings of the IEEE conference on Computer Vision and Pattern Recognition (CVPR)

Li W, Zhang Z, Liu Z (2010) Action recognition based on a bag of 3d points. In: 2010 IEEE computer society conference on Computer Vision and Pattern Recognition Workshops (CVPRW), IEEE, pp 9–14

Li W, Wen L, Choo Chuah M, Lyu S (2015) Category-blind human action recognition: a practical recognition system. In: Proceedings of the IEEE International Conference on Computer Vision (ICCV), pp 4444–4452

Li Y, Lan C, Xing J, Zeng W, Yuan C, Liu J (2016) Online human action detection using joint classification-regression recurrent neural networks. In: European Conference on Computer Vision (ECCV), Springer, pp 203–220

Lin J, Gan C, Han S (2019) TSM: Temporal shift module for efficient video understanding. In: Proceedings of the IEEE international conference on computer vision (CVPR), pp 7083–7093

Liu J, Shahroudy A, Xu D, Wang G (2016) Spatio-temporal LSTM with trust gates for 3D human action recognition. In: European Conference on Computer Vision (ECCV), Springer, pp 816–833

Mount DM, Arya S (1998) Ann: library for approximate nearest neighbour searching

Muja M, Lowe DG (2014) Scalable nearest neighbor algorithms for high dimensional data. IEEE Trans Pattern Anal Mach Intell (T-PAMI) 36

Ofli F, Chaudhry R, Kurillo G, Vidal R, Bajcsy R (2014) Sequence of the Most Informative Joints (SMIJ): a new representation for human skeletal action recognition. J Vis Commun Image Represent (JVCI) 25(1):24–38

Shahroudy A, Liu J, Ng TT, Wang G (2016) Ntu rgb+d: a large scale dataset for 3D human activity analysis. In: Proceedings of the IEEE conference on Computer Vision and Pattern Recognition (CVPR)

Shotton J, Sharp T, Kipman A, Fitzgibbon A, Finocchio M, Blake A, Cook M, Moore R (2013) Real-time human pose recognition in parts from single depth images. Communications of the ACM 56(1):116–124

Simonyan K, Zisserman A (2014) Two-stream convolutional networks for action recognition in videos. In: Advances in neural information processing systems (NeurIPS), pp 568–576

Song S, Lan C, Xing J, Zeng W, Liu J (2017) An end-to-end Spatio-temporal attention model for human action recognition from skeleton data. In: Thirty-First AAAI conference on artificial intelligence (AAAI)

Veeriah V, Zhuang N, Qi GJ (2015) Differential recurrent neural networks for action recognition. In: Proceedings of the IEEE International Conference on Computer Vision (ICCV), pp 4041–4049

Vemulapalli R, Arrate F, Chellappa R (2014) Human action recognition by representing 3D skeletons as points in a lie group. In: Proceedings of the IEEE conference on Computer Vision and Pattern Recognition (CVPR), pp 588–595

Wang C, Flynn J, Wang Y, Yuille AL (2016a) Recognizing actions in 3D using action-snippets and activated simplices. In: Thirtieth AAAI conference on artificial intelligence (AAAI)

Wang L, Xiong Y, Wang Z, Qiao Y, Lin D, Tang X, Van Gool L (2016b) Temporal segment networks: Towards good practices for deep action recognition. In: European Conference on Computer Vision (ECCV), Springer, pp 20–36

Wang P, Yuan C, Hu W, Li B, Zhang Y (2016c) Graph based skeleton motion representation and similarity measurement for action recognition. In: European Conference on Computer Vision (ECCV), Springer, pp 370–385

Weng J, Weng C, Yuan J (2017) Spatio-temporal Naive-Bayes nearest-neighbor (ST-NBNN) for skeleton-based action recognition. In: Proceedings of the IEEE conference on Computer Vision and Pattern Recognition (CVPR), pp 4171–4180

Weng J, Liu M, Jiang X, Yuan J (2018a) Deformable pose traversal convolution for 3D action and gesture recognition. In: Proceedings of the European Conference on Computer Vision (ECCV), pp 136–152

Weng J, Weng C, Yuan J, Liu Z (2018b) Discriminative Spatio-temporal pattern discovery for 3d action recognition. IEEE Trans Circuits Syst Video Technol (T-CSVT) 29(4):1077–1089

Weng J, Jiang X, Zheng WL, Yuan J (2020a) Early action recognition with category exclusion using policy-based reinforcement learning. IEEE Trans Circuits Syst Video Technol (T-CSVT)

Weng J, Luo D, Wang Y, Tai Y, Wang C, Li J, Huang F, Jiang X, Yuan J (2020b) Temporal distinct representation learning for action recognition. In: European Conference on Computer Vision (ECCV), Springer, pp 363–378

Yang X, Tian Y (2012) Eigenjoints-based action recognition using Naive-Bayes-nearest-neighbor. In: 2012 IEEE computer society conference on Computer Vision and Pattern Recognition Workshops (CVPRW). IEEE, pp 14–19

Yu G, Liu Z, Yuan J (2014) Discriminative orderlet mining for real-time recognition of human-object interaction. In: Asian Conference on Computer Vision (ACCV), Springer, pp 50–65

Yuan J, Liu Z, Wu Y (2009) Discriminative subvolume search for efficient action detection. In: Proceedings of the IEEE conference on Computer Vision and Pattern Recognition (CVPR). IEEE, pp 2442–2449

Yun K, Honorio J, Chattopadhyay D, Berg TL, Samaras D (2012) Two-person interaction detection using body-pose features and multiple instance learning. In: 2012 IEEE computer society conference on Computer Vision and Pattern Recognition Workshops (CVPRW). IEEE, pp 28–35

Zhu W, Lan C, Xing J, Zeng W, Li Y, Shen L, Xie X (2016) Co-occurrence feature learning for skeleton based action recognition using regularized deep lSTM networks. In: Thirtieth AAAI conference on artificial intelligence (AAAI)

Chapter 4
Random Forests with Optimized Leaves for Hough-Voting

Hui Liang and Junsong Yuan

Abstract Random forest-based Hough-voting techniques are important in numerous computer vision problems such as pose estimation and gesture recognition. Particularly, the voting weights of leaf nodes in random forests have a big impact on performance. We propose to improve Hough-voting with random forests by learning optimized weights of leaf nodes during training. We have investigated two ways for the leaf weight optimization problem by either applying L2 constraints or L0 constraints to those weights. We show that with additional L0 constraints, we are able to simultaneously obtain optimized leaf weights and prune unreliable leaf nodes in the forests, but with additional costs of more computational costs involved during training. We have applied the proposed algorithms to a number of different problems in computer vision, including hand pose estimation, head pose estimation, and hand gesture recognition. The experimental results show that with L2-regularization, regression and classification accuracy are improved considerably. Further, with L0-regularization, many unreliable leaf nodes are suppressed and the tree structure is compressed considerably, while the performance is still comparable to L2-regularization.

4.1 Introduction

Hough-voting is an effective technique for many classification and regression problems in computer vision. The basic concept is to achieve robust estimation by fusing the predictions cast by a set of voting elements sampled from an input image.

H. Liang (✉)
Amazon, Seattle, USA
e-mail: hulia@amazon.com

J. Yuan
Computer Science and Engineering Department, University at Buffalo,
State University of New York, Buffalo, USA
e-mail: jsyuan@buffalo.edu

Specifically, local features such as small image patches are first randomly sampled over image coordinates. Each of them is then used to obtain a local prediction with a pre-trained classification or regression model. Finally, the image-level prediction is made by fusing all those local predictions based on certain criteria, e.g., average pooling. Hough-voting techniques have found successful use cases in Hough transform (Duda and Hart 1972; Ballard 1981), implicit shape model (Leibe et al. 2004), and Hough forest (Gall and Lempitsky 2009). Among these methods, a combination of a random forest and Hough-voting has shown to be especially effective in various tasks, like hand gesture recognition (Liang et al. 2016; Keskin et al. 2012), head pose estimation (Liang et al. 2016; Fanelli et al. 2013), facial landmark localization (Yang and Patras 2013), and hand pose estimation (Liang et al. 2019; Xu and Cheng 2013). These methods prove to be more efficient and robust compared to those that rely on the global image features only and are also robust to partially corrupted observations.

Due to the uneven distribution of distinctness and noise in local features, some local features are more informative than others during Hough-voting. Therefore, in order for Hough-voting to achieve good prediction accuracy, it is important to accurately evaluate the contribution of a local prediction in image-level prediction fusion. In the context of random forests, this is represented by the weight of the leaf node. In the literature, the unequal contributions of local features can be reflected by hand-crafted prior knowledge, such as assigning more weights to edge pixels (Duda and Hart 1972; Ballard 1981; Sirmaçek and Ünsalan 2010) or certain interest points (Leibe et al. 2004), determining the weights of local features based on training variances (Yang and Patras 2013; Fanelli et al. 2013) or excluding long-range votes (Girshick et al. 2011), but they are not principled solutions. In previous work Maji and Malik (2009), Wohlhart et al. (2012), the weights of the voting local features are automatically optimized on the training data in a max-margin framework, while they mainly target object detection problems.

This chapter presents a principled way to optimize leaf weights in a random forest (Breiman 2001) for Hough-voting. Basically, we still follow conventional ways to build the tree structure of random forests (Breiman 2001; Xu and Cheng 2013). Given an input image, local features are densely sampled to aggregate local evidence for voting. During training, these local features are annotated with ground truth derived from image-level ground truth. The forest is trained to make optimal predictions for these annotated local features. During inference, the forest retrieves predictions from local features sampled from a testing image, and the fused prediction is obtained via average or mode-seeking with these votes. Different from the traditional random forest, we use a set of weights to represent the importance of different leaf nodes in the forest. That is, each leaf node in the forest includes not only a prediction, but also corresponding weight to reflect the confidence of this prediction during fusion, both of which are learned during forest training. Based on an additive fusion model of local feature predictions, we show that the leaf weight optimization problem can be formulated as a constrained quadratic programming problem when applying L2-regularization, which can be solved efficiently. In addition, we propose to enforce an additional L0-sparsity constraint on the leaf weights during optimization to suppress non-informative leaves, and thus leaf nodes with zero weight will not participate

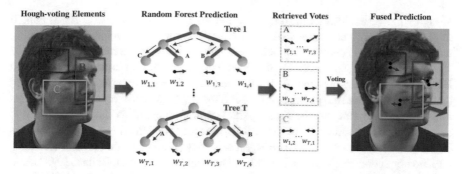

Hough-voting Elements   **Random Forest Prediction**   **Retrieved Votes**   **Fused Prediction**

Fig. 4.1 Random forest with optimized leaves in an exemplar application of head pose estimation. **a**, **b**, and **c** indicate sampled voting local features. Pink arrows at the leaf nodes indicate vote for head orientation and $w_{a,b}$ indicate the corresponding weights learned during training, where **a** and **b** are tree and leaf indices, respectively. The big red arrow denotes fused head orientation prediction

in Hough-voting. The problem to both optimize leaf weights and suppress non-informative leaves is formulated as an L0-regularized optimization problem. When the training dataset is not big, it can be solved by the Augmented Lagrange Multiplier Method (Lin et al. 2010). Particularly, to maintain independence among the trees in the random forest, we choose to optimize the leaf votes at each tree separately. Figure 4.1 illustrates the proposed optimized random forest in the application of head pose estimation.

To illustrate the effectiveness of the proposed algorithm, we have adapted it to several different tasks, including hand pose estimation, hand gesture recognition, and head pose estimation. The experimental results show that it improves the fused prediction accuracy considerably with either L2-regularization or L0-regularization, compared to un-optimized leaf weights. Further, when the dataset is not big, we could use L0-regularization to achieve similar accuracy with L2-regularization even with a large portion of suppressed leaf nodes, with the extra benefits of reduced memory usage and running time cost.

4.2   Literature Review

Hough-voting is widely used in computer vision. During training, local features sampled from training images are coded into a codebook. During testing, the local features sampled from a query image cast their votes for the fused prediction by feature matching in the learned codebook. As each leaf node in a random forest can be regarded as a codebook entry to define a mapping between local features and probabilistic votes, the random forest and its variants are also widely used in Hough-voting due to their ability of fast and highly nonlinear mapping from feature to

Hough votes (Girshick et al. 2011; Keskin et al. 2012; Xu and Cheng 2013; Fanelli et al. 2013; Yang and Patras 2013). This section reviews previous Hough-voting techniques and lays emphasis on relevant random forest-based methods.

Hough-Voting. The original Hough transform has been proposed in Duda and Hart (1972) to detect lines and curves. Its generalized version was proposed in Ballard (1981) to detect arbitrary shapes by encoding the local parts as cookbook entries and use them to vote for the shape parameters. Compared to the original Hough transform, the generalized Hough transform is capable of detecting a variety of shapes in images. However, some local image parts may produce ambiguous predictions, e.g., homogeneous regions. To this end, in Duda and Hart (1972), Ballard (1981), and Sirmaçek and Ünsalan (2010) only the edge pixels are allowed to cast votes to detect certain shapes. In Leibe et al. (2004), the Harris interest points are first detected over the whole image, and the local patches are only extracted around these points for voting-based object localization to avoid using local parts from homogeneous image regions. Nevertheless, the weights of the selected local patches are still determined via their number of activations in the codebook, which can be sub-optimal. To address this issue, in Maji and Malik (2009) the weights of the local parts are discriminatively optimized in a max-margin formulation to maximize certain object detection scores on the training images. Compared to the methods that rely on uniform weights or Naïve Bayesian weights, this method largely improves the detection performance without incurring computational overhead. A similar idea is proposed in Wohlhart et al. (2012), which associates the votes from training local patches with test local patches using a Hough forest and optimizes the weights of training local patches for voting via a max-margin formulation to improve object detection. However, these methods lay more emphasis on object detection, and are not primarily developed to improve regression or classification accuracy by fusing local predictions from Hough-voting elements.

Random Forest. Random forests have been extensively studied in the literature, and most of their variants aim to improve their performance by learning better split functions or probabilistic leaf votes (Schulter et al. 2013; Rota Bulo and Kontschieder 2014; Hara and Chellappa 2014). However, their focus is on general machine learning problems and they do not differentiate between informative and non-informative Hough-voting samples during training. In contrast, in a Hough-voting framework, e.g., body/hand/head pose estimation (Girshick et al. 2011; Xu and Cheng 2013; Fanelli et al. 2013), face landmark localization (Yang and Patras 2013), and gesture recognition (Keskin et al. 2012), it is favorable that the forest is learned to stress on the informative local parts to produce an optimal fusion strategy. While uniform weights are sometimes assigned to leaf votes in the forest for fusion (Keskin et al. 2012), some other methods have attempted empirical ways to determine the voting weights. For instance, in Girshick et al. (2011) it is found that leaf nodes containing long-range votes are unreliable to predict the body joint positions and should be excluded from fusion. In Yang and Patras (2013), the leaf vote is assigned a voting weight based on a trace of the covariance matrix of node sample annotations, and an adaptive threshold is proposed to filter out long-range votes to predict facial point positions. In Fanelli et al. (2013), the leaf nodes that have high training variances are filtered out based on an empirical variance threshold to improve accuracy. However, these strategies cannot guarantee the optimality of the fused prediction. In Ren et al. (2015), a similar quadric form is proposed to optimize the votes stored at leaf nodes in a random forest. However, the proposed algorithm differs from their work in the essential spirits. In Ren et al. (2015), the purpose is still to improve the prediction accuracy of each individual sample. This is different from the Hough-voting framework, in which we aim to improve the per-frame prediction accuracy by assuming that many voting elements do not have a positive impact on the fused predictions and their corresponding votes in the forest should be filtered out.

4.3 The Proposed Method

In the proposed algorithm, the random forest (Breiman 2001) is utilized for either classification or regression tasks via Hough-voting given a testing image I. Let Φ denote the value to be predicted, which could be a continuous variable for tasks like object pose estimation or a discrete category label for tasks like gesture recognition. The forest is an ensemble of T randomized trees, each of which is trained independently with a bootstrap training set. A randomized tree consists of a number of intermediate nodes and leaf nodes to produce a nonlinear mapping from feature space to target space. Each intermediate node of the tree has two child nodes, and each leaf node stores one or more votes for Φ and their associated voting weights. Let the set of votes stored at all the leaf nodes of tree t be $\{\hat{\Phi}_{t,k}, w_{t,k}\}_{k=1}^{K_t}$, where $\hat{\Phi}_{t,k}$ is a vote for Φ, $w_{t,k}$ is a value to represent the voting weight, and K_t is the number of votes in tree t, which can be equal to or larger than the number of leaf nodes.

Following previous work Fanelli et al. (2013), Keskin et al. (2012), and Girshick et al. (2011) on Hough-voting with random forests, the forest is learned to map the features of spatially distributed voting local parts to the probabilistic votes for Φ by minimizing the prediction errors for all the training local parts. Let the feature vector of a local part be $\mathcal{F}$. Given a testing image I, a set of voting local parts $\{p_i\}_{i=1}^{N_s}$ are randomly sampled over the region of interest in I and their feature values $\{\mathcal{F}_i\}$ are calculated, which then cast their votes for Φ independently. To this end, each local part p_i branches down each tree in the forest based on its feature value $\mathcal{F}_i$ until a leaf node is reached, and retrieves the votes stored at the reached leaf nodes. In this framework, we follow the commonly used additive fusion to aggregate these individual votes and the optimal fused prediction is obtained by

$$\Phi^* = \arg\max_{\Phi} \sum_{i=1}^{N_s} P(\Phi|p_i) = \arg\max_{\Phi} \sum_{t=1}^{T} \sum_{i=1}^{N_s} \sum_{k=1}^{K_t} \delta_i^{t,k} w_{t,k} P(\Phi|\hat{\Phi}_{t,k}), \quad (4.1)$$

where $\delta_i^{t,k}$ is an indicator function which equals 1 if a local part p_i retrieves a vote $\hat{\Phi}_{t,k}$ and zero otherwise. As discussed in Sect. 4.1, the voting weights $w_{t,k}$ are critical for the fused prediction accuracy. The next section demonstrates how it can be optimized and pruned after the forest is training to improve per-image prediction performance in the voting framework in (4.1).

4.3.1 Leaf Selection and Weight Optimization

A dataset of images $\{I_m\}_{m=1}^M$ is needed to train the random forest, each of which is annotated with ground truth $\boldsymbol{\Phi}_m$. Following a general Hough-voting scheme, we randomly sample a fixed number of N training local parts $\{p_{i,m}\}_{i=1}^N$ from each image I_m and associate them with image features $\{\mathcal{F}_{i,m}\}$. These local parts are also associated with the ground truth annotations of the images from which they are sampled, i.e., $\{\boldsymbol{\Phi}_{i,m}\}_{i=1}^N$, with the detailed description in Sect. 4.3.2. Traditionally, the forest is trained to learn a nonlinear mapping between $\{\mathcal{F}_{i,m}\}_{i=1,m=1}^{N,M}$ and $\{\boldsymbol{\Phi}_{i,m}\}_{i=1,m=1}^{N,M}$ following the procedures in Sect. 4.3.2 to minimize the prediction error with the local parts. However, the learned forest will have to contain a large number of leaf nodes to encode the appearance variations of all the training local features, while many of them are not necessarily informative for voting, e.g., homogeneous local parts that tend to produce ambiguous predictions. Also, the minimization of prediction error on the local features cannot guarantee the optimality of the fused prediction via voting.

To maintain the independence of the trees in the forest, we consider only a single tree t next and ignore the suffix t in this section for succinctness. Based on formula (4.1), the contribution of each local feature to the fused prediction is represented as a linear weighting coefficient w_k associated with the vote it retrieves, which also represents the discriminative power of the local feature. This suggests a way to gap the local-feature-based training objective and the Hough-voting-based testing objective by adjusting the leaf weights $\{w_k\}_{k=1}^K$. Let $\boldsymbol{w} = [w_1, ..., w_K]^T$ be the concatenated vector of them. The leaf weights are optimized to improve voting-based prediction accuracy, so that the votes corresponding to non-informative local features are assigned small weights and vice versa. The problem can be formulated as

$$\boldsymbol{w}^* = \arg\min_{\boldsymbol{w}} L(w) = \arg\min_{\boldsymbol{w}} \sum_{m=1}^M E(\bar{\boldsymbol{\Phi}}_m, \boldsymbol{\Phi}_m) \tag{4.2}$$

$$s.t. \ \ 0 \le \boldsymbol{w} \le u,$$

where $\bar{\boldsymbol{\Phi}}_m$ is the per-image fused prediction, $\boldsymbol{\Phi}_m$ is the ground truth, and E is their L2-norm error function. $0 \le \boldsymbol{w} \le u$ enforces all the leaf weights to be non-negative and upper-bounded with u to avoid overfitting.

Given the tree structure and the set of leaf votes $\{\hat{\boldsymbol{\Phi}}_k\}_{k=1}^K$ of the tree learned in Sect. 4.3.2, we first define a per-image fused prediction for each training image based on the sampled local features for voting to approximate that in formula (4.1) but with only a single tree. As stated before, a fixed number of N local parts are randomly sampled from each training image I_m to construct each tree of the forest. After the tree structure is learned, each of the N local parts reaches one leaf node, and multiple local parts from one image may reach the same leaf node. The fused prediction for each training image can thus be calculated based on the votes retrieved by these N parts from the tree.

By keeping track of the destination leaf nodes of each training local parts, we can define an indicator function $\delta_{i,m}^k$, which equals 1 if $p_{i,m}$ reaches $\hat{\boldsymbol{\Phi}}_k$ and zero otherwise. We further define a vector $\boldsymbol{q}_m = [q_{m,1}, ..., q_{m,K}]^T$, in which each element $q_{m,k} = \sum_{i=1}^{N} \delta_{i,m}^k$ represents the number of local parts that are from I_m and reach the k_{th} vote. $\boldsymbol{q}_m$ is normalized to sum to one. Let $\boldsymbol{\alpha} = [\hat{\boldsymbol{\Phi}}_1, ..., \hat{\boldsymbol{\Phi}}_K]^T$ be the concatenation of all leaf votes from a tree. For each training image I_m, its voting-based fused prediction $\bar{\boldsymbol{\Phi}}_m$ is defined as the weighted sum of the votes retrieved by its local parts:

$$\bar{\boldsymbol{\Phi}}_m = \sum_{k=1}^{K} q_{m,k} w_k \hat{\boldsymbol{\Phi}}_k = (\boldsymbol{q}_m \circ \boldsymbol{\alpha})^T \boldsymbol{w}, \tag{4.3}$$

where $\circ$ denotes the Hadamard product. We define two auxiliary matrices $\boldsymbol{Q}, \boldsymbol{A} \in \mathbb{R}^{M \times K}$ and a vector $\boldsymbol{g} \in \mathbb{R}^M$, where $\boldsymbol{Q} = [\boldsymbol{q}_1, ..., \boldsymbol{q}_M]^T$ records the hits on the leaf votes for all training images, each row of which corresponds to one image. $\boldsymbol{A} = [\boldsymbol{\alpha}, ..., \boldsymbol{\alpha}]^T$ stacks vector $\boldsymbol{\alpha}$ for M repetitive rows. $\boldsymbol{g} = [\boldsymbol{\Phi}_1, ..., \boldsymbol{\Phi}_M]^T$ stores ground truths of training images. Let $\boldsymbol{A}_q = \boldsymbol{Q} \circ \boldsymbol{A}$. The prediction error over all training images is represented as $\sum_m E_m = \|\boldsymbol{A}_q \boldsymbol{w} - \boldsymbol{g}\|^2$.

L2-regularization: in order to further avoid overfitting, we can add L2-regularization to leaf weights $\boldsymbol{w}$, and thus the problem can be reformulated as

$$\boldsymbol{w}^* = \arg\min_{\boldsymbol{w}} L(w) + \lambda \|\boldsymbol{w}\|_2$$
$$s.t. \quad 0 \leq \boldsymbol{w} \leq u, \tag{4.4}$$

where λ is a coefficient to control the weight of the regularization term. This is a standard linearly constrained quadratic programming problem. When the training dataset is large, the matrix $\boldsymbol{A}_q^T \boldsymbol{A}_q$ can be huge, i.e., at the magnitude near $10^4 \times 10^4$. However, as the number of training local parts per image is relatively small, and some local parts from the same image may go to the same leaf node, $\boldsymbol{A}_q$ is quite sparse. Thus, we utilize the interior-point-convex quadric programming algorithm (Gould and Toint 2004) to solve (4.4).

L0-regularization: in order to achieve the dual goal of leaf weight optimization and pruning simultaneously, we could further enforce the L0-sparsity constraint on $\boldsymbol{w}$ to reduce model complexity of the forest so that many leaf votes are suppressed. The problem can be reformulated as

$$w^* = \arg\min_{w} \sum_{m=1}^{M} E(\bar{\Phi}_m, \Phi_m)$$
$$s.t. \quad 0 \leq w \leq u, \|w\|_0 \leq S, \tag{4.5}$$

where $\|\cdot\|_0$ denotes the L0-norm and S is a scalar to control the number of nonzero elements in w. Different sparsity ratios of the number of nonzero weights over the number of all weights S/K can adjust the model complexity of the forest. Following the augmented Lagrange multiplier method (Lin et al. 2010), we introduce an auxiliary vector β of the same size to w, and convert (4.5) to the following problem:

$$w^*, \beta^* = \arg\min_{w,\beta} \left\| A_q w - g \right\|_2^2$$
$$s.t. \quad 0 \leq w \leq u, w = \beta, \|\beta\|_0 \leq S. \tag{4.6}$$

Its augmented Lagrangian form is given by

$$w^*, \beta^* = \arg\min_{w,\beta} \left\| A_q w - g \right\|_2^2 + y^T(w - \beta) + \frac{\rho}{2} \|w - \beta\|_2^2$$
$$s.t. \quad 0 \leq w \leq u, \|\beta\|_0 \leq S, \tag{4.7}$$

where y is a Lagrange multiplier and ρ is a positive regularization parameter. The solution of (4.7) can be obtained by solving the following sub-problems for w^* and β^* separately in an iterative manner until convergence. To start the iterative optimization, ρ is initialized with a small value and gradually increased to enforce increasingly strong consistency between w and β. In each iteration, β is first fixed to convert (4.7) to

$$w^* = \arg\min_{w} \left\| A_q w - g \right\|_2^2 + y^T w + \frac{\rho}{2} w^T w - \rho \beta^T w$$
$$= \arg\min_{w} w^T (A_q{}^T A_q + \frac{\rho}{2} I)w + (y^T - 2g^T A_q - \rho \beta^T)w \tag{4.8}$$
$$s.t. \quad 0 \leq w \leq u,$$

which is again a standard linearly constrained quadratic programming problem, and thus can be solved following the way in L2-regularization. Next, we fix w to solve for β^* by converting (4.7) to

$$\beta^* = \arg\min_{\beta} -y^T \beta + \frac{\rho}{2} \|w - \beta\|_2^2 = \arg\min_{\beta} \frac{\rho}{2} \left\| w + \frac{y}{\rho} - \beta \right\|_2^2$$
$$s.t. \|\beta\|_0 \leq S. \tag{4.9}$$

This problem can be very efficiently solved by element-wise comparison in β. Finally, we update y and ρ:

$$y \leftarrow y + \rho \times (w - \beta)$$
$$\rho \leftarrow \rho \alpha, \tag{4.10}$$

where $\alpha > 1$ gradually improves the convergence rate. The algorithm stops itera-
tion when $\| w - \beta \|_\infty$ is less than a threshold or a maximum number of iterations
is reached. In general, the algorithm takes about 20–30 iterations to converge in
the experiments in Sect. 4.4. As in each iteration we need to solve a quadratic-
programming problem whose time-complexity is largely determined by $A_q{}^T A_q$,
it can be slow when the training dataset is big.

Back pruning of random forest: with weights learned via formula (4.2), many
leaf votes are suppressed to have zero weights, which are non-informative in prediction. Here we define a leaf node to be completely suppressed if the weights of all
its votes are zero. For instance, when the forest is trained to predict multiple independent objectives simultaneously, e.g., two Euler angles for head pose estimation,
there could be two weights for each leaf vote for these two objectives. In the case
of classification, there is only one weight for the class labels in one leaf node. If a
certain sub-tree in a tree of the forest contains only completely suppressed leaves, it
can be removed from the forest to reduce model complexity. This can be efficiently
implemented as a post-order tree traversal algorithm. Starting from the root of each
tree, each node will check whether all the sub-trees of its child nodes are suppressed
in a recursive manner. If yes, the sub-tree with a root at this node will be labeled as
suppressed, and vice versa.

4.3.2 Details of Forest Learning and Prediction

A forest is learned with a set of feature and annotation pairs $\{\mathcal{F}_{i,m}, \boldsymbol{\Phi}_{i,m}\}_{i=1,m=1}^{N,M}$.
Despite that $\boldsymbol{\Phi}$ can be quite a general term, we are particularly interested in its
several forms including discrete category labels, Euler angles, and 2D/3D positions,
which are widely adopted in computer vision problems. Following previous work,
the annotation $\boldsymbol{\Phi}_{i,m}$ of a local feature equals $\boldsymbol{\Phi}_m$ for discrete category labels and Euler
angles, and equal the offset between the center point of $p_{i,m}$ and the ground truth
position $\boldsymbol{\Phi}_m$ for 2D/3D positions. To learn the tree structure, each tree is initialized
with an empty root node. Starting from the root node, the training samples are split
into two subsets recursively to reduce the prediction errors at the child nodes. At
the non-leaf nodes, a set of candidate split functions $\{\psi\}$ are randomly generated
as the proposals for node splitting, which can take the form $\mathcal{F}_b \leq \tau$, where $\mathcal{F}_b$ is a
randomly selected dimension of $\mathcal{F}$ by sampling the feature dimension index, and τ
is also a random threshold value to determine whether to branch to the left or right
children. Let U be the set of node samples for splitting and $\{\boldsymbol{\Phi}_j | j \in U\}$ be the set
of their annotations. The optimal split function is selected based on the following
criterion:

$$\psi^* = \arg\max_{\psi} H(U) - \sum_{s \in \{l,r\}} \frac{|U_s(\psi)|}{|U|} H(U_s(\psi)), \qquad (4.11)$$

where U_l and U_r are the two subsets of U split by ψ. The measure $H(U)$ evaluates the uncertainty of the sample annotations in U. For classification, $H(U)$ is defined as the entropy of the category label distribution of U. For regression of 2D/3D positions, we use the below measure of offset variances:

$$H(U) = \frac{1}{|U|} \sum_{j \in U} \left\| \boldsymbol{\Phi}_j - \bar{\boldsymbol{\Phi}}_j \right\|_2^2. \qquad (4.12)$$

For Euler angles, as they follow circular distribution, we adopt the following measure to evaluate their variances:

$$H(U) = 1 - \sqrt{\left[\frac{\sum_{j \in U} \cos \boldsymbol{\Phi}_j}{|U|} \right]^2 + \left[\frac{\sum_{j \in U} \sin \boldsymbol{\Phi}_j}{|U|} \right]^2}. \qquad (4.13)$$

The samples going to each branch are then used to construct a new tree node by either continuing the splitting procedure or ending up splitting to obtain a leaf node. This is done by checking whether certain stopping criteria are met, e.g., the sample annotations are pure enough, or the maximum depth is reached. For each leaf node, its vote can be represented by the average of the ground truth annotations stored at the sample set reaching it. For discrete category labels, the vote is a histogram, each bin of which corresponds to the frequency of a category in the node samples. For the 2D/3D position, the vote is defined as

$$\hat{\boldsymbol{\Phi}} = \frac{1}{|U|} \sum_{j \in U} \boldsymbol{\Phi}_j. \qquad (4.14)$$

For Euler angles, the vote is defined as

$$\hat{\boldsymbol{\Phi}} = \mathrm{atan2} \left[\frac{1}{|U|} \sum_{j \in U} \sin \boldsymbol{\Phi}_j, \frac{1}{|U|} \sum_{j \in U} \cos \boldsymbol{\Phi}_j \right]. \qquad (4.15)$$

More refined votes can also be obtained via clustering node sample annotations (Girshick et al. 2011; Yang and Patras 2013). As in Sect. 4.3.1, their weights in Hough-voting is obtained via formula (4.2). If the weight is zero, we simply store an empty vote.

During testing, the optimal fused prediction is obtained by formula (4.1). For classification, $\boldsymbol{\Phi}$ is a category label and $P(\boldsymbol{\Phi} | \hat{\boldsymbol{\Phi}}_{t,k})$ is a probability distribution histogram stored at the leaf node following (Keskin et al. 2012). Thus the objective function in (4.1) is a weighted sum of histograms and the voting-based prediction can be obtained via finding the label with the maximum probability in the fused histogram. For regression, when $\boldsymbol{\Phi}$ is a 2D or 3D position, we adopt the weighted Parzen density estimator with a Gaussian kernel to evaluate the objective function in (4.1) following (Girshick et al. 2011; Yang and Patras 2013), and define $P(\boldsymbol{\Phi}|\hat{\boldsymbol{\Phi}}_{t,k})$ as

$$P(\boldsymbol{\Phi}|\hat{\boldsymbol{\Phi}}_{t,k}) = \mathcal{N}(\boldsymbol{\Phi}; \hat{\boldsymbol{\Phi}}_{t,k} + \boldsymbol{v}_i, \delta_v^2), \qquad (4.16)$$

where δ_v^2 is an isotropic variance for all dimensions of $\boldsymbol{\Phi}$, and $\boldsymbol{v}_i$ is the center position of the local part as $\hat{\boldsymbol{\Phi}}_{t,k}$ denotes the offset between the target position and local part center. When $\boldsymbol{\Phi}$ is a Euler angle, we utilize 1D wrapped Gaussian kernel Fisher (2000) to model $P(\boldsymbol{\Phi}|\boldsymbol{\Phi}_{ik})$ within the range $[0, 2\pi]$:

$$P(\boldsymbol{\Phi}|\boldsymbol{\Phi}_{ik}) = \sum_{z \in \mathbb{Z}} \mathcal{N}(\boldsymbol{\Phi} - 2z\pi; \hat{\boldsymbol{\Phi}}_{ik}, \delta_\theta^2), \qquad (4.17)$$

which is infinite wrappings of linear Gaussian within $[0, 2\pi]$, and δ_θ^2 is the variance. In practice, the summation can be taken over $z \in [-2, 2]$ to approximate the above infinite summation (Herdtweck and Curio 2013). Therefore, for both regression of the 2D/3D position and the Euler angle, the objective function in (4.1) is still the sum of Gaussians, and the optimal solution can be efficiently obtained by the Mean-shift algorithm (Comaniciu and Meer 2002).

4.4   Experimental Results

This section presents the experimental results of the proposed algorithms with both L2-regularization and L0-regularization on several different tasks, including hand pose estimation, head pose estimation, and hand gesture recognition. Due to computational constraints, we evaluate the proposed leaf weight optimization algorithm with L0-regularization only on a relatively small dataset for hand gesture recognition.

4.4.1   Hand Pose Estimation in Depth Images

In this experiment, we test the performance of the proposed algorithm with L2-regularization on a synthesis 3D hand pose dataset of 50k depth images, each of which is annotated with ground truth global hand pose parameters. We use the 3D hand model (Liang et al. 2014) to synthesize this dataset. The hand poses for data synthesis contain variations of both global hand rotation and local finger articulation. The global hand rotation is confined within $(-20°, 60°)$ around the X-axis, $(-180°, 30°)$ around the Y-axis, and $(-60°, 60°)$ around the Z-axis, which have covered most of the natural hand rotation ranges. It is uniformly discretized into 864 viewpoints. The local finger articulation consists of 10 basic hand posture templates, as in Liang et al. (2019). For each of the 10 basic templates, the fingers are also allowed to move in small ranges, which give in total 60 static hand postures. To train each tree of the Hough forest, 200 pixels are uniformly sampled from each training image and 10000 candidate split functions are generated. During testing, 1000 pixels are uniformly sampled from the hand region for spatial voting.

The experimental results are based on single-frame evaluation as the synthesis images are generated independently. To evaluate the prediction accuracy, we perform fivefold cross-validation, and in each fold 80% of all the images are used for forest training and the rest 20% for testing. For 3D hand translation, the prediction accuracy is evaluated in terms of the average distance between the prediction and the ground truth. For 3D hand rotation angles, we follow the conventions Agarwal and Triggs (2006) to define the prediction error between prediction $\tilde{\phi}$ and ground truth ϕ as $|(\tilde{\phi} - \phi) \mod \pm 180°|$. To perform the experiment, we use the training data to learn the tree structures for several different values of maximum tree depth ranging within [8, 20] to better understand the performance of our leaf weight optimization algorithm with respect to different numbers of leaf nodes.

In Fig. 4.2, we compare hand pose estimation results obtained by optimized and uniform leaf weights, which show the prediction errors for 3D translation and rotation angles and the average per-frame time costs for different tree depths of the forest. Overall, the proposed leaf weight optimization algorithm largely improves the prediction accuracy for both 3D hand translation and rotation compared to uniform leaf weights. For hand translation, the proposed leaf weight optimization scheme reduces the prediction error by 11.6% on average. For hand rotation, even with relatively low tree depth, e.g., 8, the prediction errors with optimized leaf weights are only 17.2°, 17.9°, and 13.9° for the three rotation angles, which is even better than the performance of the depth-10 forest with uniform leaf weights. Particularly, for the θ_y rotation which is in the range $(-180°, 30°)$ and has the largest appearance ambiguity, the forest with optimized leaf weights reduces the prediction error by 49.8% on average. In Fig. 4.2e, we also present the average per-frame time costs for hand pose prediction, which shows that the proposed method does not require extra time costs compared to the forest with uniform leaf weights. The time costs do not change much with different tree depths, and are below 12 ms on average, which is sufficient for most real-time applications.

4.4.2 Head Pose Estimation in Depth Images

In this experiment, we evaluate the proposed algorithm with L2-regularization on the Biwi Kinect head pose database (Fanelli et al. 2013). The depth images in this dataset contain both the head and the upper body, and the latter is not informative for head pose estimation. Therefore, we choose to train a head region classification forest and a head pose regression forest separately to better preserve the performance of the pose regression forest. The head classification forest is trained following a similar procedure in Shotton et al. (2011) with the ground truth head mask in the dataset. The

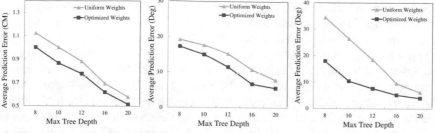

(a) Translation $\boldsymbol{v}$ prediction (b) Pitch angle θ_x prediction (c) Yaw angle θ_y prediction

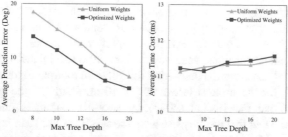

(d) Roll angle θ_z prediction (e) Avg. per-frame time cost

Fig. 4.2 Hand pose estimation results on the synthesis dataset for different values of maximum tree depth

pose regression forest is trained with the procedure in Sect. 4.3. Following Fanelli et al. (2013), we set the maximum of tree depth to be 15, and perform a fourfold, subject-independent cross-validation on this dataset. The nose localization error is defined as the Euclidean distance between prediction and ground truth in millimeters. The rotation error for yaw, pitch, and roll is the Riemannian distance between prediction and ground truth rotation angles in degree. As in Fanelli et al. (2013), we also report the direction error, which is computed by first rotating the frontal vector $[0, 0, -1]^T$ using the predicted and ground truth 3D rotation separately, and then measuring the angle between the two rotated vectors. In addition, a successful detection means that the predicted nose tip is within 20 mm from the ground truth position and that the direction error is below 15°. We choose the tree number to be 3 in the classification forest and 5 in the regression forest. The total number of trees is thus 8, which is still less than that in Fanelli et al. (2013), i.e., to train the tree structure, 8K candidate split functions are randomly generated to train each tree. The coarser depth context descriptor Liang et al. (2014) is adopted as the local feature for both head classification and pose regression. In contrast, in Fanelli et al. (2013) the average depth patch difference is used as the feature, which requires preprocessing of the entire depth image to get the integral image. A fixed stride of 5 is used to select voting pixels from the depth images, as in Fanelli et al. (2013).

In addition to Fanelli et al. (2013), we also compare our method to Papazov et al. (2015) which uses a triangular surface patch feature for head pose estimation. The results are presented in Table 4.1, which report mean and standard deviation of the errors for nose tip position and head rotation estimation, the ratio of missed prediction, and average per-frame time cost for Fanelli et al. (2013), Papazov et al. (2015), and our method with/without optimized leaf weights. N_T represents the number of triangles used for prediction in Papazov et al. (2015). Overall, the proposed method with optimized leaf weights achieved the lowest ratio of missed prediction 5.6% at the least time cost 15.2 ms. Compared to the forest with un-optimized leaf weights, the proposed method largely reduces the pose prediction error and missed ratio, i.e., 8.0 mm versus 12.5 mm for nose tip position, 3.9° versus 6.4° for 3D Euler angles, 5.6% versus 20.1% for the ratio of missed predictions, and the time costs are almost identical. In Table 4.1, we can see that our forest with optimized leaf weights largely outperforms Fanelli et al. (2013), i.e., 8.0 mm versus 12.2 mm error for nose tip position and 3.9° versus 4.2° for 3D Euler angles, while at only 1/3 the time cost. Figure 4.3 presents the average accuracy of our method and Fanelli et al. (2013) for nose position and head rotation prediction for different tolerance values of prediction error. Although for the strictest thresholds of 10 mm and 10° the accuracy of our method is lower than Fanelli et al. (2013), our overall accuracy is much higher. This may be due to the fact that we only use a coarse depth feature Liang et al. (2014) for pose prediction, which is more sensitive to noise compared to the average patch depth difference in Fanelli et al. (2013) and thus impairs the accuracy for strict thresholds. Compared to Papazov et al. (2015), our method achieves comparable results to that of $N_T = 100$ in Papazov et al. (2015), i.e., 8.0 mm versus 8.6 mm for nose tip position, 3.9° versus 3.4° for 3D Euler angles, but at only less than half the time cost. The results of Papazov et al. (2015) for $N_T = 200$ is higher than ours, while it requires five times more time costs than ours.

Table 4.1 Comparison of head pose prediction results on Biwi databased with Fanelli et al. (2013), Papazov et al. (2015), and the proposed method. Nose error is in millimeters. Direction and angle errors are in degrees

	Nose tip	Direction	Yaw	Pitch	Roll	Time (ms)
Papazov et al. (2015) $N_T = 200$	6.8 ± 14.2	3.2 ± 7.9	2.5 ± 8.3	1.8 ± 4.3	2.9 ± 12.8	75.1
Papazov et al. (2015) $N_T = 100$	8.6 ± 21.3	4.4 ± 11.8	3.5 ± 12.6	2.5 ± 6.3	4.2 ± 17.2	38.9
Fanelli et al. (2013)	12.2 ± 22.8	5.9 ± 8.1	3.8 ± 6.5	3.5 ± 5.8	5.4 ± 6.0	44.7
Ours with uniform weights	12.5 ± 13.9	9.8 ± 8.3	6.4 ± 8.1	7.2 ± 6.6	5.6 ± 6.8	15.9
Ours with optimized weights	8.0 ± 7.7	5.8 ± 4.6	3.9 ± 4.0	3.9 ± 3.5	4.0 ± 4.1	**15.2**

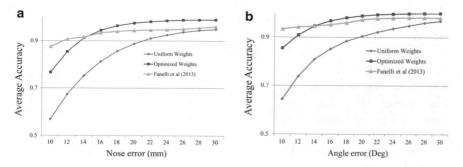

Fig. 4.3 Average accuracy for **a** nose tip position prediction and **b** head direction prediction for different error tolerance

4.4.3   Hand Gesture Recognition in Depth Images

This experiment is performed on the NTU Hand Digits dataset (Ren et al. 2013), which consists of 1000 depth images of 10 hand digit gestures, i.e., 0–9, from 10 subjects. In implementation, the ground truth gesture label is represented as a 10D vector, with all dimensions equal to 0 except the one corresponding to the ground truth label equal to 1. Thus the per-image prediction error in formula (4.2) is defined as the L2-norm of the fused histogram and this a 10D vector. The measure function $H(U)$ for tree node splitting is taken as the gesture label entropy in the node sample U. Following Zhang et al. (2013), we perform a tenfold leave-one-subject-out test in this experiment. The depth difference feature in Shotton et al. (2013) is adopted for gesture classification with a random forest, which is fast to calculate. To train the forest, 100 voting pixels are sampled from each image with their depth difference feature extracted to train each tree. The tree stops growing in conditions that its depth exceeds 20, the node samples contain only one gesture label, or the node sample is less than 50. The number of trees in the forest is set as 4. As the depth difference feature is not rotation-invariant, we utilize the method in Liang et al. (2012) to crop the hand region and find the 2D principal orientation of the forearm and rotate the hand region accordingly to perform rough 2D rotation-normalization for all training and testing images. During testing, 500 pixels are randomly sampled within the cropped hand region to vote for hand gesture, and each of them is passed to the random forest to retrieve gesture votes. Their votes are fused via formula (4.1) to get the gesture prediction of the input image.

Based on the above rotation normalization scheme (RN), we have tested the classification accuracy using random forest with uniform weights and L0-regularized weights learned via different sparsity ratios S/K within [0.05, 1.0]. Note that $S/K = 1.0$ means no sparsity constraint. The average number of leaf nodes per tree in the forest is 3678. We found that the leaf weights learned via a sparsity ratio S/K of 0.1 already outperforms uniform leaf weights in gesture recognition accuracy, i.e., 97.9% versus 97.0%. At the same time, it reduces the model complexity

Table 4.2 Comparison of recognition accuracy on the NTU hand digits dataset Ren et al. (2013)

Methods	Accuracy (%)	Time cost
Random forest + UW w/o RN (Keskin et al. 2012)	90.0	14.5 ms
Random forest + UW + RN	97.0	16.4 ms
Random forest + L0 + RN, $S/K = 1.0$	**98.0**	15.7 ms
Random forest + L0 + RN, $S/K = 0.1$	97.9	14.4 ms
Near-convex decomposition + FEMD (Ren et al. 2013)	93.9	4.0 s
Thresholding decomposition + FEMD (Ren et al. 2013)	93.2	75 ms
H3DF + SVM (Zhang et al. 2013)	95.5	N.A.
H3DF + SRC (Zhang and Tian 2015)	97.4	N.A.

of the random forest by 83.8% and reduces the classification time cost by 35.5%. Although a small value of S/K has the benefit of reduction in both model complexity of the random forest and classification time cost, leaf sparsity cannot be excessively small, which may also suppress some useful voting elements, e.g., $S/K = 0.05$ leads to the relative worse prediction accuracy of 96.0%

We also implemented the shape classification forest in Keskin et al. (2012) for gesture recognition. To this end, we discard the rotation normalization scheme in both the forest training and test stages, and assign uniform weights to all leaf votes. It only achieves 90.0% recognition accuracy on this dataset. In addition, we also compare the proposed method to other state-of-the-art methods, including Ren et al. (2013), Zhang et al. (2013), and Zhang and Tian (2015), and the results are summarized in Table 4.2, which demonstrates that the proposed method is among the state of the art. It is worth noting that Zhang et al. (2013), Zhang and Tian (2015) adopt much more complex features including the 3D depth normal, while our method only relies on the coarse depth difference feature. Such fine features can be further incorporated into our method to improve gesture recognition. Also, it is worth noting that the most time consuming part of this gesture recognition pipeline is hand segmentation, which can be largely reduced if the body skeleton information is available, e.g., from Kinect SDK.

4.5 Conclusion

This chapter presents an algorithm to optimize leaf weights and prune tree nodes in a random forest to improve classification and regression accuracy during Hough-voting. The method not only improves the fused prediction accuracy considerably, but also reduces model complexity of a random forest and running time cost. In the experiments, we show the method achieves good results for several different problems including hand gesture recognition, head orientation estimation, and hand pose estimation. Although the method is developed based on the baseline random forest (Breiman 2001), it is general enough to extend to other more advanced forests, such as Schulter et al. (2013) and Rota Bulo and Kontschieder (2014), which is left as our future work.

References

Agarwal A, Triggs B (2006) Recovering 3d human pose from monocular images. IEEE Trans Pattern Anal Mach Intell

Ballard DH (1981) Generalizing the Hough transform to detect arbitrary shapes. Pattern Recognit 13(2):111–122

Breiman L (2001) Random forests. Mach Learn 45(1):5–32

Comaniciu D, Meer P (2002) Mean shift: a robust approach toward feature space analysis. IEEE Trans Pattern Anal Mach Intell 24(5):603–619

Duda RO, Hart PE (1972) Use of the Hough transformation to detect lines and curves in pictures. Commun ACM 15(1):11–15

Fanelli G, Dantone M, Gall J, Fossati A, Gool LV (2013) Random forests for real time 3d face analysis. Int J Comput Vis 101(3):437–458

Fisher NI (2000) Statistical analysis of circular data. Cambridge University Press

Gall J, Lempitsky V (2009) Class-specific Hough forests for object detection. In: IEEE conference on computer vision and pattern recognition. IEEE, pp 1022–1029

Girshick R, Shotton J, Kohli P, Criminisi A, Fitzgibbon A (2011) Efficient regression of general-activity human poses from depth images. In: International conference on computer vision

Gould N, Toint PL (2004) Preprocessing for quadratic programming. Math Program Ser B 100:95–132

Hara K, Chellappa R (2014) Growing regression forests by classification: applications to object pose estimation. In: European conference on computer vision. Springer, pp 552–567

Herdtweck C, Curio C (2013) Monocular car viewpoint estimation with circular regression forests. In: IEEE intelligent vehicles symposium

Keskin C, Kıraç F, Kara YE, Akarun L (2012) Hand pose estimation and hand shape classification using multi-layered randomized decision forests. In: European Conference on Computer Vision, Springer, pp 852–863

Leibe B, Leonardis A, Schiele B (2004) Combined object categorization and segmentation with an implicit shape model. In: ECCV workshop on statistical learning in computer vision, pp 17–32

Liang H, Yuan J, Thalmann D (2012) 3d fingertip and palm tracking in depth image sequences. In: Proceedings of the 20th ACM international conference on Multimedia. ACM, pp 785–788

Liang H, Yuan J, Thalmann D (2014) Parsing the hand in depth images. IEEE Trans Multimed

Liang H, Hou J, Yuan J, Thalmann D (2016) Random forest with suppressed leaves for Hough voting. In: Asian conference on computer vision

Liang H, Yuan J, Lee J, Ge L, Thalmann D (2019) Hough forest with optimized leaves for global hand pose estimation with arbitrary postures. IEEE Trans Cybern

Lin Z, Chen M, Ma Y (2010) The augmented Lagrange multiplier method for exact recovery of corrupted low-rank matrices. arXiv preprint arXiv:10095055

Maji S, Malik J (2009) Object detection using a max-margin Hough transform. In: IEEE conference on computer vision and pattern recognition. IEEE, pp 1038–1045

Papazov C, Marks TK, Jones M (2015) Real-time 3d head pose and facial landmark estimation from depth images using triangular surface patch features. In: IEEE conference on computer vision and pattern recognition

Ren S, Cao X, Wei Y, Sun J (2015) Global refinement of random forest. In: The IEEE conference on computer vision and pattern recognition

Ren Z, Yuan J, Meng J, Zhang Z (2013) Robust part-based hand gesture recognition using kinect sensor. IEEE Trans Multimed 15(5):1110–1120

Rota Bulo S, Kontschieder P (2014) Neural decision forests for semantic image labelling. In: IEEE conference on computer vision and pattern recognition. IEEE, pp 81–88

Schulter S, Leistner C, Wohlhart P, Roth PM, Bischof H (2013) Alternating regression forests for object detection and pose estimation. In: 2013 IEEE international conference on computer vision (ICCV). IEEE, pp 417–424

Shotton J, Fitzgibbon A, Cook M, Sharp T, Finocchio M, Moore R, Kipman A, Blake A (2011) Realtime human pose recognition in parts from single depth images. In: IEEE conference on computer vision and pattern recognition

Shotton J, Girshick R, Fitzgibbon A, Sharp T, Cook M, Finocchio M, Moore R, Kohli P, Criminisi A, Kipman A et al (2013) Efficient human pose estimation from single depth images. IEEE Trans Pattern Anal Mach Intell 35(12):2821–2840

Sirmaçek B, Ünsalan C (2010) Road network extraction using edge detection and spatial voting. In: International conference on pattern recognition. IEEE, pp 3113–3116

Wohlhart P, Schulter S, Köstinger M, Roth PM, Bischof H (2012) Discriminative Hough forests for object detection. In: British machine vision conference, pp 1–11

Xu C, Cheng L (2013) Efficient hand pose estimation from a single depth image. In: International conference on computer vision

Yang H, Patras I (2013) Sieving regression forest votes for facial feature detection in the wild. In: IEEE international conference on computer vision. IEEE, pp 1936–1943

Zhang C, Tian Y (2015) Histogram of 3d facets: a depth descriptor for human action and hand gesture recognition. Comput Vis Image Underst 139:29–39

Zhang C, Yang X, Tian Y (2013) Histogram of 3d facets: a characteristic descriptor for hand gesture recognition. In: IEEE international conference and workshops on automatic face and gesture recognition. IEEE, pp 1–8

Chapter 5
Modeling Human Perception of 3D Scenes

Zeynep Cipiloglu Yildiz, Abdullah Bulbul, and Tolga Capin

Abstract The ultimate goal of computer graphics is to create images for viewing by people. The artificial intelligence-based methods should consider what is known about human visual perception in vision science literature. Modeling visual perception of 3D scenes requires the representation of several complex processes. In this chapter, we survey artificial intelligence and machine learning-based solutions for modeling human perception of 3D scenes. We also suggest future research directions. The topics that we cover include are modeling human visual attention, 3D object quality perception, and material recognition.

5.1 Introduction

The ultimate goal of computer graphics is to create images for viewing by people. The artificial intelligence (AI)-based methods should consider what is known about human visual perception in vision science literature. Modeling visual perception of 3D scenes requires the representation of several complex processes. In this chapter, we survey the AI-based solutions for modeling human perception of 3D scenes:

- In a complex environment, the human visual system makes use of a mechanism to address its attention to those points or objects that stand out from the rest, so

Z. C. Yildiz (✉)
Computer Engineering Department, Manisa Celal Bayar University,
45140 Yunusemre/Manisa, Turkey
e-mail: zeynep.cipiloglu@cbu.edu.tr

A. Bulbul
Computer Engineering Department, Ankara Yildirim Beyazit University,
06010 Etlik/Ankara, Turkey
e-mail: abulbul@ybu.edu.tr

T. Capin
Computer Engineering Department, TED University, Ankara, Turkey
e-mail: tolga.capin@tedu.edu.tr

© The Author(s), under exclusive license to Springer Nature Switzerland AG 2021
N. Magnenat Thalmann et al. (eds.), *Intelligent Scene Modeling and Human-Computer Interaction*, Human–Computer Interaction Series,
https://doi.org/10.1007/978-3-030-71002-6_5

67

that it can process the most significant parts of a scene. The main approaches for AI modeling of attention are discussed first.

- 3D models, whether captured by a camera or modeled offline, are generally noisy or low in quality. Furthermore, models may be exposed to several geometric modifications such as simplification, compression, and watermarking. Therefore, the problem of measuring the quality of 3D models has been a studied topic recently. In this chapter, we study the recent work on 3D visual quality assessment.
- As a part of object recognition, material recognition is successfully utilized by the human visual system. Besides helping object recognition tasks, material and specularity perception can guide us further on the quality of objects, e.g. freshness of a fruit and age of a book. Recent advances in the use of artificial intelligence on material perception are reviewed in this chapter.

5.2 Visual Attention

In real life, the human visual attention mechanism allows humans to rapidly analyze complex scenes by directing their attention to the prominent parts of the scene. This process lessens the cognitive burden. The visual attention mechanism is well-studied in cognitive sciences, and it is generally considered as having two components:

- **Bottom-up (stimulus-driven) component**: This type of attention is purely stimulus-driven and is calculated from the visual properties of a scene, such as color, intensity, orientation, and motion (see Fig. 5.1). It helps to identify salient regions of the scene. It is often referred to as *saliency* in the literature. The seminal works in visual attention (e.g. Koch and Ullman (1987); Itti et al. (1998)) and early works that follow them generally relied on cognitive approaches which extract several feature maps such as color and orientation and combine them using center-surround operations. A *saliency map* which visualizes the points in an image according to their likelihood of being attended was produced in these studies.
- **Top-down (task-driven) component**: Visual attention is also affected by the task, goal, prior experiences, semantic regions, etc. (see Fig. 5.2). The top-down component refers to this kind of attention and it is highly dependent on the viewer. Therefore, it is hard to model and not much studied in computer graphics.

5.2.1 Artificial Intelligence for Visual Attention

The main drawback of the classical approaches for visual attention is that they are based on low-level features and fail in extracting high-level features such as faces, text, and part of objects which are known to be highly effective in visual attention. On the other hand, deep neural networks may help remedy this problem by encoding such kind of semantic information internally. The results of the study by He et al.

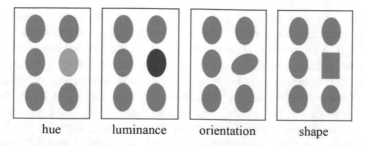

hue   luminance   orientation   shape

Fig. 5.1 Several visual properties that affect saliency

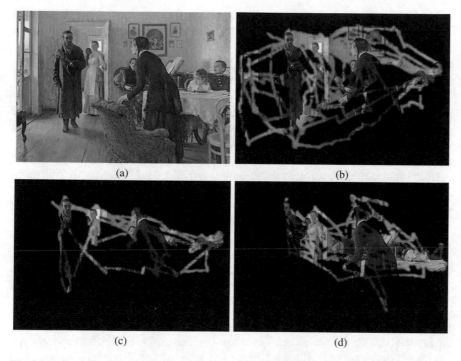

Fig. 5.2 Effect of top-down attention (adapted from Yarbus (1967)). Eye movements on Repin's painting (**a**: the stimulus, **b**: free-viewing, **c**: viewing with the task of identifying ages of people, and **d**: viewing with the task of identifying what people were doing)

(2018) where they propose a visualization method for deep saliency models to explore their internal structure validate this proposition. As a matter of fact, deep learning has opened a new era in computational modeling of visual attention, since recent findings in neuroscience and computer vision unveil the close match between deep neural network architectures and human perception Yamins et al. (2014); Zhang et al. (2018).

A recent survey on saliency prediction in the deep learning era is presented by exploring deep learning methods, datasets, benchmarks, and evaluation measures Borji (2018). A comprehensive performance analysis of the existing deep learning methods on saliency prediction over several datasets was also performed in this study. Another comparative study reviews salient object detection algorithms from different perspectives Wang et al. (2019a). Both of these works reveal that deep models ameliorate the prediction performances significantly, compared to classical methods. Several well-known deep architectures for visual attention prediction are summarized below, and interested readers are referred to the aforementioned studies for more detail.

- **Mr-CNN** Liu et al. (2015): Multi-resolution Convolutional Neural Network (CNN) contains three CNNs trained on different resolutions, followed by fully connected layers.
- **SALICON** Huang et al. (2015): This method fine-tunes pre-trained CNNs using an objective function computed according to saliency evaluation metrics. It integrates information in fine and coarse image scales.
- **DeepGaze I and II** Kummerer et al. (2014, 2017): DeepGaze I uses the well-known AlexNet architecture to generate saliency distribution, and DeepGaze II employs transfer learning by using VGG features.
- **DeepFix** Kruthiventi et al. (2017): It is a fully convolutional neural network (FCN) which also includes a novel location-biased convolutional layer to solve the problems of spatial invariance.
- **SalGAN** Pan et al. (2017): This method uses a Generative Adversarial Network (GAN) architecture containing two networks: The first one predicts saliency map and the second one discriminates whether the predicted saliency map is ground truth or predicted. The aim is to make it indistinguishable from the ground truth.
- **DVA** Wang and Shen (2018): It refers to the Deep Visual Attention model which provides multi-level saliency predictions where supervision is done in multiple layers instead of only the output layer.

Another issue in deep visual attention models is the loss function used in training the models. A wide variety of metrics are used for this purpose, such as mean squared error, area under curve, Kullback-Leibler (KL) divergence, Bhattacharya loss, and normalized scanpath saliency. Some of these metrics are computed using pixel-wise operations, some of them are distribution-based, and some are perceptually based. They all capture separate aspects of the predicted attention maps and perform differently for different methods. Bruckert et al. (2019) investigate the effect of loss functions and find out their significance on the performance. They also propose new perceptual loss functions and linear combinations of the existing functions which improve the saliency prediction performance.

Most of the studies in the literature focus on bottom-up components of visual attention. However, since they use deep learning methods, they implicitly encode high-level features such as face and text, and they address top-down visual attention to some extent. Wang et al. (2019b) attempt to develop a network for salient object detection by incorporating top-down and bottom-up components in an iterative manner. In their method, upper-layer features are progressively improved by integrating lower-level features, inspired by the interactive bottom-up and top-down processes of human visual perception.

5.2.1.1 Dynamic Visual Attention Prediction

The proposed methods on visual attention and saliency prediction are generally designed for addressing still images. However, time is another aspect that affects visual saliency. There are several studies on video saliency detection. The early approach for video saliency detection was to process individual frames and then pool them using several operations to integrate temporal information. Recent studies, on the contrary, prefer end-to-end network architectures. Bak et al. (2017) propose a two-stream spatio-temporal saliency network in which one CNN encodes spatial information by taking video frames as input and the second CNN extracts temporal information by taking the optical flow as input. They are fused with different strategies: direct averaging, max fusion, and convolutional fusion. The results show the superior performance of a convolutional fusion-based spatio-temporal saliency network over state-of-the-art methods. The main drawback of this method is its requirement of optical flow calculation which may be expensive.

Wang et al. (2017) target computational efficiency for salient object detection in videos using FCN without the need for optical flow calculation. The method uses both static images and dynamic video sequences in training. A network calculates static saliency for the frames, and the output is fed into a dynamic network along with consecutive frames. Another video saliency model called ACLNet learns static features through CNN layers and employs a Long Short-Term-Memory (LSTM) network for learning temporal saliency Wang et al. (2019c). They also introduce a benchmark called Dynamic Human Fixation 1K (DHF1K) for video saliency prediction.

5.2.1.2 Visual Attention in 3D

Similar to the evolution of 2D visual attention prediction models, early studies in mesh saliency (e.g. Lee et al. (2005)) use center-surround operations to extract low-level information as in Itti et al. (1998). Bulbul et al. (2014) propose a motion saliency method to calculate saliency in 3D animated meshes, by clustering the vertices according to their motion properties. Then the trend in this field has also shifted to utilizing deep learning. A mesh saliency detection framework based on CNN is proposed recently by Nousias et al. (2020). In this framework, ground truth saliency maps are generated using spectral and geometric analysis of the meshes for the training set. Mesh is divided into patches, and patch descriptors using Hilbert curves are extracted. Ding et al. (2019) propose a saliency detection model for point clouds by combining local and global distinctness features using an optimization framework.

Despite the enormous number of studies on 2D visual attention, there is only a handful of studies on 3D. The main reason behind this is that constructing large mesh datasets with human fixation annotations requires tedious work. This is also proven by the experimental study in which a dataset of human eye fixations on 3D printed objects is constructed Wang et al. (2018). The dataset contains 224 samples (16 objects with 14 conditions) which is small for deep architectures. They also propose a CNN model to predict gaze density maps.

To overcome the problem of unavailability of large 3D datasets, Song et al. (2019) propose a weakly supervised mesh saliency method called Classification-for-Saliency CNN, in which 3D object classification knowledge is transferred to mesh saliency. This method relies on the observation that 3D objects of the same class exhibit similar saliency distributions. Hence, they only exploit class membership annotations of 3D models, without the need for ground truth saliency data.

An interesting study on mesh saliency aims to explore the salient points of an object which are more likely to be grasped, pressed, or touched by a human Lau et al. (2016). They develop a tactile mesh saliency framework which couples learning-to-rank methods with a deep fully connected network using crowdsourced data. They also demonstrate the usage of this saliency framework in the applications such as fabrication material suggestion and rendering properties suggestion.

5.2.2 Future Directions on Visual Attention

The following future research directions may be suggested based on the literature review.

- Despite the fact that deep learning has opened a period in visual attention modeling and improved the performance of visual attention prediction by large margins, the proposed models are still far from human-level performance. Therefore, investigation of new techniques, architectures, and parameters is still required in this field.
- Since modeling bottom-up saliency in a principled way is relatively easier than top-down visual attention, the studies on top-down visual attention are very limited in contrast to bottom-up models.
- There are dozens of studies on 2D visual attention; in other respects, studies on 3D visual attention are very scarce. There are several reasons for this such as the problems during mapping 2D fixation data to 3D and laborious work for constructing 3D datasets and benchmarks. Hence, studies on modeling visual attention on 3D shapes, including triangular meshes, point clouds, and virtual environments, are strongly encouraged.
- Another important open issue in the field of visual attention is that temporal aspects are not well-elaborated in both 2D and 3D. Yet it is foreseen that animation and motion may have a severe effect on the attention maps.

- The success and generalizability of machine learning methods heavily depend on the size and quality of datasets. There is a huge amount of effort in constructing such datasets including human eye fixation data on images. The prevalence of crowdsourcing tools has also promoted this process. However, this is not the case for video and mesh saliency since it requires expensive and time-consuming work. Besides, most of the current datasets for both 2D and 3D include synthetic stimulus and omit real-world or extreme cases.
- There are many different metrics to evaluate the performance of visual attention prediction methods, as mentioned previously. Proposed visual attention prediction methods are generally compared according to a few of these evaluation metrics, thus a fair comparison between the methods is not possible. More comprehensive metrics and evaluation techniques should be considered.
- A high number of studies are done for modeling visual attention and predicting eye fixation data. Nevertheless, applications that use these predictions are very restricted and have not gone far beyond demonstrating the usage of proposed methods. They have not become part of rendering tools or commercial modeling products yet.

5.3 Visual Quality Perception of 3D Shapes

3D mesh models are exposed to several geometric modifications such as simplification, watermarking, and compression. All these modifications may introduce some artifacts on the mesh surface. Therefore, we need a measure to quantify the visibility of these distortions. There are a number of studies on the visual quality assessment (VQA) of 3D meshes.

The quality metrics can be examined under three categories based on the availability of a reference mesh. *Full-reference* (FR) metrics measure the distance of a model to an intact model considered as a reference. In *no-reference* (NR) a.k.a. *blind* quality metrics, the visual quality of the given mesh is measured directly, without a reference mesh. There are also *reduced-reference* metrics which have limited information about the reference model. We can also categorize mesh quality metrics into two as *geometric* and *perceptual*. Purely geometric metrics do not take human perception into account, while perceptual quality metrics aim to estimate the response of the human visual system (HVS). Perceptual quality metrics have been proven to be well correlated with human responses. In this chapter, we will mainly focus on the perceptual quality metrics that use AI techniques. A review of more general 3D visual quality assessment methods can be found in Bulbul et al. (2011); Lavoue and Mantiuk (2015); Muzahid et al. (2018). Surveys on perceptual quality assessment of 3D meshes are also available Lin and Kuo (2011); Corsini et al. (2013).

5.3.1 Artificial Intelligence for Visual Quality Assessment

As in many other fields, artificial intelligence and machine learning techniques are highly employed in visual quality assessment. Table 5.1 summarizes the features and methods used in visual quality studies that are discussed below.

5.3.1.1 Full-Reference Metrics

In one of the early studies, Lavoue et al. (2013) employ multi-linear regression to optimize the weights of several mesh descriptors including curvature values, dihedral angles, and geometric Laplacian for full-reference mesh quality evaluation. Chetouani (2017) proposes to fuse several widely used full-reference quality metrics using a Support Vector Regression (SVR) model to improve the correlation between human observations. Yildiz et al. (2020) perform a crowdsourcing experiment to collect mesh quality data from human observers. They define the distance between two meshes as the weighted Euclidian distance of their feature vectors, constructed using the histogram statistics of several mesh descriptors such as curvature and roughness.

Table 5.1 A summary of the studies which use AI techniques, on mesh quality assessment. (The first section in table includes full-reference metrics and the second section lists no-reference metrics.)

Previous work	Features	Methods
Lavoue et al. (2013)	Curvature values, dihedral angles, and geometric Laplacian	Multi-linear regression
Chetouani (2017)	Other full-reference metrics	Feature fusion (SVR)
Abouelaziz et al. (2018a)	CNN generated features	CNN, KL divergence
Feng et al. (2018)	Statistical descriptors of local TPDM values	SVR
Yildiz et al. (2020)	Distribution statistics of curvature values, shape index, curvedness, and surface roughness	Metric learning (SQP)
Abouelaziz et al. (2016)	Mean curvature	GRNN
Abouelaziz et al. (2017)	Mean curvature, dihedral angles	CNN
Nouri et al. (2017)	Saliency, roughness	SVR
Abouelaziz et al. (2018)	Dihedral angles	SVR
Abouelaziz et al. (2018b)	Raw pixel data of rendered mesh images + saliency (for selecting patches)	CNN
Lin et al. (2019)	Shape index, curvedness, vertex scatter, and triangular topology area	Random forest regression
Abouelaziz et al. (2020)	Deep features extracted by VGG, AlexNet, and ResNet	Ensemble of CNNs

Then they learn the weights of these features through Sequential Quadratic Programming (SQP) optimization to maximize the likelihood of observing the results in the crowdsourcing experiment.

In most of the studies, quality scores per vertex are calculated first and average weighting or Minkowski summation is used to obtain a global quality score. However, there is no consensus on which pooling strategy is better. Feng et al. (2018) propose a spatial pooling strategy to address this problem. Given a reference and a test mesh, they generate the distortion distribution and extract statistical descriptors (mean, standard deviation, max, min, and three quartiles) of the distribution as features. They use the TPDM metric by Torkhani et al. (2014) to calculate the local distortion distribution. Then they pair feature vectors with Mean Opinion Scores (MOS) for the corresponding meshes and train an SVR model to learn the relationship between the distortion distribution and quality scores.

Abouelaziz et al. (2018a) construct 2D projections of 3D meshes from different viewpoints, take small patches from the rendered images and feed them into a CNN model to obtain feature vectors for reference and test meshes. They output the Kullback-Leibler divergence between the feature vectors as the quality score.

5.3.1.2 No-Reference Metrics

Most of the metrics developed so far use a full-reference scenario, in which a reference mesh is available. However, in many practical cases (i.e. reconstruction and network transmission), a reference model may not be available. Therefore, full-reference metrics are not sufficient and there is a strong need for no-reference quality metrics. The application of machine learning techniques will also facilitate the development of no-reference quality metrics. Although machine learning methods have been successfully applied in the image quality assessment literature (e.g. Bosse et al. (2018); Bianco et al. (2018); Ma et al. (2018); Deng et al. (2017)), they are not sufficiently utilized for 3D quality. Still, there are several recent attempts for no-reference mesh quality metrics.

Mostly used AI techniques in no-reference mesh quality assessment are SVR and CNN. Nouri et al. (2017) extract multi-scale saliency and roughness maps for the meshes, then segment the meshes into superfacets, and feed them into an SVR model to calculate the quality scores. Distribution statistics of the mesh dihedral angles are also used as features in several SVR-based studies (e.g. Abouelaziz et al. (2018)). Lin et al. (2019) propose another metric that integrates concave, convex, and structural information of the mesh and learn the quality using random forest regression.

Deep learning methods have also been employed in the field of mesh quality assessment. Abouelaziz et al. (2017) train a CNN on mean curvature and dihedral angle features of the meshes, organized as 2D patches. Another CNN-based approach works on 2D patches extracted from rendered images of 3D meshes from different viewpoints Abouelaziz et al. (2018b). In this study, visual saliency information is integrated to determine informative patches that will be selected to train the model. The use of General Regression Neural Network (GRNN) is suggested to overcome the fact that available mesh quality datasets are not sufficient, based on the previous observation that GRNN yields better performance compared to RBF or backpropagation networks when dataset size is small Abouelaziz et al. (2016). They use mean curvature values as the sole feature. Recently, Abouelaziz et al. (2020) propose a blind mesh quality metric via an ensemble of CNNs and multi-linear pooling. They use saliency-based patch selection and learn features by pre-trained VGG, AlexNet, and ResNet models and combine their results using multi-linear pooling.

5.3.1.3   Evaluation of VQA Metrics

The standard evaluation of the success of the visual quality metrics is performed by calculating the correlation between metric outputs and human-assigned scores provided in public mesh quality datasets. There are several publicly available datasets for mesh quality.

- *LIRIS/EPFL General Purpose Dataset* by Lavoue et al. (2006) contains 84 distorted models of 4 reference meshes. Smoothing and noise addition were applied either locally or globally.
- *LIRIS Masking Dataset* by Lavoue (2009) includes 4 reference meshes and 24 distorted models. Local noise addition with different strengths was used as distortion.
- *UWB Compression Dataset* by Vasa and Rus (2012) comprises 5 reference models along with 63 distorted versions. Different compression techniques were applied to generate distorted models.

Table 5.2 compares the Spearman Rank Order Correlation Coefficient (SROCC) values of the above no-reference metrics on these datasets. These values are gathered from the reported results in the corresponding papers.

Table 5.2 SROCC values of different metrics on different datasets. (The values are in percentages. NA: Not available; Dataset1: LIRIS/EPFL General Purpose Dataset; Dataset2: LIRIS Masking Dataset; Dataset3: UWB Compression Dataset.)

Previous work	Dataset1	Dataset2	Dataset3
Abouelaziz et al. (2016)	86.2	90.2	*NA*
Abouelaziz et al. (2017)	83.6	88.2	*NA*
Nouri et al. (2017)	78.1	83	*NA*
Abouelaziz et al. (2018b)	88.4	92	*NA*
Abouelaziz et al. (2018)	84.6	91.1	85.5
Lin et al. (2019)	81.9	*NA*	*NA*
Abouelaziz et al. (2020)	94.4	95.8	92.7

5.3.2 Future Directions on 3D VQA

Based on the literature review on mesh visual quality assessment methods, the following limitations and future directions were identified.

- Current metrics still fall short of human-level performance, and there is room for improving the performance by investigating new features, methods, and architectures.
- It is known that motion and animation have an important effect on the perceived quality. For instance, high-speed motion hides the visibility of distortions to some extent, which is known as temporal masking. Although several methods address dynamic meshes (e.g. Vasa and Skala (2011); Torkhani et al. (2015); Yildiz and Capin (2017)), the research in this field is still far from saturated.
- Most of the metrics rely solely on geometric properties of the mesh. Nevertheless, material and lighting properties may have a strong impact on the perception of quality. Hence, texture and material properties should be incorporated into a visual quality metric. There are several recent studies in this direction (e.g. Vanhoey et al. (2017); Guo et al. (2017)).
- The metrics developed should be tested in more practical cases such as games and virtual/augmented reality applications. For instance, Nehme et al. (2020) perform an objective and subjective quality evaluation of 3D meshes with diffuse colors in virtual reality environments. Furthermore, integration of these metrics into geometric mesh processing operations such as simplification and quantization should be illustrated.
- 3D representation of models is not limited to triangle meshes. Moreover, different display technologies (HMDs, holographic displays, etc.) may be effective for the perception of quality. Quality metrics for different representations (i.e. point clouds) and display technologies should be investigated. There are recent studies that focus on point cloud visual quality evaluation (e.g. Hua et al. (2020); Cao et al. (2020)).
- No-reference quality metrics have been recently proposed, however, the studies in this field are very limited. Especially, the application of deep learning methods is limited to CNNs which require 2D image patches. Other deep learning methods and architectures should be investigated.
- Public datasets are very limited in both number and diversity of geometric distortions. A comprehensive dataset is crucial for the validity of machine learning techniques. However, designing subjective user experiments to construct such datasets is very time consuming and laborious. Leveraging full-reference metrics for that purpose may be a shortcut solution for this problem.
- The visual quality expected by the user may also depend on the task to be performed. To the best of our knowledge, there is no such study that investigates task-dependent visual quality of 3D meshes. Future work may also adopt such a top-down approach for visual quality assessment.
- Another aspect to be explored in perceptual quality assessment is aesthetics. Although aesthetics perception in images is well-studied, there are not many stud-

ies in the field of perceived aesthetics in 3D shapes. Recently, Dev and Lau (2020) proposed a perceptual aesthetics measure for 3D shapes, using crowdsourcing and a deep neural network architecture.

5.4 Visual Material Perception and Recognition

The human visual system is very successful in identifying materials. In addition to almost instantly understanding what an object is made of, e.g. paper, metal, wood, or others, we also have a reliable opinion about the finer properties of the material guiding us about, for instance, wetness of a surface, maturity of a fruit, and age of a book (Fig. 5.3). In this section, we first start with the basics of the material appearance, reflectance models, and how materials are used in Computer Graphics. Later, we review material perception research before moving into studies using artificial intelligence for material recognition. At the end of the section, available material databases and possible future directions on material research are pointed out.

5.4.1 Materials in Computer Graphics

The color of a surface point depends on the surface material, its geometry, illumination, and the surrounding environment, and is formed according to complex interactions between them. Having an accurate computational model of materials is crucial for visual recognition and realistic generation of scenes. The function defining how light is reflected at an opaque surface is called **bidirectional reflectance distribution function** (BRDF) Nicodemus (1965). This function indicates a radiance value for each pair of light and reflection directions relative to the surface normal. For matte materials such as paper or clay, the incoming light is almost homogeneously distributed to all directions resulting in a similar radiance for all viewpoints. On the other hand, shiny materials (polished metals, mirror) reflect most of the incoming light toward the mirror direction causing highly varying intensities according to a

Fig. 5.3 Material Samples. We can instantly recognize a variety of materials. In addition, we can recognize wetness of a surface or maturity of a fruit easily by material properties

viewpoint. Most real materials behave somewhere in between these two extremes. Moreover, materials like brushed metal differently reflect lights coming from varying angles, which is handled by anisotropic BRDFs Ashikhmin and Shirley (2000). Reflectance properties of materials may not be uniformly distributed over the entire surface of an object. Bidirectional texture function (BTF) Dana et al. (1999) include two more parameters for texture coordinates in addition to the four parameters of BRDFs to provide spatially changing material properties.

Earlier studies focused on finding analytic BRDF approximations Phong (1975); Ward et al. (1992); Ashikhmin and Shirley (2000). These studies usually consider the diffuse (albedo) and specular components of the materials separately and the materials are controlled by adjusting parameters such as diffuseness, specularity, and roughness. While these studies are powerful for generating various material appearances, matching the results with real-world materials is troublesome. To match real-world materials, later studies suggested measuring the reflectance properties directly from real material samples Matusik et al. (2003). In this data-driven approach, reflectance of a real material sample is captured for all pairs of reflection and lighting directions. While the data-driven methods notably increase the realism of rendering, the variety of materials is limited to the captured samples.

Another disadvantage of analytic BRDF models is the highly non-linear, therefore unpredictable, change in the perception of the resulting material upon a linear change of their parameters. To overcome this issue, Pellacini et al. (2000) proposed a method that modifies Ward's model for a perceptually meaningful parameter space where a variation of the perceived material is uniformly distributed.

Perceptually better approximating measured-BRDFs with analytic models was one of the subsequent research tracks within BRDF studies. Wills et al. (2009) defined nine types of gloss and proposed a perceptual parameterization of Ward's Ward et al. (1992) model. Fores et al. (2012) indicated using cube root metric is better than RMS-based metrics for approximating measured-BRDFs. In their study, they have conducted perceptual experiments on the MERL material database by altering the parameters of Ward Ward et al. (1992), Ashikhmin-Shirley Ashikhmin and Shirley (2000), and Cook-Torrance Cook and Torrance (1982) BRDF models. While utilizing captured data results in realistic appearances, generating new materials from the captured samples is not straightforward since linearly interpolating two materials does not generate perceptually intuitive materials. Thus, Serrano et al. (2016) proposed an intuitive editing method that considers 14 specified attributes of materials, such as soft, glossy, and ceramic-like.

5.4.2 Visual Material Perception

While the computer graphics discipline develops tools and methods for realistic simulations of materials, vision scientists study understanding how the human visual system perceives materials. Fleming (2014) provides a comprehensive review of visual perception of materials and their properties.

Although in some cases different materials convey the same image properties, it is mostly possible to have an idea about the materials included in a single image, even a local patch can be sufficient for recognizing the material Schwartz and Nishino (2019). Thus, there has been notable research interest for figuring out how to infer material information from image features. Fleming et al. (2003) states that image statistics are useful for extracting reflectance properties as long as the image and the illumination is realistic. Very different, but realistic, illumination environments result in similar image statistics over the same reflecting surface according to its material properties. Thus, it is argued that people rely on the stored assumptions, which is encouraging for machine learning-based methods. Another experimental study suggested that if the highlight color is not natural, the surface looks less glossy Wendt et al. (2010).

Glossy materials produce sharper and brighter highlights; therefore, positive skewness of image histogram correlates with surface glossiness Motoyoshi et al. (2007). While image histogram helps inferring the surface material, if the image has small bright regions such as stars or small dots, positive skewness incorrectly signals glossiness. In the same study, it is also stated that positive skewness has an aftereffect, that is, long exposure decreases perceived glossiness even when the adapted scene is a non-glossy stimulus with a positively skewed image histogram.

Recently, Adams et al. (2018) investigated the effects of illumination, tone mapping, and background information on the perceived glossiness of complex objects, and they confirm that skewed and high contrast images are perceived as glossier. Also, objects are perceived as less glossy when viewed within environments with greater contrast and skew. We may infer that background and foreground work oppositely on the perceived glossiness.

The shape of the stimulus also affects material perception Vangorp et al. (2007). Marlow and Anderson (2015) compared the perception of two images where the distribution of image intensities are the same for both images but they have stereoscopically depicted different shapes. It is observed that if the shiny regions occur where specular highlights are expected, they look more glossy.

Humans are capable of recognizing most materials very quickly and accurately. While image statistics are helpful for inferring material properties Fleming et al. (2003); Adams et al. (2018), Sharan et al. (2014) claim that material categorization is a distinct and fundamental ability of the HVS.

5.4.2.1 Effects of Motion, Stereo, and Accommodation

While the appearance of a diffuse material does not change according to a viewpoint, glossy materials reflect light and other objects around the environment more concentrated toward a direction; thus, their appearance depends on the viewpoint. Therefore, material and especially gloss perception is strongly affected by factors providing various viewpoints of the same scene.

One of these factors is motion. Temporal luminance differences due to head motion are significant for glossiness perception Sakano and Ando (2010). A similar effect is provided by a binocular vision where we see the scene from slightly different viewpoints simultaneously. If two eyes get different lightness from the same surface point, that indicates a specularity Wendt et al. (2010); Doerschner et al. (2011); Sakano and Ando (2010).

In addition to motion and stereo, perceived glossiness is also affected by accommodation Banks et al. (2014). The surface itself and the highlights can be observed at different depths which gets more perceivable as the surface gets flatter; a flat mirror exemplifies the situation most prominently. Consequently, the eye can separately focus on the surface distance or the highlights distance which gives a cue of specularity even to monoscopic viewing.

5.4.3 Artificial Intelligence for Material Recognition

Following successful research on object recognition, recognition of materials and their properties by machines have also recently gained popularity. These studies mostly work on images and deal with naming the materials such as metal, paper, and wood, or rating the level of material properties such as glossiness or roughness level. As expected, research on human material perception plays a significant role in those studies.

An earlier study by Dror et al. (2001) trains an SVM classifier for recognition of six material categories: *black matte*, *black shiny*, *chrome*, *gray shiny*, *white matte*, and *white shiny*. Firstly, training images are computer-generated by rendering a sphere model under various illuminations. Then, the trained SVM is used for classifying test images belonging to different shapes. The attributes used in the SVM include the mean, variance, skew, kurtosis, and the 10th, 50th, and 90th percentiles. The system reaches 94% accuracy over 54 computer-generated test images.

Linearly combining image statistics allows a machine vision system to estimate surface albedo with a performance close to humans Sharan et al. (2008). The attributes used in Sharan et al.'s experiment are *skewness*, *percentiles*, and *standard deviation*. They observed that this method also makes similar mistakes as humans.

Liu et al. (2010) proposed using a method called Augmented LDA to classify real-world materials according to eight image features which are *color*, *jet*, *sift*, *micro-jet*, *micro-sift*, *curvature*, *edge-slice*, and *edge-ribbon*. The experiments are performed over the 10 material categories such as fabric, leather, and paper from Flickr Material Database Sharan et al. (2013). The method achieved 44.6% classification accuracy where a random guess would succeed 10%. The same group later generated an SVM-based classifier which achieved 57.1% accuracy, using the same image features, still much less than human material classification accuracy of 84.9% Sharan et al. (2013). These results demonstrate the difficulty of recognizing real-world materials for computers.

Fleming et al. (2013) suggested using visual and semantic properties for material classification. The idea behind this approach is that we can also infer non-visual material properties by looking at an image such as softness or rigidity of the surface. In their experiment over Flickr Material Database, subjects rated each image according to 9 properties that are *glossiness*, *transparency*, *colorfulness*, *roughness*, *hardness*, *coldness*, *fragility*, *naturalness*, and *prettiness*. K-means clustering according to given ratings can reach over 90% accuracy for material classification.

In a recent study, Lagunas et al. (2019) proposed a similarity measure for material appearance. They use 100 measured BRDF samples of the MERL dataset over 15 shapes and 6 environment maps to generate a dataset of 9000 images. In a crowdsourcing environment, these images are shown in triplets, consisting of two test images and one reference image, where subjects pointed out the more similar test image to the reference. Results of the crowdsourcing experiment are used to train a deep network where a ResNet He et al. (2016) architecture is employed with an additional dense layer of 128-bit output that makes a material descriptor. The proposed system can be used for various applications including material suggestions, database visualization, clustering and summarization, and gamut mapping.

Schwartz and Nishino (2019) proposed another deep learning-based method for material recognition. Starting from the observation that humans can recognize material attributes even from small parts of an image, they use Flicker Material Database to generate local image patches, and using pairs of these patches they have conducted a crowdsourcing experiment, where the question is simply "Do these patches look different or not?" The results provide a weak supervision which is used to train a specific CNN architecture which generates a material attribute space while also performing material recognition.

Tamura et al. (2019) propose a method for a challenging sub-problem of material recognition. In this case, distinguishing mirror from glass is the problem for which several neural networks-based architectures and classifiers based on hand-crafted features are trained. All classifiers performed similar to human performance. Interestingly, however, when the authors assembled an image set for which humans make systematic errors, the trained networks couldn't follow humans and the correlation between them falls below 0.6. This result coincides with the idea that neural networks-based classifiers are good models of human vision.

5.4.4   Existing Material Datasets

Here, several material databases which are accessible and widely used for research purposes are pointed out (Fig. 5.4).

Fig. 5.4 Samples from several databases. Top row: Spheres rendered with BRDFs from the MERL database. Middle row: samples from the CUReT database. Bottom row: samples from Flickr Material Database

5.4.4.1 MERL BRDF Dataset

The Mitsubishi Electric Research Laboratories (MERL) dataset Matusik et al. (2003) contains densely measured BRDFs belonging to 100 different materials. It can be used freely for academic or research purposes.

5.4.4.2 CUReT

Columbia-Utrecht Reflectance and Texture Database Dana et al. (1999) includes measurements from 61 real-world material samples. These samples are selected to span a wide variety of geometric and photometric properties, e.g. diffuse, anisotropic, natural, and man-made. Three databases are provided. *BRDF database* contains Measured-BRDFs, *BRDF parameter database* contains Oren-Nayar Oren and Nayar (1994) and Koendering Koenderink et al. (1996) parameters fitting to the material samples, *BTF database* contains image textures of the material samples.

5.4.4.3 KTH-TIPS

KTH-TIPS (Textures under varying Illumination, Pose and Scale) material database Mallikarjuna et al. (2006) is created to extend the CUReT database in terms of scale, pose, and illumination. The extended database KTH-TIPS2 contains variations of 11 material categories.

5.4.4.4 FMD

Flickr Material Database Sharan et al. (2013) contains materials from 10 categories: *fabric*, *foliage*, *glass*, *leather*, *metal*, *paper*, *plastic*, *stone*, *water*, and *wood*. For each category there are 100 images. This dataset is a challenging one as it contains real-world variations for each material category.

5.4.5 Future Directions on Visual Material Perception

The following future research directions may be suggested based on the literature review.

- While there is a growing interest in material recognition studies, there is still room for improvement especially for challenging databases.
- Effects of viewpoint-dependent factors on material recognition remain as an open research area. How to infer materials using combined information from multiple, or differently focused, images is an interesting area of investigation.
- Using material information for different application areas may be effective and could be studied. For instance, structure from motion-based 3D reconstruction methods may consider signals coming from different materials separately taking their reflectance properties into account.
- Another application area where material information could be exploited is object recognition. The effect of material knowledge on object recognition could be investigated.
- An inverse approach to the previous item could be using object recognition to estimate the material properties.
- As humans can use material appearance to extract useful information such as freshness of fish and how slippery the surface can be, it is possible to find useful application areas in computer-based systems.

References

Abouelaziz I, El Hassouni M, Cherifi H (2016) A curvature based method for blind mesh visual quality assessment using a general regression neural network. In: 2016 12th international conference on signal-image technology & internet-based systems (SITIS). IEEE, pp 793–797

Abouelaziz I, El Hassouni M, Cherifi H (2017) A convolutional neural network framework for blind mesh visual quality assessment. In: 2017 ieee international conference on image processing (ICIP). IEEE, pp 755–759

Abouelaziz I, Chetouani A, El Hassouni M, Cherifi H (2018a) Reduced reference mesh visual quality assessment based on convolutional neural network. In: 2018 14th international conference on signal-image technology & internet-based systems (SITIS). IEEE, pp 617–620

Abouelaziz I, Chetouani A, El Hassouni M, Latecki LJ, Cherifi H (2018b) Convolutional neural network for blind mesh visual quality assessment using 3d visual saliency. In: 2018 25th IEEE international conference on image processing (ICIP). IEEE, pp 3533–3537

Abouelaziz I, El Hassouni M, Cherifi H (2018c) Blind 3D mesh visual quality assessment using support vector regression. Multimed Tools Appl 77(18):24365–24386

Abouelaziz I, Chetouani A, El Hassouni M, Latecki LJ, Cherifi H (2020) No-reference mesh visual quality assessment via ensemble of convolutional neural networks and compact multi-linear pooling. Pattern Recognit 100

Adams WJ, Kucukoglu G, Landy MS, Mantiuk RK (2018) Naturally glossy: gloss perception, illumination statistics, and tone mapping. J Vis 18(13):4

Ashikhmin M, Shirley P (2000) An anisotropic phong BRDF model. J Graph Tools 5(2):25–32

Bak C, Kocak A, Erdem E, Erdem A (2017) Spatio-temporal saliency networks for dynamic saliency prediction. IEEE Trans Multimed 20(7):1688–1698

Banks MS, Bulbul A, Albert RA, Narain R, O'Brien JF, Ward G (2014) The perception of surface material from disparity and focus cues [conference talk]. J Vis 14(10):1315

Bianco S, Celona L, Napoletano P, Schettini R (2018) On the use of deep learning for blind image quality assessment. Signal, Image Video Process 12(2):355–362

Borji A (2018) Saliency prediction in the deep learning era: an empirical investigation. arXiv:181003716

Bosse S, Maniry D, Müller KR, Wiegand T, Samek W (2018) Deep neural networks for no-reference and full-reference image quality assessment. IEEE Trans Image Process 27(1):206–219

Bruckert A, Tavakoli HR, Liu Z, Christie M, Meur OL (2019) Deep saliency models: the quest for the loss function. arXiv:190702336

Bulbul A, Capin T, Lavoué G, Preda M (2011) Assessing visual quality of 3-D polygonal models. IEEE Signal Process Mag 28(6):80–90

Bulbul A, Arpa S, Capin T (2014) A clustering-based method to estimate saliency in 3D animated meshes. Comput Graph 43:11–20

Cao K, Xu Y, Cosman P (2020) Visual quality of compressed mesh and point cloud sequences. IEEE Access 8:171203–171217

Chetouani A (2017) A 3D mesh quality metric based on features fusion. Electron Imaging 2017(20):4–8

Cook RL, Torrance KE (1982) A reflectance model for computer graphics. ACM Trans Graph (TOG) 1(1):7–24

Corsini M, Larabi MC, Lavoué G, Petřík O, Váša L, Wang K (2013) Perceptual metrics for static and dynamic triangle meshes. Comput Graph Forum, Wiley Online Libr 32:101–125

Dana KJ, Van Ginneken B, Nayar SK, Koenderink JJ (1999) Reflectance and texture of real-world surfaces. ACM Trans Graph (TOG) 18(1):1–34

Deng Y, Loy CC, Tang X (2017) Image aesthetic assessment: an experimental survey. IEEE Signal Process Mag 34(4):80–106

Dev K, Lau M (2020) Learning perceptual aesthetics of 3D shapes from multiple views. IEEE Comput Graph Appl

Ding X, Lin W, Chen Z, Zhang X (2019) Point cloud saliency detection by local and global feature fusion. IEEE Trans Image Process 28(11):5379–5393

Doerschner K, Fleming RW, Yilmaz O, Schrater PR, Hartung B, Kersten D (2011) Visual motion and the perception of surface material. Curr Biol 21(23):2010–2016

Dror RO, Adelson EH, Willsky AS (2001) Recognition of surface reflectance properties from a single image under unknown real-world illumination. In: IEEE workshop on identifying objects across variation in lighting

Feng X, Wan W, Da Xu RY, Chen H, Li P, Sánchez JA (2018) A perceptual quality metric for 3D triangle meshes based on spatial pooling. Front Comput Sci 12(4):798–812

Fleming RW (2014) Visual perception of materials and their properties. Vis Res 94:62–75

Fleming RW, Dror RO, Adelson EH (2003) Real-world illumination and the perception of surface reflectance properties. J Vis 3(5):3

Fleming RW, Wiebel C, Gegenfurtner K (2013) Perceptual qualities and material classes. J Vis 13(8):9

Fores A, Ferwerda J, Gu J (2012) Toward a perceptually based metric for BRDF modeling. Color Imaging Conf, Soc Imaging Sci Technol 2012:142–148

Guo J, Vidal V, Cheng I, Basu A, Baskurt A, Lavoue G (2017) Subjective and objective visual quality assessment of textured 3D meshes. ACM Trans Appl Percept (TAP) 14(2):11

He K, Zhang X, Ren S, Sun J (2016) Deep residual learning for image recognition. In: Proceedings of the IEEE conference on computer vision and pattern recognition, pp 770–778

He S, Borji A, Mi Y, Pugeault N (2018) What catches the eye? visualizing and understanding deep saliency models. arXiv:180305753

Hua L, Yu M, Jiang G, He Z, Lin Y (2020) Vqa-cpc: a novel visual quality assessment metric of color point clouds. In: Optoelectronic imaging and multimedia technology VII, international society for optics and photonics, vol 11550, p 1155012

Huang X, Shen C, Boix X, Zhao Q (2015) Salicon: reducing the semantic gap in saliency prediction by adapting deep neural networks. In: Proceedings of the IEEE international conference on computer vision, pp 262–270

Itti L, Koch C, Niebur E (1998) A model of saliency-based visual attention for rapid scene analysis. IEEE Trans Pattern Anal Mach Intell 11:1254–1259

Koch C, Ullman S (1987) Shifts in selective visual attention: towards the underlying neural circuitry. In: Matters of intelligence. Springer, Berlin, pp 115–141

Koenderink JJ, Van Doorn AJ, Stavridi M (1996) Bidirectional reflection distribution function expressed in terms of surface scattering modes. In: European conference on computer vision. Springer, Berlin, pp 28–39

Kruthiventi SS, Ayush K, Babu RV (2017) Deepfix: a fully convolutional neural network for predicting human eye fixations. IEEE Trans Image Process 26(9):4446–4456

Kümmerer M, Theis L, Bethge M (2014) Deep gaze i: Boosting saliency prediction with feature maps trained on imagenet. arXiv:14111045

Kummerer M, Wallis TS, Gatys LA, Bethge M (2017) Understanding low-and high-level contributions to fixation prediction. In: Proceedings of the IEEE international conference on computer vision, pp 4789–4798

Lagunas M, Malpica S, Serrano A, Garces E, Gutierrez D, Masia B (2019) A similarity measure for material appearance. ACM Trans Graph 38(4):135:1–135:12. https://doi.org/10.1145/3306346.3323036

Lau M, Dev K, Shi W, Dorsey J, Rushmeier H (2016) Tactile mesh saliency. ACM Trans Graph (TOG) 35(4):52

Lavoué G (2009) A local roughness measure for 3D meshes and its application to visual masking. ACM Trans Appl Percept (TAP) 5(4):21

Lavoué G, Mantiuk R (2015) Quality assessment in computer graphics. In: Visual signal quality assessment. Springer, Berlin, pp 243–286

Lavoué G, Gelasca ED, Dupont F, Baskurt A, Ebrahimi T (2006) Perceptually driven 3d distance metrics with application to watermarking. In: Applications of digital image processing XXIX, international society for optics and photonics, vol 6312, p 63120L

Lavoué G, Cheng I, Basu A (2013) Perceptual quality metrics for 3d meshes: towards an optimal multi-attribute computational model. In: 2013 IEEE international conference on systems, man, and cybernetics. IEEE, pp 3271–3276

Lee CH, Varshney A, Jacobs DW (2005) Mesh saliency. ACM Trans Graph (TOG) 24(3):659–666

Lin W, Kuo CCJ (2011) Perceptual visual quality metrics: a survey. J Vis Commun Image Represent 22(4):297–312

Lin Y, Yu M, Chen K, Jiang G, Peng Z, Chen F (2019) Blind mesh quality assessment method based on concave, convex and structural features analyses. In: 2019 IEEE international conference on multimedia & expo workshops (ICMEW). IEEE, pp 282–287

Liu C, Sharan L, Adelson EH, Rosenholtz R (2010) Exploring features in a bayesian framework for material recognition. In: 2010 IEEE computer society conference on computer vision and pattern recognition. IEEE, pp 239–246

Liu N, Han J, Zhang D, Wen S, Liu T (2015) Predicting eye fixations using convolutional neural networks. In: Proceedings of the IEEE conference on computer vision and pattern recognition, pp 362–370

Ma K, Liu W, Zhang K, Duanmu Z, Wang Z, Zuo W (2018) End-to-end blind image quality assessment using deep neural networks. IEEE Trans Image Process 27(3):1202–1213

Mallikarjuna P, Targhi AT, Fritz M, Hayman E, Caputo B, Eklundh JO (2006) The kth-tips2 database

Marlow PJ, Anderson BL (2015) Material properties derived from three-dimensional shape representations. Vis Res 115:199–208

Matusik W, Pfister H, Brand M, McMillan L (2003) A data-driven reflectance model. ACM Trans Graph

Motoyoshi I, Nishida S, Sharan L, Adelson EH (2007) Image statistics and the perception of surface qualities. Nature 447(7141):206

Muzahid AM, Wan W, Feng X (2018) Perceptual quality evaluation of 3d triangle mesh: a technical review. In: 2018 international conference on audio. Language and image processing (ICALIP). IEEE, pp 266–272

Nehme Y, Dupont F, Farrugia JP, Le Callet P, Lavoue G (2020) Visual quality of 3d meshes with diffuse colors in virtual reality: subjective and objective evaluation. IEEE Trans Vis Comput Graph

Nicodemus FE (1965) Directional reflectance and emissivity of an opaque surface. Appl Opt 4(7):767–775

Nouri A, Charrier C, Lézoray O (2017) 3D blind mesh quality assessment index. Electron Imaging 20:9–26

Nousias S, Arvanitis G, Lalos AS, Moustakas K (2020) Mesh saliency detection using convolutional neural networks. In: 2020 IEEE international conference on multimedia and expo (ICME). IEEE, pp 1–6

Oren M, Nayar SK (1994) Generalization of lambert's reflectance model. In: Proceedings of the 21st annual conference on computer graphics and interactive techniques. ACM, New York, NY, USA, SIGGRAPH '94, pp 239–246. https://doi.org/10.1145/192161.192213

Pan J, Ferrer CC, McGuinness K, O'Connor NE, Torres J, Sayrol E, Giro-i Nieto X (2017) Salgan: visual saliency prediction with generative adversarial networks. arXiv:170101081

Pellacini F, Ferwerda JA, Greenberg DP (2000) Toward a psychophysically-based light reflection model for image synthesis. In: Proceedings of the 27th annual conference on Computer graphics and interactive techniques. ACM Press/Addison-Wesley Publishing Co., pp 55–64

Phong BT (1975) Illumination for computer generated pictures. Commun ACM 18(6):311–317

Sakano Y, Ando H (2010) Effects of head motion and stereo viewing on perceived glossiness. J Vis 10(9):15

Schwartz G, Nishino K (2019) Recognizing material properties from images. IEEE Trans Pattern Anal Mach Intell

Serrano A, Gutierrez D, Myszkowski K, Seidel HP, Masia B (2016) An intuitive control space for material appearance. ACM Trans Graph (TOG) 35(6):186

Sharan L, Li Y, Motoyoshi I, Nishida S, Adelson EH (2008) Image statistics for surface reflectance perception. JOSA A 25(4):846–865

Sharan L, Liu C, Rosenholtz R, Adelson EH (2013) Recognizing materials using perceptually inspired features. Int J Comput Vis 103(3):348–371

Sharan L, Rosenholtz R, Adelson EH (2014) Accuracy and speed of material categorization in real-world images. J Vis 14(9):12. https://doi.org/10.1167/14.9.12

Song R, Liu Y, Rosin P (2019) Mesh saliency via weakly supervised classification-for-saliency CNN. IEEE Trans Vis Comput Graph

Tamura H, Prokott KE, Fleming RW (2019) Distinguishing mirror from glass: a 'big data' approach to material perception. arXiv:190301671

Torkhani F, Wang K, Chassery JM (2014) A curvature-tensor-based perceptual quality metric for 3D triangular meshes. Mach Graph Vis 23(1)

Torkhani F, Wang K, Chassery JM (2015) Perceptual quality assessment of 3D dynamic meshes: subjective and objective studies. Signal Process: Image Commun 31:185–204

Vangorp P, Laurijssen J, Dutré P (2007) The influence of shape on the perception of material reflectance. ACM Trans Graph 26(3). https://doi.org/10.1145/1276377.1276473

Vanhoey K, Sauvage B, Kraemer P, Lavoué G (2017) Visual quality assessment of 3D models: on the influence of light-material interaction. ACM Trans Appl Percept (TAP) 15(1):5

Váša L, Rus J (2012) Dihedral angle mesh error: a fast perception correlated distortion measure for fixed connectivity triangle meshes. Comput Graph Forum, Wiley Online Libr 31:1715–1724

Vasa L, Skala V (2011) A perception correlated comparison method for dynamic meshes. IEEE Trans Vis Comput Graph 17(2):220–230

Wang W, Shen J (2018) Deep visual attention prediction. IEEE Trans Image Process 27(5):2368–2378

Wang W, Shen J, Shao L (2017) Video salient object detection via fully convolutional networks. IEEE Trans Image Process 27(1):38–49

Wang W, Lai Q, Fu H, Shen J, Ling H (2019a) Salient object detection in the deep learning era: an in-depth survey. arXiv:190409146

Wang W, Shen J, Cheng MM, Shao L (2019b) An iterative and cooperative top-down and bottom-up inference network for salient object detection. In: Proceedings of the IEEE conference on computer vision and pattern recognition, pp 5968–5977

Wang W, Shen J, Xie J, Cheng MM, Ling H, Borji A (2019c) Revisiting video saliency prediction in the deep learning era. IEEE Trans Pattern Anal Mach Intell

Wang X, Koch S, Holmqvist K, Alexa M (2018) Tracking the gaze on objects in 3D: how do people really look at the bunny? In: SIGGRAPH Asia 2018 technical papers. ACM, p 188

Ward GJ et al (1992) Measuring and modeling anisotropic reflection. Comput Graph 26(2):265–272

Wendt G, Faul F, Ekroll V, Mausfeld R (2010) Disparity, motion, and color information improve gloss constancy performance. J Vis 10(9):7

Wills J, Agarwal S, Kriegman D, Belongie S (2009) Toward a perceptual space for gloss. ACM Trans Graph (TOG) 28(4):103

Yamins DL, Hong H, Cadieu CF, Solomon EA, Seibert D, DiCarlo JJ (2014) Performance-optimized hierarchical models predict neural responses in higher visual cortex. Proc Natl Acad Sci 111(23):8619–8624

Yarbus AL (1967) Eye movements during perception of complex objects. In: Eye movements and vision. Springer, Berlin, pp 171–211

Yildiz ZC, Capin T (2017) A perceptual quality metric for dynamic triangle meshes. EURASIP J Image Video Process 1:12

Yildiz ZC, Oztireli AC, Capin T (2020) A machine learning framework for full-reference 3D shape quality assessment. Vis Comput 36(1):127–139

Zhang R, Isola P, Efros AA, Shechtman E, Wang O (2018) The unreasonable effectiveness of deep features as a perceptual metric. In: Proceedings of the IEEE conference on computer vision and pattern recognition, pp 586–595

Chapter 6
Model Reconstruction of Real-World 3D Objects: An Application with Microsoft HoloLens

Younhyun Jung, Yuhao Wu, Hoijoon Jung, and Jinman Kim

Abstract Digital reconstruction of 3D real-world objects has long been a fundamental requirement in computer graphics and vision for virtual reality (VR) and mixed-reality (MR) applications. In recent years, with the availability of portable and low-cost sensing devices, such as the Kinect Sensor, capable of acquiring RGB-Depth data in real-time, has brought about a profound advancement of the object reconstruction approaches. In this chapter, we present our research on using RGB-Depth sensors embedded in the off-the-shelf MR devices such as the Microsoft HoloLens for object model reconstruction. As MR devices are primarily designed to use its RGB-Depth sensors for environmental mapping (via mesh geometry), it lacks the capability for object reconstruction. We fill this gap by proposing a pipeline for an automated ray-casting-based texture mapping approach to the object mesh geometry acquirable from HoloLens. Our preliminary results from real-world object reconstructions, with different sizes and shapes, demonstrate that our approach produces acceptable reconstruction quality with efficient computation.

Y. Jung (✉) · Y. Wu · H. Jung · J. Kim
Biomedical & Multimedia Information Technology (BMIT) Research Group,
School of Computer Science, The University of Sydney, Sydney, Australia
e-mail: yjun6175@uni.sydney.edu.au; younhyun.jung@gachon.ac.kr

Y. Wu
e-mail: yuwu7002@uni.sydney.edu.au

H. Jung
e-mail: hoijoon.jung@sydney.edu.au

J. Kim
e-mail: jinman.kim@sydney.edu.au

Y. Jung
School of Computing, Gachon University, Seongnam-si, Republic of Korea

J. Kim
Nepean Telehealth Technology Center, Nepean Hospital, Kingswood, Australia

© The Author(s), under exclusive license to Springer Nature Switzerland AG 2021
N. Magnenat Thalmann et al. (eds.), *Intelligent Scene Modeling and Human-Computer Interaction*, Human–Computer Interaction Series,
https://doi.org/10.1007/978-3-030-71002-6_6

6.1 Introduction

Digital model reconstruction of real-world objects and environments is becoming increasingly important to a variety of computer applications using virtual reality (VR) and mixed-reality (MR) technologies. One of the key VR digital model applications is with medical education (Wang et al. 2016; Vankipuram et al. 2013; Alfalah et al. 2019). Alfalah et al. (2019) developed an interactive VR environment with a 3D digital model of a heart structure. Here, users were allowed to perform various interactions, such as free manipulation, and disassembling of the models to present true anatomical relations of different parts of the heart. This was shown to help with understanding the complexity of the heart structures, as well as enhancing the clarity of the anatomical relations of its different parts. Other digital model applications with VR were virtual visiting, e.g., users could visit virtual museums to look at digitally reconstructed models to view arts (paintings as well as status/artefacts) (Xiao and Furukawa 2014; Kersten et al. 2017; Giangreco et al. 2019; Huiying and Jialiang 2020), visit virtual furniture stores that can offer 3D reconstructed models of their furniture products (Merrell et al. 2011; Oh et al. 2004, 2008), or virtually experience a solar system where different planets are digitally modeled and visualized (Mintz et al. 2001; Barnett 2005). There are other applications that were reliant on the use of digital models in VR, e.g., building architecture (Tang et al. 2010; de Klerk et al. 2019), industrial design (Bi and Wang 2010; Nie and Ren 2014), and cultural heritage (Santagati et al. 2013; Gonizzi Barsanti et al. 2015; Bruno et al. 2010). We suggest readers to refer to recent surveys (Kamińska et al. 2019; Berg and Vance 2017; Pareek et al. 2018) in further details on different applications of VR using digital models.

With MR, instead of only having the digital models in a virtual environment, users can complement their real-world environment with digital models that are relevant and necessary for the environment. It has been applied in the form of a superimposition of digital models in the human vision field via the use of a holographic head-mounted display (HMD) such as Microsoft HoloLens and Google Magic Leap. Medical-surgical domains are well-known MR model applications (Itamiya et al. 2018; Soulami et al. 2019; Liebmann et al. 2019). For example, (Soulami et al. 2019), the holographic display could localize digital models of tumor disease in the surgeon's view and highlight specific anatomical features for surgical guidance of patients. In earlier applications of MR, prior to the availability of the holographic displays, data augmentation, e.g., overlay of 2D images/objects was used for manufacturing applications, such as with laser-printer maintenance (Feiner et al. 1992), an object calibration (Whitaker et al. 1995), and an automotive maintenance (Halim 2018), where the information necessary for task completion were superimposed in a form of digital models. For readers interested in MR digital model applications, we refer to prior surveys (Kim et al. 2017; de Souza Cardoso et al. 2020; Eckert et al. 2019; Vávra et al. 2017).

There are two primary approaches to model reconstructions (see Fig. 6.1). The first is the multi-view approach that uses multiple overlapping images from different

Fig. 6.1 Two primary 3D real-world object reconstruction approaches: **a** multi-view approach that evolves the object's geometry derived from images acquired from RGB camera, while iteratively eroding inconsistent points from a view to another and, **b** depth sensor device that physically obtains the object geometry by using time-of-flight infrared (IR) technique

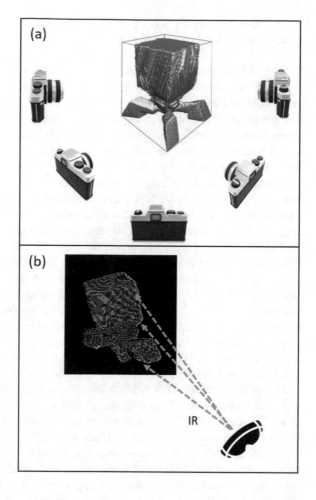

camera angles acquired from a handheld RGB sensor device, e.g., digital cameras on smartphones (Kutulakos and Seitz 2000; Broadhurst et al. 2001; Montenegro et al. 2004). In this RGB approach, typically a user walks around their environment by holding the camera and facing it to the object of interest; the object is then constantly scanned to generate and update a polygon mesh representing the surface geometry of the object as its model (Vlasic et al. 2009; Graciá et al. 2010; Xie et al. 2019). Such model reconstruction accounts for the photometric consistency of the surfaces across the input images and the recovery of photo-hull geometry that contains all possible photo-consistent reconstructions. The surface geometry of the reconstruction is eroded at the points that are inconsistent with the input images until there are consistencies between the model to the input images (Kordelas et al. 2010; Jancosek and Pajdla 2011). Finally, color textures are mapped to the geometry using the correspondence to the input images.

The second approach is through the recent affordability and availability of low-cost, handheld depth sensors that are coupled with RGB camera, (RGB-D) devices, such as the Kinect Sensor (Newcombe et al. 2011; Izadi et al. 2011; Molyneaux 2012) and Samsung Galaxy S10 Note+.[1] The additional use of the depth information is shown to be superior in model reconstruction results (Pan et al. 2016; Ruchay et al. 2018). In RGB-D approaches, the depth sensor uses time-of-flight technique to measure the object depth from the sensor origin. It emits IR rays to the objects through affiliated IR illuminators. The technique works on the IR reflective properties of the objects. It uses the known speed of light to calculate the depth of the object by measuring the round-trip time of IR light emitted by the illuminators and reflected by the objects. The depth images are converted to a point cloud, a set of data points, and the object geometry are then reconstructed by wire-framing the point vertices as triangle sub-mesh sets. The user can also obtain texture details by using the images acquired from the accompanying RGB sensor. Resulting model reconstruction provides realistic digital representation of the objects in a variety of application domains (Thomas and Sugimoto 2013; Zollhöfer et al. 2014, 2018).

Recently, off-the-shelf MR HMD devices such as the Microsoft HoloLens are equipped with a variety of built-in sensors, including a depth sensor (Liu et al. 2018; Hübner et al. 2020a). With HoloLens's real-word environment reconstruction software, it offers the feasibility to reconstruct 3D object models, which can boost up practical usage of this technology (Hübner et al. 2020b). HoloLens further provide unique applications in MR, e.g., rendering acquired models as realistic holograms and interacting with them in a real-world environment; interactions include the user control of the occlusions between the holograms and other real-world objects (Hoffman and Provance 2017), appropriate placement of the hologram into the environment (Lang et al. 2019) and/or improve the appearance of the hologram based on light reflections and ambient colors (Qian et al. 2018). Although HoloLens provide unprecedented MR interaction and holographic experiences, HoloLens is not inherently optimized for model reconstruction of real-world objects; it only scans the geometry of the objects and does not apply color textures which are important to provide the visual appearance of the objects (Lawless and Heymann 2010).

In this chapter, we describe our pipeline for model reconstruction using HoloLens. To achieve this, we introduce a new approach for automatic texture mapping; we map texture images to sub-meshes in 3D coordinates through pixel-by-pixel ray-casting to improve inaccurate texture mapping and distortion that may occur with 2D-based mapping (Dong and Höllerer 2018). We demonstrate our 3D reconstruction results using multiple real-world objects with varying complexity in size and shape.

---

[1] https://www.samsung.com/global/galaxy/what-is/3d-depth-camera/.

6.2 Microsoft HoloLens

6.2.1 *Application Programming Interfaces (API)*

6.2.1.1 Mesh Reconstruction

HoloLens obtains raw data from its sensing cameras and reconstructs polygon mesh to represent real-world object's surface geometry using the holographic processing unit (HPU). HoloLens also uses the raw data for camera location tracking, and this is used to locate the mesh in real-world coordinates. HoloLens provides two APIs to enable software development. In this section, we discuss these APIs in regard to their utility in object model reconstruction. HoloLens reconstruct polygon mesh, referred to as the Spatial Surfaces, representing the surfaces of the objects, as exemplified in Fig. 6.2. HoloLens provides Spatial-Mapping[2] API which allows for access to a set of Spatial Surfaces. Every Spatial Surface has a unique identification (ID) and applications can access and process the Spatial Surfaces using the ID.

6.2.1.2 Locatable Camera

The locatable camera[3] is an API that enables accessing the location information of each camera including 3D pose and view-spectrum, focal length, and principal point. Locatable camera API provides three transformation matrices: projection matrix; view matrix and, coordinate system matrix, enabling spatial transformations of objects captured from camera space to real-world space as illustrated in Fig. 6.3.

6.3 Model Reconstruction Pipeline

The 3D object model reconstruction pipeline is shown in Fig. 6.4. The process starts with real-world object scanning (mesh generation) using the depth sensor; texture images from the RGB camera are also acquired. Using these inputs, our proposed ray-casting approach associates the texture images with the sub-meshes. Texture dilation is then performed to avoid the inherent distortion error in the Locatable Camera.[4] Finally, the dilated textures are rendered with their corresponding meshes as holograms.

---

[2]https://docs.microsoft.com/en-us/windows/mixed-reality/spatial-mapping.

[3]https://docs.microsoft.com/en-us/windows/mixed-reality/locatable-camera.

[4]https://docs.microsoft.com/en-us/windows/mixed-reality/locatable-camera.

Fig. 6.2 The reconstructed mesh augmented on a real-world chair. The orange arrows indicate under- or over-estimation of the mesh geometry

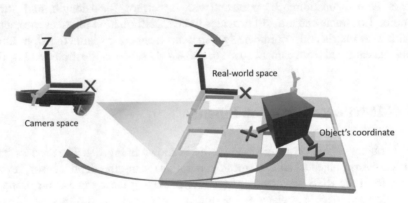

Fig. 6.3 Example of object transformations from the camera space to the real-world space

6.3.1 Pixel Ray-Casting for Texture Mapping

Ray-casting starts on the captured RGB (texture) image. A ray was cast to each pixel of the image from the camera origin, to trace the path of photon for that pixel (see Pixel Ray-casting in Fig. 6.4). Any object (meshes) intersected by the path of the projection were analyzed for occlusion. Multiple objects could have intercepted

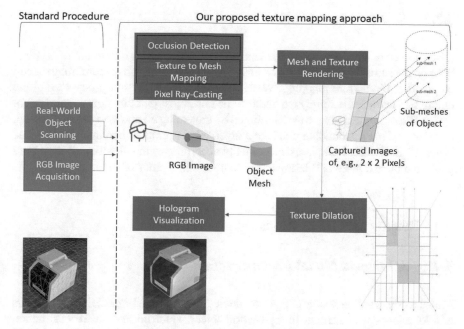

Fig. 6.4 A 3D object model reconstruction pipeline exemplified with a real-world printer object

the path, where the closest object occluded all objects behind it. We, hence, sorted all objects on the path of the projection by distance to the camera origin (starting point), and only the first object was considered. Once this process was performed on all image pixels, we obtained a mapping dictionary of every image pixel and sub-meshes.

6.3.2 Mesh and Texture Rendering

Using Spatial-Mapping API, we stitched together and rendered the sub-meshes consisting of an object of interest to visualize the geometry (surfaces) of the object. For each sub-mesh, an empty sub-texture was then generated. Using the mapping dictionary, the empty sub-textures were filled with the captured RGB images, which were then rendered onto the corresponding sub-meshes (see Mesh and Texture Rendering in Fig. 6.4).

6.3.3   Texture Pixel Dilation

Distortion error from Locatable Camera API could result in a maximum of 10-pixel delta on the actual position of a given image pixel, and some sub-textures may remain empty after the texture mapping. We introduced a pixel dilation process to fill the empty sub-textures. It simply expands all the outermost pixel in a given sub-texture by 20. The outermost pixel was determined by traversing all pixels in the sub-texture, and if any of the surrounding pixels of a given pixel is empty, then that pixel's value is copied and used by all pixels encountered according to the direction of the empty pixel (see the example of dilating a sub-texture with 8 outer pixels in Fig. 6.4).

6.4   Results and Discussions

6.4.1   3D Object Model Reconstruction

Model reconstruction results of a printer device are shown in Fig. 6.5. The user wears a HoloLens and walks around the real-world object, which initiates the reconstruction of the mesh model of the object. In Fig. 6.5b, the reconstructed mesh geometry is augmented on the object. Using the RGB camera, the color texture of the object is captured, and it was used to map it to the mesh geometry facing the camera. The

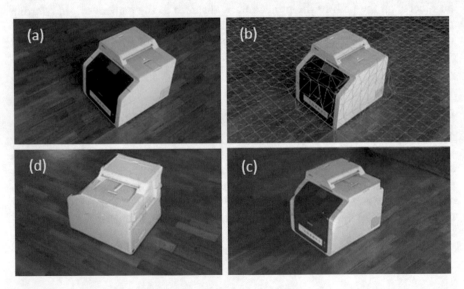

Fig. 6.5 Object model reconstruction result: **a** a real-world printer device object; **b** mesh geometry calculated by HoloLens's Spatial-Mapping API, overlaid on the object; **c** reconstructed printer object (hologram) and, **d** reconstructed hologram showing the back angle of **c**

hologram of the reconstructed model of the object is shown in Fig. 6.5c, replacing the real-world printer. In Fig. 6.5d, we present another reconstructed hologram from the back angle of the same object. The results show that the mesh representation, based on Spatial-Mapping of the HoloLens, produced accurate geometry modeling. The results also indicate that the texture mapping using our 3D ray-casting-based approach resulted in minimal distortion and was accurately fitted to the mesh geometry.

In Fig. 6.6, we present another reconstruction result using a table object. This object, shown in Fig. 6.6a, has a larger and more complex geometry than the printer object in Fig. 6.5. This large object is an example of an object exceeding the size of the RGB camera's image, such that a single color image is unable to retain all the textures needed by the mesh geometry to reconstruct the object. This is in contrast to the printer object in Fig. 6.5 which fitted within the field of view of a single image from the RGB camera. For large objects, our approach uses images captured from

Fig. 6.6 Object reconstruction results: **a** a large table object; **b** reconstructed hologram using multiple textures mapping and, **c** reconstructed hologram showing the back angle of **b**. The change in color shadow of the low part of the table is due to different lighting effects from different angles

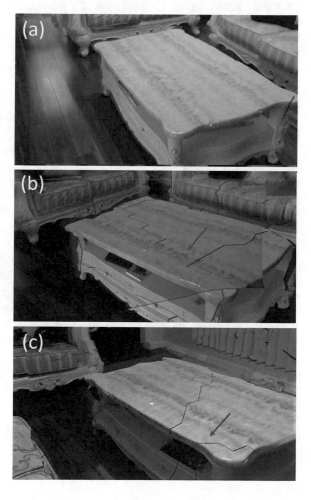

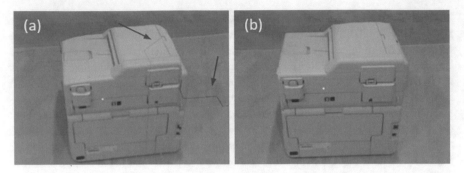

Fig. 6.7 Object model reconstruction results **a** without and **b** with the texture dilation process. We used the same printer object in Fig. 6.6, but with different side view

multiple camera angles, to ensure that all sub-meshes of the object have textures applied. In the reconstruction result shown in Fig. 6.6b, we used two captured color images to reconstruct a single angle view of the object. A different angle view of the reconstructed object (with another two captured images) is shown in Fig. 6.6c. For this example, instead of replacing the physical table, we augmented the hologram onto the physical table, to illustrate the accuracy of the spatial mesh positioning and the texture mapping quality. The black lines in the reconstruction (indicated by green arrows) are due to the edges visible from the sub-meshes. Texture dilation can be used to remove these edges; however, in our current implementation, our dilation only supports smaller objects. We refer to the video link for a demo of the real-time model reconstruction.

In Fig. 6.7, we show the object model reconstruction comparison with and without the texture dilation process. In Fig. 6.7a, we observe the black (texture unmapped) lines at the boundaries of some sub-meshes indicated by green arrows, which were then eliminated through the dilation process as shown in Fig. 6.7b.

Spatial-Mapping of HoloLens can result in under- or over-estimation of the mesh representation of the objects. An example is shown in Fig. 6.2 where the sub-meshes are not tightly represented on the chair (indicated by orange arrows). This results in some of the color textures being mapped exceeding the object (or smaller than the object), thus generating texture distortion as illustrated in Fig. 6.8. We used ray-casting to map the textures on the mesh geometry, and as such, the texture pixels from the camera rays were supposed to be mapped to the mesh of the object of interest.

6.4.2   Computation

Our pipeline computation has two components: mesh reconstruction and texture mapping. The computation time for the mesh reconstruction tended to be proportional to the complexity of the modeled objects based on their shape and size. With the

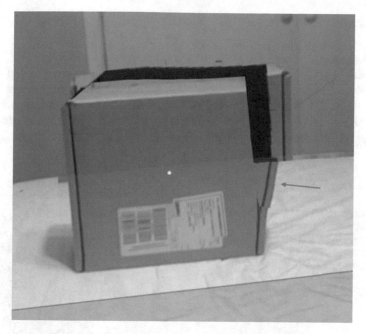

Fig. 6.8 A texture mapping distortion example from under-estimation of mesh representation by Spatial-Mapping of HoloLens (affected textures indicated by orange arrows). The box's textures were fitted to the mesh which did not adequately represent the box

simple object example of the printer (Fig. 6.5), it took 3 s, whereas the larger and more complex object of the table (Fig. 6.6) resulted in 7 s. Overall, we suggest that the mesh reconstruction has an acceptable computation time for practical usage.

The current texture mapping implementation has been done per image pixel in a serial manner. Therefore, the computation time for the texture mapping was according to $O(n*t)$, where n is the number of texture images and t is the amount of time required to map each image to sub-meshes, i.e., dependent on the pixel resolution. It took 150 s for a single texture image with the pixel resolution of 896×504, which is the default setting in our method, and then became double at 300 s for two texture images. With 1280×720 pixel resolution, a single image took 310 s. The object complexity (i.e., the number of sub-meshes), meanwhile, was not the factor to affect the texture mapping computation. This was attributed to the texture mapping occurring in 1-to-multi relation between texture pixels to sub-meshes. In total, we achieved 153 s for the complete printer object and 307 s for the table object reconstructions.

6.5   Conclusions and Future Work

In this chapter, we presented a new pipeline to digitally reconstruct real-world objects
using Microsoft HoloLens with its mesh reconstruction. We demonstrated that the
Microsoft HoloLens, the first generation of consumer-level MR device, can be used
to reconstruct 3D models of physical objects; it offers a new visual experience of
sharing these models in MR applications. Our preliminary results introduced the
capability of our pipeline but also identified multiple areas for improvements and

Fig. 6.9 **a** hexahedron-shape
air purifier object, **b** its mesh
reconstruction result from
the default sensing camera of
HoloLens we used, and **c** the
comparative result from a
high-performance sensing
camera

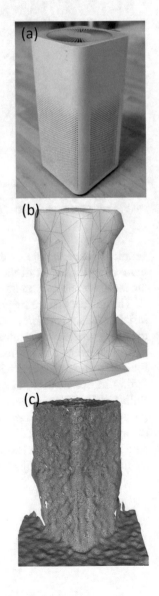

extensions. To resolve the texture distortion issue due to the underestimated mesh, we are exploring the use of 3D edge detection algorithm during ray-casting. When a ray is close to an edge of an object mesh (based on a defined distance threshold), we propose to readjust the angle of the ray casted so that the texture can be mapped more accurately to the object. As another future work, although our serial-based pixel texture mapping produced acceptable computational performance, we aim to further improve its performance by parallelizing the pixel texture mapping using the built-in graphics processing units (GPUs) in HoloLens. We suggest that the next generation of holographic MR HMD, e.g., HoloLens 2, will be equipped with enhanced sensing cameras, e.g., higher image resolution and frame rates (Terry 2019). For example, in Fig. 6.9, we show hexahedron-shape air purifier (Fig. 6.9a) and its mesh reconstruction results using two sensing cameras: the default camera of HoloLens we used (Fig. 6.9b) and a high-performance camera (Fig. 6.9c) where the geometry of the object can be preserved more precisely. Together with robust and powerful MR software development (Ungureanu et al. 2020; Vidal-Balea et al. 2020) and GPU-based parallelization technologies (Navarro et al. 2014), we can expect boosting up the proposed reconstruction pipeline in many aspects including model accuracy, visual quality, and computational efficiency. We suggest this is an interesting research direction to investigate how we can maximally use the enhanced capabilities from the new MR hardware.

References

Alfalah SF, Falah JF, Alfalah T, Elfalah M, Muhaidat N, Falah O (2019) A comparative study between a virtual reality heart anatomy system and traditional medical teaching modalities. Virtual Reality 23(3):229–234

Barnett M (2005) Using virtual reality computer models to support student understanding of astronomical concepts. J Comput Math Sci Teach 24(4):333–356

Berg LP, Vance JM (2017) Industry use of virtual reality in product design and manufacturing: a survey. Virtual Reality 21(1):1–17

Bi Z, Wang L (2010) Advances in 3d data acquisition and processing for industrial applications. Robot Comput Integr Manuf 26(5):403–413

Broadhurst A, Drummond TW, Cipolla R (2001) A probabilistic framework for space carving. In: Proceedings eighth IEEE international conference on computer vision, ICCV 2001, vol 1. IEEE, pp 388–393

Bruno F, Bruno S, De Sensi G, Luchi ML, Mancuso S, Muzzupappa M (2010) From 3D reconstruction to virtual reality: a complete methodology for digital archaeological exhibition. J Cult Herit 11(1):42–49

de Klerk R, Duarte AM, Medeiros DP, Duarte JP, Jorge J, Lopes DS (2019) Usability studies on building early stage architectural models in virtual reality. Autom Constr 103:104–116

de Souza Cardoso LF, Mariano FCMQ, Zorzal ER (2020) A survey of industrial augmented reality. Comput Ind Eng 139(106):159

Dong S, Höllerer T (2018) Real-time re-textured geometry modeling using microsoft HoloLens. In: 2018 IEEE conference on virtual reality and 3D user interfaces (VR). IEEE, pp 231–237

Eckert M, Volmerg JS, Friedrich CM (2019) Augmented reality in medicine: systematic and bibliographic review. JMIR mHealth and uHealth 7(4):e10,967

Feiner S, MacIntyre B, Seligmann D (1992) Annotating the real world with knowledge-based graphics on a see-through head-mounted display. In: Proceedings of the conference on graphics interface'92, pp 78–85

Giangreco I, Sauter L, Parian MA, Gasser R, Heller S, Rossetto L, Schuldt H (2019) Virtue: a virtual reality museum experience. In: Proceedings of the 24th international conference on intelligent user interfaces: companion, pp 119–120

Gonizzi Barsanti S, Caruso G, Micoli L, Covarrubias Rodriguez M, Guidi G et al (2015) 3D visualization of cultural heritage artefacts with virtual reality devices. In: 25th international CIPA symposium 2015, Copernicus Gesellschaft mbH, vol 40, pp 165–172

Graciá L, Saez-Barona S, Carrión D, Salvador I, Perez-Cortes JC (2010) A system for real-time multi-view 3D reconstruction. In: 2010 workshops on database and expert systems applications. IEEE, pp 235–239

Halim AA (2018) Applications of augmented reality for inspection and maintenance process in automotive industry. J Fundam Appl Sci 10(3S):412–421

Hoffman M, Provance J (2017) Visualization of molecular structures using HoloLens-based augmented reality. AMIA Summits Transl Sci Proc 2017:68

Hübner P, Clintworth K, Liu Q, Weinmann M, Wursthorn S (2020a) Evaluation of HoloLens tracking and depth sensing for indoor mapping applications. Sensors 20(4):1021

Hübner P, Weinmann M, Wursthorn S (2020b) Voxel-based indoor reconstruction from HoloLens triangle meshes. arXiv preprint. arXiv:200207689

Huiying Z, Jialiang H (2020) Virtual reality design of Chinese classical furniture digital museum. Int J Electr Eng Educ 0020720920928545

Itamiya T, Iwai T, Kaneko T (2018) The holographic human for surgical navigation using microsoft HoloLens. EPiC Ser Eng 1:26–30

Izadi S, Kim D, Hilliges O, Molyneaux D, Newcombe R, Kohli P, Shotton J, Hodges S, Freeman D, Davison A et al (2011) Kinectfusion: real-time 3D reconstruction and interaction using a moving depth camera. In: Proceedings of the 24th annual ACM symposium on User interface software and technology, pp 559–568

Jancosek M, Pajdla T (2011) Multi-view reconstruction preserving weakly-supported surfaces. In: Proceedings of CVPR 2011. IEEE, pp 3121–3128

Kamińska D, Sapiński T, Wiak S, Tikk T, Haamer RE, Avots E, Helmi A, Ozcinar C, Anbarjafari G (2019) Virtual reality and its applications in education: survey. Information 10(10):318

Kersten TP, Tschirschwitz F, Deggim S (2017) Development of a virtual museum including a 4D presentation of building history in virtual reality. Int Arch Photogramm Remote Sens Spat Inf Sci 42:361

Kim SK, Kang SJ, Choi YJ, Choi MH, Hong M (2017) Augmented-reality survey: from concept to application. KSII Trans Internet & Inf Syst 11(2)

Kordelas G, Agapito JPM, Hernandez JV, Daras P (2010) State-of-the-art algorithms for complete 3D model reconstruction. Proc Engag Summer Sch Zermatt Switz 1315:115

Kutulakos KN, Seitz SM (2000) A theory of shape by space carving. Int J Comput Vis 38(3):199–218

Lang V, Liang W, Yu LF (2019) Virtual agent positioning driven by scene semantics in mixed reality. In: 2019 IEEE conference on virtual reality and 3D user interfaces (VR). IEEE, pp 767–775

Lawless HT, Heymann H (2010) Color and appearance. In: Sensory evaluation of food. Springer, pp 283–301

Liebmann F, Roner S, von Atzigen M, Scaramuzza D, Sutter R, Snedeker J, Farshad M, Fürnstahl P (2019) Pedicle screw navigation using surface digitization on the microsoft HoloLens. Int J Comput Assist Radiol Surg 14(7):1157–1165

Liu Y, Dong H, Zhang L, El Saddik A (2018) Technical evaluation of HoloLens for multimedia: a first look. IEEE MultiMedia 25(4):8–18

Merrell P, Schkufza E, Li Z, Agrawala M, Koltun V (2011) Interactive furniture layout using interior design guidelines. ACM Trans Graph (TOG) 30(4):87

Mintz R, Litvak S, Yair Y (2001) 3D-virtual reality in science education: an implication for astronomy teaching. J Comput Math Sci Teach 20(3):293–305

Molyneaux D (2012) Kinectfusion rapid 3D reconstruction and interaction with microsoft kinect. In: Proceedings of the international conference on the foundations of digital games, pp 3–3

Montenegro AA, Gattass M, Carvalho PCP, Velho LCPR (2004) Adaptive space carving. In: Proceedings of 2nd international symposium on 3D data processing, visualization and transmission, 2004, 3DPVT 2004. IEEE, pp 199–206

Navarro CA, Hitschfeld-Kahlcr N, Mateu L (2014) A survey on parallel computing and its applications in data-parallel problems using GPU architectures. Commun Comput Phys 15(2):285–329

Newcombe RA, Izadi S, Hilliges O, Molyneaux D, Kim D, Davison AJ, Kohli P, Shotton J, Hodges S, Fitzgibbon AW (2011) Kinectfusion: real-time dense surface mapping and tracking. ISMAR 11:127–136

Nie GP, Ren GJ (2014) The application of virtual reality technology in teaching of industrial design-outline of the project for the human-computer interactive simulation of the upper limb operations. Appl Mech Mater Trans Tech Publ 464:420–423

Oh H, Yoon SY, Hawley J (2004) What virtual reality can offer to the furniture industry. J Text Appar Technol Manag 4(1):1–17

Oh H, Yoon SY, Shyu CR (2008) How can virtual reality reshape furniture retailing? Cloth Text Res J 26(2):143–163

Pan H, Guan T, Luo Y, Duan L, Tian Y, Yi L, Zhao Y, Yu J (2016) Dense 3D reconstruction combining depth and RGB information. Neurocomputing 175:644–651

Pareek TG, Mehta U, Gupta A et al (2018) A survey: virtual reality model for medical diagnosis. Biomed Pharmacol J 11(4):2091–2100

Qian L, Plopski A, Navab N, Kazanzides P (2018) Restoring the awareness in the occluded visual field for optical see-through head-mounted displays. IEEE Trans Vis Comput Graph 24(11):2936–2946

Ruchay A, Dorofeev K, Kober A (2018) Accuracy analysis of 3D object reconstruction using RGB-D sensor. In: Proceedings of the international conference information technology and nanotechnology. Session image processing and earth remote sensing, CEUR workshop proceedings, vol 2210, pp 82–88

Santagati C, Inzerillo L, Di Paola F (2013) Image-based modeling techniques for architectural heritage 3D digitalization: limits and potentialities. Int Arch Photogramm Remote Sens Spat Inf Sci 5(w2):555–560

Soulami KB, Ghribi E, Labyed Y, Saidi MN, Tamtaoui A, Kaabouch N (2019) Mixed-reality aided system for glioblastoma resection surgery using microsoft HoloLens. In: 2019 IEEE international conference on electro information technology (EIT). IEEE, pp 079–084

Tang P, Huber D, Akinci B, Lipman R, Lytle A (2010) Automatic reconstruction of as-built building information models from laser-scanned point clouds: a review of related techniques. Autom Constr 19(7):829–843

Terry E (2019) Silicon at the heart of hololens 2. In: 2019 IEEE hot chips 31 symposium (HCS). IEEE Computer Society, pp 1–26

Thomas D, Sugimoto A (2013) A flexible scene representation for 3D reconstruction using an RGB-D camera. In: Proceedings of the IEEE international conference on computer vision, pp 2800–2807

Ungureanu D, Bogo F, Galliani S, Sama P, Duan X, Meekhof C, Stühmer J, Cashman TJ, Tekin B, Schönberger JL, et al (2020) HoloLens 2 research mode as a tool for computer vision research. arXiv preprint. arXiv:200811239

Vankipuram A, Khanal P, Ashby A, Vankipuram M, Gupta A, DrummGurnee D, Josey K, Smith M (2013) Design and development of a virtual reality simulator for advanced cardiac life support training. IEEE J Biomed Health Inform 18(4):1478–1484

Vávra P, Roman J, Zonča P, Ihnát P, Němec M, Kumar J, Habib N, El-Gendi A (2017) Recent development of augmented reality in surgery: a review. J Healthc Eng

Vidal-Balea A, Blanco-Novoa O, Picallo-Guembe I, Celaya-Echarri M, Fraga-Lamas P, Lopez-Iturri P, Azpilicueta L, Falcone F, Fernández-Caramés TM (2020) Analysis, design and practical validation of an augmented reality teaching system based on microsoft HoloLens 2 and edge computing. In: Engineering proceedings, multidisciplinary digital publishing institute, vol 2, p 52

Vlasic D, Peers P, Baran I, Debevec P, Popović J, Rusinkiewicz S, Matusik W (2009) Dynamic shape capture using multi-view photometric stereo. In: ACM SIGGRAPH Asia 2009 papers, pp 1–11

Wang F, Liu Y, Tian M, Zhang Y, Zhang S, Chen J (2016) Application of a 3D haptic virtual reality simulation system for dental crown preparation training. In: 2016 8th international conference on information technology in medicine and education (ITME). IEEE, pp 424–427

Whitaker RT, Crampton C, Breen DE, Tuceryan M, Rose E (1995) Object calibration for augmented reality. Comput Graph Forum 14(3):15–27

Xiao J, Furukawa Y (2014) Reconstructing the world museums. Int J Comput Vis 110(3):243–258

Xie H, Yao H, Sun X, Zhou S, Zhang S (2019) Pix2vox: context-aware 3D reconstruction from single and multi-view images. In: Proceedings of the IEEE international conference on computer vision, pp 2690–2698

Zollhöfer M, Nießner M, Izadi S, Rehmann C, Zach C, Fisher M, Wu C, Fitzgibbon A, Loop C, Theobalt C et al (2014) Real-time non-rigid reconstruction using an RGB-D camera. ACM Trans Graph (ToG) 33(4):1–12

Zollhöfer M, Stotko P, Görlitz A, Theobalt C, Nießner M, Klein R, Kolb A (2018) State of the art on 3D reconstruction with RGB-D cameras. Comput Graph Forum 37(2):625–652

Chapter 7
Semantic Modeling and Rendering

J. Divya Udayan and HyungSeok Kim

Abstract 3D objects get more attention in various applications including computer games, movies, urban planning, training and so on. To model a large-scale 3D scene, semantic modeling method is getting more attention to efficiently handle the complexity of modeling process. Semantic modeling method could be utilized to model a large-scale scene, through interactive editing of the scene, and automatically generating complex environments. Semantic model could be also used to support intelligent behaviour on virtual scene, semantic rendering and adaptive visualization of complex 3D objects. In this chapter, methods to create semantic models from real objects are discussed. In addition, application examples of semantic models are illustrated with large-scale urban scene. Semantic modeling and rendering would provide ability to create interactive and responsive virtual world by considering its semantics in addition to shape appearances.

7.1 Introduction

Modeling and visualization of 3D objects is a great challenge in computer graphics domain. This research activity started from early era of computer graphics and is now becoming ubiquitous in the industry. Its application is widespread in many areas, specifically video games, advertisements, movies, urban planning and navigation. In brief, we have witnessed computer animated sequences turn from experimental to common practice nowadays. For 3D modeling, this has become overwhelming in many sectors such as manufacturing, medical science, urban planning, military simulations, tele-presence and remote collaborations (Petit et al. 2010).

J. Divya Udayan
Computer Science and Engineering, GITAM Institute of Technology, Visakhapatnam, India
e-mail: djayasre@gitam.edu

H. Kim (✉)
Department of Computer Engineering, Konkuk University, Seoul, South Korea
e-mail: hyuskim@konkuk.ac.kr

Large scale 3D scene modeling has been receiving increasing demand in the fields of urban design, navigation, 3D games and entertainment. As the name implies, city modeling relates to 3D modeling of buildings and its associated infrastructure. A lot of applications are made possible with this; some new synthetic or even unreal objects can be added to the original image, new viewpoints of the scene can be computed using classical rendering methods of computer graphics, etc.

The modeling cost for virtual cities is high, and the cost for modeling real city is even higher. Although a few models were created for an entire city, in a vast majority of cases the model consists of low-detailed buildings with lack of semantics. Usually, each building is represented by a coarse polygonal model associated with texture mapping. This certainly is appreciable for fly-over views, but it is inadequate for an immersive walk-through, which requires higher levels of detail, while requiring at the same time significant storage and memory capacities. In terms of modeling, some of the city models or at least some of their landmarks are highly detailed. But this is again achieved at the price of heavy human intervention.

In order to model a large-scale scene, computer vision techniques are widely used. Nowadays, research is focused towards computer vision for classification of scenes, objects and activities. However, 3D understanding has traditionally faced several impediments. Firstly, the problem of self and normal occlusion highly affects the accuracy of reconstruction output. Further, the problem persists in mapping different images of the same structures to the same 3D space and in handling the multi-modalities of these representations. Finally, acquiring ground-truth 3D datasets are expensive and are in turn training limitations for divergent approaches for representing 3D structures.

To address those issues, we can find an analogy between our human vision system and two branches of computer vision—recognition and reconstruction. The ventral stream is associated with object recognition and form representation and dorsal stream is involved in guidance of actions and recognizing the position of objects in space. For recognition, i.e. counterpart of ventral stream, it is widely accepted that the task can be divided into three levels as shown in Table 7.1 (Xiao 2012).

Conventional Modeling is focused on the low-level image features like geometrical ones; Modeling virtual objects which has pixel-wise closer to the real objects. Recently, there have been approaches to model high-level features which is semantics. Using semantics, it is possible to greatly reduce amount of data to be rendered or

Table 7.1 Different levels and different streams for both human and computer vision systems

Human vision	Computer vision	Low level	Mid-level	High level
Ventral stream	Recognition	Color value	Grouping and alignment	Semantic → Context
Dorsal stream	Reconstruction	Distance value	Grouping and alignment	Shape → Structure
Question to answer at each level	How to process signal?	Which are together?	What is where?	

simulated while preserving human perceptual details. It is also possible to model the shape using semantics so that the generated model can be easily edited and populated in the virtual world.

7.2   Semantic Modeling

Semantic 3D Modeling aims to generate a dense geometric model and at the same time it also intends to infer the semantic meaning of each parts of the reconstructed 3D model. Thus it supports meaningful representation of 3D model in the scene. For example the volume of the car can be easily extracted which is difficult if we use geometric Modeling alone which lack the knowledge about which part of the geometry belongs to the car. Semantic 3D Modeling is used in different applications like Modeling the underground and aboveground infrastructures, indoor space and artefact Modeling, city Modeling and so on.

Shape structure indicates the arrangement and associations between shape points which is prior to local geometry and low-level processing, while assessing and processing shapes at high-level. Nevertheless, this shows a greater focus on the inter and intra-semantic associations between the shape components, rather than concentrating on local geometry. Shapes' structure studies are now a basic research subject enabling shape analysis, editing and Modeling with the coming of convenient shape acquisition, easy-to-use desktop fabrication possibilities, as well as access to large repositories of 3D models. An entirely new structure-aware shape line which processes algorithms has been brought into view for the purpose of apprehending the structure of the shapes. There are fundamentally two types of algorithm, namely rule-based shape Modeling and component-based shape Modeling which have two key stages; a smart processing stage and an analysis stage. The smart processing stage employs the acquired information for synthesis, editing and exploration of new shapes, whereas the analysis stage indicates the extraction of information from input data. Nevertheless, this segment of the study manages summarisation and the presentation of principal conceptualities and methodological strategies towards effi-cient structure-aware shape processing. Subsequently, the major open challenges and barriers which belong to the technical and conceptual steps are listed in order to provide new researchers with better exploration and contribution to this research subject.

Semantic Modeling has been categorized into two stages: (i) representation of shape semantics and (ii) capture and Modeling of shape semantics.

7.2.1   Representation of Shape Semantics

Shape semantics and its representations are the procedure of capturing the appear-ance and shape of the objects within a 2D image scene on the basis of the structural information. One technique is component-based structure capturing. Component analysis exists within the depth of structure-aware shape processing which is of help in obtaining components from a shape which exists in the classical segmentation issue (Shamir 2008). The correspondence issue, which exists among a shape collection and not only a pair of shapes, is equally necessary (Van Kaick et al. 2011). Early works on local geometric analysis which comprise curvature and geodesics are presented for the purpose of focusing on both issues independently. Furthermore, the Shape Annotator Framework (Attene et al. 2009), endeavoured to help the user to generate semantic, part-based shape ontology. The data-driven method has been employed by recent enhancements, especially in structural invariants from the exemplars' set. As Golovinskiy and Funkhouser (2009) began a co-analysis method, they also initialized a consistent segmentation while achieving momentum on some fronts which are composed of style content separation (Xu et al. 2010), spectral clustering, co-abstraction, joint segmentation (Sidi et al. 2011), active learning (Kim et al. 2012) and the discovery of functional substructures (Yumer and Kara 2013). Huang et al. (2011), Wang et al. (2012) after considering more than object Modeling, assessed the scene data by using spatial contexts while applying the results of novel scene synthesis. However, the methodologies of this class can be separated into structure-aware editing approaches, symmetry driven shape analysis and co-analysis of shape sets.

7.2.2   Capture and Modeling Shape Semantics

Computer vision, computer graphics societies and rule-based shape Modeling representations in urban planning have been studied punctiliously. Initially, these were first considered as the formal design analysis, and subsequently for random creations of unique designs. They are now considered for automatic image-based reconstruction of current environments. The possibilities of these representations emanating from the computer graphics perspective are conversed in this segment and subsequently by the production of paradigms through a formal generic rule. The rule-based shape Modeling may be categorized into procedural Modeling and also inverse procedural Modeling. The procedural Modeling class receives considerable interest in digital image synthesis, while the inverse procedural Modeling concerns computer vision.

The procedural methodologies which have been observed up to the present time are of a generative nature, and are labelled Forward Procedural Modeling procedures. Unfortunately, the rule-dependent Procedural Modeling system has a serious disadvantage, being that it is more frequently descriptive, thereby suggesting a low level of intuitiveness as well as control over the results obtained. In the setting of a city having multiple structures, there needs to be a considerable number of rules, which would make it unmanageable for very large urban regions. Moreover, this could present a challenge to ordinary laymen when using such complicated volumes of data. The recently introduced Inverse Procedural Modeling procedure could be a means of solving the aforementioned anomalies. Also, resolves the problems observed regarding compact parameterised grammar rules as well as the corresponding values related to them. When this is sequentially applied, it supplies a predetermined output; consequently, it is regarded as being particularly applicable in the foreseeable future.

Inverse Procedural Modeling can be split into two fundamental categories, the first of which comprises an initiation stage of rules and grammar associated with supplying the authentic derivation together with the respective parameter. The second category is associated with recovering the grammar structures and fundamental parameters. The former category is related to optimisation tasks associated with the shape of the grammar in the necessary paradigm. Subsequently, this is required to determine a rule-set; however, since urban settings have a connection with discernible geometric patterns, it is demoted to a manageable work level. Nevertheless, if an accurate rule-set regarding the construction of an effective paradigm is to be found, this would involve dismantling a 3D paradigm into a very compact design. The objective of the Inverse Procedural Modeling methodology requires an automated provision of parameters and rules. However, this presents a challenge when taking into account regions of interest in a top down context for the purpose of anticipating a particular fundamental paradigm to be in alignment, bottom up and context free. This could occur because we have no knowledge of the actual paradigm, but just need an estimate of the grammar from the presented data. Most of the data presented and processed needs a certain level of input from the user regarding the appropriate rules.

When similar groups are paired, there is provision for various transformation spaces; furthermore, with the completion of the spaces, they are clustered together. In conclusion, the clusters are weighed and sorted in the rules generation procedure, thereby supplying the identification of the appropriate elemental sequence (Stava et al. 2010). A method was presented to extract a compact grammar from arbitrary 2D vector content. An L-System methodology is supplied for the elemental sequence, and the clusters are correspondingly updated by replacing the sequence with the new rule. This procedure replicates until just one remains, as depicted in Fig. 7.1. Vanegas (2010) have used partial symmetries for the purpose of interpreting the processes from 3D paradigms, which subsequently provide approaches for buildings and associated structures. Taking into account the argument that a complicated paradigm does not need any comprehensive definition. Benes et al. (2011) introduced the Guided Procedural Modeling concept. It is significant in bisecting the space into guides, being geometrical objects retaining particular closed restrictions.

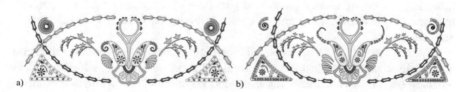

Fig. 7.1 Inverse procedural modeling by automatic generation of L-systems (Stava et al. 2010)

It is presupposed that the majority of construction programmes tend to predominate towards three orthogonal directions; namely, the Manhattan-World (MW) constraint. Moreover, Vanegas (2010) conducted a computerized presentation which used multiple images which were measured aerially towards supplying a distinct geometrically synchronized representation of the edifices, to some extent integrating their textures. This system moved towards representing buildings by using a grammar which provided for buildings which were in conformity with the MW restrictions and also added factors associated with an initial course building volume. This procedure was possible according to the dual presuppositions, the first of which is that the buildings could be represented sequentially regarding multiple floors, with individual floors bearing a series connected faces with each facet being accordingly presumed to be parallel with an MW direction. Secondly, it was taken into account that each individual Manhattan direction of the building floor would be coloured differently inside each image, as a result of the lighting provided from outside sources. Therefore, the course building envelope, which was formed, was subsequently bisected into a group of floors, each of which is regarded as being a terminal symbols in the grammar. Such symbols are then changed in order for new buildings to be in alignment with what had been observed aerially following an optimisation which passed through the parameter spaces of reasonable changes, thereby reducing the error value between preceding and recent constructions. Mathias et al. (2011) offered a technique to rebuild whole structures with IPM by using template grammars, trained detectors and Structure from Motion (SfM) systems. All of these fundamentally involved a grammar interpreter for the purpose of deciphering the proceeding stages which were to be considered. These techniques could be regarded as being a procedure to inaugurate the template by predetermining the authentic grammar parameters, enabling the generations of 3D simulations. In order to explain this, the presentation discussed a Doric temple. Ripperda and Brenner (2009) explained the challenges encountered in building a façade simply from images and data ranges without any structural information. Moreover, they recommended a particular grammar to the data in order to solve the anomalies. This procedure involved a nonchalant walk through the façade models supplied by the grammar using a reversible jump, being the Markov Chain Monte Carlo. The most recent work proposed by Wu et al. (2014) seeks to create a significant split grammar which explains a given façade layout procedure. In this case, the recommended changes involve the necessity of corresponding proposals. When such a proposal is accepted its acceptance is dependent on a probability established by the derivation of the input details. Furthermore, Bayesian learning for inverse procedural Modeling is another pioneering work, Wu et al. (2014). Additionally, inverse procedural Modeling seeks a procedural paradigm which creates a given input, and in connection with this, much research work involving encoding façade layouts has been conducted.

In the real world, it can be explained that urban spaces, in the course of time, are continually experiencing historical, cultural and economic change, which results in updating building styles. Reflecting these updates in the virtual world is certainly a challenge, even at the present time.

Each building façade have its unique structure with complicated footprints. However, architectural components of the buildings are repetitive along the vertical and horizontal directions. Such patterns are exploited by procedural Modeling systems which are encoded into a set of rules in which the textures and geometry are created, producing a compact representation of their structure. Procedural rules are typically in the style of formal grammar, including symbols which indicate each pattern and also some operations on the patterns such as repetitions and splitting. Beginning with an initial shape (known as the axiom) which is usually the building footprint, a production of rules results in the creation of the desired structure. The principal drawbacks of applying grammar-based rules are that they are typically text-based and also lack intuitiveness. The principal objective of IPM is to extract procedural rules; for example, from images in order to produce paradigms resembling the input 2D image.

7.2.2.1 Shape Analysis Based on Symmetry

Symmetry has a powerful influence in the structure-aware processing of man-made items, whereas it is expected that symmetrical structures will share a similar functionality. Symmetries exist in many of these objects. Structural symmetry detection methodologies have been used by the geometric Modeling community (Zheng et al. 2013; Fisher et al. 2011, 2012; Simari et al. 2006). The upright orientation concept, Fu et al. (2008) can be used to understand the functionality of man-made items. This tends to be an early endeavour in the structural analysis of such items. The upright orientation and symmetry show early endeavours in the acquiring of high-level semantic information from geometry.

There are generally two types of symmetries:

1. Building blocks or instances indicate the weak type of symmetry, (Kalojanov et al. 2012) which suggests a set of operations G consigning to every probability of exchanging an object's components with another by rigid transformations. This has no impact on the shape itself and, in this case, G is not a subgroup of the rigid motions.
2. Regular transformations are stronger types, Pauly et al. (2008). In this symmetry, an algebraic group formulates itself as the transformations of the geometry, thereby suggesting that geometry is superfluous in the transformations' perception as it has a similar piece which is displayed repetitively; however, building blocks themselves are instantiated as regular symmetries themselves.

Several techniques have been presented in order to locate symmetry (Simari et al. 2006; Podolak et al. 2006). These refer to the recent surveys for images (Liu et al. 2010) and also 3D geometry, Mitra et al. (2013) for a detailed discussion and survey of symmetry. Since symmetry acts as a structure model, it appears to be attractive. This is because of the agnostic attribute of the actual geometry which shows much symmetry so it can be abstracted from the concrete shape. Furthermore, this can be used in generating complex and high-level structure presumptions on greater geometry classes. This is in the same symmetry which is used for absolution of incomplete shapes by means of inferring that most symmetrical shapes are consistent with the observation, Thrun and Wegbreit (2005). Nevertheless, Mitra et al. (2007) have advocated a technique which formulates shapes symmetrically.

The hierarchical nesting of symmetries has been explored for Modeling and shape representation. Wang et al. (2011) have built a symmetry hierarchy from a man-made item especially while the object is presupposed to be divided into useful components. Firstly, self-symmetries of the components and inter-component symmetries are evaluated; subsequently, symmetry and (part) connectivity associations are established into a graphical representation. Furthermore, the compactness principle refers to work for the most basic representation. However, the consequent symmetric hierarchies are shown to replicate object semantics as well as to support structure-aware hierarchical shape editing. The consistency in the hierarchical structural representations is not determined as acquired on a set of related shapes.

7.2.2.2   Co-analysis of Shape Sets

In recent years, greater interest has been shown in the co-analysis of sets of shapes because it is of assistance in understanding a shape and its particular components and can be consistent only by observing a set of shapes having a similar functionality or semantic rather than a single observation. Nevertheless, it is accepted that further information is created by analysing a set concurrently. However, the method of using the distributed set knowledge efficiently remains uncertain. This is of assistance in obtaining an articulate and consistent structures' analysis. Unsupervised co-analysis simply relies on where the input sets of shapes are related to one another and show the same object class such as aircraft, chairs, lamps and so on. Co-segmentation indicates the central obstruction of co-analysis where the challenge is to proportion every shape resolutely in the input set concurrently. Furthermore, a labelling of the segments is obtained across the set together with proportioning the shapes into segments. Furthermore, since the components here have a similar label which fulfils the same semantic objective, their geometries may be dissimilar. Current endeavours towards co-segmentation can be classified in more detail into supervised and unsupervised methodologies.

1. Unsupervised Methodology: In comparison with supervised methodology, this appears to be rather more challenging since total knowledge needs to be obtained from the input set itself.
2. Supervised Methodology: This indicates a training set which is composed of presupposed and sufficient pre-analysed shapes which are applied in labelling a set of unknown shapes probabilistically. However, supervised methodologies satisfy the needs of co-analysis strictly because the shapes are not analysed concurrently and the results move towards a regular segmentation for shapes in every object classification.

It is necessary to accept that neither supervised nor unsupervised methodology can guarantee a perfect co-segmentation of a set because geometry is unable to express shape semantics completely. Consequently, it is impossible to capture every probable geometric variation of a component, specifically by any descriptor. Work previously undertaken by Golovinskiy and Funkhouser (2009) as shown in Fig. 7.2 strongly pre-aligns every shape within the set, and subsequently clusters the shape faces according to a fundamental graph. Such graph is related to adjoining faces in the models which are achieved subsequent to the alignment. The resulting clusters have endowed a natural co-segmentation of the shapes. The scale variation within the shape components are factored out by Xu et al. (2010), firstly by clustering the shapes into miscellaneous styles where a style indicates anisotropic component scales of the shapes. This enables them to co-segment shapes offering greater variety

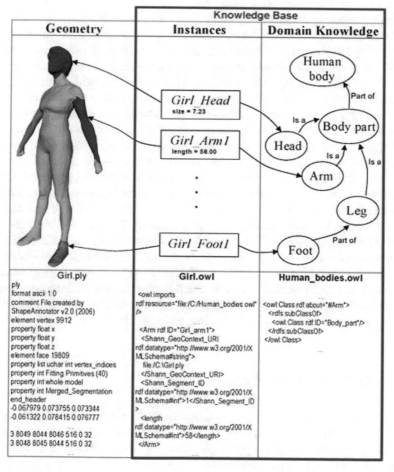

Fig. 7.2 Characterization of 3D shape parts for semantic annotation (Golovinskiy and Funkhouser 2009)

in contrast and in generating some new shapes by the transformation of various styles. However, this method is structured to manage only one specific style. The co-segmentation issue is the same as that of the clustering segments achieved from an initial over-segmentation of the shapes' set is mentioned by Sidi et al. (2011) with the application of diffusion maps. However, in comparison with the previous works, the clustering is performed in the field of shape descriptors rather than the spatial coordinates of the shapes. This methodology allows corresponding components to be managed. These are distinct in location, cardinality and pose; therefore, the factors which challenge any strategy are based on spatial alignment in geometry or direct shape clustering.

Furthermore, the exploitation of a major enabling attributes of the input set, also referred to as third-party connections, is enabled by the descriptor clustering method. There is a likelihood of developing a connection between two shapes if they obtain essentially distinct components; also, some other components exist in the set, thereby formulating a connection which gives a completed co-segmentation. The algorithm's feature Modeling factor is advanced in subsequent work which has been improved by Hu et al. (2012). Moreover, they resolve and pose a subspace clustering problem in several feature spaces instead of focusing the different features into one feature descriptor. Subsequently, Huang et al. (2011) developed a joint segmentation methodology in which a set is used in order to assist in the segmentation of individual shapes. Furthermore, they employed shape descriptors to manage rich shape discrepancies but had no target of consistent segmentation of the entire set. Consequently, this does not indicate a co-segmentation methodology. Furthermore, semi-supervised methodologies may be regarded as being unsupervised methodologies which receive greater help by input emanating from the set by user interaction. It is shown, in the most recent work, that the system involuntarily advocates restrictions which effectively filter the results while the user interactively attaches suitable limitations, according to the work undertaken by Wang et al. (2012) on active learning for co-segmentation. Subsequently, the user attaches either a must-link limitation or a cannot-link limitation among recently acquired segments. Following this, the limitations are distributed to the set while purifying the co-segmentation. In accordance with their work, a relatively small number of user limitations can direct towards perfect co-segmentation results. The COSEG dataset, which is helpful for establishing algorithms on co-segmentation, becomes obtainable through their work.

7.2.3   Applications of Shape Semantics

This research study segment manages some illustration techniques with the aim of editing current shapes. Moreover, the common feature of these illustration techniques is that they form their structure paradigm according to the analysis of a single input shape which subsequently is maintained as a soft or hard limitation. This is associated with eliminating levels of freedom in contrast with particular, unrestrained shape amendments together with the aim of making the execution of reasonable transformations convenient. When a triangle mesh is regarded as an input, the most suitable means of editing is, in fact, executing low-level mesh operations, meaning generating and removing triangles by moving vertices. Moreover, this gives the greatest level of freedom and the least structural limitations. It is accepted in practice that editing shapes by this method is unlikely; however, this can be attained to the easiest three-dimensional paradigms.

Some methodologies have been advocated for performing higher-level edits instead of relocating separate vertices affecting various vertices to be used beneficially. The Bezier basis of $3 \times 3 \times 3$ control points/B-spline is the type of free-form deformations which indicate the initial methodologies which use a volumetric, band-limited, low-dimensional basis for the imposition of smooth, low-frequency deformations to the geometry.

The structure can be free-form deformations which can preserve this structure as they are composed of a non-adaptive and local ways in which the local pieces' shape is conserved autonomously of the content, meaning that it lacks adaptivity. No global connections are considered in this situation, but only a tendency of low-frequency bending occurs totally from chaining various segments. These two factors may enable us to discover new techniques (Kraevoy et al. 2008) which consider local and adaptive deformation while using a differential free-form deformation energy which favours axis-aligned stretch. Following the consideration of differential attributes such as curvature and slippage analysis, it assesses the vulnerability of local areas while reducing the elasticity of the paradigm in vulnerable areas. Moreover, Xu et al. (2009) introduce adaptivity by adjusting the deformation penalties locally for the purpose of balancing the object's slippage attributes, further formulating deformation behaviour which often copies the behaviour of the mechanical systems; for example, joints and cylinders; moreover, the similar conceptuality of factors and components is used in both situations. The discrepancy between both situations is the creation of constraint energy because the constraints simply respond to local differential attributes of the deformation field in both situation, while the behaviour is more adaptive when compared with a standard deformation method. The iWires, (Gal et al. 2009) apply global connections. In the initial technique, crease lines in a triangle mesh are discovered. The authors call these "wires" with reference to the components of the deformation paradigm. Furthermore, these elements indicate the vertices of the wires; and among all of these components, every prominent aspect of Euclidean geometry including orthogonality, parallelity and diverse symmetries are itemised at the analysis stage. Subsequently, these attributes indicate the invariants of the deformation. On one more occasion, the user has the opportunity to manage the deformation by handles; but initially, a traditional elastic solution is calculated. Therefore, the system attempts to restore the invariants iteratively by a gluttonous algorithm which bends the wires so that they can still convene the user limitations; however, it is better to store it in its original structure. Symmetrical objects exist under a Euclidean (rigid) transformation together with parallel lines which always remain parallel and should sustain this property. Nevertheless, Zheng Y et al. (2011) advocated a similar concept in which the components are object-aligned bounding boxes of shape elements which are acquisitioned by segmentation. Totally constrained systems, as observed by Habbecke and Kobbelt (2012), have minimal interest in the context of interactive modelling because of their deficiency of design freedom and concentration over under-constrained techniques. Constraint functions (energies) are linearized while assessing their null space, Bokeloh et al. (2012) as an occurrence of the Cardinality Minimisation Problem which can resolve the optimization effectively by using concepts from compressed sensing. Their suggested techniques are separate from image-based constrained reconstruction approaches since they interactively sustain manipulation with many vertices and limitations.

7.2.4   Scheme for Generating 3D Models

In this section, exemplar cases of the scheme for the generation of 3D models from an image view are given. Usually, to reconstruct 3D models from images, constructing a point-cloud is widely used. From a point-cloud, it is not easy to extract semantics for captured 3D shapes. To rebuild both shapes and semantics, it is necessary to consider image semantics together.

It is possible to formulate the shape reconstruction from a given image view as an optimization problem. Let M be the unknown model to be reconstructed and I_l is the image facade layout. A facade layout is defined inside a rectangular domain by a set of non-overlapping rectangular regions. A rectangular region, R_i, is defined by parameters (x_i, y_i, w_i, h_i) denoting the position of the lower left corner (x_i, y_i) and size (width w_i and height h_i). A label function, $l_i(u, v)$ describes the material at position $(x_i + u, y_i + v)$ as an integer label. The term $P(M)$ imposes constraints over the infinite set of all possible solutions for generating M due to the huge space of possible models that can be generated from the input facade layout I_l. Thus the best model $\widehat{M}$ that corresponds to the image façade layout I_l can be expressed as logarithmic form using Bayes rule, Eq. (7.1):

$$\hat{M} = \arg \min_{M} \{\log P(I_l|M) + \log P(M)\} \qquad (7.1)$$

The model M is composed of the 3D components which form a structure S and rules r that generate the structure. The structure S is composed of components of the building. For example, window, door, wall, floor and so on. Every component is associated with the corresponding shape, representing a rectangular region in 2D or a mesh in 3D. Therefore the Eq. (7.1) becomes:

$$\hat{M}(S, r) = \arg \min_{M(S,r)} \{\log P(I_l|S, r, \Pi) + \log P(S) + \log P(r)\} \qquad (7.2)$$

The terms P(S) and P(r) are respectively the prior terms on the structure and rules to generate the shapes. $P(I_i|S, r, \Pi)$ corresponds to the likelihood for a given structure S and rule r where the camera models Π are fixed. $P(I_i|S, r, \Pi)$ measures the similarity between the generated 3D model and the given image facade layout I_l. The prior terms $P(S)$ and $P(r)$ are important to reduce the infinite set of possible solutions that might otherwise arise when reconstructing 3D model from 2D image. The above equation is difficult to optimize directly. Therefore, we split the optimization problem by alternatively optimizing the structure S by choosing a set of rules r^*.

We formulate the reconstruction of a 3D model from a single view 2D image as choosing a set of rules r^* which generate a building that best fits the image view in terms of projection. The energy function $E(r)$ decides the appropriateness of a given rule r with respect to the image view I. Given $E(r)$, our method of Modeling can be seen as an optimization problem expressed as Eq. (7.3).

$$r^* = \arg\min_{r \in M} E(r) \qquad (7.3)$$

In order to generate the 3D model of the building the shapes defined by the rules are projected onto the 2D image plane. On the 2D image plane a building is represented as a facade layout where the image is divided into regions R symbolic of the building components such as window, door, wall, floor and so on. For a region R and a candidate label l we can compute the probability $P(l|I)$ of each pixel location i in the image to belong to the class label l. The probability of the whole region R to belong to the class label l can be computed using the joint probability over all the pixels as given in the Eq. (7.4):

$$P(l|R) = \prod_{i \in R} P(l|I_i) \qquad (7.4)$$

This equation can be converted to energy through Boltzmann's transformation as expressed in Eq. (7.5):

$$E_l(R) = -\sum_{i \in R} \log P(l|I_i) \qquad (7.5)$$

In the procedural space, facade layouts can be described by a set of rules r^* where $r = (r_1, r_2, ..., r_m)$. Therefore, façade layout and rules are two representations of the same image view I. Therefore, the energy $E(r)$ can be written as in Eq. (7.6):

$$E(r) = \sum E(l_k|R_k) = -\sum_k \sum_{i \in R_k} \log P(l_k|I_l) \qquad (7.6)$$

i.e. the energy of a given rule with respect to the image view is computed as the sum of energies of all the regions R_k with label l_k in the image façade layout I_l provided by the rule r. Therefore, our optimization problem is minimizing the energy of all regions R_k with label l_k. Equation (7.3) can be rewritten as follows:

$$r^* = \arg\min_{r \in M} - \sum_k \sum_{i \in R_k} \log P(l_k | I_l) \tag{7.7}$$

For minimizing the energy, terminal shapes in façade layout I_l are projected onto the image view I. This projection is a one-to-one mapping between the rectangular regions in the facade layout and the corresponding regions labelled in the image view.

Facade components are extracted from the facade layout and organized as a repetitive shape tree. A meaningful grammar representation is automatically extracted from the hierarchical facade subdivision. We extend the previous approaches of procedural building models to a constraint-based framework for the recovery of the hidden parts of the building. This is an independently done work from, Divya Udayan et al. (2015a) although there are some significant similarities in both the approaches. Our work focuses more on updating a real-world building using single façade layout and building footprint. The limitation of the grammar in, Divya Udayan et al. (2015a) is that it works only for façade layouts that can be split by a single line. We have extended the grammar formulation to a more flexible and compact form that is suitable to a variety of real-world buildings. We then provide an interactive editing process for updating of the structural topology given a different view of the building, Divya Udayan and Kim (2017). The key observation of this Modeling approach is that component identification, grouping and solving for individual component fitting in a hierarchical and layered structural representation, leads to an enhanced accuracy and editing capability. Although a fully automated solution for facade encoding exists, to the best of our knowledge, no framework allows for generation of a complete building from the facade and the building footprint. In this work, we propose an interactive user-assisted solution. Beyond the 3D building reconstruction, our framework reveals the possibilities for a layered 3D facade generation, in which signboards and other functional metadata can be placed at the exact positions bringing a real life-like appearance to buildings. In addition, real footprint of the building is given as prior information in order to align the reconstructed facade geometry so that it reflects the real world. The height information is obtained either from real measurement or estimated measurement calculated from the ratio of pixels occupied by the horizontal footprint segment and the pixels occupied by the vertical height of the building image.

We demonstrate our framework on using semantic rendering of several real-world buildings with challenging footprints and we show that the procedural representation can generate similar buildings to the original that are used to populate a virtual city.

There are also several work on recognizing and Modeling semantics from image using deep-learning methods (Rahmani et al. 2017; Ren et al. 2015; Badrinarayanan et al. 2016; Liu et al. 2017). Those methods are trying to recognize façade components using learning-methods. Those approaches could generate effective segmentation on façade components. Using those segmentation, it is possible to make semantic modeling based on image features and labelled components. Figure 7.3 shows possible approaches; after segmentation, each segments are categorized and labelled using image features.

Fig. 7.3 Overall procedure of labelling façade component using deep-learning methods (Lee 2018)

These methods are also be applied to deal with components that are hidden by other obstacles Xiao et al. (2018), Lee (2016). Figure 7.4 shows example cases of segmentation.

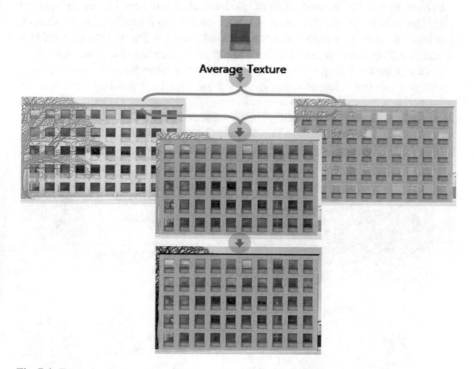

Fig. 7.4 Example of removing noise from the façade image (Lee 2016)

7.3   Examples: Rendering Complex Urban Model

Urban street environment is highly populated with 3D building information. Hence, in this section we focus on urban rendering and Modeling. The data quantity is very huge to be represented in any data representation schemes. Even if such a representation is possible, the extend of its utilization and management in various applications including navigation systems, driving simulators, urban data management, air pollution detection, traffic analysis, disaster management and so on is highly tedious and complex task. Considering a city as an enlarged aggregation of big data units which can be decomposed into numerous meaningful objects, each such entity can be represented semantically and its relationships can be expressed as a hierarchical data structure. This idea can be utilized in urban navigation applications, where the main purpose of the user is to find the destination buildings of his interest or intension. In such a scenario, providing the entire street area data to the user is not meaningful as he has to do a lot of cognitive interpretations by himself and as a result he may sometimes lose his point of interest (POI) of his destination building. Lesser the detailed content more is the usability, interactivity and easiness to find a building in a street. Based on this idea, we propose a design methodology for filtering out unnecessary information from the scene and emphasizing important areas in the street data. Thus in the design methodology we represent the entire city information hierarchically as structural semantics using different level of details for both geometry and texture. The concept of semantic LOD is shown in Fig. 7.5. This structural hierarchy is then semantically mapped to user specific functional semantics. We represent the building model as a RDF schema based on building ontology and its relationships with other building parts. The buildings are then grouped as functional clusters depending on

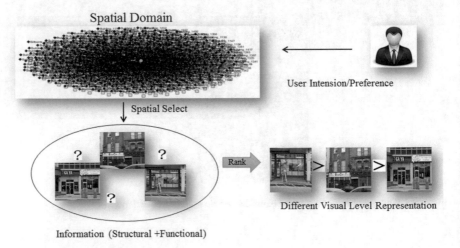

Fig. 7.5   Concept of semantic LOD

the service each building provides to the user. The approach helps to prioritize buildings depending on the functional clusters and associate them with the user intension
in real time.

The key objective of this approach is focused on:

- Development of Interoperability model for the transformation of 3D data models.
- Conceptually formulate the mapping for transformation of generated 3D model
  into CityGML semantic model of information at different levels of detail.
- To integrate application-specific semantics related to smart city service

7.3.1 Semantic Data Structure

It is necessary to devise efficient technique for multi-level information representation
and high quality visualization of the 3D city models to the user with less computational cost and at real time. The method introduces an hierarchical LOD data as
shown in Fig. 7.6, organization based on Multi-way k-d-trees that simplifies memory
management and allows controlling the level of detail that is rendered to the user.
A k-d tree (short for k-dimensional tree) is a space-partitioning data structure for
organizing points in a k-dimensional space. k-d trees are a useful data structure for
several applications, such as searches involving a multidimensional search key (e.g.
range searches and nearest neighbour searches). k-d trees are a special case of binary

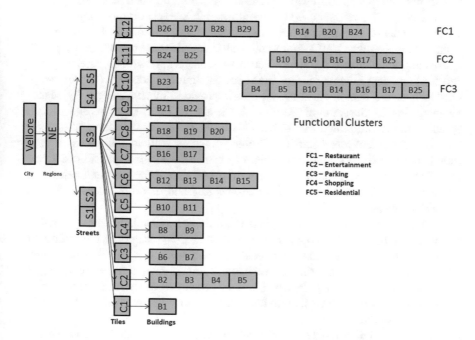

Fig. 7.6 Multi-level information hierarchy: functional level of details

space partitioning trees. In our work, we use a Multi-way k-d tree as data structure to represent semantic level of detail (LOD). In semantic LOD data structure as shown in Fig. 7.6, we represent the building semantics as structural semantics and user defined semantics. The city is decomposed into specific regions which are further sub divided into functional clusters like FC1, FC2, FC3 and so on for grouping the buildings. Each building can be further represented as multi-level information representation using both structural and texture based level of details. The user semantics consists of understanding the user's intension and then analysing the situation of the user and mapping the user intension to the functional group of buildings or to a single building.

Typically, providers and users of 3D city models are different. When a user gathers data needed for an application, he often obtains data from different sources which were collected at different times with different methods at different levels of detail and are based on differing models with regard to geometry and semantics. Hence, users face the problem of data heterogeneity. CityGML focuses on these problems. It is the international standard of the Open Geospatial Consortium (OGC) for the representation and the exchange of 3D city models since 2008. An extended version 2.0 has been adopted in 2012. Besides being an OGC standard, it has been accepted well by the software industry: tools from nearly all notable companies provide CityGML interfaces.

CityGML represents the geometrical, semantic and visual aspects of 3D city models. The principal focus is on the semantic definitions of all objects (features) that are relevant for applications of 3D city models: buildings and their parts (building parts, walls, roofs, dormers, doors, windows, etc.), transportation objects, water bodies, vegetation, terrain and furniture. Furthermore, the relations between those features (e.g. the relation of a door to the wall it contains) are represented explicitly. These common thematic definitions address the problem of semantic heterogeneity and facilitate data integration. For the representation of geometry (and topology), CityGML uses a standardized model that is provided by the Geography Markup Language GML (Groger et al. 2008) which is also an OGC standard and which is based on the markup language XML. This again facilitates data integration at the level of geometrical representation. Technically, CityGML is defined as an application schema of GML and uses GML mechanisms for defining features. Hence, CityGML fits perfectly into the concept of spatial data infrastructures, which will become more and more important for exchanging and modifying spatial data via geo-web services.

CityGML defines the semantic objects, attributes and relationships which are required by most 3D city model applications. It is a base model in the tradition of European topographic or cadastral models. For specific applications like indoor navigation, energy assessment or noise propagation simulation and mapping, CityGML can be extended by adding feature types or properties to existing feature types. For such extensions, CityGML provides a uniform mechanism called Application Domain Extension.

For semantic rendering, it could be defined multi-level information representation (both structural hierarchy and texture hierarchy) for different user context as shown

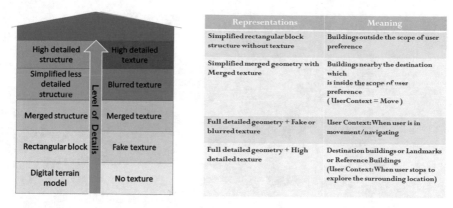

Fig. 7.7 Multi-level information representation: visual levels of details

in Fig. 7.7. User Context is defined as User Context {Move, Stop}. The building level of detail changes with different contexts and also depending on the user purpose and user gaze.

7.3.2 Database for Large-Scale Semantic Urban Rendering

The DB Schema is a structural data representation described in a formal language that supports the database management system (DBMS) and refers to the organization of data as a blueprint of how a database is constructed. The formal definition of database schema is a set of formulas (sentences) called integrity constraints imposed on a database. These integrity constraints ensure compatibility between parts of the schema. All constraints are expressible in the same language. A database can be considered a structure in realization of the database language. The states of a created conceptual schema are transformed into an explicit mapping to the database schema. This describes how real world entities are modelled in the database.

The Modeling principle of our DB schema as shown in Fig. 7.8 is based on feature taxonomy and decomposition of city into smaller components considering both the semantic and spatial aspects. The key idea is to provide a common data definition of the basic features, attributes and relations in the form of ontology for 3D building models with respect to geometric, appearance, topological and semantic properties. Buildings may be an aggregation of building parts, which allows the separation of different parts of large buildings. The class Building includes information about building class, function, usage, roof type, height (as well as individual heights for each of the building floors). Both classes may also reference one or more addresses. According to the CityGML encoding standard, building complexes such as airports or hospitals should be aggregated into CityObjectGroups. The different buildings in the group may then be given individual attributes such as 'Main Building'. The representation and the semantic structure of buildings are refined from LOD1 to LOD4.

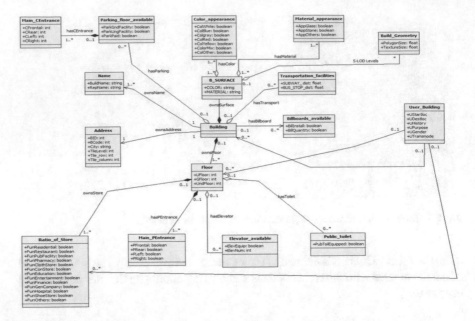

Fig. 7.8 DB schema representation

There are five different Levels of Detail (LODs) in the CityGML encoding standard. The different LODs allow for a more detailed view and a low-poly representation of city models. A CityGML file may include several models of the very same building but in different Levels of Detail, which is useful when different parts of the dataset have different sources and accuracy. Our building model consists of Name, Address, Parking availability, surface information, billboards installation, public toilet facility, number of entrances, floor details and so on.

The floor details can be classified as main entrance details, elevator availability details, public toilet and the functional ratio of stores. The surface information can be of colour appearance or material appearance details. Transportation facilities can also be included as an important information regarding the building, i.e. the distance to the nearest subway or bus stop. The building model specifies the details of the data types of each category and the manner in which they need to be stored in the data base. Association of the metadata to the building model permits for the semantic annotation of the 3D environment. Such an association helps to add high-level information that describes the properties of building parts and their relationship between them.

7.3.3   Integration of Application-Specific Semantics for 3D Smart City Services

The rapid technological evolution, which has been characterizing all the disciplines included within the wide idea of smart cities, is turning into a key element responsible for triggering genuine user—driven innovation and development. However, to completely add to the Smart City concept for a wide-scale geographical mark, it is essential to have a structure which provides for the integration of heterogeneous geo-information over a common technological context. In this regard virtual 3D city models will assume an inexorably critical part in our everyday lives and become crucial for the city information infrastructure of the modern world (Spatial Data Infrastructure). Figure 7.9 shows the interactive streaming process. The goal of interactive streaming process is to provide the user with continuous LODs to respond to the user's request quickly based on semantic LOD, (Divya Udayan et al. 2015b).

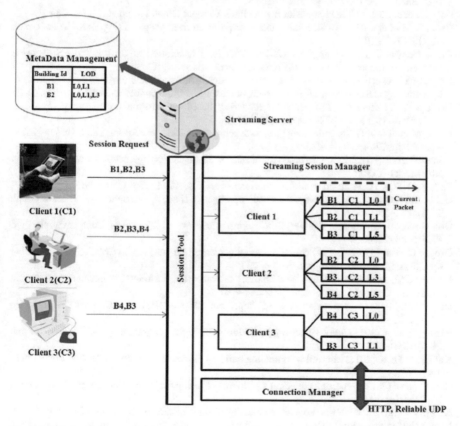

Fig. 7.9 Interactive streaming process

7.4 Conclusions

Semantic modeling and rendering methods are getting popular in computer graphics. Using semantic modeling, it is possible to generate similar looking models from a single or limited source. Compared with purely geometrical modeling, it could generate virtual world in more detailed way with less efforts. In addition, semantic modeling could give a possibility to filter complex data for effective rendering.

References

Attene M et al (2009) Characterization of 3d shape parts for semantic annotation. Comput Aided Des 41(10):756–763

Badrinarayanan V et al (2016) SegNet: a deep convolutional encoder-decoder architecture for image segmentation. In: Proceedings of CVPR'16

Benes B et al (2011) Guided procedural modelling. Comput Graph Forum 30(2):325–334

Bokeloh M et al (2012) An algebraic model for parameterized shape editing. ACM Trans Graph 31(4):78:1–78:10

Divya Udayan J, Kim HyungSeok (2017) Procedural restoration of texture and restructuring geometry from facade image. IEEE Access 6:2645–2653

Divya Udayan J et al (2015a) An image based approach to the reconstruction of ancient architecture by extracting and arranging 3D spatial components. Front Inf Technol Electron Eng 16(1):12–27

Divya Udayan et al (2015b) Semantic rendering based on information hierarchy for urban navigation. Appl Math Inf Sci 9(2L):493–504

Fisher M et al (2011) Characterizing structural relationships in scenes using graph kernels. ACM Trans Graph 30(4):34:1–34:12

Fisher M et al (2012) Example-based synthesis of 3d object arrangements. ACM Trans Graph 31(6):135:1–135:11

Fu H et al (2008) Upright orientation of man-made objects. ACM Trans Graph 27(3):42:1–42:7

Gal R et al (2009) iWires: an analyze-and-edit approach to shape manipulation. ACM Trans Graph 28(3):33:1–33:10

Golovinskiy A, Funkhouser T (2009) Consistent segmentation of 3D models. Comput Graph (Proc SMI) 33(3):262–269

Groger G et al (2008) OpenGIS city geography markup language (CityGML). OGC encoding specification, version 1.0.0, Doc. No.08–007r1

Habbecke M, Kobbelt L (2012) Linear analysis of nonlinear constraints for interactive geometric modelling. Comput Graph Forum 31(2):641–650

Hu R et al (2012) Co-segmentation of 3d shapes via subspace clustering. Comput Graph Forum 31(5):1703–1713

Huang Q et al (2011) Joint shape segmentation with linear programming. ACM Trans Graph 30(6):125:1–125:12

Kalojanov J et al (2012) Microtiles: extracting building blocks from correspondences. 31(5):1597–1606. Wiley

Kim VG et al (2012) Exploring collections of 3d models using fuzzy correspondences. Trans Graph 31(4):54:1–54:11

Kraevoy V et al (2008) Non-homogeneous resizing of complex models. ACM Trans Graph 27(5):1–9

Lee D (2016) Procedural modeling of texture and geometry from a 2D image of architectural building. Master thesis, Konkuk University

Lee W (2018) Estimation of façade components for inverse procedural modeling of building based on deep-learning methods. Master thesis, Konkuk University

Liu Y et al (2010) Computational symmetry in computer vision and computer graphics. Found Trends Comput Graph Vis 5(1–2):1–195

Liu H et al (2017) Deep facade: a deep learning approach to façade parsing. In: Proceedings of IJCAI'17

Mathias M et al (2011) Procedural 3D building reconstruction using shape grammars and detectors. In: International conference on 3D imaging, modeling, processing, visualisation and transmission, pp 304–311

Mitra NJ et al (2007) Symmetrization. ACM Trans Graph 26(3):1–8

Mitra NJ et al (2013) Symmetry in 3d geometry: extraction and applications. Comput Graph Forum (STAR Proceedings of Eurographics) 32(6):1–23

Pauly M et al (2008) Discovering structural regularity in 3d geometry. ACM Trans Graph 27(3). Article 43

Petit B et al (2010) Multicamera real-time 3d modeling for telepresence and remote collaboration. Int J Digit Multimed Broadcast 2:12 pp. Article ID 247108

Podolak J et al (2006) A planar-reflective symmetry transform for 3D shapes. ACM Trans Graph 25(3):549–559

Rahmani K et al (2017) Facade segmentation with a structured random forest. ISPRS Ann Photogramm IV-1(W1)

Ren S et al (2015) Faster R-CNN: towards real-time object detection with region proposal networks. In: Proceedings of CVPR'15

Ripperda N, Brenner C (2009) Application of a formal grammar to facade reconstruction in semi-automatic and automatic environments. In: Proceedings of AGILE conference on GI science, pp 1–12

Shamir A (2008) A survey on mesh segmentation techniques. Comput Graph Forum 27(6):1539–1556

Sidi O et al (2011) Unsupervised co-segmentation of a set of shapes via descriptor-space spectral clustering. ACM Trans Graph 30(6):126:1–126:10

Simari P et al (2006) Folding meshes: hierarchical mesh segmentation based on planar symmetry. In: Proceedings symposium on geometry processing, pp 111–119

Stava O et al (2010) Inverse procedural modeling by automatic generation of L-systems. Comput Graph Forum 29(2):665–674

Thrun S, Wegbreit B (2005) Shape from symmetry. In: Proceedings of international conference on computer vision, pp 1824–1831

Van Kaick O et al (2011) A survey on shape correspondence. Comput Graph Forum 30(6):1681–1707

Vanegas CA (2010) Building reconstruction using manhattan-world grammars. IEEE CVPR 2010:358–365

Wang Y et al (2011) Symmetry hierarchy of manmade objects. Comput Graph Forum 30(2):287–296

Wang Y et al (2012) Active co-analysis of a set of shapes. ACM Trans Graph 31(6):165

Wu F et al (2014) Inverse procedural modeling of facade layouts. ACM TOG 34:C121:1–C121:10

Xiao J (2012) 3D reconstruction is not just a low-level task: retrospect and survey, MIT9.S912: what is intelligence? Tech report

Xiao H et al (2018) Facade repetition detection in a fronto-parallel view with fiducial lines extraction. Neurocomputing 273:108

Xu W et al (2009) Joint-aware manipulation of deformable models. ACM Trans Graph 28(3):1–9

Xu K et al (2010) Style-content separation by anisotropic part scales. ACM Trans Graph 29(6):184

Yumer M, Kara L (2013) Co-abstraction of shape collections. ACM Trans Graph 31(6):158:1–158:11

Zheng Y et al (2011) Component-wise controllers for structure-preserving shape manipulation. Comput Graph Forum 30(2):563–572

Zheng Y et al (2013) Functional substructures for part compatibility. Comput Graph Forum 32(2):195–204

Chapter 8
Content-Aware Semantic Indoor Scene Modeling from a Single Image

Yinyu Nie, Jian Chang, and Jian Jun Zhang

Abstract Digitalizing indoor scenes into a 3D virtual world enables people to visit and roam in their daily-life environments through remote devices. However, reconstructing indoor geometry with enriched semantics (e.g. the room layout, object category and support relationship) requires computers to parse and holistically understand the scene context, which is challenging considering the complexity and clutter of our living surroundings. However, with the rising development of deep learning techniques, modeling indoor scenes from single RGB images has been available. In this chapter, we introduce an automatic method for semantic indoor scene modeling based on deep convolutional features. Specifically, we decouple the task of indoor scene modeling into different hierarchies of scene understanding subtasks to parse semantic and geometric contents from scene images (i.e. object masks, scene depth map and room layout). Above these semantic and geometric contents, we deploy a data-driven support relation inference to estimate the physical contact between indoor objects. Under the support context, we adopt an image-CAD matching strategy to retrieve an indoor scene from global searching to local fine-tuning. The experiments show that this method can retrieve CAD models efficiently with enriched semantics, and demonstrate its feasibility in handling serious object occlusions.

Y. Nie · J. Chang · J. J. Zhang (✉)
Bournemouth University, Poole, UK
e-mail: jzhang@bournemouth.ac.uk

Y. Nie
e-mail: ynie@bournemouth.ac.uk

J. Chang
e-mail: jchang@bournemouth.ac.uk

N. Magnenat Thalmann et al. (eds.), *Intelligent Scene Modeling and Human-Computer Interaction*, Human–Computer Interaction Series,
https://doi.org/10.1007/978-3-030-71002-6_8

8.1 Introduction and Related Work

With the rising of 3D acquisition techniques in recent years, scene modeling has attracted increasing attention in 3D reconstruction study. Digitalizing real-life environments into the virtual world enables people to access a realistic 3D representation of their living world. However, considering the complexity, occlusion and clutter of indoor rooms with complicated object interrelations, semantic-level indoor scene reconstruction will fully be understanding scene context still faces many challenges.

In modern indoor scene modeling, the main approaches can be divided into two branches by their objectives (Chen et al. 2015): 1. geometric modeling and 2. semantic modeling. Geometric modeling methods pay attention to 3D geometry recovery (e.g. point cloud or 3D mesh) while ignoring the behind scene semantics (e.g. object categories and support relations). Simultaneous Localization And Mapping (SLAM) techniques have been the main modality (Newcombe et al. 2011; Salas-Moreno et al. 2013). Products like Kinect Fusion (Newcombe et al. 2011) have reached real-time point cloud reconstruction to recover the whole scene geometry. However, high-level applications like scene understanding and roaming in robotics and human-scene interaction in augmented reality would be limited without those contextual semantics. For semantic modeling, there are two main stages: 1. Indoor content parsing; 2. Scene modeling. The former one is to extract meaningful semantic or geometric clues from the input, and the scene modeling is responsible for recovering the 3D model with the above semantics. In the following, we mainly review some prominent works in indoor content parsing, object support relationship extraction and semantic scene modeling.

8.1.1 Indoor Content Parsing

To make computers able to understand the contents from input images, essential semantic and geometric features are extracted first for scene modeling. Previous studies have explored various scene parsing methods to obtain different kinds of content-aware features for scene modeling. Traditional approaches focused on low-level features on the image itself (like edges, line segments, face normals, contours or textures, etc.) for geometric reasoning to guide a further scene modeling (Zhang et al. 2015; Liu et al. 2017). While these hand-crafted feature descriptors are limited when dealing with low-quality and texture missing images. Modern scene parsing approaches generally use convolutional neural networks (CNNs) to obtain abstract or high-level features, like scene depth maps (Laina et al. 2016), surface normal maps (Eigen and Fergus 2015), object bounding boxes or masks (Ren et al. 2015; Li et al. 2016), room layout maps (Mallya and Lazebnik 2015), etc. The latest studies considered different combinations of them to build their content parsing block for scene modeling. For example, Izadinia et al. (2017) detected object locations and room layout to support their Render-and-Match strategy for scene optimization.

Huang et al. (2018) blended depth and surface normal estimation, object detection and segmentation, with layout estimation into a matching-by-rendering process to provide a scene grammar for modeling.

In our method, three parallel Fully Convolution Networks (FCNs) (Long et al. 2015) are applied to process a single image and respectively generate a depth map, a layout edge map, and an instance segmentation map. Then a data-driven support inference method is designed to deduce the supporting relationship between indoor objects. It bridges the spatial relations between objects and provides a physical constraint for the next scene modeling.

8.1.2 Support Inference

The step of support relationship inference is inspired by the early work (Xu et al. 2013) where a freehand sketch drawing is leveraged to model semantics-enriched and well-arranged 3D scenes. In their work, co-retrieval and co-placement of 3D models are performed. Objects related to each other (e.g. a chair and a desk) are jointly processed following the cues of the sketched objects in pair. This milestone work indicated the importance of inter-object relationships. Inspired by this insight, our work contributes to this part by automatically inferring the object support relationship.

Support relationship reveals a type of geometric constraints between indoor objects to present scenes more robustly and reasonably. It originates from the fact that objects require supports to counteract the gravity. The problem if support inference from single RGB images is inherently ambiguous without any clues of the 3D geometric information. Occlusions between objects often make the supporting surfaces between two objects invisible in the field of view. However, room layout and furniture arrangement in indoor scenes generally follow some latent principles of interior design and living habits (e.g. sofas are generally supported by the floor; pillows are commonly on beds). These potential feature patterns behind scenes make the support relationship a type of priors that can be concluded and learned by browsing various types of indoor environments. Previous works addressed this problem by designing a specific optimization strategy (Silberman et al. 2012; Xue et al. 2015) considering both depth clues and image features. Apart from inferring support relations, many studies represented the support condition by object stability and indoor safety (Zheng et al. 2015; Jia et al. 2013). Moreover, the support relationships are also a kind of spatial condition in scene grammar to improve contextual bindings between objects. Some other methods implemented support inference to understand scenes with a scene graph (Liu et al. 2014; Huang et al. 2018). However, these approaches either require depth clues, or rely on hand-crafted priors. Nie et al. (2020) reformulated the support inference problem into a Visual-Question Answering (VQA) form (Antol et al. 2015), where a Relation Network is designed to end-to-end link the object pairs and infer their support relations.

8.1.3 Scene Modeling

Modeling 3D objects from an RGB image is an ill-posed problem because of the singularity in-depth disparity (Chen et al. 2015). Many existing approaches tailored specific geometric reasoning methods to deduce the object geometry first to match similar CAD models with images and place them to 3D scenes with 2D–3D alignment. For example, to obtain object positions for instance modeling, Zhang et al. (2015) used Canny Edge Detector to searching for line segments with cuboid detection to decide object proposals. With the object geometry inferred from normal maps and edges. Liu et al. (2017) extracted object geometry features using a normal-based graph for CAD model matching. However, these image-based traditional geometric descriptors are sensitive to the input quality. Latest CNN-based methods tended to follow a Render-and-Matching strategy (Izadinia et al. 2017; Huang et al. 2018). They initialized an object placement proposal and refined it iteratively until the scene rendering was similar to the input image as enough.

As object segmentation masks and the scene depth map produced by our FCNs provide enough geometric details. With support relationships as constraints, we build our scene modeling as a searching-and-matching problem to choose optimal 3D models from the dataset with best fitting their 2D projections and 3D placement to the corresponding segmentation masks and the depth map.

8.2 Overview

Our pipeline is presented in Fig. 8.1. We parse a single RGB image and output various semantics-meaningful scene contexts to help with indoor scene modeling. In the scene parsing step, we extract three feature maps (object mask map (Li et al. 2016), scene depth map (Laina et al. 2016) and layout edge map (Mallya and Lazebnik 2015)) with different FCNs to lead the next support inference. For object mask extraction, we train an instance-aware FCN architecture (Li et al. 2016) to segment object instances into 40 categories. By combining the depth map with camera intrinsic parameters and these masks, the point cloud of indoor scenes can be recovered and segmented further. While the layout edge map is provided to designate a room coordinate system for support relation inference and object modeling.

We regard object support relations as a type of physical rules that can be learned from daily priors. In this work, an indoor scene dataset (SceneNN (Hua et al. 2016)) is parsed to extract the category-level support priors. With the learned priors and 3D object locations in the point cloud, the exact instance-level support relations can be decided following an intuitive estimation.

Support relations provide a physical constraint that can make the modeled scenes more reasonable. In full scene modeling, we adopt a search-to-match strategy to find similar object models from a CAD model database, and edit them with orientation, translation and scale fine-tuning to complete the scene modeling.

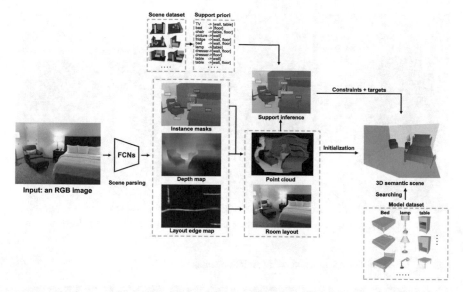

Fig. 8.1   Overview and a pipeline of our semantic modeling approach

8.3   Scene Parsing

8.3.1   Instance Segmentation

The FCN proposed by Li et al. (2016) provides an end-to-end architecture to segment
scene images into objects at the instance-level. We train this network on the NYU
v2 dataset (Silberman et al. 2012), which contains 1,449 indoor images with 40
common object categories. The official training/testing data split is adopted for the
evaluation. It shows that the mAP^r score (Hariharan et al. 2014) on the test set
is at 29.95% and 19.13% (under the IoU threshold of 0.5 and 0.7, respectively).
Then the full dataset is used for training for the scene modeling task. Figure 8.2
presents a segmentation sample using the indoor photos (Fig. 8.2a) from the SUN-
RGBD dataset (Song et al. 2015). Figure 8.2b shows that the FCN provides faithful
object masks. In the prediction step, we append a Grab-cut-based mask refining
layer (Rother et al. 2004) onto the FCN to smoothen the zig-zagged mask margin
(see Fig. 8.2c), as the mask quality will affect the object placement performance.

8.3.2   Depth Estimation

We introduce the FCN architecture from Laina (2016) to predict scene depth maps.
This network is designed based on residual learning, which requires fewer parameters
and training data. That means it runs faster in-depth inference. Again we train it on

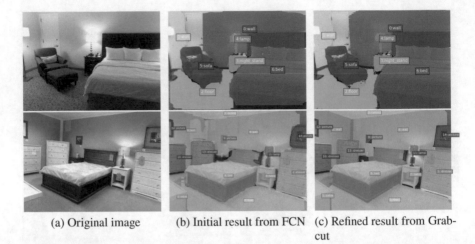

(a) Original image   (b) Initial result from FCN   (c) Refined result from Grab-
                                                          cut

Fig. 8.2 Object instance segmentation on an indoor image

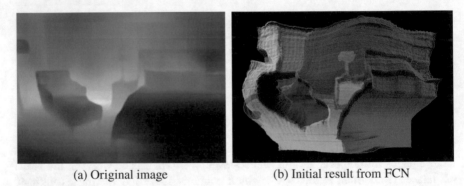

(a) Original image   (b) Initial result from FCN

Fig. 8.3 Point cloud retrieval

the NYU v2 dataset. With the predicted depth map, the camera parameters of Kinect
(Konolige and Mihelich 2011) (used in capturing NYU v2 depth maps) are taken to
recover the point cloud (see Fig. 8.3). With the object masks, the segmented point
cloud (see Fig. 8.3b) illustrates that the estimated depth is rather noisy but at least
offers spatial clues about relative position. Thus we propose the support relation
inference to obtain more robust geometric constraints.

8.3.3 Layout Estimation

Modeling and placing indoor objects into the same scene space requires a unified
scene coordinate system. In this step, we build a unified scene coordinate system
from layout estimation. Intuitively, the coordinate system decision problem can be

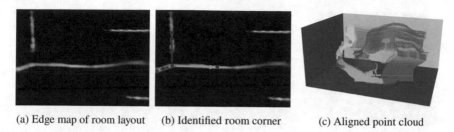

(a) Edge map of room layout   (b) Identified room corner   (c) Aligned point cloud

Fig. 8.4   Room layout estimation

converted into how to find an orthogonal room corner. Unlike the general methods (Hedau et al. 2009) which aimed at finding the room bounding box, a room corner is enough for calibrating the scene system. We first predict the probability map of room layout with the method from Mallya et al. (2015). This method is based on structured edge detection forests with an FCN to produce edge clues of room layout (see Fig. 8.4a). Secondly, we adopt an RANSAC algorithm (Nie et al. 2018) to search for a robust corner from the edge map (see Fig. 8.4b). With the room corner in the 2D image plane and point cloud information, we can recover its spatial position and rotation (relative to the camera) by fitting an orthogonal 3D corner. With the corner as the scene coordinate system, we align its horizontal plane (x-y plane) to the floor, and its z-axis upwards (see Fig. 8.4c). Then the floor and two walls can also be decided.

8.4   Support Inference

In this section, we introduce two manners of data-driven support inference: (1) support inference directly from prior statistical experiences (Nie et al. 2018); (2) learning support relationships with Relation Network (Nie et al. 2020).

8.4.1   Support Inference from Priors

This part of the work is from our previous publication (Nie et al. 2018) where representing support relations is to provide spatial constraints to make the indoor objects modeled physically reasonable. From our daily experience, there are three common observed support types between objects: support from below, from behind and from top. We here only take into account the first two types for the convenience of demonstration. Our implementation of support inference is based on the observation that support relations between daily-life furniture generally follow a series of faithful priors (e.g. the beds, tables are generally supported by the floor). Thus we parse the SceneNN (Hua et al. 2016) dataset to obtain the support priors at the category level. The co-occurrence map of all indoor objects involved in the 50 scenes is illustrated in

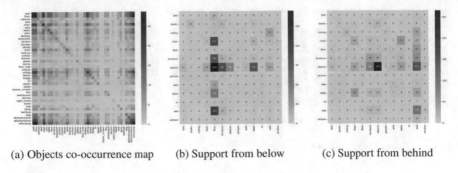

(a) Objects co-occurrence map   (b) Support from below   (c) Support from behind

Fig. 8.5 Support priors from SceneNN dataset (Nie et al. 2018)

Fig. 8.5a. The block color indicates the frequency of two objects occurred in the same scene. As an object could be supported by more general categories (e.g. lamps could be supported by tables or nightstands), we aggregate the NYU 40 object categories to 13 ones (by class mapping from Silberman et al. (2012)). Then the frequency of co-occurred object pairs with the same support relation is accumulated, resulting in Fig. 8.5b, c. The block in row i, column j means the frequency of object category i supported by category j from below or behind. The two matrices are used as support priors for instance-level support inference.

To decide the support relations for all objects in a scene, we leverage the category-level priors above to deduce support relations at the instance-level. For each target instance, with its object category, we query the two support matrices above to obtain its possible supporting categories and identify their corresponding objects that exist in the scene. With the point cloud and 3D room layout, we remove those objects that are not spatially close (at vertical or horizontal direction) to the target instance. Every object except walls, the ceiling and floor should be supported by at least one another object. We use the prior information as it not only improves the searching efficiency, but also avoids mistakes by directly using the noisy point cloud for support inference. For the details of example demonstrations, we refer readers to Nie et al. (2018).

8.4.2 Support Inference with Relation Network

The relation network introduced in this part is from our previous work (Nie et al. 2020). In contrast to directly summarizing the support statistics from a dataset, this work (Nie et al. 2020) leverages neural networks to learn support relationships from scene images and object segmentation masks. Still, two support types are considered in the implementation. That is support from behind (e.g. a picture on the wall surface) and support from below (e.g. a pillow on the bed). In the assumption of this work, every object must be supported by another object except the layout structures (i.e.

wall, ceiling and floor). For those objects that are supported by unseen instances, they are treated as being supported by one of the layout structures, i.e. walls, floor or ceiling.

Unlike those non-relational semantics (e.g. object category, mask, 3D shapes), the relational semantics (i.e. support relationship) generally refers to not only the object property features (e.g. category, shape, size), but also the contextual relations (e.g. relative placement and size, orientation) between object pairs. Based on this insight, a possible solution is to combine the object property feature pairs with specific task descriptions for support reasoning. It can be intuitively formulated as a Visual Question Answering (VQA) problem (Antol et al. 2015; Santoro et al. 2017): given the object segmentation results, which instance is supporting the query object? Is it supported from below or behind? With this formulation, a Relation Network can be configured to answer these support relationship questions by combining these image features with question texts. The architecture of Relation Network (Nie et al. 2020) is designed and illustrated in Fig. 8.6. The upstream of the Relation Network is composed of two modules that encode images (with masks) and questions, respectively. For the layer information, we refer readers to Nie et al. (2020) for the details. Here we elaborate the network design as follows.

In the **Vision** part of Fig. 8.6, the color intensities (RGB image, 3-channel) is normalized to the interval of [0, 1] and appended with the corresponding segmentation mask (instance labels, 1-channel), followed by a scale operation on image size to a $300 \times 300 \times 4$ matrix. It then generates $10 \times 10 \times 64$ CNN feature vectors after convolutions. In the **Question** part, for each object, it customizes the relational reasoning by answering two groups of questions: non-relational and relational, four questions for each. Taking the bed in Fig. 8.6 as an example, the related questions and corresponding answers are encoded as shown in Fig. 8.7. Four relational questions are designed for support inference, and four non-relational questions are designed as regularization terms to make the network able to recognize the target object the system is querying. The network is trained on the dataset of NYU v2 (Silberman et al. 2012). In a single image, maximal of 60 indoor instances with 40 categories are taken into account. Therefore, for the ith object which belongs to the jth category,

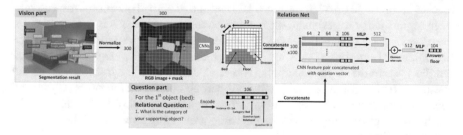

Fig. 8.6 Relation network for support inference (Nie et al. 2020). The network is composed of three parts. The vision part encodes object images for feature extraction, and the question part parses the related questions. The relation net predicts the answers given the question codes and the image features

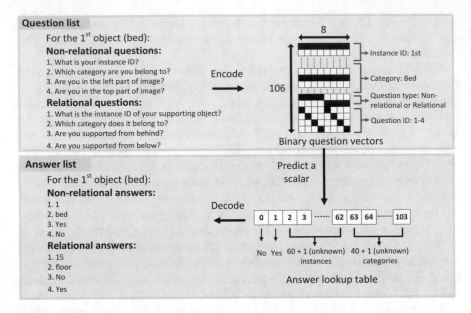

Fig. 8.7 Questions and answers for training (Nie et al. 2020)

we encode the k-th question from the mth group to a 106-d ($106 = 60 + 40 + 4 + 2$) binary vector.

The outputs of the **Vision** and the **Question** parts are concatenated. The $10 \times 10 \times 64$ CNN features from the Vision part are represented by 100 of 64-d feature vectors, which are further combined into 100×100 pairs feature vectors (64+64 dimension for each pair). The 100×100 feature pairs are appended with their 2D image coordinates (2-d) and exhaustively concatenated with the encoded question vector (106-d), then go through two multi-layer perceptrons to answer the questions. For each question, the Relation Network outputs a scalar between 0 and 103. The scalar number is further decoded into a human-language answer by indexing the lookup table as shown in Fig. 8.7. The correct rate on the testing dataset of NYU v2 reaches 80.62% and 66.82 % on non-relational and relational questions, respectively.

In segmentation experiment, the numbering of instance masks is randomly given from the object segmentation, which undermines the network performance on the first relational question (i.e. *what is the instance ID of your supporting object?* see Fig. 8.7). In the implementation, (Nie et al. 2020) used the last three relational questions to predict the category of the supporting object and the support type, and keep the first one as a regularization term. The exact supporting instance can be identified by maximizing the prior supporting probability between the target object and its neighbors:

$$O_{j^*} = \underset{O_j \in \mathcal{N}(O_i)}{\mathrm{argmax}} \ P(\mathcal{C}(O_j)|\mathcal{C}(O_i), T_k), \ \mathcal{C}(O_j) \in \mathcal{SC}(O_i), \tag{8.1}$$

where O_i and $\mathcal{N}(O_i)$ respectively denote the ith object and its neighboring objects. Room layout structures (i.e. walls, floor and ceiling) are neighboring to all objects. $\mathcal{C}(O_j)$ is the category label of object O_j. $\mathcal{SC}(O_i)$ is the top-5 category candidates of O_i's supporting object, and T_k represents the support type, $k = 1, 2$ (i.e. support from below or behind). Hence $P(\mathcal{C}(O_j)|\mathcal{C}(O_i), T_k)$ indicates the probability of $\mathcal{C}(O_j)$ supporting $\mathcal{C}(O_i)$ by T_k. The prior probability P is calculated by counting from the training data (see Nie et al. (2020) for further details). The supporting instance is represented by O_{j^*}. With this procedure, it can improve the testing accuracy on the four relational questions by a large margin (from 66.82 to 82.74%).

8.5 Scene Modeling

We propose a global-to-local method to search and edit models from the database for scene modeling. We search for CAD models that have a similar shape with the object masks (in the global searching step) and edit their geometry properties (including the position, orientation and size) for local fine-tuning. The CAD models are chosen from Google 3D Warehouse, and we preprocess them by alignment and label them with the categories in line with NYU v2.

8.5.1 Model Matching Formulation

The point cloud is too noisy to deduce object orientation but at least indicates spatial position and height clues. While object masks provide edge and contour information to indicate object orientation. Therefore, we use point cloud to initialize 3D position and model scales (see Fig. 8.8, height size is initialized by the point cloud), and use object masks to optimize the orientation, and subsequently adjust the 3D position and scales.

Under the scene coordinate system built in Sect. 8.3.3, for each target object, we denote its point cloud, 2D image mask, supporting models from behind or below, and

Fig. 8.8 Point cloud and the matched model

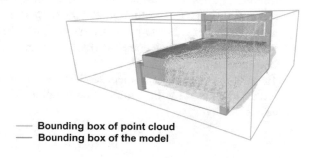

—— **Bounding box of point cloud**
—— **Bounding box of the model**

CAD model for matching as $\mathbf{P}_i$, $Mask_i$, $\mathbf{M}_i^H$, $\mathbf{M}_i^L$ and $\mathbf{M}_i$, respectively. $i = 1, 2, ..., n$, n denotes object number. The model scales $\mathbf{S}$, spatial position $\mathbf{p}$ and the horizontal orientation θ are variables for optimization. With the camera parameters used in layout decision and point cloud retrieval, the projection from 3D space onto the image plane can be obtained and we denote it by $\mathtt{Proj}(*)$. Following the development of Nie et al. (2018), the model matching problem can be formulated by minimizing

$$\max_{\theta, \mathbf{S}, \mathbf{p}} \mathtt{IoU}\{\mathtt{Proj}[\mathbf{R}(\theta) \cdot \mathbf{S} \cdot \mathbf{M}_i + \mathbf{p}], Mask_i\},$$

$$\mathbf{R} = \begin{bmatrix} \cos(\theta) & -\sin(\theta) & 0 \\ \sin(\theta) & \cos(\theta) & 0 \\ 0 & 0 & 1 \end{bmatrix}, \mathbf{S} = \begin{bmatrix} s_1 & 0 & 0 \\ 0 & s_2 & 0 \\ 0 & 0 & s_3 \end{bmatrix}, \mathbf{p} = \begin{bmatrix} p_1 \\ p_2 \\ p_3 \end{bmatrix}, \tag{8.2}$$

where $\mathtt{IoU}$ score is to measure the matching accuracy. The insight behind is that the perspective projection of the reconstructed 3D objects should be consistent with their 2D segmentation results. We design the constraints from support relations and point cloud as the following.

1. Support constraint from below
   This constraint is to make the object model attached on the upper surface of its supporting model from below (see Eq. (8.3)).

$$\mathrm{mean}[\mathbf{R}(\theta) \cdot \mathbf{S} \cdot \mathbf{M}_i + \mathbf{p}]_{x,y} >= \min[\mathbf{M}_i^L]_{x,y}$$

$$\mathrm{mean}[\mathbf{R}(\theta) \cdot \mathbf{S} \cdot \mathbf{M}_i + \mathbf{p}]_{x,y} <= \max[\mathbf{M}_i^L]_{x,y} \tag{8.3}$$

$$\min[\mathbf{R}(\theta) \cdot \mathbf{S} \cdot \mathbf{M}_i + \mathbf{p}]_{z|x,y} = \max[\mathbf{M}_i^L]_{z|x,y}$$

2. Support constraint from behind
   There commonly is a high relevance between object orientations if one of them supports another from behind. We denote the orientation angle of the supporting model $\mathbf{M}_i^H$ by θ_i^H. The constraints can be written as

$$\theta \in \{\theta_i^H + k \cdot \pi/4 | k = 0, 1, ..., 7\}$$

$$\mathrm{dist}(\mathbf{M}_i, \mathbf{M}_i^H)_{x,y,z} < \mathbf{d}_1 \tag{8.4}$$

where $\mathtt{dist}$ is to get the shortest distance in x,y and z-axis between $\mathbf{M}_i$ and $\mathbf{M}_i^H$, and $\mathbf{d}_1$ is the threshold. It means the supporting object should stay close to the supported one. For objects that are not supported from behind by any one, we loose the orientation constraint by $\theta \in \{k \cdot \pi/4 | k = 0, 1, ..., 7\}$.

3. Constraint from point cloud
   The position and scale of object models are first initialized by point cloud and further fine-tuned by the optimization iteration. The scale of object height can be decided by

$$s_3^* = \frac{\max(\mathbf{P}_i)_z - \max(\mathbf{M}_i^L)_z}{\max(\mathbf{M}_i)_z - \min(\mathbf{M}_i)_z}. \tag{8.5}$$

To handle occlusions, we use the height difference between the tops of object point cloud and its supporting object $(\max(\mathbf{P}_i)_z - \max(\mathbf{M}_i^L)_z)$ to estimate the real height. We set the geometric center of the point cloud $\mathbf{P}_i$ as $\mathbf{p}_i^c$, and the constraints are designed as

$$
\begin{aligned}
\left|\mathbf{p} - \mathbf{p}_i^c\right| < \mathbf{d}_2, s_1 \in [\rho_1^L \cdot s_3^*, \rho_1^U \cdot s_3^*], \\
s_2 \in [\rho_2^L \cdot s_3^*, \rho_2^U \cdot s_3^*], s_3 \in [\rho_3^L \cdot s_3^*, \rho_3^U \cdot s_3^*]
\end{aligned}
\tag{8.6}
$$

where $\mathbf{d}_2$ is to ensure that the model $\mathbf{M}_i$ overlaps the point cloud $\mathbf{P}_i$, and $\{(\rho_k^L, \rho_k^U) | k = 1, 2, 3\}$ are used to adjust the model scales.

The optimization problem described above is built for both global model searching and local fine-tuning. Following the support hierarchy, every supported object should be built after its supporting objects.

8.5.2   Global-to-Local Model Search and Refinement

Searching CAD models from the database demands high efficiency in finding out similar shapes in the parametric space to match masks. In this implementation, we introduce the DIRECT algorithm (Jones et al. 1993) to solve the above model matching problem (8.2) to first find out a model without extensive model property refining. The DIRECT algorithm is a gradient-free and deterministic-search method that can handle global optimization with bound constraints. The main idea of this method is to scale the search domain to a hypercube and subdivide it into smaller hyperrectangles step by step to find the global optima, thus it shows an advantage in handling a large parametric space. Therefore we use it to decide the exact object model first. To fine-tune the model property, we use the preliminarily optimized results from the DIRECT algorithm to initialize a local optimization process (with BOBYQA algorithm (Powell 2009)). The model property (size, orientation and position) will be refined after few iterations.

8.6   Experiment and Discussions

We present some reconstruction samples on SUN-RGBD dataset (Song et al. 2015) in Fig. 8.9. The parameter configuration is detailed in Appendix, and the performance and limitations are discussed below.

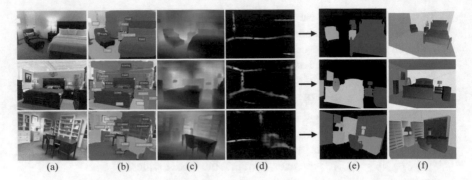

   (a)   (b)   (c)   (d)   (e)   (f)

Fig. 8.9 Semantic modeling results. **a** Test images; **b** Instance masks; **c** Depth maps; **d** Layout edge maps; **e** 2D Projections of matched models; **f** Retrieved semantic scenes

8.6.1 Performance Analysis

Figure 8.9b shows that most objects get well segmented with refined masks. The average depth estimation error (Fig. 8.9c) is at rel score: 0.463, rms score: 1.642, log10 score: 0.276 (Laina et al. 2016). It shows noisier on the SUN-RGBD dataset comparing with the work (Laina et al. 2016) on the NYU v2 dataset. Figure 8.9d illustrates the searched room corners. With it as the coordinate system, every object is modeled by matching their perspective projection (Fig. 8.9e) with corresponding masks (Fig. 8.9b). The reconstruction results in Fig. 8.9f illustrate that our method can recover a plausible semantic scene from an RGB image. Objects that are partly occluded can also be estimated with a reasonable position and size.

The time cost depends on scene complexity. The segmentation and object modeling efficiency are linearly relative to the object quantity. Taken a scene with 5 objects as an example, scene segmentation costs 3.83 s in average (as the grab-cut method refines object masks by sequence), and fine-tuning models costs 58.25 s on average. The layout estimation only costs 0.29 s per image with Nvidia GTX 1080 GPU and Intel Xeon E5-1650 CPU.

8.6.2 Discussions

Although our method appears robust in handling noisy inputs, it is still sensitive to the performance of scene parsing steps. We find the most vulnerable part is the layout edge map estimation. If a room is over-cluttered, the layout edge map could be too unclear for room corner decision (see Fig. 8.10b). For these cases, few manual interactions (e.g. choose a room corner by hand, see Fig. 8.10c) will largely improve the layout estimation accuracy.

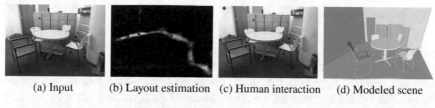

| (a) Input | (b) Layout estimation | (c) Human interaction | (d) Modeled scene |

Fig. 8.10   Scene modeling by human interaction

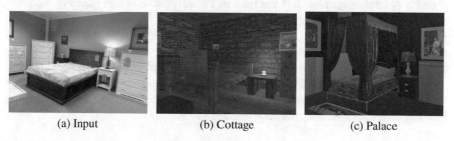

| (a) Input | (b) Cottage | (c) Palace |

Fig. 8.11   Furniture replacement (Nie et al. 2018)

8.7   Conclusions

A modern indoor scene modeling streamline is introduced in this chapter. We demonstrate the feasibility of Fully Convolutional Networks in instance segmentation, depth prediction and layout estimation. On this basis, support relations between instances provide powerful hierarchical constraints for object modeling, enabling our method to be robust in noisy point cloud input and make scenes modeled physically reasonable. Our experiments show the objects in reconstructed scenes can be recovered with plausible geometry property, like sizes, positions and orientations, even in seriously occluded cases. Based on semantic information, our work can facilitate more high-level applications like human-scene interaction for augmented reality and semantic-level scene editing. In the future, based on semantic scenes, scene-editing applications (e.g. furniture replacement) will be developed for VR devices, which enables people to experience realistic 3D indoor scenes with different decoration styles (see Fig. 8.11).

Acknowledgements The research leading to these results has been partially supported by the VISTA AR project (funded by the Interreg France (Channel) England, ERDF), the China Scholarship Council and Bournemouth University.

Appendix: Parameter Decision

In image segmentation and room corner searching, the training configurations and parameters setup are followed with Li et al. (2016) and Nie et al. (2018). In object modeling, we set $\mathbf{d}_1 = [0.5, 0.5, 0.5]^T$ (in meters, the same below) for normal objects. For those supported by a wall, $\mathbf{d}_1$ is set as $[0.2, \infty, \infty]^T$ or $[\infty, 0.2, \infty]^T$ depending on the orientation of the wall. $\mathbf{d}_2$ is set as $[1.0, 1.0, 0.5]^T$ as the point cloud is noisier in horizontal plane than in the vertical direction (see Fig. 8.8). For model scales, we set $\rho_1^L = \rho_2^L = \rho_3^L = 0.8, \rho_1^U = \rho_2^U = 1.2$, and $\rho_3^U = 1.0$. While for objects whose top part is occluded, the point cloud could underestimate the model height size. We hence change the lower bounds to $\rho_1^L = \rho_2^L = \rho_3^L = 1.0$, and the upper bounds to $\rho_1^U = \rho_2^U = \rho_3^U = 2.0$ or more. In global searching, the maximal iterations number is limited to 50, while in the local matching, generally we do not set the maximal iteration number to ensure convergence, the only stopping criteria is set as when the absolute tolerance reaches 10^{-3}.

References

Antol S, Agrawal A, Lu J, Mitchell M, Batra D, Lawrence Zitnick C, Parikh D (2015) Vqa: visual question answering. In: Proceedings of the IEEE international conference on computer vision, pp 2425–2433

Chen K, Lai Y-K, Hu S-M (2015) 3d indoor scene modeling from rgb-d data: a survey. Comput Visual Media 1(4):267–278

Eigen D, Fergus R (2015) Predicting depth, surface normals and semantic labels with a common multi-scale convolutional architecture. In: Proceedings of the IEEE international conference on computer vision, pp 2650–2658

Hariharan B, Arbeláez P, Girshick R, Malik J (2014) Simultaneous detection and segmentation. In: European conference on computer vision. Springer, pp 297–312

Hedau V, Hoiem D, Forsyth D (2009) Recovering the spatial layout of cluttered rooms. In: 2009 IEEE 12th international conference on computer vision. IEEE, pp 1849–1856

Hua B-S, Pham Q-H, Nguyen DT, Tran M-K, Yu L-F, Yeung S-K (2016) Scenenn: a scene meshes dataset with annotations. In: 2016 fourth international conference on 3D vision (3DV). IEEE, pp 92–101

Huang S, Qi S, Zhu Y, Xiao Y, Xu Y, Zhu S-C (2018) Holistic 3d scene parsing and reconstruction from a single rgb image. In: Proceedings of the European conference on computer vision (ECCV), pp 187–203

Izadinia H, Shan Q, Seitz SM (2017) Im2cad. In: 2017 IEEE conference on computer vision and pattern recognition (CVPR). IEEE, pp 2422–2431

Jia Z, Gallagher A, Saxena A, Chen T (2013) 3d-based reasoning with blocks, support, and stability. In: 2013 IEEE conference on computer vision and pattern recognition, pp 1–8

Jones DR, Perttunen CD, Stuckman BE (1993) Lipschitzian optimization without the lipschitz constant. J Optimizat Theory Appl 79(1):157–181

Konolige K, Mihelich P (2011) Technical description of kinect calibration. http://www.ros.org/wiki/kinect_calibration/technical

Laina I, Rupprecht C, Belagiannis V, Tombari F, Navab N (2016) Deeper depth prediction with fully convolutional residual networks. In: 2016 fourth international conference on 3D vision (3DV). IEEE, pp 239–248

Li Y, Qi H, Dai J, Ji X, Wei Y (2016) Fully convolutional instance-aware semantic segmentation. arXiv:1611.07709

Liu M, Guo Y, Wang J (2017) Indoor scene modeling from a single image using normal inference and edge features. Visual Comput 1–14

Liu T, Chaudhuri S, Kim VG, Huang Q, Mitra NJ, Funkhouser T (2014) Creating consistent scene graphs using a probabilistic grammar. ACM Trans Graph (TOG) 33(6):211

Long J, Shelhamer E, Darrell T (2015) Fully convolutional networks for semantic segmentation. In: Proceedings of the IEEE conference on computer vision and pattern recognition, pp 3431–3440

Mallya A, Lazebnik S (2015) Learning informative edge maps for indoor scene layout prediction. In: Proceedings of the IEEE international conference on computer vision, pp 936–944

Newcombe RA, Izadi S, Hilliges O, Molyneaux D, Kim D, Davison AJ, Kohi P, Shotton J, Hodges S, Fitzgibbon A (2011) Kinectfusion: real-time dense surface mapping and tracking. In: 2011 10th IEEE international symposium on mixed and augmented reality (ISMAR). IEEE, pp 127–136

Nie Y, Chang J, Chaudhry E, Guo S, Smart A, Zhang JJ (2018) Semantic modeling of indoor scenes with support inference from a single photograph. Comput Animat Virtual Worlds 29(3–4)

Nie Y, Guo S, Chang J, Han X, Huang J, Hu S-M, Zhang JJ (2020) Shallow2deep: indoor scene modeling by single image understanding. Patt Recognit 103

Powell MJ (2009) The bobyqa algorithm for bound constrained optimization without derivatives. Cambridge NA report NA2009/06, University of Cambridge, Cambridge

Ren S, He K, Girshick R, Sun J (2015) Faster r-cnn: towards real-time object detection with region proposal networks. Adv Neural Inf Process Syst 91–99

Rother C, Kolmogorov V, Blake A (2004) Grabcut: interactive foreground extraction using iterated graph cuts. ACM Trans Graph (TOG) 23:309–314

Salas-Moreno RF, Newcombe RA, Strasdat H, Kelly PH, Davison AJ (2013) Slam++: simultaneous localisation and mapping at the level of objects. In: Proceedings of the IEEE conference on computer vision and pattern recognition, pp 1352–1359

Santoro A, Raposo D, Barrett DG, Malinowski M, Pascanu R, Battaglia P, Lillicrap T (2017) A simple neural network module for relational reasoning. In: Advances in neural information processing systems, pp 4967–4976

Silberman N, Hoiem D, Kohli P, Fergus R (2012) Indoor segmentation and support inference from rgbd images. In: Computer vision-ECCV 2012, pp 746–760

Song S, Lichtenberg SP, Xiao J (2015) Sun rgb-d: a rgb-d scene understanding benchmark suite. In: Proceedings of the IEEE conference on computer vision and pattern recognition, pp 567–576

Xu K, Chen K, Fu H, Sun W-L, Hu S-M (2013) Sketch2scene: sketch-based co-retrieval and co-placement of 3d models. ACM Trans Graph (TOG) 32(4):123

Xue F, Xu S, He C, Wang M, Hong R (2015) Towards efficient support relation extraction from rgbd images. Inf Sci 320:320–332

Zhang Y, Liu Z, Miao Z, Wu W, Liu K, Sun Z (2015) Single image-based data-driven indoor scene modeling. Comput Graph 53:210–223

Zheng B, Zhao Y, Yu J, Ikeuchi K, Zhu S-C (2015) Scene understanding by reasoning stability and safety. Int J Comput Vision 112(2):221–238

Chapter 9
Interactive Labeling for Generation of CityGML Building Models from Meshes

Pradeep Kumar Jayaraman, Jianmin Zheng, Yihao Chen, and Chee Boon Tan

Abstract While 3D building models inherently contain semantic information that is useful for industrial applications such as urban planning and construction analysis, the data of the buildings obtained from acquisition and modeling processes are often mere geometry/graphics information. This paper considers the problem of converting 3D building models from a graphical format such as Wavefront OBJ to CityGML which includes semantic information. The problem is challenging due to the lack of explicit semantic information in graphical models. We present a recommendation-based approach to generate CityGML files. The basic idea of the approach is to automatically/semi-automatically group faces of the building models and recommend them to the user for labeling. The underlying technique is based on geometric clustering and graph-cut-based selection that is able to effectively group faces of the same semantic attributes. Our method is efficient and reliable since it involves the user to make use of human's perception about the shape for labeling and meanwhile reduces the user's interaction by grouping and recommending faces using geometric algorithms. The experiments demonstrate that the proposed approach can substantially speed up the generation of CityGML models.

P. K. Jayaraman · J. Zheng (✉) · Y. Chen
School of Computer Science and Engineering, Nanyang Technological University,
50 Nanyang Ave, Singapore 639798, Singapore
e-mail: asjmzheng@ntu.edu.sg

P. K. Jayaraman
e-mail: pradeepkj@ntu.edu.sg

Y. Chen
e-mail: michaelchen@ntu.edu.sg

C. B. Tan
Government Technology Agency of Singapore, 1 Fusionopolis View, 07-01,
Singapore 138577, Singapore
e-mail: wayne_tan@tech.gov.sg

© The Author(s), under exclusive license to Springer Nature Switzerland AG 2021
N. Magnenat Thalmann et al. (eds.), *Intelligent Scene Modeling and Human-Computer Interaction*, Human–Computer Interaction Series,
https://doi.org/10.1007/978-3-030-71002-6_9

9.1 Introduction

A 3D city model is a 3D geometric representation of a city or an urban environment with terrain attributes, detailed texture, geometry and topology of city objects such as buildings, and semantic information as well. While such models have been used for visualization, they are also valuable for many other purposes beyond visualization and are increasingly used in a large number of domains, for example, Geographic Information Systems (GIS) (Biljecki et al. 2015) and Land Administration (Floros et al. 2017). Advanced information and modelling technologies allow 3D city models to be infused with different sources of static, dynamic and real-time city data and information. This paper is focused on building models and their semantics modeling in format conversion.

3D building models are derived from various techniques such as photogrammetry (Suveg and Vosselman 2004), laser scanning (Tomljenovic et al. 2015) and conventional 3D modeling (for example, using SketchUp Pro software), which eventually result in graphics models that describe the geometry and topology of the buildings. One common and typical format for 3D graphics models is Wavefront OBJ, which is widely used in computer graphics and supported by various modeling and graphics software packages. While graphics models are sufficient for visualization, applying GIS analysis on these data requires further information in the form of semantic labels (for example, tags describing the kind of surface patches—wall, roof, floor, etc.). Such information is useful in a variety of applications including urban planning, real estate, and disaster modeling, as well as helpful in creating software tools for practical purposes such as measuring the surface area of roofs for solar panel installation, analyzing the bending of roads for traffic safety, and estimating the cost of painting a building from its total wall surface area. However, the OBJ format does not contain this kind of information explicitly and many GIS software packages do not support OBJ.

Currently, the integration of semantics into 3D building models is typically achieved through structural-oriented Building Information Modeling (BIM)/Industry Foundation Classes (IFC) or the semantic-oriented City Geography Markup Language (CityGML). BIM is a rich intelligent digital repository that uses an object-oriented approach to describe geometry, semantics and relationships in the building industry, and IFC serves as a reference model standard for BIM. IFC not only represents structural components of a BIM model but also supports advanced processes marking the course of the construction within the life cycle of the BIM model. CityGML is an official standard of Open Geospatial Consortium (OGC) for the representation and exchange of 3D city data with different Levels of Detail (LoD) (Groeger and Plumer 2012; Gröger et al. 2012; Kolbe et al. 2008). It is a widely accepted concept in GIS for modelling and exchanging 3D city-related urban objects and landscape models. It defines the classes and relations for the most relevant topographic objects in cities and regional models with respect to their geometrical, topological, semantical and appearance properties. Various research and commercial efforts have been initiated to integrate BIM and GIS (Breunig et al. 2020). Meanwhile, there is research towards the conversion from graphics models (for example, in OBJ format) to CityGML or IFC, which is beneficial in practice. In fact, the use of computer graphics software to handle 3D GIS data for GIS applications has shown great potential (Scianna 2013), and on the other hand, semantic information also plays an important role in computer graphics visualization (Zhang et al. 2014).

This paper presents a novel method for converting 3D meshes of buildings from graphics format, Wavefront OBJ, to semantics-enabled 3D format, CityGML. While automatically extracting geometric features and semantic information and assigning them to the 3D models is appealing, it is full of challenges. Some automatic methods have been proposed using both geometric and topological information conveyed in the graphics models (Diakité et al. 2014; Biljecki and Arroyo Ohori 2015), but they are not very reliable and only apply to the models with simple building elements. Thus we seek an alternative approach to provide an efficient and reliable solution. To annotate semantics in CityGML, we need to assign predefined labels of CityGML to the faces of a 3D model to describe the urban objects. For example, a building has to be partitioned into various parts such as roof, door, window, and floor by assigning the relevant XML like tags (`bldg:WallSurface`, `bldg:RoofSurface`, `bldg:Window`, `bldg:Door`, `bldg:FloorSurface`, etc.) to the corresponding faces. Our approach is to progressively label the faces of the building model. The key idea is to automatically or semi-automatically merge faces of the same tags into a group as much as possible and then bring the group to the user for labeling, which aims to maximize the power of advanced algorithms for geometric clustering and minimize the user interaction. For this purpose, different criteria and segmentation methods are used for effective segmentation. In this way, we can substantially increase the processing speed while ensuring reliable labeling, which is demonstrated by experiments. Moreover, our approach degrades gracefully for models containing geometric noise and also works with models composed of multiple parts, which can pose problems to purely heuristic methods that usually have strong assumptions on the geometry and topology of the building models.

9.2   Related Work

3D building modeling is an active research topic in various disciplines such as GIS, BIM, and graphics as well. There have been a lot of works and efforts in converting building models from one format to another. This can improve interoperability between different formats of building models and thus benefit different demands in applications. Boeters et al. (2015) considered an LoD 2 labeled CityGML file and introduced a new level-of-detail called LoD 2+ that includes coarsely detailed interiors of buildings in addition to the already defined coarse exteriors in LoD 2. Nagel et al. discussed and identified conceptual requirements for converting CityGML to IFC models Nagel et al. (2009), and Stouffs proposed a formal framework for semantic and geometric conversion from IFC models into CityGML LoD 3/4 building models using a triple graph grammar approach which extracts both geometric and semantic information as available in the IFC models to create CityGML (Stouffs 2018). El-Mekawy et al. (2012) examined the semantic mapping between IFC and CityGML, and proposed a meta-based unified building model for the conversion between both representations.

Compared to the conversion between two representations both having semantic attributes, converting a graphical model without explicit semantic attributes to a CityGML model is much more difficult. Relatively such conversion is much less well investigated. In general, the conversion process requires feature extraction and semantic information recovering from building models. Bauer et al. (2003) presented a method to extract features on façades point cloud, and Pu and Vosselman (2006) proposed to extract semantics like walls, doors, and windows from laser scanning. Boulch et al. (2013) proposed a semantic parsing scheme on CAD models using an expressive formalism based on attribute grammars and constraint. Diakité et al. (2014) semantically annotated graphics models by representing them as a combinatorial map and performing a depth-first search region growing based on simple but sensible heuristics, for example, floors are horizontal, walls are vertical and windows are within walls. The method is based on the topology of the model and assumes that the geometry is not only clean, but that each semantic part is modeled as a separate component in the input model. Kavisha et al. (2015) attempted to convert building models in the COLLADA format to CityGML for developing a solar radiation model. They mainly considered the problem of automatically extracting and labeling roof surfaces using simple heuristics and also assumed that the input model was geometrically clean.

Learning techniques seem to be attractive for this conversion process due to the nature and complexity of the problem. Rook et al. (2016) proposed a method to use features such as height, and orientation of normal vectors to train a support vector machine (SVM) to classify LoD 2 building models. Slade studied the problem of automating the semantic and geometric enrichment of 3D building models by using histogram of oriented -gradients-based template matching (Slade 2018). Scalable methods were developed to automatically enrich 3D building models with windows and doors and detect the architectural styles of windows and doors using geometry-based heuristics and SVM-based machine learning. Xiong et al. (2013) proposed a system to semantically label LIDAR point cloud data of buildings by voxelizing them first, and then applying a learning-based approach to predict semantic labels. However, this requires a labeled dataset, which is generally difficult to procure for 3D building data, especially for LoD 3 and above.

9.3 Overview of the Proposed Approach

Our problem can be described as follows: given a 3D triangular mesh model of a building in typical graphics file format Wavefront OBJ, we want to create a CityGML file for this building model. The input model does not have to be a single manifold and can often be composed of multiple parts, but each part must be a manifold. Since an OBJ file does not contain explicit semantic information and a CityGML file does, the key is how to recognize semantics from the OBJ file and add semantic labels in order to output a CityGML file.

9.3.1 Wavefront OBJ Models

The OBJ file format is a simple data-format for object definition, which was developed in1980s by Wavefront Technologies for its Advanced Visualizer animation package. It can define common 3D mesh models, and also support higher-order freeform geometries such as Bézier and B-spline surfaces. In this work, we only focus on triangular mesh models for which the OBJ file stores vertex data, face data given by a set of vertex indices, and possibly vertex normals and texture coordinates as well. Refer to Fig. 9.1 for a triangular mesh and its OBJ file, where

- "v x y z" specifies a geometric vertex and its x, y, z coordinates;
- "vn x y z" specifies a normal vector with components x, y, and z;
- "vt u v" specifies a texture vertex and its u, v coordinates;
- "f v1/vt1/vn1 v2/vt2/vn2 v3/vt3/vn3" specifies a face element with its vertex reference numbers $v1$, $v2$, $v3$, texture vertex reference numbers $vt1$, $vt2$, $vt3$, and vertex normal reference numbers $vn1$, $vn2$, $vn3$.

Nowadays OBJ is ubiquitous in 3D modeling and computer graphics, and supported by most 3D graphics software. It provides a simple and compact set of geometry information of 3D objects, which is sufficient for 3D modeling and visualization. However, it can be seen from Fig. 9.1 that semantics support is very limited in OBJ and there is no standard way to differentiate faces or components in terms of semantics.

9.3.2 CityGML Models

CityGML is an XML-based format for the representation of 3D urban objects with thematic and semantic information. It provides thematic classes to store different classes of objects such as buildings and tunnels, and structures 3D models into semantically meaningful parts by assigning an attribute to each surface. Thus the semantic-geometric relations of 3D objects in an urban environment are available, which facilitates spatial analysis and other applications as well.

The CityGML file format supports a level-of-detail (LoD) modeling for urban structures, particularly buildings:

LoD 0: the building is represented by a simple base plane, on which aerial images may be textured.

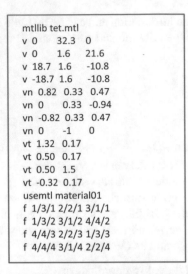

```
mtllib tet.mtl
v 0      32.3   0
v 0       1.6   21.6
v 18.7   1.6   -10.8
v -18.7  1.6   -10.8
vn 0.82  0.33  0.47
vn 0     0.33  -0.94
vn -0.82 0.33  0.47
vn 0     -1    0
vt 1.32  0.17
vt 0.50  0.17
vt 0.50  1.5
vt -0.32 0.17
usemtl material01
f 1/3/1 2/2/1 3/1/1
f 1/3/2 3/1/2 4/4/2
f 4/4/3 2/2/3 1/3/3
f 4/4/4 3/1/4 2/2/4
```

Fig. 9.1 A triangular mesh of a tetrahedron (right) and its wavefront OBJ file (left)

LoD 1: the building is represented by a simplified outer shell defined by a single prismatic extrusion solid (generally a cuboid).

LoD 2: builds upon LoD 1 and includes simplified roof structures, chimneys, balconies, and dormers.

LoD 3: includes geometrically detailed outer shells for buildings and detailed roofs distinguishing between various roof shapes. Doors and windows are also represented as planar objects.

LoD 4: the building geometry is much more detailed than LoD 3, and may also include movable and non-movable building elements such as furniture and detailed interiors.

These LoDs describe the spatio-semantic relations corresponding to the real-world counterparts.

In this work, we mainly focus on LoD 3 semantic labelings for building models, which require a relatively fine-grained segmentation. Our method, however, can be applied for other LoDs since it is interactive in nature and does not make strong assumptions about the input model.

9.3.3 Outline of the Algorithm

The geometric data in the OBJ file are first directly converted to CityGML, but all faces in the generated CityGML at this moment are non-classified. Then the main process in the conversion problem is to assign the correct CityGML tag to each face of the building model. While manually selecting and labeling the faces can be very

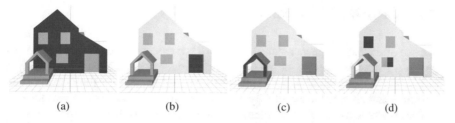

(a)   (b)   (c)   (d)

Fig. 9.2 Groups of faces are recommended to the user for labeling one by one

tedious, we propose a strategy to employ a recommendation-based approach that selects and displays groups of faces to the user for labeling one-by-one in an attempt to reduce tedium. As shown in Fig. 9.2, from left to right groups of faces shown in magenta are gradually recommended to the user for labeling.

More specifically, our algorithm proceeds in the following steps:

(1) Since CityGML LoD 3 represents the exterior of a building, the outer hull of the building model is extracted. In case the model contains multiple components, the models can be modified to construct a single outer hull if required.
(2) Construct a face adjacency graph from the outer hull of the models, which will facilitate the subsequent geometric processes.
(3) Find an unlabeled face and search for more faces using a breadth-first manner in the face adjacency graph and based on similarity of their normal vectors (Sect. 9.4.3) to form a group. The group of faces is then recommended to the user for labeling. Note that for better visualization, the camera is oriented to point at the center of each group. Moreover, the view direction of the camera is aligned to be roughly horizontal (by clamping the camera position's azimuthal angle in spherical coordinates) to avoid disorienting movements.
(4) The user can accept the recommended group of faces and assign a tag, or choose to improve the selection using other criteria (Sect. 9.4.3) or using an interactive approach (Sect. 9.4.4). The process repeats steps (3) and (4) until all faces have been labeled.

9.4 Geometric Processing for Interactive Labeling

This section explains the geometric processes that are used for interactive labeling described in the preceding section.

9.4.1 Outer Hull Extraction

It is quite often that designers create models in a component-wise manner for modeling convenience. As a result, the created 3D building models often contain multiple components, which we call *parts*. This might be problematic for those conversion algorithms that assume the target CityGML model to have a single outer surface.

In cases where the input is not a single manifold mesh, but has multiple parts, we provide two options. The first option is to treat each part as an individual object and let the user handle all parts one by one. The second option is to merge the parts and construct a single outer hull of the model (see Fig. 9.3). This option is of more interest for converting 3D models into CityGML files with LoD1, LoD2 or LoD3, but needs a process of outer hull reconstruction. We assume that each part of the mesh is free of holes, and reconstruct the outer hull by adapting Zhou et al.'s method (Zhou et al. 2016). First, all face–face intersections are resolved to ensure that each intersection among the parts is strictly along an edge without self-intersections. Then the ambient space is clearly partitioned into "cells" by the faces of the model, with the cell that is completely outside of the model called the "infinite cell". The outer hull is defined as the set of faces that are adjacent to the infinite cell.

9.4.2 Face Adjacency Graph

For the outer hull of a manifold model, we create a face adjacency graph to propagate the user's selection to nearby faces. Consider the input 3D triangle mesh M, which is a collection of vertices, edges and faces (V, E, F). The face adjacency graph G is

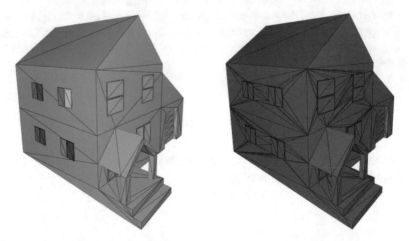

Fig. 9.3 Outer hull reconstruction. Left: a building model with multiple parts; Right: the model is modified to have a single outer full of the surface

a dual of the mesh M, and is defined such that each node is a face $f_i \in F$, and each edge connects faces f_i and f_j if they share a common edge $e_{ij} \in E$. The advantage of using a face adjacency graph compared to the original mesh is that the semantic parts can be cleanly segmented as a group of faces, as opposed to a group of vertices that are shared multiple faces. Moreover, the boundaries of semantic regions can be naturally defined according to the weight of the edges defined to be small for adjacent faces that have a tendency to represent a single semantic part, and large otherwise.

9.4.3   Criteria for Semantic Grouping

When the user selects a face f_i in the mesh, we would like to select a larger set of faces S such that $f_i \subset S$. We define below three criteria tailored for a polygonal building like models that can be potentially used for adding the neighboring face to the current selection (see Fig. 9.4).

Smoothness of Normals $N(f_i, f_j)$: Neighboring faces whose normal vectors are similar are likely to belong to the same semantic group. Quantitatively, this criterion can be checked by computing the difference between 1 and the absolute value of the dot product of the corresponding unit face normals $\hat{\mathbf{n}}_i$ and $\hat{\mathbf{n}}_j$:

$$N(f_i, f_j) = 1 - |\hat{\mathbf{n}}_i \cdot \hat{\mathbf{n}}_j|.$$

This criterion will include the faces that are connected and have similar normals.

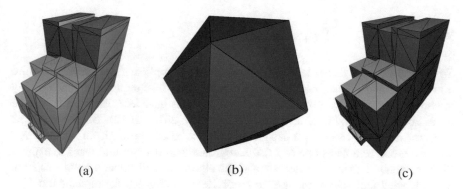

(a)   (b)   (c)

Fig. 9.4 Criteria for selecting multiple faces connected to user's selection. The criteria can be iteratively computed starting from the seed face in a breadth-first-search manner. **a** *Coplanarity* expands the user's selection if the adjacent face normals are comparable to the seed face normal. **b** *Smoothness of normals* expands the user's selection if the unit normal vectors vary smoothly among neighboring faces. **c** *Relative-to-up* selects all connected faces that are similarly oriented with respect to the "up" vector of the model

Coplanarity $C(f_i, f_j)$: Faces that are connected and are roughly coplanar are likely to form a semantic group, such as a portion of a wall, floor, roof, etc. This criterion can be checked quantitatively by computing the smoothness of normals defined above, but with respect to a fixed seed face f_s, $N(f_s, f_j)$, $\forall f_j \in F$. Conventionally, coplanarity is defined using the scalar triple product. For a triangle with vertices **p**, **q**, and **r** and the centroid **s** of the other face f_j, the vectors $\mathbf{q} - \mathbf{p}, \mathbf{r} - \mathbf{p}, \mathbf{s} - \mathbf{p}$ can be used for this purpose. However, we found this definition to be sensitive to the scale of the mesh as well as the individual triangles with no upper bounds. Hence, it is difficult to define a threshold for which coplanarity is consistent throughout the model.

Relative-to-up: Building models are oriented and have an "up" orientation usually aligned with the virtual world's y-axis. Incidentally, faces that are aligned similarly with respect to the up vector tend to form a semantic group. If we approximate a building model coarsely with a cuboid, then the walls of the building have normal vectors perpendicular, while roofs and floors have normal vectors parallel and anti-parallel, respectively, with respect to the unit "**up**" vector. This can be measured as

$$R(f_i, f_j) = |\hat{\mathbf{n}}_\mathbf{i} \cdot \mathbf{up} - \hat{\mathbf{n}}_\mathbf{j} \cdot \mathbf{up}|.$$

For simple models, the three criteria on their own appear to be useful for segmenting and labeling faces by a breadth-first search which propagates if the criteria are within a threshold. For complicated models with fine-grained geometric detail, it is difficult for these individual criteria to give efficient grouping or selections. Hence we combine them into an optimization model in the next subsection.

9.4.4   Graph-Cut-Based Selection

To support efficient face selection for models with complicated geometric structure and details, fine-grained control is often necessary. In computer graphics, many automatic or interactive mesh segmentation methods have been developed (Attene et al. 2006; Kalogerakis et al. 2010; Zhang et al. 2011, 2012). Borrowing some ideas from the prior work, we design a graph-cut-based approach for our purpose, where the user annotates one or a few foreground and background faces to express his/her intention about the selection and the algorithm will select a few faces from the unlabeled face set for the user to label. Refer to Fig. 9.5 for an example. The user just casually chooses a few faces from the roof as the foreground seeds and a few faces from the wall as the background seeds. The algorithm segments out more roof faces for labeling. The user can iteratively refine the seeds until the desired segmentation has been achieved. Moreover, we can further simplify the user's input in our graph-cut-based algorithm. The user can only specify one or a few faces as

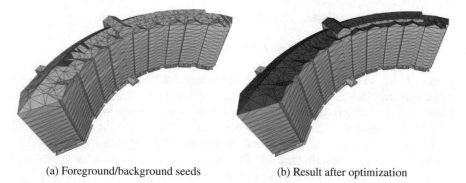

(a) Foreground/background seeds   (b) Result after optimization

Fig. 9.5 Graph-cut-based selection. Left: the user inputs where magenta-colored faces represent the foreground while cyan-colored faces represent the background; Right: magenta-colored faces represent the selected face by the algorithm

the foreground. The algorithm will select an un-classified face that is far away from these seeds as the background, and then run the graph-cut. Figure 9.7e, f shows such a process.

The underlying model of the graph-cut is to minimize an energy function over the set of all possible labeling l for faces:

$$E(l) = E_{data}(l) + \lambda E_{smooth}(l)$$

where l is a function that assigns a label—foreground (0) or background (1) to each face (resp. every node of the graph G), and *lambda* is a tradeoff factor. Usually we simply set $\lambda = 1$.

Data term: The data term $E_{data}(\ell)$ represents the cost of violating our confidence that a node is likely to belong to one of the two labels. We use a simple data term which gives the cost of 0 to the seed faces whose labels are the same as the user-selected labels, the cost of 1000 to the seed faces whose labels are opposite to the user-selected one, and the cost of 0 to all other faces. Hence, the sum of these costs for all faces represents the data term E_{data}. It is also possible to use complex data terms, for example, based on the distribution of normals and textures of the selected faces.

Smoothness term: The smoothness term is to ensure that the boundaries of the segmentation tend to snap to the boundaries of semantic groups of faces and the sharp edges in the mesh. To compute the smoothness term, we first compute a weight for each edge of the graph G such that it is large for an edge shared by semantically similar faces, and small otherwise.

Given two adjacent faces f_i and f_j, we define a distance between them:

$$d(f_i, f_j) = w_G \, d_G(f_i, f_j) + w_N \, N(f_i, f_j) + w_R \, R(f_i, f_j),$$

where $N(f_i, f_j)$ and $R(f_i, f_j)$ are the smoothness of normals and relative-to-up criteria defined in Sect. 9.4.3, d_G is the approximate geodesic distance between two faces f_i and f_j defined by the sum of lengths of the line segments joining the centroid of f_i to the midpoint of the shared edge between f_i and f_j, and then to the centroid of f_j, and w_G, w_N, w_R are the weights. We normalize d_G by its average computed from all pairs of neighboring faces in the model. This is to account for the scale of the mesh as well variance in the size of individual triangles which is usually high in man-made CAD-like models. Generally, we set w_G, w_N and w_R to 1, 0.5 and 1, respectively, but the values can be adjusted.

We then convert $d(f_i, f_j)$ into edge weights of the graph:

$$w_{ij} = \exp\left(-\left(\frac{d(f_i, f_j)}{\text{avg}(d(f_i, f_j))}\right)^2\right).$$

Finally the sum of all the terms of the label penalty between two adjacent faces i and j multiplied by the edge weight defines the smoothness term: $E_{smooth} = \sum_{i \in F, j \in N(i)} w_{ij} \, \mathbf{1}(l(i) \neq l(j))$, where $N(i)$ represents the set of faces that are adjacent to face i, and $\mathbf{1}$ is the indicator function that outputs 1 if its expression is true, and 0 otherwise. Hence this smoothness term satisfies the Potts potential.

9.5 Experiments

We have implemented the algorithm using C++ and developed a prototype for converting OBJ models to CityGML models (see Fig. 9.6 for the interface of the prototype). The graph-cut is implemented using the approximate optimization algorithm proposed by Kolgomorov et al. (2004). The system allows the user to load an OBJ file, perform interactive labeling, and export a CityGML file that has been partially or completely labeled. The prototype also allows the user to load a CityGML file and edit the semantics of the CityGML model by performing interactive labeling.

Figure 9.7a shows a house model in OBJ format, which contains 12542 vertices, 20542 triangles, and 1129 parts. Figures 9.7b–f demonstrate some individual selection processes. In particular, Fig. 9.7b, d shows the selection results (highlighted in magenta) based on "Coplanarity", "Smoothness of Normals", and "Relative-to-up", respectively, where the user just specifies one triangle as the seed. Figure 9.7e depicts one triangle specified by the user as a foreground seed for the graph-cut-based selection, and Fig. 9.7f shows a group of faces returned by the algorithm. It can be seen that these faces all belong to a wall. Hence these faces are labeled as "wall" as shown

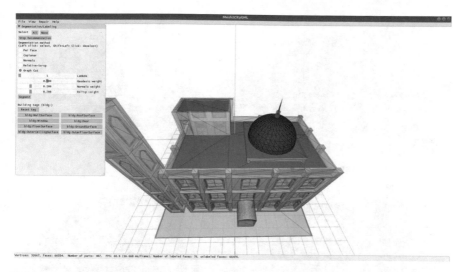

Fig. 9.6 Interface of the prototype

in Fig. 9.7g. Continuing the process, we eventually label all the faces and generate a CityGML model, as displayed in Fig. 9.7h. In general, the graph-cut-based selection tool is more efficient and also easier to fine-tune the selection.

Figure 9.8 shows another three models, which are all successfully converted to CityGML format from OBJ format by our prototype tool. The statistics of the models is given in Table 9.1. The time of interactive conversion for each of the four models presented in this section is less than 30 minutes, which demonstrates the efficiency of our method and tool.

9.6 Conclusion

We have presented a solution to the problem of converting building models represented by Wavefront OBJ to CityGML by (semi-)automatically grouping the faces of building models and interactively labeling them with semantic and thematic information as defined by the CityGML standard. The basic idea of our method is to involve the user to make use of human's ability in recognizing the semantic attributes of the building elements and meanwhile to reduce the user's interaction by developing geometric optimization algorithms. The prototype built upon the method shows the efficiency and simplicity of the process. Moreover, our method does not make strong assumptions about the geometry or topology of the mesh and is interactive. Hence, it can be used as a standalone tool, as well as in conjunction with other methods that are learning or heuristic based, to simplify the task of generating a CityGML file.

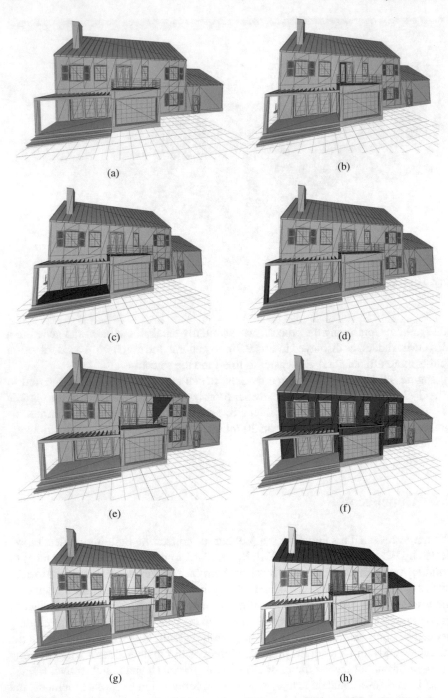

Fig. 9.7 Geometric processing for the conversion of a house model from OBJ to CityGML

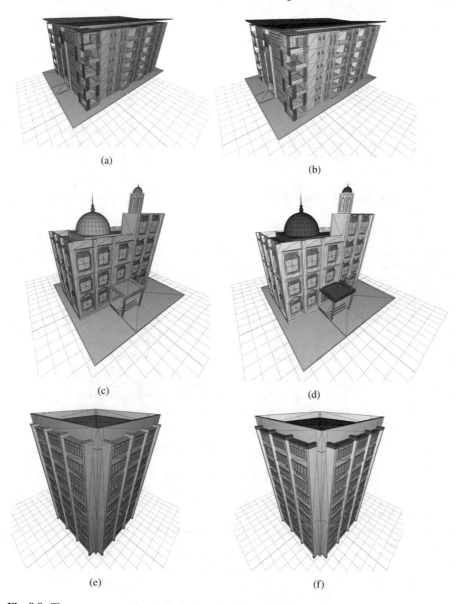

(a)

(b)

(c)

(d)

(e)

(f)

Fig. 9.8 Three more examples. Left: the input OBJ models; Right: the output CityGML models

Table 9.1 Statistics of the three models in Fig. 9.8

Models	# of vertices	# of faces	# of parts
Figure 9.8a	29381	50638	2325
Figure 9.8c	32667	66554	407
Figure 9.8e	20401	35452	665

Acknowledgements This research is supported by the National Research Foundation under Virtual Singapore Award No. NRF2015VSG-AA3DCM001-018.

References

Attene M, Katz S, Mortara M, Patane G, Spagnuolo M, Tal A (2006) Mesh segmentation—a comparative study. In: Proceedings of the IEEE international conference on shape modeling and applications 2006. IEEE Computer Society, Washington, DC, USA, SMI '06, p 7. https://doi.org/10.1109/SMI.2006.24

Bauer J, Karner K, Schindler K, Klaus A, Zach C (2003) Segmentation of building models from dense 3D point-clouds. In: 27th workshop of the Austrian Association for pattern recognition, pp 253–259

Biljecki F, Arroyo Ohori K (2015) Automatic semantic-preserving conversion between OBJ and CityGML. In: Eurographics workshop on urban data modelling and visualisation, pp 25–30

Biljecki F, Stoter J, Ledoux H, Zlatanova S, Coeltekin A (2015) Applications of 3D city models: state of the art review. ISPRS Int J Geo-Inf 4:2842–2889

Boeters R, Ohori KA, Biljecki F, Zlatanova S (2015) Automatically enhancing CityGML LOD2 models with a corresponding indoor geometry. Int J Geograph Inf Sci 29(12):2248–2268. https://doi.org/10.1080/13658816.2015.1072201

Boulch A, Houllier S, Marlet R, Tournaire O (2013) Semantizing complex 3D scenes using constrained attribute grammars. In: Proceedings of the eleventh Eurographics/ACMSIGGRAPH symposium on geometry processing, Eurographics Association, SGP'13, pp 33–42

Breunig M, Bradley PE, Jahn M, Kuper P, Mazroob N, Roesch N, Al-Doori M, Stefanakis E, Jadidi M (2020) Geospatial data management research: Progress and future directions. ISPRS Int J Geo-Inf 9(2) https://doi.org/10.3390/ijgi9020095, https://www.mdpi.com/2220-9964/9/2/95

Diakité AA, Damiand G, Gesquière G (2014) Automatic semantic labelling of 3D buildings based on geometric and topological information. In: Proceedings of 9th international 3D GeoInfo conference (3DGeoInfo), Karlsruhe Institute of Technology, Dubaï, United Arab Emirates, 3D GeoInfo conference proceedings series

El-Mekawy M, Östman A, Hijazi I (2012) An evaluation of IFC-CityGML unidirectional conversion. Int J Adv Comput Sci Appl 3(5)

Floros G, Tsiliakou E, Kitsakis D, Pispidikis I, Dimopoulou E (2017) Investigating semantic functionality of 3d geometry for land administration. In: Abdul-Rahman A (eds) Advances in 3D geoinformation. Lecture notes in geoinformation and cartography. Springer. https://doi.org/10.1007/978-3-319-25691-7_14

Groeger G, Plumer L (2012) CityGML: interoperable semantic 3D city models. ISPRS J Photogramm Remote Sens 71:12–33

Gröger G, Kolbe TH, Nagel C, Häfele KH (2012) OGC city geography markup language (CityGML) Encoding Standard. Tech. rep, Open Geospatial Consortium

Kalogerakis E, Hertzmann A, Singh K (2010) Learning 3D mesh segmentation and labeling. ACM Trans Graph 29(4):102:1–102:12. https://doi.org/10.1145/1778765.1778839

Kavisha (2015) CityGML based interoperability for the transformation of 3D data models. Master's thesis, Andhra University, Visakhapatnam

Kolbe T, Nagel C, Stadler A (2008) CityGML: a framework for the representation of 3D city models from geometry acquisition to full semantic qualification. In: Proceedings of ISPRS congress

Kolmogorov V, Zabin R (2004) What energy functions can be minimized via graph cuts? IEEE Trans Pattern Anal Mach Intell 26(2):147–159. https://doi.org/10.1109/TPAMI.2004.1262177

Nagel C, Stadler A, Kolbe HT (2009) Conceptual requirements for the automatic reconstruction of building information models from uninterpreted 3D models. In: Academic track of geoweb 2009 conference

Pu S, Vosselman G (2006) Automatic extraction of building features from terrestrial laser scanning. In: International archives of the photogrammetry, remote sensing and spatial information sciences, pp 33–39

Rook M, Biljecki F, Diakité AA (2016) Towards automatic semantic labelling of 3D city models. ISPRS Ann Photogram, Remote Sens Spat Inf Sci IV-2/W1:23–30. https://doi.org/10.5194/isprs-annals-IV-2-W1-23-2016

Scianna A (2013) Building 3D GIS data models using open source software. Applied Geomatics 5(2):119–132. https://doi.org/10.1007/s12518-013-0099-3

Slade J (2018) Automatic semantic and geometric enrichment of city GML 3D building models of varying architectural styles with HOG-based template matching. PhD thesis, Cardiff University, United Kingdom

Stouffs R (2018) A triple graph grammar approach to mapping IFC models into CityGML building models. In: Proceedings of the 23rd CAADRIA conference, vol 2, Tsinghua University, Beijing, China, pp 41–50

Suveg I, Vosselman G (2004) Reconstruction of 3D building models from aerial images and maps. ISPRS J Photogram Remote Sens 58(3):202–224. https://doi.org/10.1016/j.isprsjprs.2003.09.006, Integration of Geodata and Imagery for Automated Refinement and Update of Spatial Databases

Tomljenovic I, Höfle B, Tiede D, Blaschke T (2015) Building extraction from airborne laser scanning data: an analysis of the state of the art. Remote Sens 7(4):3826–3862. https://doi.org/10.3390/rs70403826

Xiong X, Adan A, Akinci B, Huber D (2013) Automatic creation of semantically rich 3D building models from laser scanner data. Autom Constr 31:325–337. https://doi.org/10.1016/j.autcon.2012.10.006

Zhang F, Tpurre V, Moreau G (2014) Applying level-of-detail and perceptive effects to 3D urban semantics visualization. In: Proceedings of the Eurographics workshop on urban data modelling and visualization, pp 31–36

Zhang J, Zheng J, Cai J (2011) Interactive mesh cutting using constrained random walks. IEEE Trans Vis Comput Graph 17(3):357–367. https://doi.org/10.1109/TVCG.2010.57

Zhang J, Zheng J, Wu C, Cai J (2012) Variational mesh decomposition. ACM Trans Graph 31(3):21:1–21:14. https://doi.org/10.1145/2167076.2167079

Zhou Q, Grinspun E, Zorin D, Jacobson A (2016) Mesh arrangements for solid geometry. ACM Trans Graph (TOG) 35(4)

Chapter 10
ToolY: An Approach for the Combination of Motion Capture and 3D Reconstruction to Present Tool Usage in 3D Environments

Evropi Stefanidi, Nikolaos Partarakis, Xenophon Zabulis, Paul Zikas, George Papagiannakis, and Nadia Magnenat Thalmann

Abstract Visualization techniques for the usage of tools, handicrafts, and assembly operations are employed for demonstrating processes (e.g., assembly instructions). Until today, most commonly used techniques include written information, sketches in manuals, video instructions, etc. The evolution of technology nowadays has generated mature methods for transforming movement to digital information that can be processed and replicated. Motion capture together with 3D reconstruction techniques can provide new ways of digitizing handicrafts. At the same time, Virtual Humans can be used to present craft processes, as well as to demonstrate the usage of tools. For this, the tools utilized in these processes need to be transferred to the digital world. In this paper, we present ToolY, a 3D authoring platform for tool usage

E. Stefanidi (✉)
University of Bremen, Bremen, Germany
e-mail: evropi@uni-bremen.de; evropi@ics.forth.gr; evropi@miralab.ch

E. Stefanidi · N. Partarakis · X. Zabulis · P. Zikas · G. Papagiannakis
Institute of Computer Science, Foundation for Research and Technology—Hellas (FORTH), Heraklion, Greece
e-mail: partarak@ics.forth.gr

X. Zabulis
e-mail: zabulis@ics.forth.gr

P. Zikas
e-mail: zikas@csd.uoc.gr

G. Papagiannakis
e-mail: papagian@ics.forth.gr; papagian@csd.uoc.gr

E. Stefanidi · N. Magnenat Thalmann
MIRALab, University of Geneva, Geneva, Switzerland
e-mail: thalmann@miralab.ch; nadiathalmann@ntu.edu.sg

G. Papagiannakis
Department of Computer Science, University of Crete, Heraklion, Greece

N. Magnenat Thalmann
Institute of Media Innovation, Nanyang Technological University, Singapore, Singapore

© The Author(s), under exclusive license to Springer Nature Switzerland AG 2021
N. Magnenat Thalmann et al. (eds.), *Intelligent Scene Modeling and Human-Computer Interaction*, Human–Computer Interaction Series,
https://doi.org/10.1007/978-3-030-71002-6_10

presentation in 3D environments, to demonstrate simple operations (e.g., usage of a hammer, scissors, screwdriver), where the tools are the product of 3D reconstruction. The movement of the Virtual Humans derives from motion capture, while for the movement of the tools, a novel approach is used, for inducing the tool motion from the human motion capture. The products of ToolY are Virtual Environments that can be experienced in 3D or through immersion in Virtual Reality.

10.1   Introduction

"A picture is worth a thousand words" (Wikipedia 2019). It is a known fact that humans like visualization, and that the human mind understands concepts easier when text is accompanied by some sort of visual medium (Dewan 2015). To date, most handicraft and assembly operation tutorials mainly consist of text, as well as demonstrative pictures, with indicators and arrows aiming to direct the reader. However, performing simple handicraft tasks, assembling furniture, and any process requiring the use of handheld tools can often be a struggle, resulting in fear or reluctance to perform such tasks, as well as incorrect execution and even accidents. Thus, the issue of how to go beyond pictures and texts arises, in order to demonstrate tool usage processes effectively. While video tutorials exist on the Internet for handicrafts or processes that involve the use of tools, immersion could lead to more efficient demonstration and training: Virtual Reality (VR) has been proven an effective learning technique (Hussein and Nätterdal 2015). Benefits of learning in a Virtual Environment (VE) include: (i) experiencing physical properties such as shape and size directly, (ii) the ability to change the point of view to access new or unusual perspectives (Ferrington and Loge 1992), (iii) it is a low-cost alternative to creating full-scale physical training scenarios, (iv) training scenarios that can be run repeatedly can be simulated, and (v) monitoring of progress during training sessions can be included to evaluate learners' skills (Ieronutti and Chittaro 2007).

Apart from Virtual Reality, the evolution of technology has led to methods that successfully transform movement to digital information that can then be processed and replicated. For this, technologies such as Motion Capture (MoCap) can be utilized. Furthermore, 3D reconstruction can transform physical objects into their digital representation, which along with Virtual Humans (VHs), can be used to demonstrate processes that involve tools. These two methods together (MoCap and 3D reconstruction) can lead to digitization, not only of the human motion while performing the task, but also of the tool being used. The movement of the practitioner can be recorded by MoCap techniques such as IMU-based or Visual Tracking methods. Although the objects, i.e., the tools being used in the process, as well as the environment in which the handicraft is performed, can be digitized through 3D reconstruction, MoCap cannot capture the actual movement of the tools easily (e.g., in the case of deformable tools). Adding to this issue is the fact that these tools, as well as the Avatars representing the VHs, and the scenes representing the surrounding environment, might be captured with different technologies. Thus, a platform is needed, to integrate all these technologies and content, in order to create engaging demonstration and training experiences of handheld tool usage processes.

In this paper, we propose a solution, by presenting a platform for authoring tool usage experiences in 3D environments, regarding simple operations, which combines motion capture and 3D reconstruction. These tasks are presented by the VHs, whose movement derives from the MoCap, while for the movement of the tools, a novel approach is used, for inducing the tool motion from the human MoCap. In this chapter, we focus on handheld tools e.g., hammer, screwdriver, scissors, etc., which are free to move in any direction. Some important issues that need to be taken into account, regard the grip of the tools by the VHs, the realistic motion of the tool, as well as multiplexing MoCap powered motion with other animations of the VH (e.g., when the VH is moving and hammering at the same time). Our platform is the editor, where the user can create these experiences, and then deploy them, for use by anyone who wants to experience the usage of a tool in a process that concerns handicraft. In this research work, the Unity 3D game engine is used as the main development platform, which simplifies the loading of different 3D model formats. This is considered important as MoCap data, 3D digitization, Avatars, 3D models of the environment, etc., are produced by different technologies and tools. In this context, it is important to maximize compatibility so as to be able to easily integrate content from multiple sources without increasing the complexity of the produced technology.

10.2 Related Work

10.2.1 Key Technologies

Motion Capture Technologies

Motion Capture (or MoCap) technologies measure the motion of subjects in three dimensions, based on wearable markers whose location in 3D is estimated by corresponding sensors. Two main technologies are used, optical-based MoCap, and inertial measurement units (IMU) MoCap. Unlike normal video, MoCap directly measures positional and orientational components of human motion. The results accurately encapsulate human motion in 3D and, therefore, provide a comprehensive representation of the recorded motion.

MoCap technologies provide a complete 3D area where only the marked objects are tracked while ignoring the rest of the scenery. In optical-based systems, it is possible to have an unobstructed view of a large area, if multiple cameras are used in a structured environment without many occlusions (typically a studio). The IMU MoCap systems are a bit different in the sense that they do not directly measure position and displacement, but acceleration. Each IMU is comprised of an accelerometer, a magnetometer, and a gyroscope (Bachmann et al. 2004; Brigante et al. 2011) that provide acceleration measurements in 3D with respect to Earth's magnetic field.

Although they provide more indirect measurements and are sensitive to magnetic interference, they can provide practical solutions in environments with multiple occlusions, such as in a craft workshop, because the wearable markers are the sensors as well. Thereby no structured environment is required. Visual Tracking technologies use camera-type sensors to record a subject's motion, and for this reason, are quite unobtrusive. These sensors are typically video cameras (RGB sensor), possibly with the addition of a depth camera[1] (RGBD sensor). Motion is estimated in 3D, by processing the visual stream, distinguishing the subject from the rest of the imaged scene, and fitting a 3D deformable model into the acquired visual data. The cost of the unobtrusive nature of these methods is the treatment of occlusions and the inference of subject motion that is not imaged, due to these occlusions. These methods have been the focus of multiple works in Computer Vision and considerable progress has already been achieved in the last decade.

Regardless of the technology used to acquire the recordings, the resulting data are a chain of coordinate frames and the difference in position and orientation between them. In our context, we follow a generic approach, meaning we can support the results of any motion capture technology. This is of great value, as any visualization of movement comes from an abstraction of the movements, which can then be used in various domains, ranging from cartoon movement to instructions on how to assemble furniture.

3D Reconstruction for Digitization

3D reconstruction is the process of capturing the shape and appearance of real objects. The capabilities of the different technologies vary in terms of several criteria that must be considered and balanced when formulating appropriate campaign strategies. The 3D reconstruction of physical objects has been improved with laser scanning and photogrammetry, digitizing tangible artifacts for cultural heritage and archeological sites. Each methodology proposes a different approach to face the challenge of digitization for visualization or preservation purposes. Papaefthymiou et al. (2018) compared the latest software and hardware techniques for rapid reconstruction of real humans using RGB and RGBD cameras suitable for Virtual, Augmented (AR), or Mixed Reality (MR) experiences. In the context of our approach, we can use any 3D reconstruction that results in a correct, 3D model of a tool. We are namely not bound by any restrictions regarding which 3D reconstruction technique will be used.

10.2.2   Motion Visualization

Motion visualization in 3D has been achieved using various approaches, such as key frame extraction, converting a skeleton-based motion or animated mesh to a

---

[1] Depth cameras are standard RGB cameras that use a separate sensor that emits infrared (IR) light in a specific pattern and reads the deformation as it is being reflected back, producing a depth image that shows the distance of surfaces imaged by the RGB camera from the depth sensor.

key frame-based representation (Huang et al. 2005), or by selecting a representative moment from a performance and producing a narrative image as output (Wang et al. 2019). For human motion, "action summarization" is often used, producing motion effects in still image frames (Assa et al. 2005). An important parameter is depth information of animations for summarization of 3D animations in a single image, extracting the most important frames from the animation sequence based on their contribution to the overall motion-gradient (Lee et al. 2012).

10.2.3 Authoring Tools for Experiences and Tool Usage Demonstration

An authoring tool encapsulates various functionalities and features for the development of a specific product. The software architecture of such a system empowers users/programmers with the necessary tools for content creation to (a) support users with intuitive and easy to use methodologies (visual scripting, editors) and (b) provide advanced users with enhanced tools to extend the capabilities of the system.

M.A.G.E.S ™ (Papagiannakis et al. 2018) is a platform for tool usage demonstration, proposing a VR SDK to deliver psychomotor VR surgical training. The system generates a fail-safe environment for mastering skills and tracking abilities. The platform supports a visual scripting editor, scene customization plugins, custom VR software patterns, and Unity editor tools for rapid prototyping of VR training scenarios. In addition, the M.A.G.E.S ™ platform offers ToolManager, a unique plugin designed for usage and manipulation of tools in VR environments. Utilizing ToolManager, a developer can transform any 3D model of a tool (pliers, hammer, scalpel, drills, etc.) into a fully functional and interactive asset, ready to use in VR applications. After the tool generation, users can interact with it in the VE and use it to complete specific tasks following recorded directions. ToolManager supports additional features, such as the re-initialization of the tool if the user drops it accidentally, sound effects and animations for electric tools, and finally flashing visual indicators to inform the user which tool to select to complete a task among others.

Recent approaches focus on the creation of tools to enhance the development with additional features. In more detail, ExProtoVAR (Pfeiffer-Leßmann and Pfeiffer 2018) is a lightweight tool to generate interactive experiences in AR, for designers and non-programers who do not have much technical background in AR interfaces. ARTIST (Kotis 2019) is a platform featuring methods and tools for real-time interaction between non-human and human characters to generate reusable, low cost, and optimized MR experiences. This project proposes a code-free development environment for the deployment and implementation of MR applications while using semantic data from heterogeneous resources. RadEd (Xiberta and Boada 2016) features a new web-based teaching framework with an embedded smart editor to create case-based exercises for image interaction, such as attaching labels and selecting specific parts of the image, and taking measurements. It is an assistive tool for complex training courses like radiology.

In the context of this research work, an alternative approach is presented that allows the inference of simple tool usage based on the postures obtained from MoCap data. Using this approach, the 3D model of a tool can be associated with the Avatar representing the VH in the VE, by applying suitable rotation and translation operations.

10.2.4 Embodied Agents—Virtual Humans

Virtual characters, and in particular VHs, constitute an important aspect of 3D applications, due to our familiarity with a human-like individual. They have already been used in literature as narrators (Zikas et al. 2016a), virtual audiences (Chollet et al. 2016), and in our case demonstrators of tool usage. We can distinguish two different styles in the representation of VHs: (a) human-like and (b) cartoon style Avatars, each one serving a different purpose and fitting into specific applications.

In the context of VEs, VHs have already been utilized for explaining physical and procedural human tasks (Rickel and Johnson 1999), simulating dangerous situations (Traum and Rickel 2002), group and crowd behavior (Zikas et al. 2016b), and assisting users during navigation, both by showing where relevant objects/places are and by providing users with additional information (Chittaro et al. 2003). Moreover, VHs offer a possible solution to the problem of unstructuredness (Economou et al. 2000), which requires the user to take the initiative both in exploring the environment and interacting with its parts. This lack of proper assistance clashes with the traditional learning scenario, where a real teacher structures the presentation of material and learning activities (Hertz-Lazarowitz and Shachar 1990). VHs can provide a solution by acting as an embodied teacher. While it is not feasible to provide a human tutor for every learner in the real world, embodied agents can aid anyone with access to a computer, enabling an individualized instruction for a massive number of learners.

Regarding the different styles of VHs, human-like avatars are more closely related to users due to their natural appearance. However, imperfect human-likeness can provoke dislike or strangely familiar feelings of eeriness and revulsion in observers, a phenomenon known as the uncanny valley (Mori 1970). The same principle is applied not only in the visual representation of a VH, but also in the way of moving in 3D space. Studies suggested that interaction and animation can overcome the valley in affinity due to matching and common human non-verbal cues (Seymour et al. 2017). VHs are usually more complex to animate since they consist of humanoid skeletons with more joints than cartoon Avatars. The animation process needs to be precise and with high realism to avoid the uncanny valley effect. In contrast, cartoon style Avatars represent a simplified version of human characters, leading to low complexity in generation and animation processes. Cartoon Avatars are mainly used in applications designed with a similar cartoony style to match their environment.

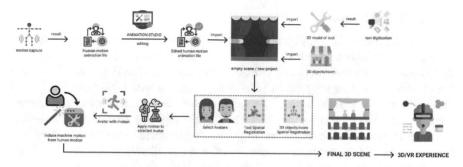

Fig. 10.1 Overview of our pipeline

However, this design style reflects limitations on the usage of cartoon Avatars in realistic environments, making human-like Avatars ideal for such scenarios.

In our platform, we decided to use realistic, human-like VHs for a number of reasons. First of all, tools are designed to be handled by humans, thus making the human hand ideal to interact with them in a natural way. Most cartoon style Avatars do not have five fingers to avoid the uncanny valley, resulting in poor and unrealistic handling capabilities with tools. Additionally, we wanted to develop a realistic representation of tool usage, i.e., a simulation for interacting with tools in 3D environments; thus, utilizing human-like Avatars was the preferred choice.

10.3   The Proposed Pipeline: From Motion Capture to Motion Visualization

This section presents our pipeline, from the MoCap of the human movement to an authored 3D scene which includes the Avatar(s), the tools, and various 3D objects, as well as the motion of the Avatar and the tool they use. In the beginning, this scene is empty, and subsequently, the Avatar, the tool, and finally the surrounding environment (room and 3D objects) are added. Furthermore, the Avatar may use different tools throughout the execution of a Motion Vocabulary Item (MVI), or interchange between tools. An MVI is used in the context of this research work to represent an instance of a movement that is encoded in a BVH file and can be used to represent a specific action or part of an action. MVIs can be combined and interleaved to represent entire procedures and are considered building blocks of a Motion Vocabulary (MV). The MV in turn can be used to create "sentences" that encode different actions and procedures. As a result, the MV can be used to encode a wider variation of actions and combinations of actions than the initial MoCap data used for its implementation. An overview of our pipeline is visible in Fig. 10.1.[2]

---

[2]This Figure has been designed using resources from Flaticon.com.

Step 1: Motion Capture

The first requirement is a MoCap file, which represents the human movement. As was analyzed in the Related Work section, there are various ways to procure a MoCap, and all of them can work in our context. For the purposes of testing TooltY, we used MoCap files that were the product of motion capturing with a NANSENSE©[3] R2 motion capture suit, in the context of motion capture sessions that took place during the second plenary meeting of the Mingei H2020 EU project at Haus der Seidenkultur in Krefeld Germany[4]. For the hammering activity presented in the TooltY demo, we used an open BVH dataset from outworldz[5] and specifically package 60–75[6] file 62_08.bvh. The product is a BVH animation file, which is used in our editor.

Step 2: Tool Digitization

Another prerequisite is the digitized form of the tool(s) that will be used. For this, various approaches for 3D reconstruction for digitization can be used, as described in the corresponding section in the Related Work presentation. The result of the digitization is a 3D model that represents the surface geometry and appearance of the object and is, typically, encoded as a textured mesh of triangles (e.g., in VRML or FXB file format). While we can use the model of any digitized tool, some cases require post-processing. For instance, in the case of scissors, post-processing is needed to make the tool deformable, in order to introduce joints that describe its deformation. In the context of experiments, several 3D models were used coming both from 3D reconstructions of physical objects and from online sources.[7] For complementarity, we used 3D models of both non-deformable (i.e., hammer) and deformable (i.e., scissors) tools.

Step 3: Editing of the MoCap (BVH file) in Animation Studio

For editing the MoCap animation files, we use a BHV editor, developed in-house, called Animation Studio (Partarakis et al. 2020). Animation Studio allows visualization, editing, and annotation of 3D animation files, obtained by motion capture or visual tracking. In the case of visual tracking, temporally corresponding video can be also edited. The application allows the user to isolate animation segments and the associated video for further annotation, as well as the synthesis of composite animation files and videos from such segments. Pertinent annotation software exists in the linguistics domain (The Language Archive) but does not stream for video and motion capture. Using Animation Studio, segments of the BVH input can be isolated and exported to test different "atomic" scenarios (e.g., hand movement when hammering a nail), simplify the input, or to allow the in-depth analysis of certain scenarios. For

---

[3] https://www.nansense.com/.

[4] https://seidenkultur.de/.

[5] https://www.outworldz.com/Secondlife/Posts/CMU/.

[6] https://www.outworldz.com/Secondlife/Posts/CMU/cmuconvert-daz-60-75.zip.

[7] www.thingiverse.com.

the demo of ToolY, Animation Studio was used to create the MVIs for the case of operating a hammer and scissors.

Step 4: Start ToolY

When starting ToolY, first a new project has to be created, which loads an empty scene. After editing the MoCap files, they can be imported to ToolY, along with the 3D models for tools and any desired objects. ToolY has some predefined ready-to-use content that users can browse through in their corresponding collections: Avatars, Human Motions, Tools, Rooms, and 3D Objects. Additionally, users can choose to add their own files to any of these collections.

Step 5: Selecting an Avatar

The Avatar representing the VH plays a very important role in our concept, as it is the actor executing the movements representing the tool usage, thus bringing the whole process to life. The user can choose from a selection of available Avatars. ToolY is built using the Unity 3D game engine, and thus Avatars created using a plethora of 3D Computer Graphics and Animation Creation editors can be imported (e.g., 3DStudioMax, Fusion 360, etc.). For the purposes of the ToolY demo presented by this research work, Poser Pro 11,[8] as well as Adobe Fuse,[9] were employed for the creation of the two (2) Avatars visible in Fig. 10.2. These avatars were exported from Poser and Fuse and then imported to the developed platform as resources that can be selected and assigned to a simulation scenario. The user can also choose to upload their own Avatar to use as the VH, provided that it is rigged (i.e., it has a humanoid skeleton). After an Avatar for the VH has been selected, it can be added to the scene.

Step 6: Application of motion to the Avatar

After a suitable Avatar has been chosen, the user can apply on it a single or multiple human motion animations. Each animation is mapped through the correspondence of the joints, between the humanoid-type rig (skeleton) of the Avatar, and the joints of the humanoid skeleton resulting from the motion capture. The result of this process can be previewed both using the selected Avatar and in the form of a primitive Avatar animation. The latter is used to help users visualize animation problems (e.g., elbows are getting inside the body when movement is previewed using a certain avatar). This could mean for example, that the avatar's torso is too narrow. This is a well-studied problem in Computer Graphics, known as motion retargeting, with various research solutions (Monzani et al. 2000; Dariush et al. 2008; Hecker et al. 2008). In the scope of this work, we decided to solve the problem offline, by utilizing Unity's Avatar Muscle & Settings,[10] for configuration of the degrees of freedom of joints in the skeleton of the Avatar. In more detail, it allows tweaking of the character's range of motion to ensure the character deforms convincingly, free from visual artifacts or self-overlaps. However, we would like to explore other possibilities for online

---

[8] https://www.posersoftware.com/.

[9] https://www.adobe.com/gr_en/products/fuse.html.

[10] https://docs.unity3d.com/Manual/MuscleDefinitions.html.

Fig. 10.2 Screenshot of the 2 VHs inside TooltY, holding (**a**) a hammer and (**b**) scissors

motion retargeting in our future work, to minimize the manual and offline tweaking the users of TooltY are required to perform. An example of an Avatar operating a hammer can be seen in Fig. 10.3.

Step 7: Introducing a tool

The user can add to the scene any digitized tool from the available collection of tools, corresponding to the selected human motion animation for the Avatar, as well as their own 3D models of tools.

Fig. 10.3 Screenshots of a VH holding and operating a hammer

Tool $\mathbf{o}$ is represented by a mesh of triangles, which are encoded in 2 lists. The first list is the list of vertices, denoted by $\mathbf{l_v}$ and the second is the list of triangles, denoted by $\mathbf{l_t}$.

To add a tool, the following are required:

- A grip point $\mathbf{p_a}$ on the hand of the Avatar.
- A preferred grip on the tool, denoted as $\mathbf{g}$.
- Two points on the front and back faces of the desired grip point of the tool, denoted as $\mathbf{p_f}$ and $\mathbf{p_b}$, respectively.
- A grip center $\mathbf{p_c}$ is automatically calculated as the mid-point of $\mathbf{p_f}$ and $\mathbf{p_b}$.
- The projection of $\mathbf{p_c}$ to the top side of the bounding box of the tool $\mathbf{o}$, denoted as $\mathbf{p_g}$, also automatically calculated.

Regarding $\mathbf{p_a}$, $\mathbf{g}$, $\mathbf{p_f}$ and $\mathbf{p_b}$, they are already calculated when referring to tools in the available collection, otherwise they need to be provided by the user adding their own 3D model.

Below, translations are encoded as 3×1 matrices and rotations as 3×3 rotation matrices.

The coordinate frame of the hand $\mathbf{C_h}$ is the coordinate system on the selected joint of the Avatar (in our case, its hand) at the current configuration of the avatar. This frame is determined at each moment in time, by the animation that the avatar executes.

A grip $\mathbf{g}$ is a configuration of the Avatar's hand that is represented by a series of rotations of the Avatar's joints. The number of rotations is determined by the skeleton of the Avatar and the values of these rotations by the animation that the avatar executes.

A tool posture is the rotation that orients the tool in the hand of the Avatar as intended by this posture. The posture is represented by rotation matrix $\mathbf{R}$. Matrix $\mathbf{R}$ aligns the $\mathbf{C_h}$ with $\mathbf{C_o}$, by rotating the tool in-place, by $\mathbf{R}$. The rotation center is $\mathbf{p_c}$, and R needs to be an "in place" rotation to avoid rotation about the world center. R is determined by the current orientation of the hand. It should be noted that we choose to rotate around $\mathbf{p_c}$, since that is the point from which the Avatar holds the tool.

Let $\mathbf{b_o}$ the bounding box of tool $\mathbf{o}$. The user names the faces of $\mathbf{b_o}$ as front/back, top/bottom, and left/right. This determines the coordinate frame $\mathbf{C_o}$ for tool $\mathbf{o}$. This frame is represented by rotation matrix $\mathbf{R_o}$ that aligns the $\mathbf{C_o}$ to the world coordinate frame. In the case of tools in the available collection, these have already been calculated, i.e., the user does not need to use the User Interface to name these points.

Typically, the Avatar and the 3D model of the tool are not in the same scale, metric unit, and coordinate system. Tool $\mathbf{o}$ is brought to the correct scale by scaled by factor $\mathbf{s}$; the scaled tool is denoted as $\mathbf{o_s}$. Let $\mathbf{s}$ the scalar that adjusts the scale and metric unit of the model.

To emulate the grip of a tool, grip $\mathbf{g}$ is applied to the avatar.

The transformation that brings the tool in the hand of the Avatar is as follows:

Let $\mathbf{x}$ a 3D point of $\mathbf{o}$.

Let $\mathbf{T} = \mathbf{p_a} - \mathbf{p_c}$ the translation that brings $\mathbf{p_c}$ and $\mathbf{p_a}$ to coincidence.

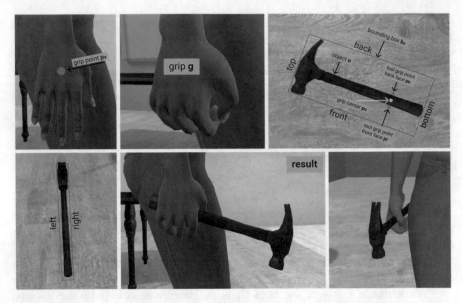

Fig. 10.4 Display of grip points and resulting attachment of hammer to the VH hand

The required (see above) in-place rotation is applied to **o** about $\mathbf{p_c}$. The operation required is $(\mathbf{R*(x-p_c))} + \mathbf{p_c}$, where '*' denotes matrix multiplication.

In the case of our demo in Unity, where the VH is operating a hammer, it is important to note that the default pivot is the center of the mesh of the object, and it is according to this point that any transformation is applied on the object. Therefore, in order to manipulate the object by $\mathbf{p_c}$, we created an intermediate (invisible) object, as a parent in the hierarchy of the tool, while preserving the world coordinates of the tool. Thus, transformation formulas are applied to the custom pivot point, instead of directly on the object.

Figure 10.4 below aims at explaining the aforementioned concepts, notations, and operations.

Step 8: Addition and spatial registration of surrounding environment/3D objects

The user can add to the scene 3D objects, either from the available collection or by importing new ones. Such objects can either be craft workspace objects (i.e., pieces of furniture) or the room (surrounding environment) itself i.e., the 3D environment where the scene is set. As with the 3D models of the tools, the room and the objects imported may derive from heterogeneous sources and models, and thus spatial registration may need to take place, i.e., the 3D models may need to be scaled, rotated, or translated.

Step 9: Tool manipulation from human motion

We do not have MoCap for the movement of the tools, so we induce the tool motion, from the human motion. We argue that it is easier and more cost-efficient to induce the tool's motion since the tool may not be rigid (e.g., scissors) or/and might not be usable if we add motion capture instrumentation on it. For example, if sensors for motion capturing are put on a scissor, it might not be possible for the operator to hold it and use it easily or as they would normally do. Our approach aims to solve such issues, by allowing generalization, as we can induce the motion of any simple handheld tool, by that of the humans, deriving from the MoCap.

Step 10: Play the scene in 3D

After following these steps, the user can choose to play the scene, i.e., trigger the execution of the animations that comprise the MV. Thus, the VH comes to life, enacting the use of the tool, in the desired 3D environment. We argue that the proposed approach provides positive feedback regarding its validity and the possibility to further generalize and extend it. This could ultimately lead to an improved version of TooltY, where any handicraft process involving the manipulation of simple hand tools can be authored and visualized.

Step 11: Experience the scene in 3D or VR

After the 3D scene is ready, it can be deployed for use in 3D or VR, where users can have immersive experiences regarding the handicraft procedure in question. Namely, TooltY produces VEs that can be experienced in 3D or through immersion in VR, where the VHs demonstrates how to execute a handicraft, step by step. In more detail, users experiencing this can see the hands of the Avatar in VR, showing them the tools they need to use and how to operate them, to complete an action correctly.

10.4   Results and Contribution

The result of this research work is TooltY, an authoring platform that allows the authoring of tool-usage experiences. These scenes can subsequently be exported as 3D or VR immersive experiences, so that simple handicrafts can be demonstrated to the user.

Regarding the implementation of the authoring platform, it was developed in Unity, and presents the following main functionalities:

- Allows users to use existing Avatars available in the platform's collection, or upload new ones to the collection, for use as the VHs enacting the tool-using task.
- Allows users to use existing tools available in the platform's collection, or upload new ones to the collection, for the objects used in the handicraft they wish to demonstrate.
- Allows users to use existing rooms and objects available in the platform's collection, or upload new ones to the collection, for the room used as a background scene and the objects in this room.
- Allows users to use existing MoCap files for the VHs, or upload new ones to the collection, for the human motion.

- When uploading new content, users have to configure specific details:
  - Avatars need to have a humanoid skeleton (if they don't have one the user needs to add it),
  - For the tools, they need to define p_a, g, p_f, p_b, and the faces of the bounding box b_o as front/back, top/bottom, and left/right, as explained in Step 7 of the TooltY pipeline.
- Users can add Avatars and tools to the scene, link them, and select the suitable human motion for the VH, to enact the tool usage. The desired tool is correctly positioned in the hand of the Avatar, by performing translation and rotation operations, as described in Step 7 of the TooltY pipeline.
- Users can add different background scenes (rooms) and objects to the scene.
- Users can export the final scene, for 3D and VR immersive experience of the tool usage.

To achieve high-quality rendering for the displayed tools, we utilized global illumination as the main rendering pipeline. Our approach focuses on high-quality visualization of used tools, aiming to deliver a realistic interaction with handheld tools, improving the visuals, and providing a high-fidelity final product. We applied the same rendering techniques to the VHs, highlighting the interaction with the available tools.

Our methodology follows a modular pipeline, thus transferring the generated 3D application to a VR immersive experience is straightforward. The proposed solution contains a list of well-defined steps to generate an animated human-tool behavior. TooltY facilitates an authoring tool regardless of the deployed medium since the same principles are applied for both 3D and VR applications. To prepare the generated scene for VR, minimal changes are needed including the initialization of a VR camera into the VE representing the headset. In addition, TooltY generates a fully personalized virtual world, giving users the ability to customize both the human character along with the tool, as well as the surrounding 3D environment. This customization process improves the virtual scene, offering a realistic representation of the environment, ideal for VR integration.

10.5   Future Work

This paper has presented an authoring platform for combining motion capture with 3D reconstruction, to present tool usage in 3D environments, in contexts such as handicrafts and assembly operations. The usage of these tools is carried out by Virtual Humans, whose movements are the result of the MoCaps, using digitized tools from the 3D reconstruction. For the motion of the tools, a novel approach is used, for inducing the tool motion from the human motion capture. This work is part of a broader research effort, conducted in the context of the Mingei project.

Our future work includes (i) the further development of the current VR experience to incorporate a VR training module, so that users can be immersed in a learning environment, where the technique and usage of each tool can be demonstrated and subsequently executed by the user, including feedback (ii) exploring the effects the tool usage could have on the scene (e.g., how the hammer is deforming a nail), and (iii) the addition of a Storytelling module, where a second VH can explain the usage of the tool and its story, and optionally narrate its usage through history during the demonstration. For the orchestration of the narration, as well as the dialogue between the VHs, the CasandRA framework (Stefanidi et al. 2019) will be used. Finally, we plan to conduct user evaluation experiments, to assess the usability of the authoring platform, as well as of the produced immersive module, and the ability of the users to learn how to perform a handicraft with its help.

Acknowledgements This work has been supported by the EU Horizon 2020 Innovation Action under grant agreement No. 822336 (Mingei). The authors are grateful to project partner ARMINES (Association pour la Recherche et le Developpement des Methodes et Processus Industriels) for the acquisition of MoCap data, and to the practitioner community of the Association of Friends of Haus der Seidenkultur (HdS), Krefeld, Germany for their collaboration. Finally, the authors would like to thank Nikolaos Patsiouras for his contribution to the technical discussions and development of the Toolt Y demo.

References

Assa J, Caspi Y, Cohen-Or D (2005) Action synopsis: pose selection and illustration. ACM Transa Graphics (TOG) 24:667–676

Bachmann ER, Yun X, Peterson CW (2004) An investigation of the effects of magnetic variations on inertial/magnetic orientation sensors. In: IEEE international conference on robotics and automation, 2004. Proceedings. ICRA'04. 2004. IEEE, pp 1115–1122

Brigante CM, Abbate N, Basile A et al (2011) Towards miniaturization of a MEMS-based wearable motion capture system. IEEE Trans Industr Electron 58:3234–3241

Chittaro L, Ranon R, Ieronutti L (2003) Guiding visitors of Web3D worlds through automatically generated tours. In: Proceedings of the eighth international conference on 3D Web technology. pp 27–38

Chollet M, Chandrashekhar N, Shapiro A, et al (2016) Manipulating the perception of virtual audiences using crowdsourced behaviors. In: International conference on intelligent virtual agents. Springer, pp 164–174

Dariush B, Gienger M, Arumbakkam A, et al (2008) Online and markerless motion retargeting with kinematic constraints. In: 2008 IEEE/RSJ international conference on intelligent robots and systems. IEEE, pp 191–198

Dewan P (2015) Words versus pictures: leveraging the research on visual communication. Partnership: Can J Lib Inform Pract Res 10

Economou D, Mitchell WL, Boyle T (2000) Requirements elicitation for virtual actors in collaborative learning environments. Comput Educ 34:225–239

Ferrington G, Loge K (1992) Virtual reality: a new learning environment. Comput Teacher 19:16–19

Hecker C, Raabe B, Enslow RW et al (2008) Real-time motion retargeting to highly varied user-created morphologies. ACM Trans Graph (TOG) 27:1–11

Hertz-Lazarowitz R, Shachar H (1990) Teachers' verbal behaviour in cooperative and whole-class instruction. Cooperat Learn Theory Res 77–94

Huang K-S, Chang C-F, Hsu Y-Y, Yang S-N (2005) Key probe: a technique for animation keyframe extraction. Visual Comput 21:532–541

Hussein M, Nätterdal C (2015) The benefits of virtual reality in education. A comparison Study

Ieronutti L, Chittaro L (2007) Employing virtual humans for education and training in X3D/VRML worlds. Comput Educ 49:93–109

Kotis K (2019) ARTIST-a real-time low-effort multi-entity interaction system for creating reusable and optimized MR experiences. Res Ideas Outcomes 5:

Lee H-J, Shin HJ, Choi J-J (2012) Single image summarization of 3D animation using depth images. Comput Anim Virtual Worlds 23:417–424

Monzani J-S, Baerlocher P, Boulic R, Thalmann D (2000) Using an intermediate skeleton and inverse kinematics for motion retargeting. In: Computer graphics forum. Wiley Online Library, pp 11–19

Mori M (1970) Bukimi no tani [the uncanny valley]. Energy 7:33–35

Papaefthymiou M, Kanakis ME, Geronikolakis E, et al (2018) Rapid reconstruction and simulation of real characters in mixed reality environments. In: Digital cultural heritage. Springer, pp 267–276

Papagiannakis G, Lydatakis N, Kateros S, et al (2018) Transforming medical education and training with vr using mages. In: SIGGRAPH Asia 2018 Posters. pp 1–2

Partarakis N, Zabulis X, Chatziantoniou A et al (2020) An approach to the creation and presentation of reference gesture datasets, for the preservation of traditional crafts. Appl Sci 10:7325

Pfeiffer-Leßmann N, Pfeiffer T (2018) ExProtoVAR: a lightweight tool for experience-focused prototyping of augmented reality applications using virtual reality. In: International conference on human-computer interaction. Springer, pp 311–318

Rickel J, Johnson WL (1999) Animated agents for procedural training in virtual reality: perception, cognition, and motor control. Appl Artif Intell 13:343–382

Seymour M, Riemer K, Kay J (2017) Interactive realistic digital avatars-revisiting the uncanny valley

Stefanidi E, Leonidis A, Partarakis N, Antona M (2019) CasandRA: a screenplay approach to dictate the behavior of virtual humans in AmI environments. In: International conference on human-computer interaction. Springer, pp 57–66

The Language Archive ELAN: annotation tool for audio and video recordings. In: ELAN: annotation tool for audio and video recordings. https://archive.mpi.nl/tla/elan. Accessed 19 Nov 2020

Traum D, Rickel J (2002) Embodied agents for multi-party dialogue in immersive virtual worlds. Proc First Int Joint Conf Auton Agents Multiagent Syst 2:766–773

Wang M, Guo S, Liao M et al (2019) Action snapshot with single pose and viewpoint. The Visual Comput 35:507–520

Wikipedia (2019) A picture is worth a thousand words. In: Wikipedia. https://en.wikipedia.org/w/index.php?title=A_picture_is_worth_a_thousand_words&oldid=909812483. Accessed 19 Nov 2020.

Xiberta P, Boada I (2016) A new e-learning platform for radiology education (RadEd). Comput Methods Programs Biomed 126:63–75

Zikas P, Bachlitzanakis V, Papaefthymiou M, et al (2016a) Mixed reality serious games and gamification for smart education. In: European conference on games based learning. Academic Conferences International Limited, p 805

Zikas P, Papaefthymiou M, Mpaxlitzanakis V, Papagiannakis G (2016b) Life-sized Group and Crowd simulation in Mobile AR. In: Proceedings of the 29th international conference on computer animation and social agents, pp 79–82

Chapter 11
Generating 3D Facial Expressions with Recurrent Neural Networks

Hyewon Seo and Guoliang Luo

Abstract Learning-based methods have proved effective at high-quality image synthesis tasks, such as content-preserving image rendering with different style, and the generation of new images depicting learned objects. Some of the properties that make neural networks suitable for such tasks, for example, robustness to the input's low-level feature, and the ability to retrieve contextual information, are also desirable in 3D shape domain. During last decades, data-driven methods have shown successful results in 3D shape modeling tasks, such as human face and body shape synthesis. Subtle, abstract properties on the geometry that are instantly detected by our eyes but are nontrivial to synthesize have successfully been achieved by tuning a shape model built from example shapes. Recent successful learning techniques, e.g., deep neural networks, also exploit this shape model, since the regular grid assumption with 2D images does not have a straightforward equivalent in the common shape representation in 3D, thus do not easily generalize to 3D shapes. Here, we concentrate on the 3D facial expression generation task, an important problem in computer graphics and other application domains, where existing data-driven approaches mostly rely on direct shape capture or shape transfer. At the core of our approach is a recurrent neural network with a marker-based shape representation. The network is trained to estimate a sequence of pose change, thus generate a specific facial expression, by using a set of motion-captured facial expression sequences. Our technique promises to significantly improve the quality of generated expressions while extending the potential applicability of neural networks to sequence of 3D shapes.

H. Seo (✉)
CNRS-University of Strasbourg, Strasbourg, France
e-mail: seo@unistra.fr

G. Luo
East China Jiaotong University, Nanchang, China
e-mail: luoguoliang@ecjtu.edu.cn

© The Author(s), under exclusive license to Springer Nature Switzerland AG 2021
N. Magnenat Thalmann et al. (eds.), *Intelligent Scene Modeling and Human-Computer Interaction*, Human–Computer Interaction Series,
https://doi.org/10.1007/978-3-030-71002-6_11

11.1 Introduction

Facial shape modeling is a long-sought subject in computer graphics and computer animation, with interesting applications in many areas. Traditionally, facial shape has been sculpted or interactively designed by CG artists by using CG softwares that are equipped with geometric shape interpolation Kalra et al. (1992) or physics-based simulation of muscle actions (Terzopoulos and Waters 1990). During 90s computational methods started to appear that aim at automatic reconstruction of 3D shape models from 2D photo images (Lee et al. 2000) or 3D range scans (Lee et al. 1995). Often, only the static shape can be modeled realistically, and the animation of the reconstructed models has been handled as a separate process with devoted techniques for motion capture. Recent evolutions in the technology for capturing moving shapes have changed this paradigm, with multi-view acquisition systems that allow the simultaneous capture of shapes and motions (DeCarlo and Metaxas 1996; Pighin et al. 1999). Similarly, recent 4D (3D + time) laser-scanners now enable the capture of 3D human face geometry under motion (Beeler et al. 2011; Cosker et al. 2011). These techniques can be assisted by deformation transfer or animation retargeting (Noh and Fidaleo 2000; Blanz et al. 2003; Vlasic et al. 2006), which helps reuse the captured animation on new facial models. This line of research has evolved to data-driven methods that make use of a set of 3D shape datasets and the priors collected from the data shapes. A common strategy employed by data-driven methods is to learn the model by performing a dimension reduction, often principal component analysis (PCA), on a dataset of face scans. It goes with several different names such as subspace, or morphable model (MM) or statistical model, all of which refer to a same technique that captures shape and texture variations in observed human faces with a set of basis. Based on the *linear model* that captures shape and texture variations in observed human faces with a set of basis, they offer powerful modeling functionalities: A complete 3D model can be reconstructed by using only a single 2D photo as input, and generation of new face models or modifying existing ones can be performed by adjusting a few parameters whose mapping to a full facial model has been found from the database. We summarize MM in Sect. 11.2.1, and review other shape representations considerable for facial modeling in Sect. 11.2.2.

These days, recent deep learning techniques start to replace linear function approximators with deep neural networks (DNNs) in facial modeling tasks, to achieve improved performance. Most of these methods, on the other hand, have focused on the optimal 2D to 3D shape estimation, i.e., generation of a 3D shape from a 2D input photo showing a face of arbitrary pose. Typically, the neural network learns and estimates the basel face model (BFM) parameters (Paysan et al. 2009) of the 3D face model from 2D photos (Garrido et al. 2016; Jiang et al. 2018). Compared to linear models like BFM, the DNN uses larger datasets spanning a large variety of not only shape and texture, but also pose or expression so that the network can learn the corresponding parameters of the 3D shape from an arbitrary, 'in-the-wild' facial image. More importantly, it can learn *nonlinear model*, the variation of facial shapes due to the facial identity, and due to the expression or pose change of a face. In Sect. 11.2.3, we review state-of-the-art facial modelers adopting DNNs.

One observation is that through all these works, the expression has been modeled as separate, independent entity from the shape identity. The expression-driven facial deformation is learned as a separate phenomenon from their shape identity-driven variation, and then the two modalities are combined when a new shape is synthesized. Similarly, from an observable shape that often comes with the shape identity and the expression mixed together, a modeler decouples the two entities. Conveniently, the extracted expression component from one person can be easily combined with or transferred to another facial shape, to depict the same semantic expression on the new shape identity. This model is very powerful yet simple, but it cannot capture the potential correlation between two modalities. For example, the shape change elicited by a smiling expression on a young Asian face will be the same as on an old, Caucasian face. In Sect. 11.2.3, we address a more challenging alternative, i.e., modeling the subtle correlation between the facial expression sequence and the shape identity.

11.2 Facial Shape Modeling

11.2.1 Facial Shape Space

In their 3D morphable model work that are also known as the basel face model (BFM), Blanz and Vetter (1999) have constructed a subspace for facial identity variation to reduce the dense facial geometry (several thousand vertices per face). Using a common polygon mesh representation, each vertex's position and color vary between example faces, but its semantic identity remains the same—A vertex located at the tip of the nose in one face should be located at the tip of the nose in all faces. To obtain a consistent representation across all examples, they use a modified version of 2D optical flow in the cylindrical parameterization of head scans. Consequently, a face is represented by a shape-vector $\mathbf{S} = (x_1, y_1, z_1, x_2 \ldots y_n, z_n)^T \in R^{3n}$ and a texture-vector $\mathbf{T} = (r_1, g_1, b_1, r_2 \ldots g_n, b_n)^T \in R^{3n}$, containing the coordinates and the color values of its n vertices, respectively. From the m exemplar faces that are in correspondence, PCA is applied to m shape vectors and m texture vectors. The facial shape is then described in the space of a reduced dimension, as a vector of weights α to the eigenshapes $\mathbf{s}_i$ i.e., the eigenvectors of the covariance matrix of $\mathbf{S}_i$. The facial color is similarly described as a vector of weights β to the eigencolors $\mathbf{t}_i$:

$$\mathbf{S}(\bar{\alpha}) = \bar{\mathbf{S}} + \sum_{i=1} \alpha_i \cdot \mathbf{s}_i, \ \mathbf{T}(\bar{\beta}) = \bar{\mathbf{T}} + \sum_{i=1} \beta_i \cdot \mathbf{t}_i,$$

where $\bar{\mathbf{S}}$ and $\bar{\mathbf{T}}$ denotes the mean shape and texture, respectively. In this facial subspace, arbitrary new faces can be generated by varying these parameters (vectors of weights) that control the shape and texture. Model fitting to a given image is formulated as an optimization by minimizing the image-space discrepancy between the input 2D image and the rendered image of the 3D face synthesized with the current parameter set. Thanks to the learnt linear model, the solution space becomes compact and constrained, thus solvable by common optimization techniques.

High-level facial attributes (femaleness, concave or hooked nose, thickness of eyebrow, etc.) have been shown to be manipulated by forming shape and texture vectors ΔS and ΔT that, when added to or subtracted from a face, will change a specific attribute while keeping all other attributes as constant as possible. Such attribute vectors are computed as weighted sums of manually labeled faces. Expression is handled as one of facial attributes. Formally,

$$\Delta S = \sum_{i=1} \mu_i (S_i - \bar{S}), \ \Delta T = \sum_{i=1} \mu_i (T_i - \bar{T}), \qquad (11.1)$$

where μ_i is the attribute value labeled to (S_i, T_i), and $\bar{S}, \bar{T}$ are mean shape and texture vectors.

11.2.2 Other Shape Representations

The 3D shape representation methods can be categorized into the global and the local feature based. The global shape descriptors, such as the shape histogram (Ankerst et al. 1999) and histogram of gradient (Scherer et al. 2010), are based on the global statistical analysis to represent an entire object (Ankerst et al. 1999; Scherer et al. 2010). On the contrary, local feature descriptors detect local distinctive features, which are more precise and robust against the occlusions. Below we summarize a number of local shape representations that have been adopted for the 3D face data.

Key-points: The representative points for 3D faces can be either the distinctive points based on the quantified measurement of the tension, normal, curvature of each point, or the anatomical landmarks on/around eyes, nose, mouth, etc. For example, shape diameter function is the averaged radial segment length at each point (Shapira et al. 2008); Heat Kernel Signature measures the energy of heat distribution which reflects the local surface shape at each point (Sun et al. 2009); Spin image encodes each point with respect to the normal vector (Johnson 1997); shape index (histogram of surface normal) can be used to detect the landmarks at the eye corners and the nose tip (Canavan et al. 2015). The key-point extraction process, however, can be computationally heavy and sensitive to occlusions.

Feature-curve: Based on the precise nose tip point detection, typical feature curves of 3D face include the iso-depth contour, the iso-geodesic curve, and the radial curves. The quality of these curves highly relies on the correctness of the nose tip detection, and occlusions may cause the incompleteness of the curves (Samad and Iftekharuddin 2016).

Local surface based: The local surface-based feature descriptors are normally based on the local statistics of the regional geometrical properties such as normal, geodesic distance, curvatures, etc. (Li and Zhang 2007). Compared to the key-point-based methods, such methods are more robust for representing facial expressions.

We note that most of the existing feature representations for 3D faces are for facial recognition, but they may be not directly applicable for 3D face reconstruction or synthetics. For example, given a 3D face model of point clouds, we can easily compute the per-vertex curvatures, which can be applied to visualize the 3D face and recognize the facial expression. However, the reverse process is not quite possible, i.e., one cannot reconstruct the 3D face by using the computed curvatures.

11.2.3 Modern Facial Modelers Using DNN

Recently, the revolutionary development of deep learning started to replace linear function approximators with deep neural networks to achieve drastically improved performance. Most of these methods, on the other hand, are devoted to the generation of a 3D shape from a 2D input photo showing a face of arbitrary pose. Typically, the neural network learns and estimates the BFM parameters of the 3D face model from 2D photos (Garrido et al. 2016; Jiang et al. 2018). Compared to linear models like BFM (Sect. 11.2.1), the DNN uses larger datasets spanning a large variety of not only shape and texture, but also pose or expression so that the network can learn the corresponding parameters of the 3D shape from an arbitrary, 'in-the-wild' facial image. More importantly, it can learn nonlinear model, the variation of facial shapes due to the facial identity, and to the expression or pose change of a face.

E2FAR (End to end 3D Face Reconstruction with DNN) by Dou et al. (2017) shows how a trained DNN takes a 2D facial image as input and predicts the optimal identity and expression parameters to minimize the error in the 3D space—the difference between the reconstructed 3D face and the ground truth (the shape that has been used to produce the 2D input image) (Dou et al. 2017). They make use of the BFM without any encoder that extracts shape parameters from input images and concentrate on learning the mapping function $f : I \rightarrow \alpha_d, \alpha_e$, that maps the 2D image I to the BFM shape parameters. With only shapes considered, and the network learns (1) identity parameters α_d, and (2) expression parameters α_e.

Model-based deep convolutional facial autoencoder (MOFA) (Tewari et al. 2017) shows a good example of commonly adopted NN architecture, i.e., the combination of a CNN encoder and model-based decoder. The CNN encoder learns to extract semantically meaningful parameters from a single image. Similarly to Dou et al. (2017), they use the facial subspace based on the Basel Facial Model, and once again, pose, shape, expression, texture, illumination are parametrized independently. Given a scene description in the form of a semantic code vector, the decoder generates a synthetic image of the corresponding face. The loss function is defined as a photometric error between the synthesized image and the input image. The error combines three error terms, landmark error; photometric error, and statistical regularization error, as is often the case in similar optimization setting (Fig. 11.1).

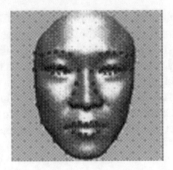

Fig. 11.1 83 markers have been defined in our facial mocap data (BU-3DFE) (Yin et al. 2006)

Nonlinear 3D face morphable model (Nonlinear 3DMM) operates in a similar fashion, with the decoder-encoder architecture (Tran and Liu 2018). They train their own encoder to extract feature descriptors on the given scene, and use texture image instead of per-vertex color for the sake of better preservation of spatial relation among pixels. Given a set of 2D facial images, an encoder is learned to estimate the shape, texture and projection parameters, and two DNs (decoders) to decode the estimated parameters to a 3D shape and texture, respectively, with an objective that the rendered image with the encoded parameters can approximate the original image well.

Among a few works that adopt other representation than BFM is that of Jackson et al. (2017). They convert the 3D face surface into binary 3D voxels, i.e., the voxels crossed by face surface with 1s, otherwise 0s. The conversion of the unstructured 3D face model into the structured volume form allows a direct adaptation of the advanced DNNs to 3D face data. In specific, they use DNNs to encode the projection process from 3D voxels to 2D images (Yang et al. 2017; Jackson et al. 2017). However, due to the computational costs, the size of the volume is kept small.

11.3 Facial Animation Modeling

Facial animation modeling has evolved along a similar path as the facial shape modeling, i.e., from interactive key-framing to capture-based reconstruction. Thanks to recent evolutions in the technology for capturing moving shapes, it is now possible to acquire full 4D shapes of human faces including geometry, motion, and appearance with advanced multi-view acquisition systems. However, most current techniques focus on modeling the shape instances in a frame-by-frame manner, and do not model the temporal aspect of the shape evolution.

Flame (Faces Learned with Articulated Model and Expressions) presents an extension of BFM to 4D facial model (Li et al. 2017). Given a 4D scans, displacements from a 3D template shape are modeled for each frame as a function of three decoupled parameters describing the shape identity, head pose, and expression. The temporal evolution is not modeled, i.e., the facial parameters have been found for each frame. Formally, the mapping function is defined as

$$M(\beta, \theta, \psi) : \mathbb{R}^{|\beta| \times |\theta| \times |\psi|} \rightarrow \mathbb{R}^{3N},$$

where β, θ, ψ are the shape identity, head pose, and expression parameters, and N is the number of vertices of the template shape. The facial parameters are found for each frame, i.e., the temporal evolution of the found parameters is not modeled

In their work on the facial reenactment, Kim et al. (2018) also reconstruct a sequence of 3D facial models from a video input, by fitting the BFM to each frame: The identity parameter set is estimated in the first frame and is kept constant throughout the frames, and all other parameters are estimated every frame. Again, the reconstruction as well as estimation is limited to the spatial domain of the facial shape.

In facial animation transfer (Blanz et al. 2003; Vlasic et al. 2006; Thies et al. 2015), source and target sequences of facial poses are analyzed to separate the identity, pose, and expression components in a frame-by-frame manner. Typically, the expression component is extracted from the source video and transferred to replace that of the target video. However, the transferred, expression-driven shape change is a direct function of the source face and its expression, neglecting the shape identity of the target face.

11.4   Learning-Based Generation of 3D Facial Expression Sequences

We build a facial expression estimator model by training a neural network that learns to generate facial expression sequences. Unlike existing methods that treat the expression data as a set of shape instances, we aim at modeling the temporal evolution of the facial shape. RNN seemed appropriate as it can learn temporal relation between consecutive frames. Initially, we considered generative adversarial network (GAN) (Goodfellow et al. 2014) as well, which has shown a superior performance on generating high-quality images based on the raw 2D image input (Goodfellow et al. 2014; Brock et al. 2019). However, this would require the additional preprocessing of time-normalization of the facial expression dataset, and its learning capability on temporal dependency may not be as good as RNN. For these reasons, we have adopted RNNs for our work.

11.4.1   RNN on Time Series Data

Our work builds on the recent success of deep neural networks in sequence data analysis. In particular, RNNs achieved promising results in processing and modeling sequential, time series data, such as text-to-text translation (Sutskever et al. 2014; Cho et al. 2014), scene description (Vinyals et al. 2015), and music composition (Boulanger-Lewandowski et al. 2012). Unlike many feedforward neural networks, an RNN maintains hidden internal states that is not only dependent on the current input, but also relies on the previous hidden state and hence the previous inputs. It takes inputs, updates its internal state through recurrent connection that spans adjacent time steps, and generates outputs at every time step iteratively. Therefore, the history of inputs affects the generation of outputs. Formally, the fixed-length hidden state $h(t)$ is updated with the current input $x(t)$ by using a nonlinear function f:

$$h(t + 1) = f(h(t), x(t)). \tag{11.2}$$

RNN training is similar to feedforward network straining in the sense that network parameters are updated incrementally via backpropagation. Since RNNs include recurrent edges that span adjacent time steps the same parameters are shared across all time steps, gradients at the current time step would affect gradient computation at the previous time steps. This process is called backpropatation through time (BPTT). In our work, we build our RNNs using LSTM units, which preserves gradients well through BPTT/layers and thus can deal well with long-term dependencies.

11.4.2   Learning to Generate 3D Facial Animations

Overview. Here, we leverage the well-known capability of a recurrent network to capture temporal information, in order to model the facial expression sequence modeling. We set our goal to generate new sequences to animate an arbitrary facial shape by using a trained network. We could have employed generative adversarial networks (GANs) instead (Goodfellow et al. 2014; Brock et al. 2018), but it would be computationally more expensive and less reliable for ensuring temporal fluidity. Indeed, an RNN is not only capable of learning temporal relation between frames but also more suitable for handling sequential data with arbitrary lengths. The main inspiration of our work comes from recent advances in neural image caption (NIC), which makes use of a deep CNN that encodes a given image into a fixed length vector representation, and uses the vector as the initial hidden state of a decoder RNN that generates the target caption sentences. Here, we propose to directly use the landmark locations of a neutral face as the initial input to a decoder RNN, as the representation of the facial geometry (landmark coordinate vectors) lies in the same dimensional space as the sequence data (landmark displacement vectors). Expression-specific prior is assumed, that is, each network is devoted to one specific facial expression elicited by a basic emotion.

Data preparation. We have used the facial mocap data from Binghamton University (BU-3DFE) Yin et al. (2006), consisting of 606 facial expression sequences captured from 101 people (58 females and 43 male subjects). For each subject, six universal facial expressions (anger, disgust, fear, happiness, sadness, and surprise) are elicited, whose shape and texture have been recorded at a video frame rate of

Fig. 11.2 Deep recurrent neural network architecture of our facial animation synthesizer. The rounded rectangles represent LSTM cells, each containing 128 neurons, and the rectangles fully connected layer. The solid lines represent weighted connections and the dashed lines predictions. The predicted marker displacements y_t are fed as input to RBF nets, which computes a deformation field

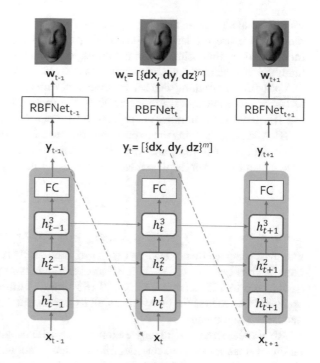

25 fps. Also provided is a sequence of 3D coordinates of 83 markers located on the face (Fig. 11.2). With a number of exceptions, most sequences begin and end with neutral head/face expression poses.

We use the marker displacements (i.e., offset coordinates from the previous frame), rather than absolute coordinates. Thus, from the original sequence data containing the ordered list of landmark coordinates, we generate landmark displacement data. Initially, we tried to decouple the head motion from the expression-driven deformation and removed the rigid motion in the landmark displacement data. However, we found from some early experiments that the head motion encoded in the landmark displacements actually increases the expressivity of generated expressions. This is especially noticeable in 'surprise' expression, where many subjects lean their heads slightly backward and so does the generated expression when the head motion had been included in the training data. Thus, we use the original landmark displacement data including the head motion. Thus, from the original data containing the ordered list of marker positions, we generate pose-oblivious marker coordinate displacement.

Each sequence contains a varying number of frames. In the 'happy' dataset, for example, the sequence length varies from 69 to 115 frames. We uniformized the length of the sequence by choosing a constant as the number of frames for all sequences. A sequence data with longer frames has been cut at the end, and the one with shorter frames has been zero-padded until the end.

Data representation. Since we aim to model the sequence as a whole instead of modeling each frame individually, we must employ a light-weight representation for the facial shape and avoid using vectors/matrices of large dimensionality. In our modeler, we use the landmark-based shape representation in order to maintain a moderate data dimension. A facial expression is then represented as a sequence of landmark displacement vectors applied to each landmark point on a rest pose.

Formally, our training data can be described with the input and output pairs $(\mathbb{X}, \mathbb{Y})$. Let $\mathbb{X}$ be the input observations and $\mathbf{X}^i \in \mathbb{X}$ a sample from our observation, where $i \in 1, \ldots n$; n is the number of subjects in the dataset.

$\mathbf{X}^i \in \mathbb{M}_{f \times 3m}$ contains the expression sequence from the i-th subject, where $f+1$ is the number of frames, and m is the number of landmarks, respectively. It is an ordered set of marker displacement vectors, as written by

$$\mathbf{X}^i = \begin{bmatrix} x_1^i & x_2^i & \ldots x_t^i \end{bmatrix}^T,$$

where $x_j^i = \begin{bmatrix} dx_{1,j}^i, dy_{1,j}^i, dz_{1,j}^i, \ldots, dz_{m,j}^i \end{bmatrix}$ is a row vector of size $3m$ denoting the landmark displacements between $(t+1)$-th frame t-th frame $(t = 1, \ldots f)$. In our data, $\mathbf{X}^i$ has been recorded with 83 markers and its sequence length f has been normalized to 135, so it is 135×249 (83 times 3) dimensional. We have tried to apply PCA to reduce the data dimension to dozens but the gain in computation time had been insignificant.

RNN to learn the facial expression. Given a 3D face mesh (in a rest pose) whose landmark locations have been identified, a neural network is trained to predict the sequence of marker displacements, which will animate the given mesh when added to the given mesh sequentially. Formally, the variable number of facial expression poses (as represented by landmark displacement vectors) previously seen by the network are expressed by a fixed length hidden state h_t, which is updated with the current input x_t by using a nonlinear function, i.e., $h_{t+1} = h(h_t, x_t)$. The output y_t is evaluated as a linear function of the hidden state, i.e., $y_t = g(h_t)$, which can be implemented as a fully connected (FC) layer.

Figure 11.3 illustrates the predictor network architecture used in this paper: A long short term memory (LSTM) network consisting of multiple LSTM layers with a fully connected (FC) decoder unit. LSTM is a variant of RNN which preserves gradients well while backpropagating through time/layers and thus can deal with long-term dependencies. The input to the network is the current displacement vector $\mathbf{x}_t = \left(dx_1^t, dy_1^t, \ldots, dz_m^t \right)$ encoding x, y, and z offsets of each landmark. The input vector $\mathbf{x}_t$ is passed to weighted connections to a stack of recurrently connected hidden layers to compute first the hidden vector sequences $\mathbf{h}^n = \left(h_1^n, \ldots, h_T^n \right), n = 1 \ldots 3$ and then the output vector $\mathbf{y}_t$. $\mathbf{y}_t$ is the predicted landmark displacement vector in the next time step, $\mathbf{x}_{t+1}$, and is used to predict the next marker displacement by being fed as input to the network in the next time step. During the training of network, we directly minimize the sum of squared error over the predicted displacements and the ones from the observation data. Thus, we define our loss function that measures the mean squared error over the displacements.

$$L_{\text{disp}} = \sum \|\mathbf{y}_t - \mathbf{x}_{t+1}\|^2$$

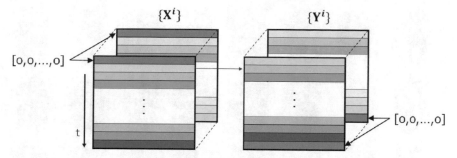

Fig. 11.3 Training data. Input data block, **X**, is the compilation of individual expression sequences, in the form of dx, dy, and dz. The initial frames (colored in grey) are set to 0. The output data block, **Y**, has been generated by shifting the **X** vector

Fig. 11.4 Given a sequence of marker set and a static mesh, we generate a sequence of deformed mesh driven by the marker locations

where $\mathbf{y}_t$ is the predicted output at time t, and $\mathbf{x}_{t+1}$ is the corresponding ground truth at time $t + 1$.

In our experiments, we trained each expression network with 3 hidden layers with 128 hidden units and a dense output layer, by using Tensorflow (Tensorflow) deep learning library (Abadi et al. 2015). The hidden layers used the *tanh* nonlinear function, although other activation functions could have been used. Figure 11.4 shows the blocks of training data in Tensorflow. The displacement vectors from all subjects are compiled together; to form the input dataset **X**. The first element $\mathbf{x}_1$ of every expression sequence is set to a null vector. The output data blocks, **Y**, have been generated by left-shifting **X**.

The model parameters were tuned by using Adam optimization method, with the learning rate $\alpha = 0.001$ and default values for the other parameters: $\beta_1 = 0.9$, $\beta_2 = 0.999$ and $\varepsilon = e^{-8}$. Although deep RNNs are known to take a long time to train, thanks to the compressed nature of the marker-based facial animation data, we were able to train our RNNs in approximately 30 min, with 10 000 epochs over 101 samples with batch size 5.

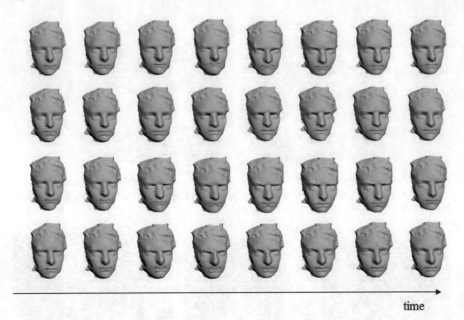

time

Fig. 11.5 Snapshots of 'Anger' expression sequences generated by our model

Each output vector y_t is used to parametrize an RBF network over the Euclidian space, which computes a deformation of the full face mesh (see the next subsection).

Marker to full mesh deformation. The trained RNN networks generate a sequence of displacement vector for the marker set, from which we compute a sequence of deformed mesh of given face shape (Fig. 11.5). Among many available techniques that we could use for the mesh warping, we use radial basis function (RBF) networks, a universal solver for scattered interpolation problems (Powell 2007). Consider a real valued function $w_x(\mathbf{v}) : \mathbb{R}^3 \rightarrow \mathbb{R}$ that approximates the deformation (along x-axis, without losing the generality) of the face mesh given a sparse set of function values known at marker locations $\{w_x(\mathbf{v}^i) = d_x^i \mathbf{s}\}$ where $\mathbf{v}^i$ is the location of the i-th maker and d_x^i denotes its displacement along x-axis. Note that the RBF works on a multidimensional domain as a scalar function, thus, we compute $w(\mathbf{x})$ for each dimension, i.e., $w_x(\mathbf{x})$, $w_y(\mathbf{x})$, and $w_z(\mathbf{x})$ for the displacement along each coordinate. $w_x(\cdot)$ is assumed to be as a weighted sum of radial basis function and a linear term, i.e.,

$$w_x(\mathbf{v}) = \sum_i^m q_i \cdot \phi\left(\left\|\mathbf{v} - \mathbf{v}^i\right\|\right) + p(\mathbf{v}) \tag{11.3}$$

where $\phi : \mathbb{R}^3 \rightarrow \mathbb{R}$ is a radial-based function (Gaussian in our case), q_i are scalar weights of ith kernel, $\mathbf{v}^i \in \mathbb{R}^3$ are the kernel centers of RBF, m is the number of interpolants, and $p(\mathbf{x})$ is a polynomial. To determine q_i and $p(\mathbf{x})$, we use the known function values at interpolates, i.e., the displacements at marker locations, as written by $w_x(v^i) = d_x^i$, $j = 1, \ldots, m$. This results in a linear system

$$
\begin{bmatrix} w_x\left(\mathbf{v}^1\right) \\ \vdots \\ w_x\left(\mathbf{v}^m\right) \end{bmatrix} = \begin{bmatrix} \phi_{11} & \cdots & \phi_{1m} \\ \vdots & \ddots & \vdots \\ \phi_{m1} & \cdots & \phi_{mm} \end{bmatrix} \begin{bmatrix} q_1 \\ \vdots \\ q_m \end{bmatrix} = \begin{bmatrix} d_x^1 \\ \vdots \\ d_x^m \end{bmatrix}
\tag{11.4}
$$

where $\phi_{ij} = \exp\left(-\frac{\|\mathbf{v}^i - \mathbf{v}^j\|}{2\sigma^2}\right)$. As the matrix $\boldsymbol{\phi}$ can be computed from the Gaussian evaluation using marker distances as input, and the displacement vector $\mathbf{d}_x$ is known, the weight vector $\mathbf{q}$ can be found by solving for the linear system, i.e., $\mathbf{q} = \boldsymbol{\phi}^{-1} \cdot \mathbf{d}_x$ which determines the function $w_x(\cdot)$.

Once the warp functions $w_x(\cdot)$, $w_y(\cdot)$, $w_z(\cdot)$ are found, we can evaluate them at each vertex location of the full mesh so that it conforms to the displaced markers. The warping functions should be solved for every frame, since each frame yields new interpolants. With the number of markers less than 100, it can be solved efficiently by using the LU decomposition.

Results. Figure 11.6 shows some of the expression sequences generated by our 'Anger' network. Note that we have applied the marker displacement prediction to a same face geometry, to mask off the visual effects originating from different shape identities. The deformations deriving a specific facial expression are learned properly and gives plausible results. This is despite the fact that the captured marker data is sometimes very noisy, and that the shape variety of facial models is large.

The overall evaluation is a neural-net inference followed by RBF warping of a full mesh. The training and evaluation for the marker-to-mesh deformation is performed in a per-frame basis. Each frame takes about 0.1 s for a mesh comprised of 10 000 vertices, accounting for a total time of only a few seconds for the generation of an entire sequence.

11.5 Discussion

We have presented a deep learning method that models a facial animation as a temporal entity, i.e., a sequence of deformations applied to a facial mesh as represented by sparsely sampled marker location. It distinguishes itself from existing modelers where a static expression pose is learned. Instead of modeling the facial animation in a frame-by-frame basis, the temporal evolution of deformation comprising a specific expression is modeled as a whole. Our technique offers a promising solution for the facial expression sequence modeling, significantly improving the quality of generated expression while extending the potential applicability of neural networks to 4D shape data (time-varying shapes).

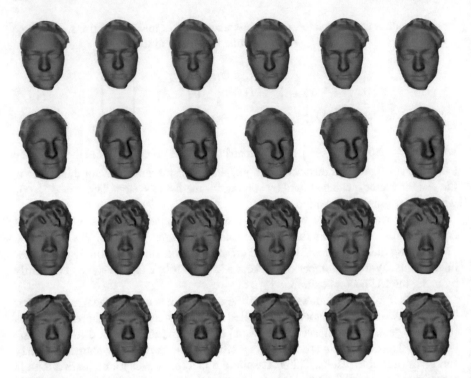

Fig. 11.6 Facial expression sequences generated by our shape-oblivious network have been applied to different faces

References

Abadi M, Agarwal A, Barham P, Brevdo E, Chen Z, Citro C, Corrado GS, Davis A, Dean J, Devin M, Ghemawat S, Goodfellow IJ, Harp A, Irving G, Isard M, Jia Y, Józefowicz R, Kaiser L, Kudlur M, Levenberg J, Mané D, Monga R, Moore S, Murray DG, Olah C, Schuster M, Shlens J, Steiner B, Sutskever I, Talwar K, Tucker PA, Vanhoucke V, Vasudevan V, Viégas FB, Vinyals O, Warden P, Wattenberg M, Wicke M, Yu Y, Zheng X (2015) Tensorflow: large-scale machine learning on heterogeneous distributed systems. arXiv:1603.04467

Ankerst M, Kastenmüller G, Kriegel HP, Seidl T (1999) 3D shape histograms for similarity search and classification in spatial databases. Lect Notes Comput Sci, pp 207–226

Beeler T, Hahn F, Bradley D, Bickel B, Beardsley P, Gotsman C, Sumner R, Gross M (2011) High-quality passive facial performance capture using anchor frames. ACM Trans Graph 30:75. https://doi.org/10.1145/2010324.1964970

Blanz V, Vetter T (1999) A morphable model for the synthesis of 3D Faces. SIGGRAPH'99 Proc. of the 26th annual conference on computer graphics and interactive techniques 187–194. https://doi.org/10.1145/311535.311556

Blanz V, Basso C, Poggio T, Vetter T (2003) Reanimating faces in images and video. Comput Graph Forum 22(3):641–650. https://doi.org/10.1111/1467-8659.t01-1-00712

Boulanger-Lewandowski N, Bengio Y, Vincent P (2012) Modeling temporal dependencies in high-dimensional sequences: application to polyphonic music generation and transcription. arXiv:12066392, https://academic.microsoft.com/paper/1819710477

Brock A, Donahue J, Simonyan K (2018) Large scale GAN training for high fidelity natural image synthesis. arXiv:1809.11096

Brock A, Donahue J, Simonyan K (2019) Large scale gan training for high fidelity natural image synthesis. In: ICLR 2019 : 7th international conference on learning representations. https://academic.microsoft.com/paper/2893749619

Canavan SJ, Liu P, Zhang X, Yin L (2015) Landmark localization on 3D/4D range data using a shape index-based statistical shape model with global and local constraints. Comput Vis Image Underst 139:136–148. https://academic.microsoft.com/paper/1667484106

Cho K, van Merrienboer B, Gulcehre C, Bahdanau D, Bougares F, Schwenk H, Bengio Y (2014) Learning phrase representations using RNN encoder-decoder for statistical machine translation. arXiv:14061078, https://academic.microsoft.com/paper/2950635152

Cosker D, Krumhuber E, Hilton A (2011) A facs valid 3D dynamic action unit database with applications to 3d dynamic morphable facial modeling. In: 2011 international conference on computer vision, pp 2296–2303. https://doi.org/10.1109/ICCV.2011.6126510

DeCarlo D, Metaxas D (1996) The integration of optical flow and deformable models with applications to human face shape and motion estimation. In: 2013 IEEE conference on computer vision and pattern recognition, IEEE computer society. Los Alamitos, CA, USA, p 231. https://doi.org/10.1109/CVPR.1996.517079, https://ieeecomputersociety.org/10.1109/CVPR.1996.517079

Dou P, Shah SK, Kakadiaris IA (2017) End-to-end 3D face reconstruction with deep neural networks. In: 2017 IEEE conference on computer vision and pattern recognition (CVPR), pp 1503–1512. https://academic.microsoft.com/paper/2605701576

Garrido P, Zollhöfer M, Casas D, Valgaerts L, Varanasi K, Pérez P, Theobalt C (2016) Reconstruction of personalized 3D face rigs from monocular video. ACM Trans Graph 35(3):28. https://academic.microsoft.com/paper/2398381847

Goodfellow IJ, Pouget-Abadie J, Mirza M, Xu B, Warde-Farley D, Ozair S, Courville AC, Bengio Y (2014) Generative adversarial nets. In: Advances in neural information processing systems, vol 27, pp 2672–2680. https://academic.microsoft.com/paper/2099471712

Jackson AS, Bulat A, Argyriou V, Tzimiropoulos G (2017) Large pose 3D face reconstruction from a single image via direct volumetric CNN regression. arXiv:170307834, https://academic.microsoft.com/paper/2951863354

Jiang L, Zhang J, Deng B, Li H, Liu L (2018) 3D face reconstruction with geometry details from a single image. IEEE Trans Image Process 27(10):4756–4770. https://academic.microsoft.com/paper/2593956217

Johnson AE (1997) Spin-images: a representation for 3D surface matching. https://www.ri.cmu.edu/publications/spin-images-a-representation-for-3-d-surface-matching/

Kalra P, Mangili A, Thalmann NM, Thalmann D (1992) Simulation of facial muscle actions based on rational free form deformations. Comput Graph Forum 11(3):59–69. https://doi.org/10.1111/1467-8659.1130059, https://onlinelibrary.wiley.com/doi/abs/10.1111/1467-8659.1130059

Kim H, Garrido P, Tewari A, Xu W, Thies J, Niessner M, Pérez P, Richardt C, Zollhöfer M, Theobalt C (2018) Deep video portraits. Int Conf Comput Graph Interact Tech 37(4):1–14. https://academic.microsoft.com/paper/2806833697

Lee WS, Gu J, Thalmann N (2000) Generating animatable 3D virtual humans from photographs. Comput Graph Forum 19. https://doi.org/10.1111/1467-8659.00392

Lee Y, Terzopoulos D, Waters K (1995) Realistic modeling for facial animation. In: Proceedings of the 22nd annual conference on computer graphics and interactive techniques, association for computing machinery. New York, NY, USA, SIGGRAPH '95, pp 55–62. https://doi.org/10.1145/218380.218407

Li T, Bolkart T, Black MJ, Li H, Romero J (2017) Learning a model of facial shape and expression from 4D scans. ACM Trans Graph 36(6):194. https://academic.microsoft.com/paper/2769666294

Li X, Zhang H (2007) Adapting geometric attributes for expression-invariant 3D face recognition. In: IEEE international conference on shape modeling and applications (SMI '07), pp 21–32. https://academic.microsoft.com/paper/2095595190

Noh JY, Fidaleo D (2000) Animated deformations with radial basis functions. In: In ACM virtual reality and software technology VRST, pp 166–174

Paysan P, Knothe R, Amberg B, Romdhani S, Vetter T (2009) A 3D face model for pose and illumination invariant face recognition. https://doi.org/10.1109/AVSS.2009.58

Pighin F, Szeliski R, Salesin DH (1999) Resynthesizing facial animation through 3D model-based tracking. In: Proceedings of the seventh IEEE international conference on computer vision, vol 1, pp 143–150. https://doi.org/10.1109/ICCV.1999.791210

Powell MJD (2007) A view of algorithms for optimization without derivatives 1. https://academic.microsoft.com/paper/2187467903

Samad MD, Iftekharuddin KM (2016) Frenet frame-based generalized space curve representation for pose-invariant classification and recognition of 3D face. IEEE Trans Hum-Mach Syst 46(4):522–533. https://academic.microsoft.com/paper/2344785877

Scherer M, Walter M, Schreck T (2010) Histograms of oriented gradients for 3D object retrieval. https://academic.microsoft.com/paper/2467579536

Shapira L, Shamir A, Cohen-Or D (2008) Consistent mesh partitioning and skeletonisation using the shape diameter function. Vis Comput 24(4):249–259. https://academic.microsoft.com/paper/1989540182

Sun J, Ovsjanikov M, Guibas LJ (2009) A concise and provably informative multi-scale signature based on heat diffusion. Symp Geom Process 28(5):1383–1392. https://academic.microsoft.com/paper/2100657858

Sutskever I, Vinyals O, Le QV (2014) Sequence to sequence learning with neural networks. arXiv:14093215, https://academic.microsoft.com/paper/2949888546

Terzopoulos D, Waters K (1990) Physically-based facial modelling, analysis, and animation. J Vis Comput Animat 1(2):73–80

Tewari A, Zollhöfer M, Kim H, Garrido P, Bernard F, Pérez P, Theobalt C (2017) Mofa: model-based deep convolutional face autoencoder for unsupervised monocular reconstruction. arXiv:170310580, https://academic.microsoft.com/paper/2952080583

Thies J, Zollhöfer M, Nießner M, Valgaerts L, Stamminger M, Theobalt C (2015) Real-time expression transfer for facial reenactment. ACM Trans Graph 34(6). https://doi.org/10.1145/2816795.2818056

Tran L, Liu X (2018) Nonlinear 3D face morphable model. In: 2018 IEEE/CVF conference on computer vision and pattern recognition, pp 7346–7355. https://academic.microsoft.com/paper/2796822548

Vinyals O, Toshev A, Bengio S, Erhan D (2015) Show and tell: a neural image caption generator. In: 2015 IEEE conference on computer vision and pattern recognition (CVPR), pp 3156–3164. https://academic.microsoft.com/paper/1895577753

Vlasic D, Brand M, Pfister H, Popovic J (2006) Face transfer with multilinear models. ACM Trans Graph 24. https://doi.org/10.1145/1185657.1185864

Yang J, Liu Q, Zhang K (2017) Stacked hourglass network for robust facial landmark localisation. In: 2017 IEEE conference on computer vision and pattern recognition workshops (CVPRW), pp 2025–2033. https://academic.microsoft.com/paper/2736728583

Yin L, Wei X, Sun Y, Wang J, Rosato MJ (2006) A 3D facial expression database for facial behavior research. In: The 7th international conference on automatic face and gesture recognition (FGR06), pp 211–216. https://academic.microsoft.com/paper/2137306662

Part II
Human Computer Interaction (HCI)

Chapter 12
Facilitating Decision-Making with Multimodal Interfaces in Collaborative Analytical Sessions

Yasin Findik, Hasan Alp Boz, and Selim Balcisoy

Abstract In collaborative visual analytics sessions, participants analyze data and cooperate toward a shared vision. These decision-making processes are challenging and time-consuming. In this chapter, we introduce a system for facilitating decision-making in exploratory and collaborative visual analytics sessions. Our system comprises an assistant analytical agent, a multi-display wall and a framework for interactive visual analytics. The assistant agent understands participants' ongoing conversations and exhibits information about the data on displays. The displays are also used to manifest the current state of the session. In addition, the agent answers the participants' questions either regarding the data or open-domain ones, and preserves the productivity and the efficiency of the session by confirming that the participants do not deviate from the session's goal. Whereas, our visual analytics medium makes data tangible, hence more comprehensible and natural to operate with. The results of our qualitative study indicate that the proposed system fosters productive multi-user decision-making processes.

12.1 Introduction

In data analytical sessions participants introduce a problem, generate a hypothesis, and test the hypothesis on the data (Keim et al. 2008). Nonetheless, these decision-making processes are complex, last longer than anticipated and consequently lack the desired outcome. Thus, an auxiliary system that mitigates the aforementioned

Y. Findik · H. A. Boz · S. Balcisoy (✉)
Sabanci University, Istanbul, Turkey
e-mail: balcisoy@sabanciuniv.edu

Y. Findik
e-mail: yasinfindik@sabanciuniv.edu

H. A. Boz
e-mail: bozhasan@sabanciuniv.edu

© The Author(s), under exclusive license to Springer Nature Switzerland AG 2021   199
N. Magnenat Thalmann et al. (eds.), *Intelligent Scene Modeling and Human-Computer Interaction*, Human–Computer Interaction Series,
https://doi.org/10.1007/978-3-030-71002-6_12

problems would be advantageous for data analytical sessions. For this system to be practical in decision-making, it should be naturalistic to interact with and should elicit our intrinsic learning and understanding skills.

For instance, newborns explore the world around them not by using a mouse or a keyboard, but by touching objects with their hands. Hence, the most intuitive way to interact with data is by seeing and touching it. Nonetheless, traditional human–computer interaction techniques do not fulfill this necessity. Data visualization techniques aim to facilitate the analysis of complex data by helping people derive meaning from data by stimulating the sense of sight. While a large number of studies in visual analytics have focused on assisting the analytical process of complex data by visualization, considerable limitations still persist. These limitations are accentuated especially when collaborative work is involved in the analytical process.

Just as infants' innate instinct to question caregivers about the surroundings, people learn more about the data, not only through sight and touch, but also with the help of a companion that has knowledge about it. While this companion may be a human being, it can be a computer too. With current developments, conversational agents are increasingly taking the role of assistants in our daily lives. Such assistant with domain knowledge is beneficial in collaborative analytical processes, as well. During these processes the assistant can answer the questions asked by the participants regarding the data, it can also support/reject their idea by giving an explanation after understanding their conversation. Moreover, the assistant may play a crucial role in preserving the productivity and efficiency of the session, by making sure the participants do not deviate from the session goal.

We present a system that both assists the meeting participants during the analytical process and also enables interactive visual analytics. Figure 12.1 shows the overview

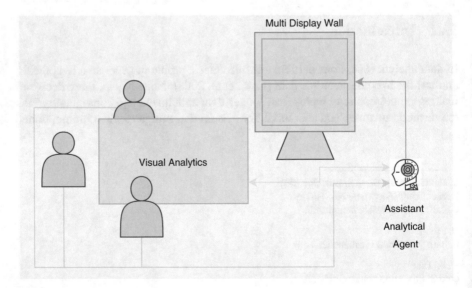

Fig. 12.1 System overview

of the system. Participants using the platform interact with the data by touching it and also communicate with an assistive analytical agent through natural language. Our system encourages collaboration among the participants, forges exploration through data, and preserves the meeting time-line and effectivity By combining the analytical agent with visual analytics, to the best of our knowledge, our study presents the first multimodal visual analytics system, that fosters more productive and faster multi-user decision-making processes.

12.2   Related Work

The system described in this chapter employs concepts in visual analytics, natural language interfaces and their fusion. Here we review related work in those areas.

12.2.1   Collaborative Visual Analytics

In collaborative decision-making processes, visual analytics aids data comprehension and analysis (Kaya et al. 2018). To facilitate decision-making in collaborative sessions, developing a cooperative platform is one of the motivations of this work. Collaborative data analysis is defined as a task where two or more people work together, rather than a single person task. Traditional computer software usually does not support collaborative work, but in recent years a plethora of studies have focused on collaborative work (Li et al. 2006; Hou et al. 2008; Bortolaso et al. 2014). The success of such platforms is largely dependent on the participants seeing each other during the collaboration (Fan et al. 2014). Thus, tabletop systems are increasingly being used in collaborative environments, since they provide an ideal medium for both communication and data visualization. These systems, through facilitating the collaborative working environment and fostering idea sharing, mitigate many communication problems (Scott et al. 2003; Shen et al. 2003, 2006), thoroughly discussed in (Girard and Robin 2006; Vivacqua et al. 2011).

Furthermore, tabletop systems present a naturalistic interface for data visualization and interaction. Studies in educational sciences and developmental psychology have shown that physical objects enhance people's ability to learn and understand (Apple 2019; Wilson and Margaret 2002). One of the main goals of this work is to increase the use of this innate learning motivation of humans, to facilitate visualizations understanding and to foster interaction with it. Almost all of the visualization tools to this end require prior visual knowledge and indirect interaction, such as a mouse and a keyboard. For these reasons, these tools can only be used by the end user after a long learning period. The visualization part of this work aims to make data visualization easier for the end-users to comprehend and interact with it. Due to the advantages listed above, we leverage a tabletop setup as a medium for visual analytics.

12.2.2   Natural Language Interfaces

By using natural language as a means of communication, conversational agents are increasingly being used as daily assistants (e.g. Apple's Siri 2019), Amazon's Alexa (Amazon 2019), Microsoft's Cortana (2019)). The common usage of these systems is as reminders that facilitate daily life and chores. An assistant can be physical (i.e. robots) or virtual (i.e. virtual agents). Some applications of robots as assistive technologies, mainly developed for physical support, are: smart wheelchairs, walking assistants, external skeletons and robotic butlers (Magnenat-Thalmann and Zhang 2014; Guizzo and Goldstein 2005; Yanco and Holly 2001; Graf et al. 2004). Communication devices and robotic pets (Beck et al. 2003; DiSalvo et al. 2003) are developed for social purposes. Whereas, reminder devices and sensor monitoring platforms provide cognitive assistance (Scanaill et al. 2006). Studies (Cesta et al. 2007; Jung et al. 2005) show that natural language interfaces, such as conversational agents, are beneficial since they invoke human social behaviors and help communication.

For instance, Bickmore et al.'s study (2005) experiments with a virtual agent. It evaluates the responses of elderly users to relational agent Laura. Laura's aim is to give health advice to the elderly. The main purpose of the agent's interaction is to establish a relationship with the users along with social dialogue, empathy, humor and self-disclosure. Findings of the study demonstrate that the agent was considered by the participants as a speech partner on health and health behavior. It was also considered as reliable, friendly and a good health consultant.

The aforementioned studies emphasized how the assistant agent could help people in various ways as a physical robot or as a virtual agent. The focus of the assistant analytical agent in this study is to monitor the collaborative analytical process, speed it up if necessary and increase its productivity by analyzing the meeting environment, extracting meeting notes and understanding participants' conversations. Cognitive Assistant that Learns and Organizes (CALO) (Tur et al. 2010) is an example of a study on such analytical agents. The authors of CALO argue that automated summarization of the meeting and issuance of the decisions increased the efficiency and improved the productivity of the meeting for participants and non-participants. Whereas, (Thompson et al. 2011) highlights the contribution of the assistant agent for the organization of the meeting.

12.2.3   Natural Language Interfaces for Visual Analytics

On top of touch, being able to operate visual interfaces through natural language also, establishes a more naturalistic interaction, since people express questions more easily through natural language than through system commands. In their recent study, Henkin et al. (Henkin and Turkay 2018) discuss the benefits of this multimodal data analysis. Still, integration of natural language interfaces or agents to visual analytics systems is an area in its infancy and there are very few studies in the field.

For example, *Evizeon* (Hoque et al. 2018) is a visual analytics system that supports interaction through natural language. While *Evizeon* allows advanced data querying through natural language, it is not designed for multiple users, nor for meeting environments. Hence, it does not foster faster decision-making in any way. Ehnes et al. (2009) provide an example of a system including both a tabletop and a supporting agent. However, in contrast to ours, this study's aim is not to assist participants with the analytical process. Its purpose is to automatically retrieve the discussed documents and display them on the table.

In this context, our study presents a novel multimodal visual analytics system, that fosters more productivity and facilitates multi-user decision-making processes.

12.3 System Analysis

Our system comprises an assistant analytical agent, a multi-display wall and a framework for interactive visual analytics (VA). In this section, we describe how our system enhances the multi-user decision-making process through its multiple facets.

12.3.1 Analytical Agent

This work aims to facilitate decision-making in collaborative visual analytics sessions by introducing an analytical agent. The role of the agent in this scenario is to extract the meaning of the conversation among the subjects and to present related schemes or diagrams. It also responds to the subjects' questions, either regarding the data or open-domain ones. Consequently, the agent complements the visual analytical process.

The analytical agent module of the system utilizes a multi-display wall consisting of two monitors to communicate with the participants. Here, we list facets of the assistant analytical agent which facilitate and enrich the decision-making process of the participants.

12.3.1.1 Interactivity

The analytical agent interacts with the participants, the data and the VA system. The analytical agent-data and the analytical agent-VA system communications depend on the users' utterances. According to the user choices, the analytical agent takes action on data or changes what the VA system shows to the users. Figure 12.2 depicts the interactions and the relations of system components.

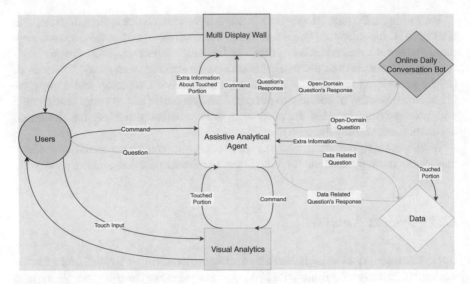

Fig. 12.2 Relations and interactions among system components

Human–Analytical Agent Interaction

The analytical agent utilizes a microphone and a contemporary automatic speech recognition (ASR) system for speech recognition.

Users directly ask questions to the analytical agent either about the topic of the meeting or open-domain ones. If the question is related to the data, the analytical agent analyzes the sentence in a rule-based fashion and gives the proper response to the user's request. If a user asks an open-domain question such as: "How are you today?", the analytical agent directs these kinds of questions to an online freely available daily conversation bot, takes the answer from them and shows it to the users.

To prevent prolonged sessions and promote faster decision-making, the analytical agent also participates as an active listener during the meeting. If it deduces which part of the data is being discussed by the users, it calculates related charts and shows them in the multi-display wall. Moreover, if the analytical agent detects that the users deviate from the meeting topic for a time interval longer than a threshold, it politely warns the meeting leader about the deviation.

Analytical Agent–Data Interaction

If the analytical agent decides or users want the analytical agent to make operation on data, it interacts with the data using its sub-modules for specific operations. Besides, when users touch the data on the VA system, the analytical agent calculates relevant charts on the touched portion of the data and displays them on the multi-display wall.

Analytical Agent-VA System Interaction

One of the monitors in the multi-display wall displays the analytical agent's version of the data. Essentially, this version is tailored by the deductions the analytical agent makes from the conversations, and its reasoning on what might be helpful for the participants to see. Whereas, the VA system shows the version of the data that the participants modify themselves.

The analytical agent copies its monitor's version of the data to the VA system, if it is commanded by the users to do so. Users can also go back to the previous version of the data on the VA system, if they want to. This feature provides the users with the opportunity to manipulate with more than one version of the data, to examine it and to draw comparisons among the versions.

12.3.1.2 Participant Identification

In order for the interaction to feel more naturalistic and customized, the analytical agent aims to acquire the participants' names. While they can remain anonymous, if participants choose to provide their names, the analytical agent addresses them by their names during the meeting. In addition to creating a warmer meeting environment, this feature enables the agent to take notes for each participant by using their name rather than the numeric ids. Consequently, the meeting notes become more comprehensible for future references.

12.3.1.3 Meeting Summarization

The analytical agent listens to each user during the meeting and also takes note of all conversations with user id/name, time-stamps and user's emotion, if it exists. Moreover, if the users emphasize specific ideas to the agent to note them, the analytical agent logs these as a decision taken during the meeting. Besides dialogs, the analytical agent can note interested users, and also takes note of users' interests by considering where they participate in the conversation. According to the users' actions, the analytical agent can infer which part of the data attractive for which user and is able to utilize this information in future meetings.

Users who were not present at the analytical session, but interested in the meeting minutes, can access information about the meeting status such as decisions taken or more interested region of the data, and they can also obtain information about its attendants like which user tend to disrupt the meeting or which users are more willing to contribute using these notes. Since the analytical agent will know more about the users and data using these notes, the productivity of the next meetings is increased. More importantly, these notes are invaluable for the meeting leader.

12.3.1.4   User Engagement

A successful decision-making process requires engagement from all of the present participants. Hence, keeping participants engaged during the meeting is one of the analytical agent's responsibilities. The agent captures input on user engagement from their speech and VA system interaction frequencies. Having identified the less engaged participants, the agent aims to increase their engagement by directing questions to them.

The frequency of the users' utterances during the meeting is one of the user engagement indicators. After detecting infrequently speaking participants, the analytical agent asks motivating questions to them like "What is your opinion on the discussed issue?" to get their attention.

The analytical agent also detects the less engaged participants on the VA system by their touch frequency. After identifying the less engaged users, the analytical agent asks questions or gives suggestions to these users such that to give an answer they must touch the VA system, such as, "To see the further information on *performance*, you can change the filter on the VA system".

12.3.1.5   Session Coordination

Meeting management is a key factor for an effective meeting. The meeting leader has specific duties during the meeting. On top of helping the attendees to stay focused and productive, the leader should make a follow-up plan for the analytical process.

Analytical agent's mission is not to be the meeting leader, but to alleviate the difficulties of leadership by helping the leader of the meeting, so that the leader can focus on more important tasks. Therefore, the analytical agent assists the attendees to stay focused and effective.

The hardest part of helping the meeting leader is session coordination. Directly interfering with users' speech and stopping them causes attendees to feel offended. To prevent that, the analytical agent just provides the information about the meeting status on the screen without taking much attention. Thus, the meeting leader can easily follow-up on this information.

In a session, users can introduce more than one problem and work toward their solutions. After finding solutions for a problem or getting commands from users to do so, the analytical agent will note the problem and its solutions in a file to be used for meeting summarization.

12.3.2   Visual Analytics System

As one of the mediums for visual analytics in our system, we exploit a tabletop, essentially a projector and a bare wooden surface of a table with no additional electronic appliances.

The tabletop system can correspond to at most six users at the same time. The system is able to handle the entire touch action independent of the user's settlement. In other words, users can interact with the table from every position. Below we list the features that accentuate the efficacy of our tabletop as a medium for visualization.

12.3.2.1 Communication

Research shows that interactions with the data by using touch and hand gestures make data easier for people to understand and explore rather than depending solely on conventional inputs, such as mouse and keyboard. Touch and hand gestures address the users' perception naturally (Ishii et al. 2012). Further, studies indicate that face-to-face interactions lead to a faster and more effective decision-making process (Blenke et al. 2013). Our system provides a medium for the participants to communicate face-to-face with each other, in addition to providing a naturalistic touchable interface. Therefore, the decision-making is promoted, by both the actualization of face-to-face communication of the participants and the higher understanding of data through a touchable interface.

12.3.2.2 User Friendliness

To use the tabletop system, attendees do not need to be instructed. They should only know that the data shown on the table is touchable and the conventional hand gestures for zooming in/out and panning. Users do not need additional time to learn how to use the application. This provides an important advantage to users so that they can simply adapt to the tool and interact with the data (Coombs et al. 2000).

12.3.2.3 Responsiveness

The responsiveness is another significant property of the tabletop system. Latency is the imperative point for these kinds of interactive systems. Users should not spend much time to get an answer or result from their actions (Card et al. 1991). In view of the significance of responsiveness, we designed our system so that it responds instantly (with a latency of at most 1.57 ms) to the users' commands, both touch and gestures.

12.4 Data Overview

Internal production data on 2044 branch offices for the years 2015–2016 was donated to us from an insurance company of an OECD (Organization for Economic Co-operation and Development) country. In this study, we utilize this data which provides information about the branch offices of this particular insurance company, along with their location (latitude and longitude). The data carries information on the standing of the branch offices in terms of different segments, namely *governance*, *performance* and *response*.

The *governance* segment indicates the relation between the change in the total premium volume of the head office produced by the product group and the premium volume changes performed in the same outcome group at the branch office.

The *performance* segment displays how close a branch office is to its estimated potential. The potential metric is calculated by the rate of actual production to the potential derived from the premiums of similar branches.

Finally, the *response* segment is an indicator that shows how long the branch office has reacted and accommodated itself to the change in sales strategies of the head office based on product groups.

For each segment, there exists a further division into *red*, *yellow* and *green* sub-segments. This division differentiates the standing of the branch office in the stated segment (i.e. *performance*, *governance* or *response*) compared to the average score of all branch offices in that particular segment. *Red* indicates lower than, *yellow* close to or equal to and *green* higher than the average.

12.5 System Description

The hardware setup of the system is demonstrated in Fig. 12.3. The assistant analytical agent setup consists of Kinect for Xbox One (Wikipedia 2019) as an RGB-depth camera, a microphone to capture users speech and a multi-display wall. The setup of the VA system is comprised of an additional Kinect for Xbox One that serves as an RGB-D camera, an HD projector and a wooden table without any sensor or electronic parts.

12.5.1 Analytical Agent

The analytical agent assists the decision-making process of the meeting through speech, data analysis and data visualization. It takes input either from speech, sight, or touch (from VA). Its software is a distributed system, comprised of five sub-modules ranging from data processing to user tracking. The various modules used in the implementation of the assistant analytical agent are described below.

12.5.1.1 Speech Recognition

To obtain the speech of users, the system uses a single microphone. At the beginning of the study, we used multiple microphones to get clearer speech. However,

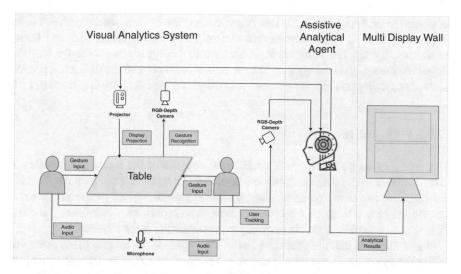

Fig. 12.3 The hardware setup of the system, including the relationship and data flow among its components

taking multiple audio streams from microphones and processing them causes the system a huge amount of computation time. In other words, the analytical agent can either deduce a more extensive analysis about the current topic without any loss of speech or miss some of the detail of the analysis but give the users quick responses according to their discussions. Since human–computer interaction systems are predominantly affected by the degree of responsiveness (Ushirobira et al. 2016), we opted for providing quicker responses rather than more thorough ones.

The audio coming from the microphone is captured from the sub-module as a stream. To convert speech to text, we used Google Speech-To-Text API (Google 2019).

12.5.1.2   Conversation Mining

The analytical agent is named Jason, to be able to discern the questions and commands that are directed to him during the meeting. An utterance starting with the "Jason" keyword, is embedded into a vector representation using the average of word2vec embeddings (Mikolov et al. 2013) of its words. This utterance embedding is compared to the embeddings of a set of predefined domain questions by using cosine similarity. The utterance is regarded as a domain-related utterance if the cosine similarity with any of the questions in the set is above a certain threshold. The open-domain (i.e. not related to the meeting) utterances are directed to an online conversation bot for the response. Whereas, the domain-related utterances are further classified in a rule-based fashion into data and visual requests. The data requests are requests that require an operation on data, such as "Jason, can you show the branch offices with red color response?". Whilst, visual requests require only a change of view, such as "Jason, zoom into city A". The utterances not directed to the agent are also analyzed. If at the end of the analysis the agent is able to extract the topic and the discussed portion of the data, it displays related schemes and diagrams on the multi-display wall.

12.5.1.3 Visualization

The visualization part of the analytical agent consists of the meeting environment visualization and the data visualization, depicted in Fig. 12.4. The agent displays the meeting room from its point of view, including the utterances of the participants transcribed to text with an ASR. In addition, this display also visualizes schemes/diagrams about the data that is currently being touched on the tabletop.

While the users can filter the data on the VA system by its interface, they can also utilize the agent as an interface for data interaction. In addition, the agent enables more complex filters than the VA system. For instance, users can ask to see the branch offices which have green *governance* closest to yellow. The agent filters and displays the data on a map on one of its monitors, but can also copy this filtered version of the data to the VA system, on participants' request.

12.5.1.4 User Registration and Tracking

For reliable user tracking, Kinect's position should be arranged so that it can see the entire meeting room. The intended purpose of this Kinect is to detect participants' real-positions and their emotions. Kinect can detect the real-position of each user in the meeting room if only the most part of the users' bodies are in its field of view. After detecting the bodies, Kinect provides the emotion for each user according to their facial expressions.

Further, we address the speaker recognition issue by utilizing users' positions and speech activity angle. We use Kinect to detect the angle of speech activity from which we calculate the current speaker's location. Consequently, the agent keeps track of real-time of which utterance is uttered by which participant, the locations of all participants and their emotions at a given time-stamp.

12.5.1.5 The Agent's "Mind"

The agent's "mind" is the master sub-module that connects all the other sub-modules as shown in Fig. 12.5a. We name it "the mind", since just like a mind in a body, it takes input from all senses (i.e. hearing, sight, touch) and then decides where to route it. In our scenario, the hearing is accomplished through microphones, seeing through Kinect's visual input, and touch through the tabletop. After taking the raw input from its "senses", the agent routes this input to the designated sub-modules for

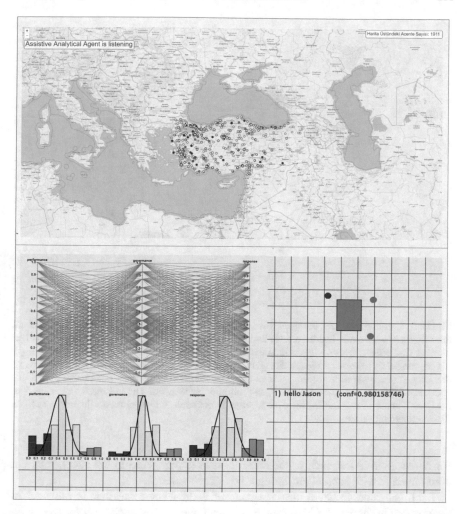

Fig. 12.4 The multi-display wall. The top display visualizes the agent's version of data. The bottom display shows extra information about the data, including charts. It also visualizes the meeting environment, with the current speaker highlighted in red

processing (e.g. audio stream to speech recognition). Afterwards, it decides whether the processed output should be further routed to other sub-modules (e.g. processed data to visualization), or whether it should be logged in the meeting notes. At the end of the meeting, the agent generates the notes which include users' speech transcriptions with time-stamps, users positions and emotions during the meeting, users actions such as table touching, and the problems discussed and solutions generated.

Essentially, the agent's mind enables inter-sub-module communication as it contains an intrinsic socket server. When each of the sub-modules starts, they send their identification to the mind. The top message in Fig. 12.5b. depicts a sample message

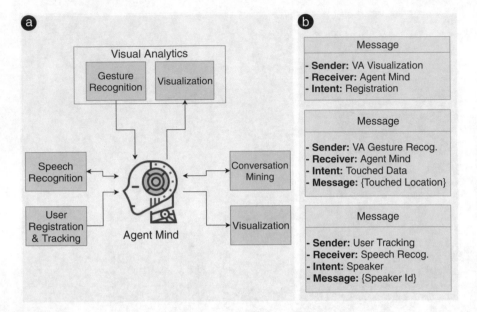

Fig. 12.5 Communication of the agent with sub-modules. **a** The relationship between the agent and the sub-modules. Double-headed arrows indicate modules that act both as a sender and a receiver, whereas single-headed arrows depict modules that solely receive messages from the agent. **b** Sample messages sent from sub-modules to the agent. The first one shows a sample registration message that each sub-module sends to the agent at the beginning of the session. The second message is addressed from the Gesture Recognition sub-module to the agent. The last message is sent from the User Tracking sub-module. Since the receiver is not itself, the agent routes the message to the Speech Recognition sub-module

for registration. After each of the sub-modules is registered to the agent, they can communicate with each other through the agent's mind.

Each sub-module has a message handler. Whenever a message is received by a sub-module, its handle is triggered. In other words, the socket server uses push notification rather than pull notification (Burgstahler et al. 2014). An example of such a message is the second message in Fig. 12.5b. If a sub-module needs to send a message to another sub-module, the message should contain the receiver sub-modules's name, sender sub-modules's name and the message itself. The agent then routes the message to the designated destination (see Fig. 12.5b).

12.5.2 Visual Analytics System

The tabletop serves as a medium for visual analytics, which takes input through gestures. Its software includes two sub-modules responsible for data visualization and gesture recognition, respectively.

12.5.2.1 Data Visualization

As described in Sect. 12.4, we visualize the branch offices of a given segment of our insurance company data on a map by using their longitude and latitude information. In our data, a segment can be either *performance, governance* or *response*. When a segment is chosen, its sub-segments are displayed as *red, yellow* or *green* based on the selected segment.

12.5.2.2 Gesture Recognition

A Processing (Reas and Fry 2006) sub-module processes the interaction for the tabletop part. All its user input comes via the RGB-D camera of Kinect, then its output is sent to the projector. For each frame, the RGB-D camera produces infrared and depth maps. These maps are processed in real-time for gesture detection. For instance, let D_0, I_0, D_1 and I_1 be depth(D) and infrared(I) maps for frames at t_0 and t_1, respectively. Afterwards, the difference between two temporal images is computed separately for the two maps as $(\Delta D) = |D_0 - D_1|$ and $(\Delta I) = |I_0 - I_1|$. The obtained delta images are converted into binary images by passing through a threshold τ. These two binary images are then combined into a single image C by an OR operation $C = (\Delta D > \tau) \vee (\Delta I > \tau)$. Finally, C is supplied to the FingerTracker library, which returns hand contours and fingertip locations.

Note that we cannot use the hand detection functionality of Kinect since to use it Kinect needs to find a body in its field of view. Because of our Kinect's location, Kinect has a bird's-eye view, consequently cannot detect bodies.

Touch Detection

For touch detection, we leverage a base depth image (D_b), taken when there is no user touching the table, or any other obstruction present. During the interaction, when the finger tracker module notifies about an update on the index finger's position at pixel p, the depth values of the neighbor pixels of p for the current frame are aggregated into an average depth value of d_f. We also calculate the aggregated average depth value of the neighborhood of p in the base depth image d_b. We check whether the difference between $|d_f - d_b|$ is below a threshold, which in turn indicates the index finger touched the table. Taking the average was necessary due to the noise induced by the RGB-depth camera.

Figure 12.6a depicts user touch on the table. After user touch is detected, according to its location, the application gives a proper response. If the touched location on the map contains a certain amount of branch offices, further detail (e.g. name, other segment values) about those branch offices are displayed. However, if the number of branch offices in that area is higher than a threshold, the system zooms in the touched area.

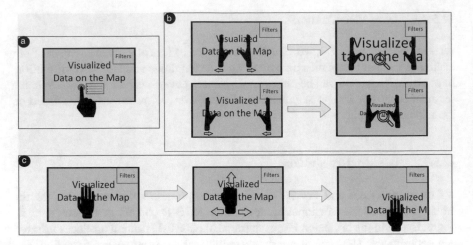

Fig. 12.6 Hand gestures for user–tabletop interaction. **a** Clicking/table-touching. **b** Zooming-in and zooming-out. **c** Panning

Through touch, in addition to obtaining extra information, users can also filter the data by selecting the appropriate check-boxes in the upper-right corner of the tabletop. The data can initially be filtered by segment (i.e. *performance*, *governance*, *response*), and further by categories (i.e. *red*, *green*, *yellow*).

Besides filter buttons, the interface contains a previous button. This button is necessary while interacting with the analytical agent, as it makes it possible to display the version of the data prior to the filters applied from the analytical agent's side.

Zoom detection

Whenever a user extends two arms over the table, the finger tracker module detects these two arms as fingers. After depth calculation same as with the touch detection part, if the difference $|d_f - d_b|$ is above a certain threshold zoom module will be activated. Changes in the distance between the arms in time determine zoom type; whether the user wants to zoom-in or zoom-out. Zoom-in and zoom-out hand gestures are shown in Fig. 12.6b.

In other words, the proximity of the user's arms manages the zoom level. For instance, if the user starts to bring their arms closer together, the tool begins to zoom-in according to the distance between the arms. Whereas, if the user increases the distance between the arms, the module will zoom-out.

Panning detection

Whenever a user opens their hand over the table, the finger tracker module detects the fingertip locations. After depth calculation, same as with the touch detection part, if the difference $|d_f - d_b|$ is above a certain threshold and the total amount of detected fingers is five, panning module will be activated. In other words, the signal for panning module initiation is seeing five fingers within a predefined distance above the table (see Fig. 12.6c). After initiating the panning module, when the user makes their hand a fist, the panning module will start the drag and drop process. The user will drag the map with their fist to the desired location, until the fist is opened which marks the drop event. Consequently, the location of the map's focus will be changed according to the user's fist movement.

12.6 Qualitative Evaluation

In order to evaluate our system and its impact on collaborative decision-making, we conducted a qualitative study with 17 participants. In total there were 5 groups, 3 of them consisting of 3 participants each and 2 of them consisting 4 participants each. The participants were classified into two categories, with one of them novice users (C_1) and the other being domain experts (C_2) . The domain experts were the two groups of 4 people we invited from the management team of the insurance company which provided the data to us. The other category (C_1) constituted of undergraduate students from the university. We reported this category as "novice users (users without domain knowledge)".

12.6.1 Evaluation with Novice Users (C_1)

C_1 consists of three groups of students, all participants of the groups were novice, without any knowledge about the visualized data and the business domain. We asked them to compare their experience obtained from analyzing data with tabletop only (C_{1-t}) and their experience analyzing the data with the analytical agent and the tabletop (C_{1-a}). We gave the participants two decision-making tasks, one to be completed with C_{1-t} and the other with (C_{1-a}). During the experiment, we monitored the participants, but did not intervene with their decision-making process.

C_{1-t}-related discoveries

When participants interacted with the tabletop only, our presence was required to give information about the meaning of the data. For instance, they asked what the colors represented, what the points visualized on the map and the definition of domain-related concepts. Post-study interviews with the students revealed that the need for the presence of a domain expert (as were we in this case) was a huge drawback of C_{1-t}. Two of the students reported that although C_{1-t} provided ease of collaboration and was an engaging medium for discussions, when they moved their hands over the table (especially for zoom or panning), a portion of visualization was occluded. Yet, that was the exact portion the participants were discussing about.

C_{1-a}-related discoveries

When the analytical agent was added to the sessions, participants did not direct their questions to us anymore. While interacting with the data on the tabletop, they asked the agent about their meaning. Hence, the analytical agent replaced the human domain expert needed in C_{1-t}. While the participants were discussing the interaction with the data, the analytical agent showcased basic hypotheses based on previous analytical sessions. For example, it showed the most used filters by prior participants. Overall, students were successful in interacting with and analyzing the data. They reported that "At the beginning of the session Jason was very informative. However, when we started testing our own hypothesis, the figures and charts shown by the agent were sometimes too complex to understand". The two students who mentioned the occlusion drawback of C_{1-t}, said that "When we moved our hands to zoom or pan action, the map on the table was occluded by our hands. However, in this session, since we can use the agent to complete such actions, we do not have to use our hands all the time when we want to zoom or pan".

When asked to contrast their experience in C_{1-t}, with their experience in C_{1-a}, the students found the guidance of the agent as helpful for data exploration and analysis. While none of the students explicitly stated that the agent facilitated decision-making, all of them preferred the agent condition over the tabletop only condition. "I was very lost when interacting only with the tabletop, the agent clarified what the data meant and what could be done with the data", a participant said.

12.6.2 Evaluation with Domain Experts (C_2)

Participants of the two groups in C_2 had in-depth knowledge about the data and the business domain. We conducted two sessions with each group. In the first session, participants interacted only with the tabletop (C_{2-t}). Whereas, in the second session they interacted with the analytical agent (C_{2-a}) also. We requested them to contrast their experiences between the two conditions. Participants were also encouraged to report inadequate aspects of or desiderata for the platform.

C_{2-t}-related discoveries

Participants of both groups reported that (C_{2-t}) accelerates resource planning and hypothesis testing tasks compared to their regular workflow. They emphasized that whether it facilitates decision-making certainly depends on the scenario. One of the participants stated "I can easily collaborate using the tabletop. It also provides a suitable setting for discussion and hypothesis testing. However, it would be beneficial to see multiple maps, as I wanted to compare data between two cities and I could not accomplish that".

The main inference from experts' experience with (C_{2-t}) was that they saw it as a compelling visualization tool if showing the data to managers, or other less involved parties. However, they were concerned about it not bringing too much value to their everyday workflow.

C_{2-a}-related discoveries

In the second session, when interacting with the analytical agent also, domain experts indicated that C_{2-a} allowed more natural interactions with the data. A participant said, "Interacting with the data through speech helped me ask complex queries". Another participant said that "In our everyday workflow, we conduct statistical analysis manually. The figures and charts shown by the agent were really helpful to understand the distribution of the data on the fly". However, three participants noted that the agent recommended hypothesis and information about the discussed topics were sometimes very simple. The participant who stated the problem of not being able to see multiple maps simultaneously in C_{2-t}, enjoyed the added monitor to the interaction. She said, "Seeing the table and the agent monitors at the same time, gave me an opportunity to compare two cities' data". Participants particularly highlighted meeting summarization notes and the ability to learn previous hypotheses and analyses from past notes. The experts noted that qualitative past meeting notes meetings, would potentially shorten the decision-making time. That is, because a lot of previously explored hypotheses come up in the current meeting. Having the past exploration results at hand, hence makes notes of particular importance.

When requested to compare their experience in C_{2-a} with their experience in C_{2-t}, the experts highlighted the agent as being helpful for testing hypotheses, analyses and meeting summarization. A participant noted: "While the tabletop was a good visualization medium, the agent further improved it as a useful interface for queries".

12.7 Discussion

In this chapter, we introduce a system for facilitating decision-making in exploratory and collaborative visual analytics sessions. The system is comprised of a tabletop and an analytical agent. We conduct qualitative evaluations with expert and novice users, by having them interact with the tabletop only and tabletop combined with the agent.

Our qualitative study indicates that both novice and expert participants found the agent condition more helpful for data exploration and decision-making over the tabletop-only condition. Further, two drawbacks of the tabletop as stated by the participants were: (1) occlusion of parts of visualization while interacting with the data and (2) the inability to show more than one map at the same time. The second drawback can be overcome by a different interface design which allows multiple maps to be shown at the same time. However, the first drawback is inherent to the tabletop, and cannot be alleviated.

On the other hand, our results also indicate that the agent brings solutions to the two tabletop drawbacks stated above. By using the extra monitor, the agent can assist in displaying multiple maps and showing the same map in the case of occlusion. We observed from our experiments that the assistant analytical agent's advantages can be gathered under these themes: exhibiting extra information which helps the users to create hypothesis, showing charts and figures that make participants test their hypothesis, guiding them for decision-making processes and generating meeting summarization notes.

We conducted studies with participants with different domain expertise, to evaluate whether the system was useful independent of participant domain-knowledge level. Our user studies indicate that experienced users understood the agent's data analysis, such as charts, graphs and figures easier than novice users. As future work, we might update our system to account for user expertise. The more experienced users will be shown more complex data, whereas a simplified version of the same data will be shown to novice users.

Overall, our user study results demonstrate that the system proposed in this chapter is a useful tool in collaborative visual analytics sessions. By widening the exploration space and making data analysis easier, our system facilitates decision-making.

12.8   Conclusion

In this chapter, we presented a system comprised of a tabletop and an assistant analytical agent to support multiple user analytical decision-making processes. Our aim was to establish an environment suited for facilitating and fostering more productive decision-making processes.

The assistant analytical agent visualizes data on displays, answers attendees' requests, has conversations with them and helps the meeting leader on managing meetings. It also attempts on engaging the disengaged participants by raising questions of interest to increase the productivity of the meeting. The analytical agent creates notes on problems discussed and solutions generated during the meeting. Consequently, the agent assists the participants to have more productive meetings and exploring data from different points of view.

Overall, our system presents a context for collaboration, exploration and facilitates decision-making in multi-user analytical sessions.

Acknowledgements We acknowledge Flaticon.com for providing hand gesture icons. This work was partially supported by TUBITAK (Scientific and Technological Research Council of Turkey) project number 114E516.

References

Apple (2019) Siri. https://www.apple.com/siri. In: Bara F et al (2004) The visuo-haptic and haptic exploration of letters increases the kindergarten-children's understanding of the alphabetic principle. In: Cognitive development 19.3, pp. 433–449. ISSN: 0885-2014. https://doi.org/10.1016/j.cogdev.2004.05.003

Beck, Alan et al. (2003). "Robotic pets and the elderly". In: Project overview

Bickmore, Timothy W. et al. (2005). "Acceptance and Usability of a Relational Agent Interface by Urban Older Adults". In: CHI '05 Extended Abstracts on Human Factors in Computing Systems. CHI EA '05. Portland, OR, USA: ACM, pp. 1212-1215. isbn: 1-59593-002-7. https://doi.org/10.1145/1056808.1056879.

Blenke, Lawrence R (2013). The role of face-to-face interactions in the success of virtual project teams. Doctoral Dissertations

Bortolaso, Christophe et al. (2014). "The E?ect of View Techniques on Collaboration and Awareness in Tabletop Map-Based Tasks". In: Proceedings of the Ninth ACM International Conference on Interactive Tabletops and Surfaces. ITS '14. Dresden, Germany: ACM, pp. 79-88. isbn: 978-1-4503-2587-5. doi: https://doi.org/10.1145/2669485.2669504

Burgstahler, D. et al. (June 2014). "Switching Push and Pull: An Energy E?cient Noti?cation Approach". In: 2014 IEEE International Conference on Mobile Ser- vices, pp. 68-75. https://doi.org/10.1109/MobServ.2014.19.

Card, Stuart K et al. (1991). "The information visualizer, an information workspace". In: Proceedings of the SIGCHI Conference on Human factors in computing sys- tems. ACM, pp. 181-186

Cesta, Amedeo et al. (2007). "Supporting Interaction in the ROBOCARE Intelligent Assistive Environment." In: AAAI Spring Symposium: Interaction Challenges for Intelligent Assistants, pp. 18-25

Coombs Steven J (2000) The Psychology of User-friendliness: The use of Infor- mation Technology as a Re?ective Learning Medium. Korean Journal of Thinking & Problem Solving 10(2):19–31

DiSalvo, C. et al. (Nov. 2003). "The Hug: an exploration of robotic form for intimate communication". In: The 12th IEEE International Workshop on Robot and Human Interactive Communication, 2003. Proceedings. ROMAN 2003. Pp. 403-408. https://doi.org/10.1109/ROMAN.2003.1251879.

Ehnes, J. (May 2009). "A tangible interface for the AMI Content Linking Device - the automated meeting assistant". In: 2009 2nd Conference on Human System Interactions, pp. 306-313. https://doi.org/10.1109/HSI.2009.5090997.

Fan, Min et al. (2014). "Exploring how a co-dependent tangible tool design supports collaboration in a tabletop activity". In: Proceedings of the 18th international conference on supporting group work. ACM, pp. 81-90

Girard, Philippe and Vincent Robin (2006). "Analysis of collaboration for project de- sign management". In: Computers in Industry 57.8. Collaborative Environments for Concurrent Engineering Special Issue, pp. 817-826. issn: 0166-3615. doi: https://doi.org/10.1016/j.compind.2006.04.016

Google, (2019) Google Speech-To-Text. Accessed: 2019–01-22. url: https : / /cloud.google.com/speech-to-text

Graf, Birgit et al. (Mar. 2004). "Care-O-bot II-Development of a Next Generation Robotic Home Assistant". In: Autonomous Robots 16.2, pp. 193-205. issn: 1573- 7527. https://doi.org/10.1023/B:AURO.0000016865.35796.e9.

Guizzo, E. and H. Goldstein (Oct. 2005). "The rise of the body bots [robotic ex- oskeletons]". In: IEEE Spectrum 42.10, pp. 50-56. issn: 0018-9235. doi: 10 . 1109/MSPEC.2005.1515961

Henkin, R. and C. Turkay (Mar. 2018). "Towards Multimodal Data Analytics: Inte- grating Natural Language into Visual Analytics". In: Multimodal Interaction for Data Visualization Workshop at AVI 2018

Hoque, E. et al. (Jan. 2018). "Applying Pragmatics Principles for Interaction with Vi- sual Analytics". In: IEEE Transactions on Visualization and Computer Graphics 24.1, pp. 309-318. issn: 1077-2626. https://doi.org/10.1109/TVCG.2017.2744684.

Hou, J. et al. (Dec. 2008). "A Methodology of Knowledge Management Based on Ontology in Collaborative Design". In: 2008 Second International Symposium on Intelligent Information Technology Application. Vol. 2, pp. 409-413. https://doi.org/10.1109/IITA.2008.503.

Ishii Hiroshi et al (2012) Radical atoms: beyond tangible bits, toward trans- formable materials. Interactions 19:38–51

Jung, Jin-Woo et al. (June 2005). "Advanced robotic residence for the elderly/the handicapped: realization and user evaluation". In: 9th International Conference on Rehabilitation Robotics, 2005. ICORR 2005. Pp. 492-495. doi: 10 . 1109 / ICORR.2005.1501149

Kaya, Erdem et al. (2018). "Low-?delity prototyping with simple collaborative tabletop computer-aided design systems". In: Computers & Graphics 70, pp. 307- 315. issn: 0097-8493. https://doi.org/10.1016/j.cag.2017.07.026.

Keim, Daniel et al. (2008). "Visual analytics: De?nition, process, and challenges". In: Information visualization. Springer, pp. 154-175

Li, Min et al. (Sept. 2006). "Real-Time Collaborative Design With Heterogeneous CAD Systems Based on Neutral Modeling Commands". In: Journal of Computing and Information Science in Engineering. https://doi.org/10.1115/1.2720880.

Magnenat-Thalmann, Nadia and Zh?un Zhang (2014). "Social robots and virtual humans as assistive tools for improving our quality of life". In: Digital Home (ICDH), 2014 5th International Conference on. IEEE, pp. 1-7

Microsoft, (2019) Cortana. Accessed: 2019–01-27. url: https://docs.microsoft.com/en-us/cortana/skills

Mikolov, Tomas et al. (2013). "Distributed representations of words and phrases and their compositionality". In: Advances in neural information processing systems, pp. 3111-3119

Reas Casey, Fry Ben (2006) Processing: programming for the media arts. AI & SOCIETY 20(4):526–538

Scanaill, Cliodhna Ni et al. (Apr. 2006). "Review of Approaches to Mobility Tele- monitoring of the Elderly in Their Living Environment". In: Annals of Biomedical Engineering 34.4, pp. 547-563. issn: 1573-9686. https://doi.org/10.1007/s10439-005-9068-2

Scott, Stacey D. et al. (2003). "System Guidelines for Co-located, Collaborative Work on a Tabletop Display". In: ECSCW 2003. Ed. by Kari Kuutti et al. Dordrecht: Springer Netherlands, pp. 159-178. isbn: 978-94-010-0068-0

Shen, Chia et al. (2003). "UbiTable: Impromptu Face-to-Face Collaboration on Horizontal Interactive Surfaces". In: UbiComp 2003: Ubiquitous Computing. Ed. by Anind K. Dey et al. Berlin, Heidelberg: Springer Berlin Heidelberg, pp. 281- 288. isbn: 978-3-540-39653-6

Shen, C. et al. (Sept. 2006). "Informing the Design of Direct-Touch Tabletops". In: IEEE Computer Graphics and Applications 26.5, pp. 36-46. issn: 0272-1716

Thompson, P. et al. (June 2011). "Agent based facilitator assistant for virtual meet- ings". In: Proceedings of the 2011 15th International Conference on Computer Supported Cooperative Work in Design (CSCWD), pp. 335-341. doi: https://doi.org/10.1109/SCWD.2011.5960095

Tur, G. et al. (Aug. 2010). "The CALO Meeting Assistant System". In: IEEE Trans- actions on Audio, Speech, and Language Processing 18.6, pp. 1601-1611. issn: 1558-7916. https://doi.org/10.1109/TASL.2009.2038810.

Ushirobira, R. et al. (June 2016). "A forecasting algorithm for latency compensation in indirect human-computer interactions". In: 2016 European Control Conference (ECC), pp. 1081-1086. https://doi.org/10.1109/ECC.2016.7810433.

Vivacqua Adriana et al (2011) BOO: Behavior-oriented ontology to describe participant dynamics in collocated design meetings. Expert Systems with Applications 38:1139–1147. https://doi.org/10.1016/j.eswa.2010.05.007

Wikipedia, (2019) Kinect for Xbox One. Accessed: 2019–01-22. https://en.wikipedia.org/wiki/

Wilson M (2002) Six views of embodied cognition. Psychon Bull Rev 9(4):625–636. ISSN: 1531-5320. https://doi.org/10.3758/BF03196322

Yanco A, Holly (2001) Development and testing of a robotic wheelchair system for outdoor navigation. In: Proceedings of The IEEE—PIEEE

Chapter 13
Human—Technology Interaction: The State-of-the-Art and the Lack of Naturalism

Evangelia Baka and Nadia Magnenat Thalmann

Abstract The current chapter serves as a state-of-the-art, presenting the limitations of the existing technology used in the broad area of human–computer interaction up to now. Although different kind of agents have been used to contribute to several domains, like education, health, entertainment, both in virtual and physical environments, the virtual character or robot that will make a human feel as comfortable as interacting with another human has not been reported yet. What is mainly missing from the up to date state-of-the-art is the direct comparison of all these technologies with the original human–human communication. What we need to do is to keep studying the human–human communication and not only features of the HCI as what is missing is how we, as humans, react in several contexts of communication. Through this kind of research, we can contribute to the enhancement of naturalism of every kind of agent, offering a higher level of understanding and affection in the context of everyday communication.

13.1 Introduction

Published in Mind in 1950, Alan Turing's original proposal raised questions on the intelligence of the machines, with the most famous question to be "Can machines think?". This inspired a lot of researchers to start examining the potentials of human–computer interaction (HCI), leading to a point where technology has started to be actively involved in the communication process.

E. Baka (✉) · N. Magnenat Thalmann
MIRALab, University of Geneva, Geneva, Switzerland
e-mail: ebaka@miralab.ch

N. Magnenat Thalmann
e-mail: thalmann@miralab.ch; nadiathalmann@ntu.edu.sg

N. Magnenat Thalmann
Institute of Media Innovation, Nanyang Technological University, Singapore, Singapore

To decipher and interpret the features and the boundaries between humans and technology, a first step is to compare human–human interaction with the one between humans and machines. The research of human–human communication can reveal the most useful information for enhancing the HCI field and thus, it can clearly be stated as a starting point. It has already been proved that people are more willing to discuss and even disclose private information when computers follow and present human-based conversation rules (Nass and Moon 2000).

Baylor (2011) stated the three main factors that can characterize a natural social interaction between a human and an agent. What we characterize as agent, based on what Ferber defined, is "a physical or virtual entity that can act, perceive its environment (in a partial way) and communicate with others, is autonomous and has skills to achieve its goals and tendencies" (Ferber 1999). Thus, according to Baylor's research, social interaction is portrayed by the appearance of the agent, i.e. cartoon or realistic figures, the communication features, such as gestures or facial expressions and the content of the dialogue. All this research has been based on Bandura's first theoretical social cognitive learning theory, where he supports that people learn behaviors and norms be imitating other people who react in the same way. Trying to boost this imitation, researchers are trying to create more realistic avatars or robots to facilitate the human interaction with the technology. This realism is based on human responses and reactions and human appearance.

13.2 Human Perception During HCI

13.2.1 The Role of Human Likeness

There are several hypotheses tested for the human likeness. The most commonly used are the uncanny valley, the atypical feature, the category conflict, and the similarity hypothesis. The first one, the **uncanny valley hypothesis (UVH)**, described by Professor Mori, suggests that when a character just resembles a human, without being one, creates awkward feelings in human observers (Mori 1970). The higher the human likeliness, the stronger the sensation of eeriness. There are several promoters of this hypothesis, supporting that an agent, avatar, or a robot, is better to be cartoon-based rather than having a physical appearance in order to be more preferred by a human (Baylor 2011). Research on virtual representation has proved that too much anthropomorphism can lead to negative effects, less trust, and discomfort (Nowak 2004). Recently, Stein and Ohler (2017) supported the extension of this theory as the "uncanny valley of the mind" where they argue that it is also the human-like behavior of the agent, "behavioral anthropomorphism" as they call it, that can cause negative reactions (Stein and Ohler 2017). Some researchers also support that it is not only the high degree of human-like appearance that can trigger this hypothesis but also a possible mismatch between the form and the behavior (Nowak and Fox 2018). However, Mori et al (2012) expressed their doubts, proving that if the agent is designed in a way that is hardly distinguishable from a real person, then the valence becomes positive again (Mori et al. 2012). The morphology of an agent, aligned with the uncanny valley hypothesis, may indeed influence the perception and the behavior of a person during an interaction, but the degree depends on the task. People prefer more human-like morphology when they refer to social roles or to real-time interaction for example (Edwards et al. 2019). An evaluation of UVH was conducted by Lupkowski and Gierszewska in their recent work, where they used 12 computer-rendered humanoid models to test the human perception and the UV effect (Lupkowski and Gierszewska 2019). For their purpose, they used a subscale of the NARS questionnaire regarding the human traits. The main points of their research are firstly, that the highest comfort level was noticed for a cartoon-based character and secondly that the belief of a person in human uniqueness can directly affect his/her attitude toward an agent; the higher the belief, the more nervous the person toward the agent.

The **typical feature hypothesis** supports that atypical features of the stimulus may influence the perception (Borst and Gelder 2015). Burleigh et al. noticed that the eye size constitutes such a feature. Moreover, they found that whenever human likeness was high, eeriness was low (linear relationship) (Burleigh et al. 2013). Third, the **category conflict hypothesis** (Borst and Gelder 2015) suggests that *"when human likeness of the stimulus is comprised of a morph between two categories, the stimuli in the middle of this scale are perceived as ambiguous, leading to a negative effect"*. Yamada et al. tested also this hypothesis, concluding that the most ambiguous image reflects to an increased processing time (Yamada et al. 2013). Lastly, the **similarity hypothesis** by Rosenberg-Kima et al. (2010) predicts that the gender similarity (male or female) and the attractivity of an agent have a more positive effect on the motivational outcome. This hypothesis was confirmed by Shiban et al. (2015) who used a young female agent and an older male one to test the effects on performance and motivation in learning process (Fig. 13.1).

However, the big question here is if it is the appearance of the agent who influences the perception and the performance of the user, or it is also their behavior in combination with a contextual environment. Are there measurable benefits for the

Fig. 13.1 The uncanney valley as described by Mori et al. (2012), depicting the relationship between the natural resemblance and the affinity for it. The dotted line represents the effect of the presence of movement

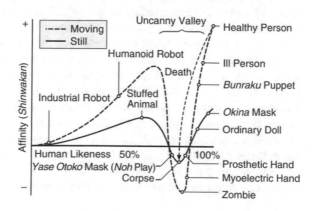

user and can we reach a level where a virtual avatar or a robot can really simulate the human behavior so that we can really compare the different cases and come to a conclusion about the usability of such agents?

Nevertheless, the majority of studies, having examined the role of human likeness, have been based in questionnaires suitable for such purposes. As Kätsyri et al. also mentioned, these kinds of studies cannot easily clear up the existing vagueness of this field, so psychophysiological studies are of need (Kätsyri et al. 2015). Ratajczyk et al. continued the work of Lupkowski and Gierszewska mentioned above, using electrodermal activity (EDA) and response time measurement to evaluate the UV effect and the human perception toward the same 12 characters, assessing also the role of their environment (background). Another interesting recent example is the one of Ciechanowski et al. who used facial electromyography (EMG), respirometer, electrocardiography, and EDA to examine the human-nonhuman interaction process between a human and a chatbox (Ciechanowski et al. 2019).

13.2.2   The Role of Embodiment and Presence

Intelligent systems have two critical features that can affect human's perception during HCI: **embodiment** and **presence**. Embodiment was defined by Pfeifer and Scheier (1999) as a *term which refers to the fact that "intelligence cannot merely exist in the form of an abstract algorithm but requires a physical instantiation, a body"*. The level of embodiment is dependent on the nature of the agent (physical, virtual, or even a combination of both), the morphology (i.e. human-like or cartoon-based), as well as the modalities it can support and the extent to which these modalities can be carried out (Li 2015). Other variables, like gestures, speech speed, and haptic stimuli, may also be considered as aspects of an agent's embodiment.

Whereas embodiment concerns the agent and its relationship with its environment, presence deals with the way this agent is presented to others. Milgram et al (1995) defined physical and digital presence as a situation where the embodied agent can be touched, saying specifically *"whether primary world objects are viewed directly or by means of some electronic synthesis process"*. Zhao categorized physical and digital presence as *copresence* and *telepresence,* respectively (Zhao 2003). Copresence, as a term in a sociological framework, describes the conditions under which humans interact with each other (Zhao 2003). Under the umbrella of HCI and HRI, copresence refers to how the agent is displayed to the user. Zhao (2003) used two dimensions to describe the copresence. The first one refers to *"the mode of being with others"* and concerns features that can physically shape a human interaction whereas the second one refers to *"the sense of being with others"*, linked to the feeling and the subjectivity of the user (Zhao 2003). We need though to differentiate physical embodiment and physical presence (copresence) as an agent, that may have physical embodiment, may not have a physical morphology presented to the user (Li 2015). There are several researchers who tried to evaluate the role and the influence of presence and embodiment in virtual environments or in robotics (Li 2015; Lee et al. 2006; Mollahosseini et al. 2018).

So, here we can pose the first question, regarding the effect of physical presence. Do people react differently in an interaction with a copresent agent (robot) compared to a telepresent one?

Researches up to now have proven that psychological responses between these two situations differ due to a variety of reasons. Initially, one reason is the size of the agent and consequently the influence it can have (Hoffman and krämer 2011). Robots that are physically present have usually a bigger size than a virtual agent displayed in a screen. As Huang et al. have mentioned, taller individuals tend to provoke a bigger social influence (Huang et al. 2002) and thus, the larger size of the physical robot may be more imposing, having a stronger impact.

Distance is one of the main aspects of presence, as Zhao also supported (Zhao 2003), which can be divided into the physical and the electronic proximity. This leads to the second reason which is the physical distance between the user and the agent, as physical proximity is normal to have different effects compared to the electronic one (Shinozawa et al. 2005). Moreover, the interaction with a physical agent allows a better understanding of its morphology and motion, creating a more familiar environment with the user. In general, it has been shown that physical presence can improve the user's behavior as well as increase the level of enjoyment and trust (Li 2015).

In the case of the same appearance, a recent survey showed that the 79% of the up to date studies favored a robot that is copresent compared to a telepresent one (Li 2015).

The next question derives as a continuation of the latter and examines the effect of physical embodiment. Do people react differently interacting with a physical agent compared to a virtual one?

One reason for which the embodiment may result to the psychological processing of the user is the degree of realism (Hoffman and Krämer 2011). Han et al. compared, with the use of functional Magnetic Resonance Imaging (fMRI), real and virtual visual worlds through the observation of movie or cartoon clips, aiming to provide information on how we perceive characters in real and virtual worlds (Han et al. 2005). They concluded that the perception of real-world characters triggers the medial prefrontal area (MPFC) of the brain and the cerebellum which act as an online representation and empathy of mental states of others, whereas cartoon clips of humans and non-human agents activated the superior parietal lobes which are associated with attention when referring to actions (Han et al. 2005). The cartoon-based clips also engaged the occipital area of the brain which is linked with the visual attention mechanism. The latter has also been proven by the study of Baka et al. (2018) where, with the use of an electroencephalography device (EEG), they showed that the occipital area, among a physical, a virtual identical to the physical and a virtual cartoon-based environment, reacts differently only under the cartoon-based environment, being synchronized in an alpha state (8–12 Hz). The alpha state activity, in that case, is associated with the recruitment of visual attention mechanisms.

Studies that have examined the influence of physical embodiment separately from the physical presence, comparing telepresent robots to virtual avatars, reported no significant results (Li 2015).

However, what if the physical embodiment and the physical presence are combined? The majority of the studies have supported that people prefer the physical presence of a robot than a virtual avatar (Li 2015), having also significant effects in several behavioral responses like performance, attention (Looije et al. 2012) and response speed (Jost et al. 2012). However, gesturing has been proved to play an important role in the response of people during HCI. Thus, to complement the above, people prefer copresent agents, compared to telepresent robots or virtual agents, but only when they use gestures to complete their interaction (Hasegawa et al. 2010).

In general, Jamy Li proved though his survey that physical presence plays a greater role in psychological responses to an agent than the physical embodiment. So, it seems that no matter the nature of the embodiment (virtual or physical) which constitutes a feature of the character, the presence is the one that can directly influence the response and behavior of the people (Li 2015). That is, what matters is how the agent will be presented to the user and finally, how the embodiment can allow that. However, there is a limitation in this field as there are no studies that have used avatars of high-level naturalism, decreasing the effect of human appearance. Moreover, the exploration of how additional variables like gesturing or voice features can influence humans' responses is also clearly missing from the up to date bibliography.

13.2.3   Other Features that Can Influence Human's Perception During HCI

Another important feature that has been tested in such interactions is the role of the eye gaze. Eye gaze is one of the most important features of the human behavior while a social interaction as it can serve several purposes and functions like enhancing the attention, revealing emotional information, preserving engagement. Therefore, it has been proved that the physical presence plays a greater role in the gaze's perception compared to physical embodiment and thus a robot's eye gaze can be more accurate than the one of a virtual agent (Mollahoseini et al. 2018).

Studies that have examined and proved that through facial expressions the behavioral and emotional intentions of another person can be predicted, started around 1973 (Ekman 1973). It has been shown that observers tend to activate similar facial muscle activity with the speakers intended facial expressions (Kunecke et al. 2014). This reaction has been characterized as Rapid Facial Reaction (RFS) [Moody] constituting an affective reaction that can occur automatically after the stimulus presentation. The majority of such studies have used a congruent direction of gaze and body using an eye-tracking system for the gaze, EMG for the face muscles, and a questionnaire for the self-assessment (Schrammel et al. 2009). However, the importance of body's direction started to raise questions and more recent studies (Marschner et al. 2015; Kluttz et al. 2009) examined the influence of the difference in body and gaze direction. Thus, although it has been shown that the gaze is one of the major indicators of socio-communicative dimensions, it has been finally proved that only when combined and congruent with body orientation, it can modulate emotional experience and attention.

Humans can express different kind of emotions while interacting with different type of agents, under the same circumstances. A priori, the communication between human beings has been guided and facilitated by the existence of emotions. Emotions, as an inherent internal procedure, are the mirror of what we feel, allowing us to perceive and understand our environment, including ourselves. It has been proven that people experience more positive emotions when interacting with a virtual agent that provides positive feedback instead of a negative one (Pour et al. 2010). Mollahosseini et al. (2018) studied the perception of people toward facial expressions of a virtual agent, a copresent retro-projected robot, a telepresent robot and a video recording of a human and they found that the emotion recognition rates differentiated among the several agent conditions. In other words, humans perceived, and consequently expressed, differently the emotions based on the nature of the agent (Mollahosseini et al. 2018). Lazzeri et al. (2015) also proved that emotions that are expressed through facial expressions can be better perceived on a robotic agent than a virtual one (Lazzeri et al. 2015). On the contrary, virtual agents seem to be more effective when it concerns visual speech due to the computer graphics that can provide a better accuracy on the realism and the animations (Mollahosseini et al. 2018).

13.3 Human—Robot Interaction (HRI)

There have been a lot of research trying to decipher the human behavior and perception when interacting with robots instead of other humans. There are even movies that describe such interactions and, even if we consider them as science fiction films, we are at a point where people have started communicating and meeting social robots in a real-life context incorporating personal or professional roles (Edwards et al. 2019).

It has already been shown that the first reaction of people toward an initial communication with a social robot is a feeling of uncertainty and decreased anticipation (Edwards et al. 2019). However, Edwards et al. suggested that this behavior is a result of the deviating social communication pattern, that leads to the alteration of the "script" and expectations during a human–human interaction. Humans, unconsciously, follow a script when interacting with each other, adapted to various social situations. One of the roles of HRI research though is to decode these scripts and allow similar behaviors to take place during a human–robot interaction.

Communication has been described by Kellerman (1992) as a "heavily-scripted procedure" (Kellerman 1992). In the framework of this procedure, humans are used to interact with another humans, creating an anthropocentric expectancy in the communication. However, despite these expectations, it has been supported that people tend to treat computer or other social intelligent technology as if they were people, by applying similar social scripts as the ones used during a human–human interaction. Reeves and Nass (1996) first illustrated this opinion with their Computers Are Social Actors (CASA) paradigm, showing that people mindlessly relate to machines and apply social rules as if they were indeed real people, even if they are aware of their incapability to embody emotions and intentions (Reeves and Nass 1996). Reeves and Nass, in the same study, also suggested that people treat televisions like real people. This was confirmed by Nass and Moon (2000), who examined user's responses to different kind of televisions and they concluded that humans perceive them also as social actors (Nass and Moon 2000). In general, Nass and Moon supported that people tend to focus on the social cues, even if they are a few, bypassing the asocial features of the entities. CASA has been already involved in several studies in a broader field of research including AI and social robots. Recently, Mou and Xu (2017) compared the initial human-AI social interaction with the one between humans in terms of personality traits and communication attributes (Mou and Xu 2017). They support that their outcome complements the CASA paradigm as they found that people can change their behavior toward social actors if they are aware that they will interact with an AI.

Edwards et al. (2019) showed that the human-like morphology can satisfy this anthropocentric expectancy during an interaction. They also confirmed the hyper-personal model, launched by Walther (1996), based on which computer-mediated communication can sometimes surpass a face-to-face interaction in terms of intimacy and liking (Walther 1996). Thus, they concluded that according to the context of the discussion an interaction with a robot can increase the level of attribution of social presence and decrease the degree of uncertainty.

While the boundary between human–computer and human–human interaction is described by CASA concept, social psychologists maintain doubts regarding the psychological invariance that can characterize a person across several different situations. This is the so-called personality paradox or consistency paradox, describing that a person can present different personality traits and behaviors under different circumstances. Attempting to solve this paradox, in the framework of human–computer interaction, Mischel and Shoda developed the Cognitive—Affective Processing System (CAPS) (Mischel and Shoda 1995). Mischel wanted the psychologists to think like mechanics and valuate people's responses according to particular conditions. According to this model, the personality system encompasses mental representations consisting of various cognitive-affective units (CAUs) that include a person's goals, beliefs, values, affective responses, and memories (Mischel 2004). Different CAUs can be activated under different conditions and different context, shaping accordingly the behavior of the individual. Consequently, when interacting with a machine, some people may feel more confident during the interacting process whereas others can feel confused and frightened. Therefore, based on the CAPS model, when interacting with a machine, humans' behavior and reaction should be different than the one presented when communicating with another human (Mou and Xu 2017).

However, it has been shown that putting robots in an anthropomorphic framework, by giving to them a personal name and even a story to follow, can affect human's behavior and reaction toward them (Edwards et al. 2019).

13.3.1 Social Robots and Their Features

The idea of robots, as mechanical agent serving specific purposes, has started a very long time ago, described even in Greek mythology. However, robots with natural language features, able to participate in a conversation, appeared in the 1990s, with the example of MAIA (Antoniol et al. 1993) and RHINO (Burgard et al. 1998). These kinds of robots were developed to cover a specific range of applications and consequently had some limitations, like the limited nonverbal communication, the difficulty in the perception of human speech, the specific pre-defined range of responses (Mavridis 2015). All these restraints of the 90 s have become the inspiration of the next years' research trying to understand and enhance the features of human–machine interaction.

Robots have been tested in several roles serving various applications where verbal and nonverbal communication are needed, like assistance and companionship (Wada and Shibata 2007; Dautenhahn et al. 2006), receptionist (Makatchev et al. 2010), educational purposes (Li et al. 2016; Kanda et al. 2009), museum robots, and tour guides (Yamazaki et al. 2012; Evers et al. 2014), or even involved in art, like musicians (Petersen et al. 2010) and dancers (Kosuge et al. 2003). In all the above applications, the main goal is the fluidity in the communication between the human and the machine, for any verbal or nonverbal feature. To succeed this, researchers had to address limitations like breaking the "simple command only" barrier, coordination of motion and nonverbal communication, affective interaction, multiple speech acts, mixed-initiative dialogue, etc. (Mavridis 2015) On the contrary, this kind of restraints have already been addressed in the virtual world since the early seventies, with the Winograd's SHRDLU program that could support different speech acts and basic mixed-initiative dialogue (Winograd 1972). Due to the lack of the physical entity of a robot, VR was easier to be developed faster and in a different way than the area of robotics. We can assume that this is why people are more used to this technology, expressing also a higher preference toward it. Nevertheless, the main difference between robots and virtual agents is the physical embodiment.

Birmingham et al. examined a new role for robots, as mediator in a multi-party support group (Birmingham et al. 2020). The role of the robot was to motivate people to speak to each other and overcome their stress by increasing the sense of trust. Participants however declared at the end that the robot made the discussion mechanical, with lack of real flow and they noticed the specific features of the robot responsible for that. As the authors used a Nao robot, the participants noticed clearly the lack of humanity first of all in the expressions of its face. Thus, in line with other studies, facial expressions play a crucial role for an efficient interaction. For example, Zawieska et al. highlighted the importance of facial expressions as the majority of their participants attributed the intelligent behavior of the robot used for their experiment to its facial expressions (Zawieska et al. 2012). Moreover, Birmingham et al. found that the sound of the robot was not natural and consequently, non-native speakers had a difficulty to understand its voice.

One of the most important items that has been addressed by both worlds, is the affective/emotional aspect. Affection during human interaction plays a crucial role as it is directly associated with learning processes, persuasion, and empathy (Mavridis 2015). Pioneering work in this domain was made on virtual avatars like Steve (Johnson et al. 2000) or Greta (Rosis et al. 2003) that became the inspiration for Cynthia Breazeal to develop the Kismet robot, an expressive mechanomorphic robot head with perceptual and motor modalities that can support multiple facial expressions (Breazea and Velásquez 1998; Breazeal 2003].

Second most important feature is the one of motor and nonverbal communication coordination. People, when interacting with each other, they use several kind of motor actions head nods, hand gestures, gaze movements and of course lip-syncing (Mavridis 2015). There has been also stated that humans use lip information to perceive better a communication, the so-called McGurk effect (Mavridis 2015). Thus, to support even the basic level of naturalness during an interaction, agents should be able to use some of these features to accompany their sound production.

Social robotics is a rapidly increasing field aiming to develop robot capable of socio-emotionally interacting and communicating with humans serving several domains like education, health, and entertainment (Mollahosseini et al. 2018). The researches and recent technologies are trying to define the best choice between robots and virtual agents, best suited for the needs of social interaction (Table 13.1).

13.4 Humans and Virtual Avatars

Over the last years, the use of Virtual Agent (VA) has started to be known for its effectiveness over the use of real human, boosting users' motivation and even performance. Thus, the question of whether to implement a virtual agent or a robot is still under a lot of investigation and is considered to be totally dependent on the requirements of the task to be performed. The main advantages of a VA, as they have been stated until now, are the overall little cost of use, the easiness and flexibility of its use as it can be used anytime and from anywhere, the dynamical anytime changes of its appearance, as well as further possibilities that it can offer as collecting and examining real-time physiological data, such as facial or movement expressions (Li 2015; Yokotani et al. 2018). For the better understanding of this comparison (Virtual vs real human), we need to mention two, almost recent, terms. The first one, the *agency belief*, refers to the reaction of people toward VAs and specifically to the extent to which they can believe that a VA represents a real human (Lucas et al. 2014) whereas the second one, the *behavioral realism*, concerns the degree to which a VA can really behave like a real human (Blascovich 2002).

Table 13.1 Examples of social robots from several domains in a chronological order

Robot's name	Reference	Year	Type	Role
WABOT	Sugano and Kato	1987	Humanoid	Piano player
PARO	Shibata et al	1997	Baby seal	Social reintegration of elderly people
Care-O-bot	Graf et al	2004	Non-humanoid	Home assistance for elderly people
RI-MAN	Odasima et al	2006	Humanoid	On-site caregiver/lifting humans
ROBOTA	Billard et al	2007	Humanoid	Robot-assisted therapy for autistic children
IROMEC	Marti et al	2009	Non-humanoid	Children companion for knowledge enhancement
KASPAR	Dautenhahn et al	2009	Humanoid	Robot-assisted therapy for autistic children
SHIMON	Hoffman and Weinberg	2010	Humanoid	Playing of percussive instruments
NADINE	Kokoro and Thalmann/Ramanathan et al	2013 (2019)	Humanoid	Social companion
JIBO	Breazeal and Faridi	2016	Non-humanoid	Personal assistant
SOPHIA	Hanson Robotics/Weller	2017	Humanoid	Social companion

It has been shown that different levels of agency belief and behavioral realism serve different purposes. For example, VA's low behavioral realism is considered to be suitable for interviews settings (Rizzo et al. 2016). Specifically, voice-only interviews have been proved to be more effective than face to face ones, helping participants to feel more comfortable to speak with higher level of self-disclosure (Bailenson et al. 2006). Moreover, participant's low agency belief seems also to be more effective in such cases (Lucas et al. 2014). On the other hand, Baylor and Kim (Baylor and Kim 2009) showed that a physically present agent can provoke better motivational results than a voice or a text box under learning circumstances. There are several studies supporting that embodied talking agents can enhance the engagement of the user (Mollahosseini et al. 2018). However, Mayer and Dapra showed that an agent can have a positive effect on a user only when the voice it supports is human-like and not a machine voice (Mayer and DaPra 2012).

13.4.1 Conceptualization and Perception of Avatars

Virtual Reality Environments, with their virtual characters, can offer opportunities and enable manipulations that may be difficult, or even impossible, to happen in a natural environment. In these environments, users can control, embody, and interact through avatars in several contexts, shaping the field of computer-mediated communication (Nowak and Fox 2018). The use of an avatar, in such kind of communication, plays a crucial role as avatars can be used as a means of influence in a variety of contexts like health communication, interpersonal communication, nonverbal communication, advertising, etc. (Nowak and Fox 2018). It can also support more complex behaviors and actions, enhancing the nonverbal communication through gestures or body movements.

Every avatar has each own characteristics that can include for example appearance, behaviors, or abilities and can be specified based on several factors like the users' preference and their previous experiences in such environments as well as the technological capabilities of the system. However, as Nowak and Fox. (2018) mentioned, the term "avatar" is used by many researchers without being properly defined, causing sometimes misinterpretations in the framework of the relevant studies.

The origin of the word "avatar" is derived from the Hinduism and specifically from the Sanskrit word for "descent" (Nowak and Fox 2018). In this concept, an avatar is the incarnation of a deity on earth, being able to experience the human aspects. Nowadays, and for more than twenty years, avatars have been acknowledged as digital representations. The term became popular mainly though the novel of Neal Stephenson (1992), who used it repeatedly to refer to characters being in digital environments (Nowak 2004). Following to that, a lot of researchers gave several definitions to this term trying to include the features like the appearance, the abilities, the degree of realism or the anthropomorphism. Therefore, some definitions include terms like "cartoon-based" or "two dimensional" but these are continuously evolving as the technologies advance. We often hear terms like "embodied avatar", "virtual human", "agent". In every case, there are two main points that are served; the avatar can represent the user in a computer-mediated environment, and it can provide the experience of interaction with the environment of another user. The most recent definition is the one of Nowak and Fox (2018) where "*an avatar is a digital representation of a human user that facilitates interaction with other users, entities, or the environment*" (Nowak and Fox 2018). They chose to use a broad definition that can be used as an umbrella, independent of any specifications or characteristics.

The characteristics of an avatar can directly influence the user's perception. For example, based on the Information Processing Theory, people can get easier affected and can pay higher attention to sources that consists of dynamism (McGuire 1985). Aspects that can influence a person's perception of an agent being in a virtual environment can be technical based, like the anthropomorphism or the realism, or in a more social context, like the gender, the age and the ethnicity.

Minutely, anthropomorphism includes the perception of any human trait or quality such as emotions, behavior, cognition presented in any human or non-human entity. It can be mainly increased by the image of the avatar as well as its behavior (Nowak and Fox 2018). There are a lot of studies on how anthropomorphic representations can influence the communication, showing that the higher level of it can lead to a more natural and persuasive (Heyselaar et al. 2017), more attractive (Gong 2008) interaction, with an increased level of social presence and engagement (Kang and Watt 2013). Furthermore, realism is the perception of how a situation, or an object, can be realistic, and it is often mixed up with the term of anthropomorphism. In the context of realism, an avatar can be judged based on its appearance, the rendering, the naturalness, and the fluidity of its movements and way of speaking.

On the other hand, given that avatars are perceived as social entities based on CASA (Reeves and Nass 1996), there are also social factors that can influence the perception of the users. First of all, the most common categorization humans use to do is the determination of gender. As Lakoff (1987) said people tend to attribute a gender to others even when physical or biological information is not available (Lakoff 1987) and probably this is an instinctual procedure as they believe that they can understand others or predict behaviors. Studies have proven that gender in specific contextual virtual environments play a role in human's reaction. For example, children prefer a male voice when it regards football and a female when to princesses or make-up (Lee et al. 2007) whereas adults prefer a young female avatar compared to an older male one for educational purposes (Shiban et al. 2015). Moreover, people often try to decipher the ethnicity of a person as they believe they can predict her/his behavior (Nowak and Fox 2018). A study of Eastwick and Gardner (2009), among others, showed that people were influenced of the existence of black and white people in a virtual environment (Eastwick and Gardner 2009).

Another study that proved the role of gender combined with the self-similarity in a gaming environment, is the one of Lucas et al. (2016) where men preferred to be represented by their own avatar whereas women preferred a stranger. This study is the only research up to date who has used a photorealistic self-similar avatar to study the effect of the appearance of the avatar in the performance and the perception of the user under a gaming environment. Lucas et al. tried to answer the question of the importance of the self-relevance of a virtual human under a specific context and although the difference in the gender they found, they noticed that the self-similarity provokes a bigger engagement and connection between the user and the avatar. Similar recent study is the one of Wauck et al. (2018) who used a more natural photorealistic self-similar avatar in a gaming context but with better technology features with which they respected even the gender aspect and they used different animations (male and female) for the two sexes. Their results indicated that there is no difference in the performance of the user based on the appearance of the avatar and no effect on gender as well. They attribute that to the better technology they used with which they avoided any negative effect on user's experience. However, further investigation it is needed under different environment and context to verify or contradict all these results.

13.5   Conclusions

No matter the technology, robotics, and virtual agents can improve the accessibility of various contents. Robots and other intelligent systems are able to improve the quality of human life by providing an assistance in intensive and difficult situations or even an independence in the way of living for people who have the need, like elderly or people with motor/cognitive disabilities. Nowadays, agents have the ability to embody and fill social roles (Spence 2019). An embodied agent can be a physical robot or a virtual character that has an identifiable body and can use modalities like voice, gestures, or facial expressions to communicate. The main differences between a virtual and a robotic agent is the physiology of the human face, the natural neck motion, the shared gaze but mostly the physical presence (Spence 2019).

Although the continuous effort of the existing studies to enhance the domain of human–computer interaction by addressing all the aforementioned features, it seems that the fluidity and the naturalness of the interaction has not yet been achieved. This has as a consequence for people to still prefer the human communication in any content. Jamy Li et al (2016) for example compared robotic and virtual agents through a video setting in an educational content, as instructors (Li et al. 2016). However, they showed that attitude was more positive toward human compared to robots, but agents have the potential to act as an alternative with the strict requirement that they are designed well. Moreover, Yi Mou and Kun Xu showed that people tend to be more open, self-disclosing, outgoing and in general more positive when interacting with another people compared to an AI agent (Mou and Xu 2017). The same was verified by the study of Shechtman and Horowitz (2003), who found that when people were talking to a human instead of a computer, they tend to be more talkative and spend more time to the conversation (Shechtmann and Horowitx 2003).

This preference can also be an outcome of the low degree of naturalism. Fischer et al. (2011) for example, found that people laughed when they had to respond in a robot's greetings, admitting that they found the movement unusual during their interaction (Fischer et al. 2011).

The current state-of-the-art aims to present the limitations of the existing technology used in the broad area of human–computer interaction up to now. Although different kind of agents have been used to contribute to several domains, like education, health, entertainment, both in virtual and physical environments, the virtual character or robot that will make a human feel as comfortable as interacting with another human has not been reported yet. Undoubtedly there are a lot of factors that should be taken into account when an agent is prepared to be used in the context of human-technology interaction, as stated before, but the most difficult part is the optimal selection and combination of these factors. What is mainly missing from the up to date state-of-the-art is the direct comparison of all these technologies with the original human–human communication. What we need to do is to keep studying the human–human communication and not only features of the HCI as what is missing is how we, as humans, react in several contexts of communication. The extraction of human features in such a context, like voice characteristics as range of frequencies, volume and timbre, gestures or body movements executed by feet or the body trank and even more physiological features like brain or muscle signals can complement the existing technologies and studies. Moreover, the way humans react to computer-mediated characters and to virtual environments can be a tool to decipher and understand existing human communication theories that can also support the aforementioned.

Thus, through this kind of research and by creating models for the human verbal and nonverbal communication, we can contribute to the enhancement of naturalism of every kind of agent, offering a higher level of understanding and affection in the context of everyday communication.

References

Antoniol G, Cattoni R, Cettolo M, Federico M (1993) Robust speech understanding for robot telecontrol. In: Proceedings of the 6th international conference on advanced robotics, pp 205–209

Bailenson JN, Yee N, Merget D, Schroeder R (2006) The effect of behavioral realism and form realism of real-time avatar faces on verbal disclosure, nonverbal disclosure, emotion recognition, and copresence in dyadic interaction. Presence: Teleoper Virtual Environ 15(4):359–372. https://doi.org/10.1162/pres.15.4.359

Baka E, Stavroulia KE, Magnenat-Thalmann N, Lanitis A (2018) An EEG-based evaluation for Comparing the sense of presence between Virtual and Physical Environments. In Proceedings of computer graphics international 2018 (CGI 2018). ACM, New York, USA, p 10. https://doi.org/10.1145/3208159.3208179

Baylor AL (2011) The design of motivational agents and avatars. Edu Tech Res Dev 59(2):291–300

Baylor AL, Kim S (2009) Designing nonverbal communication for pedagogical agents: when less is more. Comput Hum Behav 25(2):450–457

Billard A, Robins B, Nadel J, Dautenhahn K (2007) Building Robota, a mini-humanoid robot for the rehabilitation of children with autism. Assist Technol 19(1):37–49. https://doi.org/10.1080/10400435.2007.10131864

Birmingham C, Hu Z, Mahajan K, Reber E, Mataric MJ (2020) Can I trust you? A user study of robot mediation of a support group. ArXiv preprint arXiv:2002.04671

Blascovich J (2002) A theoretical model of social influence for increasing the utility of collaborative virtual environments. In: Proceedings of the 4th international conference on collaborative virtual environments. ACM, New York, NY, USA, pp 25–30. https://doi.org/10.1145/571878.571883

Breazeal C (2003) Emotion and sociable humanoid robots. Int J Hum Comput Stud 59(1):119–155

Breazeal C Faridi F (2016) U.S. patent application no. 29/491,780

Breazeal C, Velásquez J (1998) Toward teaching a robot "infant" using emotive communication acts. In: Proceedings of the 1998 simulated adaptive behavior workshop on socially situated intelligence, pp 25–40

Burgard W, Cremers AB, Fox D, Hähnel D, Lakemeyer G, Schulz D, Steiner W, Thrun S (1998) The interactive museum tour-guide robot. In: Proceedings of the fifteenth national conference on artificial intelligence. AAAI-98

Burleigh TJ, Schoenherr JR, Lacroiz GL (2013) Does the uncanny valley exist? An empirical test of the relationship between eeriness and the human likeness of digitally created faces. Comput Hum Behav 29:759–771

Ciechanowski L, Przegalinska A, Magnuski M, Gloor P (2019) In the shades of the uncanny valley: an experimental study of human–chatbot interaction. Futur Gener Comput Syst 92:539–548

Dautenhahn K, Walters M, Woods S, Koay KL, Nehaniv CL, Sisbot A, Alami R, Siméon T (2006) How may I serve you? A robot companion approaching a seated person in a helping context. In: Proceedings of the 1st ACM SIGCHI/SIGART conference on human-robot interaction. ACM, pp 172–179

Dautenhahn K, Nehaniv CL, Walters ML, Robins B, Kose-Bagci H, Mirza NA, Blow M (2009) Kaspar–a minimally expressive humanoid robot for human–robot interaction research. Appl Bionics Biomech 6(3–4):369–397 de Borst A, de Gelder B (2015) Is it the real deal? Perception of virtual characters versus humans: an affective cognitive neuroscience perspective. Front Psychol 6:576. https://doi.org/10.3389/fpsyg. 2015.00576

Eastwick PW, Gardner WL (2009) Is it a game? Evidence for social influence in the virtual world. Soc Influ 4:18–32. https://doi.org/10.1080/15534510802254087

Edwards A, Edwards C, Westerman D, Spence PR (2019) Initial expectations, interactions, and beyond with social robots. Comput Human Behav 90:308–314. https://doi.org/10.1016/j.chb. 2018.08.042

Ekman P (1973) Darwin and facial expression: a century of research in review. Academic Press, New York NY

Evers V, Menezes N, Merino L, Gavrila D, Nabais F, Pantic M, Alvito P, Karreman D (2014) The development and real-world deployment of frog, the fun robotic outdoor guide. In: Proceedings of the 2014 ACM/IEEE international conference on human-robot interaction, ser. HRI'14. ACM, New York, NY, USA, p 100. https://doi.org/10.1145/2559636

Ferber J (1999) Multi-agent systems: an introduction to distributed artificial intelligence, vol 1. Addison-Wesley, Reading

Fischer K, Foth K, Rohlfing K, Wrede B (2011) Mindful tutors: linguistic choice and action demonstration in speech to infants and a simulated robot. Interact Stud 12(1):134–161

Gong L (2008) How social is social responses to computers? The function of the degree of anthropomorphism in computer representations. Comput Hum Behav 24:1494–1509. https://doi.org/ 10.1016/j.chb.2007.05.007

Graf B, Hans M, Schraft RD (2004) Care-O-bot II—development of a next-generation robotic home assistant. Auton Robot 16(2):193–205. https://doi.org/10.1023/B:AURO.0000016865.35796.e9

Han S, Jiang Y, Humphreys GW, Zhou T, Cai P (2005) Distinct neural substrates for the perception of real and virtual visual worlds. Neuroimage 24(3):928–935

Hasegawa D, Cassell J, Araki K (2010) The role of embodiment and perspective in direction-giving systems. In: Proceedings of the AAAI fall workshop on dialog with robots

Hess U, Adams RB, Kleck RE (2007) Looking at you or looking elsewhere: the influence of head orientation on the signal value of emotional facial expressions. Motiv Emot 31(2):137–144

Heyselaar E, Hagoort P, Segaert K (2017) In dialogue with an avatar, language behavior is identical to dialogue with a human partner. Behav Res Methods 49:46–60. https://doi.org/10.3758/s13428-015-0688-7

Hoffmann L, Krämer NC (2011) How should an artificial entity be embodied? In: HRI 2011 Workshop, p 8

Hoffman G, Weinberg G (2010) Shimon: an interactive improvisational robotic marimba player, CHI 2010, April 10–15, 2010, Atlanta, Georgia, USA. ACM 978-1-60558-930-5/10/04

Huang W, Olson JS, Olson GM (2002) Camera angle affects dominance in video-mediated communication. In: CHI'02 extended abstracts on human factors in computing systems. ACM, pp 716–717

Johnson WL, Rickel JW, Lester JC (2000) Animated pedagogical agents: face-to-face interaction in interactive learning environments. Int J Artif Intell Educ 11(1):47–78

Jost C, André V, Le Pévédic B, Lemasson A, Hausberger M, Duhaut D (2012) Ethological evaluation of Human–Robot interaction: are children more efficient and motivated with computer, virtual agent or robots? In: Proceedings of IEEE ROBIO international conference on robotics and biomimetics

Kanda T, Shiomi M, Miyashita Z, Ishiguro H, Hagita N (2009)An affective guide robot in a shopping mall. In: Proceedings of the 4th ACM/IEEE international conference on human-robot interaction, ser. HRI'09. ACM, New York, NY, USA, 2009, pp 173–180 [Online]. Available: https://doi.org/ 10.1145/1514095.1514127

Kang SH, Watt JH (2013) The impact of avatar realism and anonymity on effective communication via mobile devices. Comput Hum Behav 29:1169–1181. https://doi.org/10.1016/j.chb.2012. 10.010

Kätsyri J, Förger K, Mäkäräinen M, Takala T (2015) A review of empirical evidence on different uncanny valley hypotheses: support for perceptual mismatch as one road to the valley of eeriness. Front Psychol 6:390

Kellerman KL (1992) Communication: Inherently strategic and primarily automatic. Commun Monogr 59:288–300. https://doi.org/10.1080/03637759209376270

Kluttz NL, Mayes BR, West RW, Kerby DS (2009) The effect of head turn on the perception of gaze. Vis. Res. 49(15):1979–1993. https://doi.org/10.1016/j.visres.2009.05.013

Kosuge K, Hayashi T, Hirata Y, Tobiyama R (2003) Dance partner robot-MS Dancer. In: 2003 IEEE/RSJ international conference on intelligent robots and systems, IROS 2003, Proceedings, vol 4. IEEE, pp. 3459–3464

Kunecke J, Hildebrandt A, Recio G, Sommer W, Wilhelm O (2014) Facial EMG responses to emotional expressions are related to emotion perception ability. PLoS ONE 9(1):e84053. https://doi.org/10.1371/journal.pone.0084053

Lakoff G (1987) Women, fire, and dangerous things: what categories reveal about the mind. The University of Chicago Press, Chicago, IL

Lazzeri N, Mazzei D, Greco A, Rotesi A, Lanata A, De Rossi DE (2015) Can a humanoid face be expressive? A psychophysiological investigation. Front Bioeng Biotechnol

Lee KM, Jung Y, Kim J, Kim S (2006) Are physically embodied social agents better than disembodied social agents? The effects of physical embodiment, tactile interaction, and people's loneliness in human–robot interaction. Int J Hum Comput Stud 64(10):962–973

Lee KM, Liao K, Ryu S (2007) Children's responses to computer-synthesized speech in educational media: gender consistency and gender similarity effects. Hum Commun Res 33:310–329. https://doi.org/10.1111/j.1468-2958.2007.00301.x

Li J (2015) The benefit of being physically present: A survey of experimental works comparing copresent robots, telepresent robots, and virtual agents. Int J Hum Comput Stud 77:23–37. https://doi.org/10.1016/j.ijhcs.2015.01.001

Li J, Kizilcec R, Bailenson J, Ju W (2016) Social robots and virtual agents as lecturers for video instruction. Comput Hum Behav 55:1222–1230. https://doi.org/10.1016/j.chb.2015.04.005

Looije R, van der Zalm A, Neerincx MA, Beun RJ (2012) Help, I need some body the effect of embodiment on playful learning. In: RO-MAN. IEEE, pp 718–724

Lucas GM, Gratch J, King A, Morency L-P (2014) It's only a computer: virtual humans increase willingness to disclose. Comput Hum Behav 37:94–100. https://doi.org/10.1016/j.chb.2014.04.043

Lucas G, Szablowski E, Gratch J, Feng A, Huang T, Boberg J, Shapiro A (2016) The effect of operating a virtual doppleganger in a 3D simulation. In: Proceedings of the 9th international conference on motion in games. ACM, pp 167–174

Łupkowski P, Gierszewska M (2019) Attitude towards humanoid robots and the uncanny valley hypothesis. Found Comput Decision Sci 44(1):101–119

Makatchev M, Fanaswala I, Abdulsalam A, Browning B, Ghazzawi W, Sakr M, Simmons R (2010) Dialogue patterns of an Arabic robot receptionist. In: 2010 5th ACM/IEEE international conference on human-robot interaction. HRI, pp 167–168

Marschner L, Pannasch S, Schulz J, Graupner ST (2015) Social communication with virtual agents: the effects of body and gaze direction on attention and emotional responding in human observers. Int J Psychophysiol 97(2):85–92. https://doi.org/10.1016/j.ijpsycho.2015.05.007

Marti P, Moderini C, Giusti L, Pollini A (2009) A robotic toy for children with special needs: From requirements to design. In: Proceedings of the IEEE Kyoto 2009, 11th IEEE international conference on rehabilitation robotics June 23–26–2009, Kyoto, Japan

Mavridis N (2015) A review of verbal and non-verbal human-robot interactive communication. Robot Auton Syst 63(P1):22–35. https://doi.org/10.1016/j.robot.2014.09.031

Mayer RE, DaPra CS (2012) An embodiment effect in computer-based learning with animated pedagogical agents. J Exp Psychol Appl 18(3):239

McGuire WJ (1985) Attitudes and attitude change. In: Lindzey G, Aronson E (eds) Handbook of social psychology. Random Hou, New York, NY, pp 233–346

Milgram P, Takemura H, Utsumi A, Kishino F (1995) Augmented reality: A class of displays on the reality-virtuality continuum. In: Photonics for industrial applications. Int Soc Optics Photon 282–292

Mischel W (2004) Toward an integrative science of the person. Annu Rev Psychol 55:1–22

Mischel W, Shoda Y (1995) A cognitive-affective system theory of personality: reconceptualizing situations, dispositions, dynamics, and invariance in personality structure. Psychol Rev 102:246–268

Mollahosseini A, Abdollahi H, Sweeny TD, Cole R, Mahoor MH (2018) Role of embodiment and presence in human perception of robots' facial cues. Int J Hum Comput Stud 116:25–39. https://doi.org/10.1016/j.ijhcs.2018.04.005

Moody EJ, McIntosh DN, Mann LJ, Weisser KR (2007) More than mere mimicry? The influence of emotion on rapid facial reactions to faces. Emotion 7(2):447–457

Mori M (1970) The uncanny valley. Energy 7:33–35. [Republished in IEEE Robotics and Automation Magazine, June 2012, 98–100]

Mori M, MacDorman KF, Kageki N (2012) The uncanny valley [from the field]. Robot Autom Mag IEEE 19(2):98–100

Mou Y, Xu K (2017) The media inequality: comparing the initial human-human and human-AI social interactions. Comput Hum Behav 72(March):432–440. https://doi.org/10.1016/j.chb.2017.02.067

Nass C, Moon Y (2000) Machines and mindlessness: social responses to computers. J Soc Issues 56:81–103. https://doi.org/10.1111/0022-4537.00153

Nowak KL (2004) The influence of anthropomorphism and agency on social judgment in virtual environments. J Comput-Mediat Commun. https://doi.org/10.1111/j.1083-6101.2004.tb00284.x

Nowak KL, Fox J (2018) Avatars and computer-mediated communication: a review of the definitions, uses, and effects of digital representations. Rev Commun Res 6:30–53. https://doi.org/10.12840/issn.2255-4165.2018.06.01.015

Odashima T, Onishi M, Tahara K, Takagi K, Asano F, Kato Y, Nakashima H, Kobayashi Y, Luo ZW, Mukai T, Hosoe S (2006) A soft human-interactive robot—RI-MAN—. In: Video proceedings of the IEEE/RSJ international conference on intelligent robots systems, Beijing, China, p 1

Petersen K, Solis J, Takanishi A (2010) Musical-based interaction system for the waseda flutist robot. Auton Robots 28(4):471–488

Pfeifer R, Scheier C (1999) Understanding intelligence. MIT Press, Cambridge, MA, Powers

Pour PA, Hussain MS, AlZoubi O, D'Mello S, Calvo RA (2010) The impact of system feedback on learners' affective and physiological states. Intelligent tutoring systems. Springer, Berlin Heidelberg, pp 264–273

Ramanathan M, Mishra N, Thalmann NM (2019) Nadine humanoid social robotics platform. In: Computer graphics international conference. Springer, Cham, pp 490–496

Reeves B, Nass C (1996) The media equation: how people treat computers, television, and new media like real people and places. CSLI Publications, Stanford, CA

Rizzo A, Shilling R, Forbell E, Scherer S, Gratch J, Morency L-P (2016) Autonomous virtual human agents for healthcare information support and clinical interviewing. In: Luxton DD (ed) Artificial intelligence in behavioral and mental health care. Academic Press, San Diego, pp. 53–79. https://doi.org/10.1016/B978-0-12-420248-1.00003-9

Rosenberg-Kima RB, Plant EA, Doerr CE, Baylor AL (2010) The Influence of computer-based model's race and gender on female students' attitudes and beliefs towards engineering. J Eng Educ 99(1):35–44

Rosis FD, Pelachaud C, Poggi I, Carofiglio V, Carolis BD (2003) From Greta's mind to her face: modeling the dynamics of affective states in a conversational embodied agent. Int J Hum–Comput Stud 59(1):81–118

Schrammel F, Pannasch S, Graupner ST, Mojzisch A, Velichkovsky BM (2009) Virtual friend or threat? The effects of facial expression and gaze interaction on psychophysiological responses and emotional experience. Psychophysiology 46(5):922–931. https://doi.org/10.1111/j.1469-8986.2009.00831.x

Shechtman N, Horowitz LM (2003) Media inequality in conversation: How people behave differently when interacting with computers and people. In: Proceedings of the SIGCHI conference on human factors in computing systems. ACM, pp 281–288

Shiban Y, Schelhorn I, Jobst V, Hörnlein A, Puppe F, Pauli P, Mühlberger A (2015) The appearance effect: Influences of virtual agent features on performance and motivation. Comput Hum Behav 49:5–11. https://doi.org/10.1016/j.chb.2015.01.077

Shibata T, Yoshida M, Yamato J (1997) Artificial emotional creature for human-machine interaction. In: IEEE international conference on systems, man and cybernetics, vol 3. IEEE, pp 2269–2274

Shinozawa K, Naya F, Yamato J, Kogure K (2005) Differences in effect of robot and screen agent recommendations on human decision-making. Int J Hum Comput Stud 62(2):267–279

Spence PR (2019) Searching for questions, original thoughts, or advancing theory: human-machine communication. Comput Hum Behav 90:285–287. https://doi.org/10.1016/j.chb.2018.09.014

Stein JP, Ohler P (2017) Venturing into the uncanny valley of mind: the influence of mind attribution on the acceptance of human-like characters in a virtual reality setting. Cognition 160:43–50. https://doi.org/10.1016/j.cognition.2016.12.010

Sugano S, Kato I (1987) WABOT-2: autonomous robot with dexterous finger-arm—Finger-arm coordination control in keyboard performance. IEEE Int Conf Robot Autom. https://doi.org/10.1109/ROBOT.1987.1088025

Wada K, Shibata T (2007) Living with seal robots—its sociopsychological and physiological influences on the elderly at a care house. IEEE Trans. Robot. 23(5):972–980

Walther JB (1996). Computer-mediated communication: impersonal, interpersonal, and hyperpersonal interaction. Commun Res 23:3–43. https://doi.org/10.1177/009365096023001001.

Wauck H, Lucas G, Shapiro A, Feng A, Boberg J, Gratch J (2018) Analyzing the effect of avatar self-similarity on men and women in a search and rescue game. In: Proceedings of the 2018 CHI conference on human factors in computing systems. ACM, p 485

Weller C (2017) Meet the first-ever robot citizen, a humanoid named Sophia that once said it would destroy humans. Business Insider Nordic Haettu 30:2018

Winograd T (1972) Understanding natural language. Cogn Psychol 3(1):1–191

Yamada Y, Kawabe T, Ihaya K (2013) categorization difficulty is associated with negative evaluation in the uncanny valley phenomenon. Jpn Psychol Res 55:20–32

Yamazaki A, Yamazaki K, Ohyama T, Kobayashi Y, Kuno Y (2012) A techno- sociological solution for designing a museum guide robot: regarding choosing an appropriate visitor. In: Proceedings of the seventh annual ACM/IEEE international conference on human-robot interaction, ser. HRI'12. ACM, New York, NY, USA, pp 309–316. [Online]. Available: https://doi.org/10.1145/2157689.2157800

Yokotani K, Takagi G, Wakashima K (2018) Advantages of virtual agents over clinical psychologists during comprehensive mental health interviews using a mixed-methods design. Comput Hum Behav 85(March):135–145. https://doi.org/10.1016/j.chb.2018.03.045

Zawieska K, Moussa MB, Duffy BR, Magnenat-Thalmann N (2012) The role of imagination in Human-Robot Interaction. In: 25th annual conference on computer animation and social agents (CASA 2012)

Zhao S (2003) Toward a taxonomy of copresence. Presence: Teleoper Virtual Environ 12(5):445–455

Chapter 14
Survey of Speechless Interaction Techniques in Social Robotics

Manoj Ramanathan, Ranjan Satapathy, and Nadia Magnenat Thalmann

Abstract With recent developments in the field of artificial intelligence, machine learning, and deep learning, the field of social robotics has gained momentum. Any social robot requires to interact with human and its environment. Any human–robot interaction involves two aspects, speech-based and speechless interactions. Among the two, the latter is an essential requirement to make the social robot appear convincing and believable. In this study, we bridge the robotics hardware with the non-speech components of communication. We discuss the notion of a digital ecosystem with a social robot is a powerful one, connecting the conceptual framework of biological ecology with the swiftly expanding digital world. Traditional speechless interaction considers mainly non-verbal communication cues like gazing, user action/gesture-based interaction, body language, emotion, personality detection. But in current scenario with social robotics finding more applications in healthcare (autism care), education (for deaf and dumb), office work (insurance), etc., other speechless communication techniques can also be considered and integrated into them. By reading, the robot will be able to understand any document or online content, which can help the robot to tell stories, interact with speech-impaired people, handle incoming mails and parcels. Any robot can have simple online communication like email, tweets, and status updates to sophisticated communication frameworks like Facebook, Twitter,

M. Ramanathan (✉) · N. Magnenat Thalmann
Institute for Media Innovation, Nanyang Technological University, 50 Nanyang Drive,
Singapore 637553, Singapore
e-mail: manoj005@e.ntu.edu.sg

N. Magnenat Thalmann
e-mail: nadiathalmann@ntu.edu.sg

R. Satapathy
School of Computer Science and Engineering, Nanyang Technological University,
50 Nanyang Avenue, Singapore 639798, Singapore
e-mail: ranjan002@e.ntu.edu.sg

241

N. Magnenat Thalmann et al. (eds.), *Intelligent Scene Modeling and Human-Computer Interaction*, Human–Computer Interaction Series,
https://doi.org/10.1007/978-3-030-71002-6_14

and Gmail. In this review, we look at speechless interaction methods and corresponding reaction models in social robotics not restricting to non-verbal cues, but also include how HRI is impacted by the internet, which is relatively new research domain.

14.1 Introduction

In recent times, the field of robotics has seen a tremendous rise and applications in several fields. From menial labor tasks, robots are being considered for complex tasks such as playing ping pong (Wikipedia 2018c) and chess (PALROBOTICS 2018). Robotics and automation have shown significant progress even in life saving scenarios such as disaster recovery (Murphy et al. 2011, 2016; Billah et al. 2008), surgery assistive robots (Camarillo et al. 2004). With the advent of deep learning and artificial intelligence (AI), there is an increase in robots with capabilities that include cognitive computing and social context understanding. The long-term goal of creating social robots that are competent and capable partners for people is quite a challenging task. They will need to be able to communicate naturally with people using both verbal and non-verbal signals. With advancements in technology and AI, the capabilities of robots have increased manifold. There has been specific increase in cognitive and social cue understanding. Over the last decade, this has given rise to important branch of robotics, namely, social robotics. Feil-Seifer and Matatic (2005) is one of the earliest works that broadly considers robotics under two categories, assistive and socially interactive robotics. While assistive robots focus on providing support through physical interaction, socially interactive robots entertain through social interactions. Feil-Seifer and Matatic (2005) also talks about the evolution of a new type of social robotics, namely, socially assistive robotics, which can be seen as an subset of the above-mentioned broad categories. The development and evolution of social robotics, ethical considerations have made it essential for such a robot to interact with humans and be able to perceive its surroundings in a reliable manner. Due to the nature of their work, it is essential for them to understand social cues and maintain communication protocols in all situations.

Initially, social robots were considered for applications such as work as consumer guides (Sabelli and Kanda 2016), teachers (Han et al. 2015), health and elderly care (Ge et al. 2011; Orejana et al. 2015). But with development of AI and deep learning methods to understand the environment using different sensing modalities, it is now possible to provide more human-like functionalities to social robots. Due to this, humanoid robots are being considered in different workplaces and a variety of job scope. For example, Nadine, a social humanoid robot, was employed as a customer service agent by an insurance company to answer queries and help their customers (Mishra et al. 2019). The morphology of a robot or embodiment plays an important role in social expectations (Fong et al. 2003; Feil-Seifer and Matatic 2005). Due to this, the design and capabilities of a humanoid robot such as Nadine (Ramanathan et al. 2019) is very different compared to a PARO robot (Shibata 2012).

For a social robot, human–robot interaction is of primary importance. A social robot must have a convincing and reliable human–robot interaction. For this purpose, a social robot must be capable of two characteristics:

1. firstly, perceive and react to all verbal and non-verbal cues, and
2. secondly, proactively show mixed initiative between human and robot.

Humans use a wide variety of non-verbal cues to communicate different aspects such as emotion, comfort, willingness, and involvement in tasks, etc. It is essential for a social robot to understand such non-verbal cues and also be able to imitate such non-verbal behaviors seamlessly in any communication. This would enrich and provide a realistic and holistic human–robot interaction. Apart from this, the social robot must be able to interact and understand its environment. This ability to seamlessly link up with the environment and use them as cues during human interaction goes a long way to improve the interaction experience. Authors in Mavridis (2015) talk about desiderata for a social robot and also looks at different verbal and non-verbal cues used in human–robot interaction. In this chapter, we broadly classify interactions into two classes speech-based and speechless. Speech-based interactions are quite commonly used verbal means of communication with social robots and other assistive devices such as Amazon Alexa, Google Home, and Apple Siri. But for a convincing interaction, speechless communications are also essential.

Speechless communication is an essential component of a social robot in creating reliable and believable human–robot interaction. But these speechless interaction cues are less research topic in the field of social robotics. Several non-verbal cues such as gaze, empathy, haptics or tactile sensitivity, and body language play an essential role in robot interaction. The social robot must be able to perceive and quantify the user's non-verbal cues and if required, be able to show or emulate similar non-verbal communication. Several studies (Langer et al. 2019; Flandorfer 2012) have shown the importance of such speechless interaction cues in building trust and user acceptance.

Figure 14.1 shows various components that are involved in speechless communication of social robots. Each of the components plays an essential role in reliable interaction experience with the robot. As mentioned above, these cues convey important behavioral traits and can give clues on comfortness, willingness of the user, emotions, etc. Understanding these cues in social interaction plays an essential role in designing how the robot reacts to different scenarios, applications. It is also necessary for the robot to portray similar speechless communication traits to make the human–robot interaction holistic. Non-verbal cues such as maintaining eye contact or gaze, to emulate empathy or show emotions based on user inputs, reacting actions and gestures of users, etc., help to keep the interaction realistic. For realistic humanoid robots like Nadine (Ramanathan et al. 2019), Sophia (Goertzel et al. 2017), these cues have to be designed and quantified very carefully. This allows them to maintain a good rapport with the user, which in turn can allow leading to user acceptance.

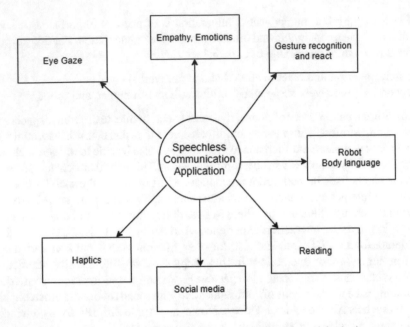

Fig. 14.1 Different attributes of speechless interaction techniques in social robotics

For human beings, reading and writing are two simple speechless communication methods that we use commonly. However, such interactions are often ignored or not considered for a social robot. With the development of OCR, it is now possible to understand the text from images. This in turn, can be integrated into robots allowing them to read documents, online content and open up a new way of communication. Social media is having a strong influence on communication and interaction among the world's population. For a social robot, which aims to interact with users, social media has opened up a new way of speechless social communication. A social media presence could range from a simple text-based email to more complex data-sharing networks such as Twitter, Instagram, and Facebook. Developing such speechless communication methods adds a new dimension to research and also the robot's ability. Both speechless and speech-based methods need to be correlated and synchronized for efficient human–robot interaction. For instance, a robot should be able to convey emotions not only through facial expressions and gestures but also in tone and pitch of its speech. In the following sections, we present a review of the current state of the art in the above-mentioned speechless interaction techniques in social robotics. Also, we provide insights on limitations and possible future research directions in each of the speechless interaction techniques.

14.2   Related Work

A social robot is required to interact with human users and also understand its environment. Due to the nature of their work, they need to understand social cues and maintain communication protocols in all situations. Fong et al. (2003) provides a taxonomy of essential design methods and system components used for building socially interactive robots. Fong et al. (2003) also provides an initial set of social characteristics that such a robot should have such as express/perceive emotions, exhibit personalities, maintain dialogue, establish social relations, learn/develop social competencies use natural cues such as gaze and gestures.

Feil-Seifer and Matatic (2005) also provides essential metrics and criteria for socially interactive and socially assistive robots. For socially interactive robots, Feil-Seifer and Matatic (2005) defines embodiment, emotion, dialogue, personality, human-oriented perception, user modeling, socially situated learning, intentionality as essential components. Moreover, for socially assistive robotics, these components must be extended to include more categories such as user population, the task to perform, the sophistication of interaction, the role of an assistive robot. Sim and Loo (2015) provides a review of assessment and evaluation methodologies used for modeling human–robot interaction for socially assistive robots. Any social robot's success has to be evaluated based on the human–robot interaction experience. An important consideration for any social robot design is user acceptance, building trust and confidence with the users. Langer et al. (2019) provided a comprehensive study focusing on the trust of socially assistive robots used for rehabilitation. Langer et al. (2019) also provides methods and guidelines for building, measuring, and evaluating trust in the HRI. Flandorfer (2012) studies impact and effects of sociodemographic factors such as age, gender, education/technical experience, family status, and cultural background in user acceptance of robots. Langer et al. (2019), Flandorfer (2012) showed that speechless communication and non-verbal interactions play an essential role in user acceptance.

Speechless communication not only includes non-verbal interaction cues but also focuses on some less researched verbal cues like multimodal natural language such as reading. Traditionally, researchers mainly focused on eye gaze (Mutlu et al. 2009; Karreman et al. 2013), affective system (emotions) (Zhang et al. 2015; Meghdari et al. 2016; Mavridis et al. 2011) and gesture-based interactions (Sakagami et al. 2002; Chrungoo et al. 2014; Vieira et al. 2012). But with more realistic human-like social robots applied to real workplaces and job scopes, they must be able to handle more human-like functionalities, realistic social situations and several other speechless means of communication. For example, there is extensive research on iCub (Metta et al. 2008) robot to employ tactile interactions with it. Authors in Argall and Billard (2010) provide a survey on tactile human–robot interactions. Another form of interaction considered is proxemics (Nakauchi and Simmons 2002; Chidambaram et al. 2012; Holthaus et al. 2011). Nakauchi and Simmons (2002) used proxemic cues in a mobile robot to maintain personal space in an environment with people, especially when standing in a queue. The operating environment and objects in it also can act as cues. Recognizing objects can help a robot to interact with the objects in the environment (Sakagami et al. 2002; Wikipedia 2018c; PALROBOTICS 2018; Fang et al. 2018).

14.3 Gaze Behavior

An important cue in any communication is eye gaze. It plays an important role in any day-to-day activity. For a social robot, eye gaze helps to enrich the human–robot interaction as it helps to keep the user interested in the conversation. Also, it increases the credibility of the robot. The gaze behavior denotes a range of social meanings during an interaction. Maintaining eye contact with the user is essential to make social robots appear more natural and vivid.

A social robot needs to interact with single or multiple users at any stage. The design of eyes for a social robot is always essential to make it believable. The movement of eyes and body posture play a significant role in any interaction. Ruhland et al. (2014) studied the importance of eye and gaze animation of virtual agents. Most social robots can handle single person interactions easily. Ramanathan et al. (2019), Wikipedia (2018b), IshiguroLab (2018) are capable of following faces and maintaining eye contact during an interaction. When there are multiple people in line of sight, how to divide attention of robot between participants is an open-ended problem. Several researchers have attempted to handle multiple-party interactions. For instance, Karreman et al. (2013), conducted an experiment with a museum tour guide robot (FROG), which interacted with 3 participants and showed exhibits. FROG had a simple screen to show its eye with a cardboard cylinder as body. The robot was required to divide attention between participants and museum exhibits. Mutlu et al. (2009) used robovie for a three-way communication and assigned conversational roles (addresse, bystander, overhearer) for each participant based on the gaze cues. Most of the studies so far have been conducted in simple and control setting with two or three participants only.

Apart from the user, operating environment places also control the gaze coordination. Thus scene recognition and understanding play an important role in eye gaze. For a realistic workplace setting, it would be necessary to understand the environment for designing the gaze. For instance, suppose a robot needs to make a presentation or address an audience, the gaze behavior would be completely different than a simple multi-party interaction. Such research problems are still open-ended. Objects and interesting events also can control gaze of the robot. Results in Karreman et al. (2013) show that the participants had a better human–robot interaction when the robot's gaze was divided between them and the museum exhibits during the tour.

For realistic human-like robots such as Ramanathan et al. (2019), Wikipedia (2018b), IshiguroLab (2018), gaze coordination is an essential part of their design. Due to the realistic appearance, the expectations for such robots would be high. Humanoid robots need to perceive the environment and control their gaze accordingly.

14.4 Affective System—Emotion Engine

Any person can be characterized by their own personality and emotions. Subconsciously people convey different messages through their display of emotions. Changes in emotion can be in the form of facial expressions, change in tone and pitch of speech and gestures. For a social humanoid robot, it is essential to have an emotion engine that would be able to perceive the situation (user and environment) and vary its emotion and behavior accordingly. For this reason, a fully expressive face would be essential in the design of social robot. Robots like Meghdari et al. (2016) designed for health care purposes include a simple monitor based face which is not enough to show intricate and complex facial expressions, whereas robots like Wikipedia (2018b), Oh et al. (2006), IshiguroLab (2018) have a fully expressive human face capable of showing numerous facial expressions.

Gauging user's interest and emotions in a conversation are essential social cues for a social robot. The emotions and expressions can be measured in a multimodal way using videos or images, speech intonations, etc. Software such as Affectiva (AFFECTIVA 2018) allows to determine facial emotions from videos. By using facial landmarks, it can also compute user's involvement, curiosity, etc., and provide detailed analysis of the face during a conversation. Speech or audio signals can indirectly be affected by emotions. Vocal cues such as tone, pitch, prosody, etc., vary with emotions and can be used for identifying user emotions. Opensmile (Eyben et al. 2010) is an open-source audio feature extraction toolkit that has been extensively for automatic emotion recognition. Emotions are intertwined with speech and audio signals, therefore, it would be necessary for any social robot also to show emotions and expressions via its speech as well. To show such non-verbal vocal cues, the text-to-speech (TTS) module must allow for easy customizations and should support several emotion tags. For instance, CereVoice Engine SDK (CereProc 2019) allows tuning and TTS manipulation, emotional synthesis control, and includes vocal gestures such as laughs, etc. Chidambaram et al. (2012) showed that combining vocal non-verbal cues (tone and expressions) with other bodily non-verbal cues such as gaze and gestures resulted in a better human–robot interaction than when using only one of them.

In addition to emotions, there are two other important aspects that can influence the effect of dynamics in an interaction. They are moods and personalities of the agents involved. Therefore, in order to model an effective system, we need to consider long-term interaction aspects such as personality and mood. Zhang et al. (2015) showed how Nadine social robot's emotion, mood, and personalities are changed during a conversation. Their system design is based on a three-dimensional PAD space (Pleasure, Arousal, and Dominance), where pleasure denotes valence of effect, arousal represents physical excitedness of effect and dominance indicates the initiative of effect. This allows Nadine to exhibit different personalities, emotions very easily. The model also allows to modify the intensity of each emotion thus making the robot show subtle emotions.

Such subtle emotions become necessary for a social robot as they are being considered for several applications such as healthcare and elderly care (Ge et al. 2011; Meghdari et al. 2016; Shibata 2012), customer service agents (Mishra et al. 2019), receptionists (Holthaus et al. 2011), consumer guides (Sabelli and Kanda 2016), teachers (Han et al. 2015), etc. Emotion, mood and personality of the robot need to vary according to each application to ensure customers or patients are happy with the service. Building a customizable or generic module to handle all possible affect dynamics is needed. Mavridis et al. (2011) developed a humanoid robot that can mainly handle 4 different face expressions, but also included the ability to interpolate and mix them if needed.

14.5 Recognize and React to Actions/Gestures

Humans have the innate ability to understand social signals and cues during any interaction. We subconsciously can process lots of such signals to make our decisions. A social robot needs to have such abilities to process different subtle social signals to understand its user. User's action or gesture is an effective social signal during any human–robot interaction as it provides essential and hidden clues to user's body language, user intentions, and his/her current behavior. As a contextual cue during conversation, it can help to react differently to user actions. For a natural social interaction, a social robot should be able to recognize subtle gestures and action of user. By understanding user intentions or predicting their behavior, the social robot can be prepared to help them in a better way. When human and robot are involved in a task together, recognizing user actions/gestures becomes essential. While social robot (Ge et al. 2011) was able to recognize simple hand gestures, a task-based robot (Sakagami et al. 2002) are able to recognize simple 2D and 3D gestures based on Bayesian model using hand, face, front and side profiles of body. Chrungoo et al. (2014) used a histogram of direction vectors of each user's skeleton joint movements to represent actions and used the recognized actions to test on P3Dx mobile robot platform.

So far in social robots and human–robot interaction, only very simple actions are considered. Keller et al. (2016) considered only 2 actions, whereas Vieira et al. (2012) used pointing gestures to control the movement of a robot. For a social robot, complex actions would also have to be considered. Also for designing humanoid or human-like robots, it would be necessary to modify behaviors and reactions (verbal and non-verbal) to enhance human–robot interaction based on actions and current context. Action recognition is a complex task that is affected several factors such as view point changes, occlusion, cluttered background, etc. (Ramanathan et al. 2014). In a realistic scenario, handling these challenges for a robot will be much more difficult as the quality of action recognition will determine the quality of human–robot interaction as well.

The next step is for the robot to react or respond in an appropriate manner. Especially for humanoids or human-like robots, this is a challenging task. The reaction or response depends on several factors such as who is performing the action, current conversation or interaction context, etc. We might have to account for other subtle factors like user emotions, robot emotions, final goal or task to be completed. Defining reactions for simple actions like hand waving, might be easy but complex actions would require proper understanding of context and generate appropriate verbal or non-verbal response. Developing such a reaction model would be challenging as many factors contribute to making that decision. For example, Nadine (Ramanathan et al. 2019) is capable of responding to simple actions such as waving and is restricted to only verbally inform about other recognized actions. Some other major concerns include 'which actions should a robot react to?', 'Is there enough data to train for required actions'. Therefore it is necessary to develop a generic module for actions, that can be generalized to untrained actions, generate verbal and non-verbal responses to actions considering the interaction context, etc.

14.6 Natural Language Communication with Robots Using Reading

Languages have been traditionally developed as means of communication. Natural language communication is a common way of interaction between any 2 people or human–robot. Speech-based natural language communication is a more researched field and has seen tremendous rise in HRI. Speechless means of natural language communication with robot is a less mature field. For instance, with development of OCR techniques (GoogleCloudPlatform 2018; Library 2019), it is possible understand natural language from images. With OCR it is possible to develop modules that would help a robot to read documents or ID cards, etc., thus opening a new paradigm of research in speechless communication which will still include natural language processing tasks such as named entity recognition, and parts of speech.

Michaud and Letourneau (2001) employed character recognition techniques in Pioneer 2 mobile robot to make it understand symbols. They tracked the color regions in the image to identify likely symbol region, followed by recognition and understanding of symbols, which they used to control the activities of robot. Similarly, Letourneau et al. (2003) enabled a Pioneer 2 robot with ability to read simple textual messages. Letourneau et al. (2003) used traditional methods of image binarization, image, color segmentation and character recognition to read these messages. It mainly focused on correct character or word recognition rather than how the robot should process it after understanding. Pioneer 2 is a mobile robotic platform with wheels and a camera mounted on top of it. For a humanoid robot interactions, development of speechless communication such as reading is more challenging. Mavridis et al. (2011) showed an initial work where they incorporated IbnSina humanoid android robot with OCR. The robot was able to perform only one basic operation which was to read out aloud. Nadine (Wikipedia 2018) is capable of registering people from their ID cards at workplace, receive parcels for employees using OCR techniques.

With development of more humanoid or human-like robots, reading/writing-based natural language interaction can be explored even more. For now only a very few applications have been tested out for humanoid robots. Understanding the characters written and context around it could be essential for realistic human–robot interaction. For example, recognizing if the robot is reading from a book or newspaper can help in understanding what is being read and how the information has to be handled. Pan et al. (2010) performed document layout analysis to identify texts, tables, pictures and determined the reading order for a reading robot. Several applications such as communication with speech-impaired, storyteller can be explored for humanoid robots with development of reading capabilities. The applications will determine how the text has to be read and what is to be done with it. For example, in case of a storyteller, the robot has to read from the book but convey it to the audience as a narrator with emotions, empathy. Such storytelling experience would make human–robot interaction more immersive. Bae et al. (2012) developed an empathizing and adaptive storytelling module for a virtual human. The virtual human was already fed with the text of the story and all required emotion tags. The aim was to study the listener's response and experience with the storytelling.

Apart from such application, natural language-based constraints can also be imposed on OCR. For example, developing multilingual reading capabilities, understanding encrypted messages, microtext or acronyms, etc., seamlessly for a robot would not be easy. Other factors such as lighting and hand-written characters can also affect the performance of OCR making it difficult to read.

14.7 Internet and the HRI

In this section, we discuss how internet has changed the human–robot interaction. Authors in Mavridis et al. (2010) aim at creating a pool of shared episodic memories that both can co-refer. The proposed architecture is an online companion of human which helps in connecting to facebook and provides with updates about the facebook account. The facebot cannot work on its own without the intervention of human. Human-Robot Cloud (Mavridis et al. 2012) is an extension of cloud computing to robots. It expands robot's capabilities manifold by incorporating cloud computing capabilities to it. Though the support is extended with the help of human. It raises questions of quality control with human involvements. Roboearth (Waibel et al. 2011) promises to connect all the robots over internet so that they can share and transfer the knowledge among one another. The limitation is the hardware. Robotics hardware needs to leapjump exponentially so as to become alike humans. For example, a robot programmed to serve will be limited by it's hardware if asked to do surgery which requires precision to nanometre scale.

Social media sites are now omnipresent and most communication between people happens over the internet. Such online speechless communication is less considered for social robots. But with advancement in technologies and applications social robots are considered for, it would be necessary for them to interact via social media or emails using online resources. This has led to a new way of research and communication with social robots. For instance, people could communicate with Sophia (Wikipedia 2018b) robot in twitter with '#AskSophia'. Sophia interacts with people and answers their questions over twitter. Nadine (Mishra et al. 2019) interacts with people with Skype, Email and can post in Facebook. She is linked to the internet allowing her to access online resources to find out answers. This makes Nadine a receptionist social robot which is the need of the hour. Social robots do not just interact with humans physically but also over social media. With the advent of social media, they also need to understand the texting languages (Satapathy et al. 2017).

Zeller et al. (2020), Ma et al. (2012) used social media strategies to improve human–robot interaction. Zeller et al. (2020) developed social media strategies to make the hitchhiking robot, hitchBOT, to reach out more audience than the ones it meets in the roads. hitchBOT has social media accounts in Facebook, Twitter, Instagram, and a website of its own. Using these means hitchBOT's origins, personality, goals and travels could be shared with everyone. This inturn helped to instill interest and emotional engagement with the hitchBOT. Similarly, Ma et al. (2012) used social media platforms such as SMS, instant messenger, Google Calendar, and Facebook accounts to establish communication between humans and vaccum robot Roomba and a surveillance robot.

The addition of internet to robotics has opened up new and promising research areas. Though, all the current work focus on robots as a companion to human beings. They provide daily updates and help in make the online life automated. Even though they can share knowledge online, they are still limited by hardware capabilities.

14.8   Haptics in Social Robotics

An integral and essential part of human interaction involves using the sense of touch and perceiving the same with the largest organ of a human body, namely, human skin. Human touch is a very powerful and effective way of communication. Hertenstein et al. (2009) showed how effective human touch could be in conveying emotions during an interaction. The tactile interaction has also now evolved even into our usage of technology. Everyday devices such as digital assistants or mobiles have evolved to support touch, and gesture-based interactions (Cirillo et al. 2017). Due to this, human–robot interaction has also started to evolve and allow tactile communication.

For robots to sense and quantify touch, an essential requirement is the development of tactile sensors capable of sensing touch and contact with objects. A vital research avenue of haptics-based human–robot interaction is focused on the development of tactile sensors capable of acting as a medium of touch and communication. The robot's artificial skin should be able to house these tactile sensors based on the touch interaction required to be recognized. Fritzsche et al. (2011) developed a tactile sensor as pressure-sensitive skin that can be placed in the entire robot body. The sensors are equipped with cushioning elements to reduce the risk of serious injuries in physical human–robot interaction. Beside safety-related functions, the sensitive skin offers touch-based robot motion control which simplifies human–robot interaction.

Cirillo et al. (2017) talks about a distributed tactile sensor developed initially to allow robots to avoid unintentional collision in HRI by estimating the contact force can be used for recognizing social haptic gestures. The haptic gestures allow for a more comprehensive HRI with the robot. Cirillo et al. (2017) developed a flexible tactile sensor that can be fitted to any robot part. This will allow for an easy and scalable solution for haptic-based interactions. The touch-based human–robot interaction allowed three types of gesture recognition. The first one is used to recognize gestures that are applied with static contact on the sensor surface. A simple set of four static tactile gestures were only considered in the static touch-based gestures. The other two methods are used to recognize dynamic and more complex touch gestures.

Mastrogiovanni et al. (2012) talks about the low and high-level perspective of tactile based human–robot interaction. While the low level focuses on estimating and detecting contact forces with objects, the high level focuses on developing cognitive understanding and processes based on touch-based interactions. Initial years of haptics-based research focused on detecting contact forces and avoiding object collision during navigation. But recent years of development as given rise to tactile-based interaction with social robots. This requires an understanding of touch-based communication in social scenarios and interaction. The robot must be capable of understanding the social cues based on touch-based interaction. Simple experiments have been conducted with Telenoid robot (Ogawa et al. 2011) and KISMET robot (Breazeal and Scassellati 1999) to show the importance of recognizing tactile based gestures in human–robot interaction. Simple gestures such as hugging in Telenoid robot (Ogawa et al. 2011) and stroking in KISMET robot (Breazeal and Scassellati 1999) helped in improving the interaction. Metta et al. (2008) introduced iCub humanoid robot, similar to a child robot, that can sense and interact using touch.

Based on the study of Hertenstein et al. (2009), Andreasson et al. (2018) investigated communication of affective emotions by the use of touch in human–robot interaction. A very basic and simple humanoid Nao robot was used for this purpose. Experiments were conducted with participants (both male and female) to show eight different emotions using touch-based interaction with Nao. Features such as touch duration, touch intensity, touch location and touch-types were analyzed and used for differentiating the various emotions. In total, 23 different types of touches were used by the participants. The results showed a link between the different emotions and how the touch patterns are used for communicating them. A significant output of the experiment was the differences in touch patterns between male and female participants for communicating the same emotions. Andreasson et al. (2018) also discuss and provide insights on placement and design of tactile sensors based on application or task, participant gender, types of touches to noted, appearance, the shape of the robot, interaction context, placement of robot, age group to be handled.

An important consideration on developing haptics-based interaction is the embodiment of the social robot and application for which the social robot has to be developed. A humanoid robot such as Nadine (Ramanathan et al. 2019), Sophia (Goertzel et al. 2017) require realistic design of tactile interactions. However, for Paro robot (Shibata 2012) that appears like a Seal the haptics-based interaction would be different. Lee et al. (2006) discusses the effects of allowing touch-based interaction with social robots considering their embodiment.

Mastrogiovanni et al. (2012), Andreasson et al. (2018) showed how the application of the social robot such as caregiver, housekeeping, working partners play a significant role in the design of touch-based interactions. Cooney et al. (2014) discussed the communication of affective emotions using touch in human–robot interaction of companion robots. Cooney et al. (2014) also showed that touch-based interaction could not be ignored in a social robot. Therapeutic and health care applications have seen an increase in usage of social robotics. Tactile interactions can offer several important cues in effective communication. They can also act as clues for therapeutic care. The humanoid robots in Taheri et al. (2014) are programmed and teleoperated via Microsoft Kinect Sensor and Phantom Omni Haptic Robot to elicit reactions consisting of imitation of humans by the humanoid robots and vice versa. Also, Taheri et al. (2014) elaborates on the therapeutic items that were designed to improve joint attention and imitation in autistic children through using humanoid robots. Authors in Kim and Follmer (2019) use haptic feedback in abstract, ubiquitous robotic interfaces. They also introduce preliminary evaluations of SwarmHaptics, a new type of haptic display using a swarm of small, wheeled robots. Readers can refer to Argall and Billard (2010) for a comprehensive review and evolution of tactile based human–robot interactions.

14.9 Conclusion

Human–robot interaction involves the common intention of all the involved partners. Based on the knowledge of human's intention when they look around their environment, robots can plan their actions that will lead to reaching a common goal. Hence, they need to be able to perceive and understand the surroundings, make decisions, plan their future actions, learn, and reflect upon themselves and their environment. The field of social robotics has gained importance in recent years due to advancements in the field of artificial intelligence and robotic hardware. Due to this, they are being applied and considered for more human-like job scopes in different workplaces. Developing such human-like capabilities for social robots (especially humanoids) requires careful design of both speech-based and speechless modes of communication. In this chapter, we provide an overview of speechless interaction techniques in social robotics. In addition to the non-verbal interaction cues such as gaze and affective system, we focus on less talked about topics such as multimodal natural language reading, haptics, the internet, and social media-based communication for social robots. We discuss reading as a skill-set for humanoid robots. The uses include receptionist to read and process paperwork. We also show how the internet has changed the course of research in social robotics, which has obvious limitations, including dependability on the internet. This chapter discusses effective systems to interact with human beings. Though the emotional connection with humans is an important aspect, the hardware limitations of skin and degree of freedom of motors is a big challenge in the research community. We discuss haptic-based communication by supporting touch and gesture-based interactions. It uses a set of static or dynamic tactile gestures.

The chapter is an introduction to the research done for non-verbal communication. It encompasses all the aspects of non-verbal communication. The current state of research is exciting but has limitations. Limitations which are mostly in the hardware, as it is challenging to build a human using wires, silicon, and metal.

Acknowledgements This research is supported by the BeingTogether Centre, a collaboration between Nanyang Technological University (NTU) Singapore and University of North Carolina (UNC) at Chapel Hill. The BeingTogether Centre is supported by the National Research Foundation, Prime Minister's Office, Singapore under its International Research Centres in Singapore Funding Initiative.

References

AFFECTIVA (2018) Affdex sdk for windows and linux. https://developer.affectiva.com/

Andreasson R, Alenljung B, Billing E, Lowe R (2018) Affective touch in human-robot interaction: conveying emotion to the nao robot. Int J Soc Robot 10:473–491

Argall D, Billard G (2010) A survey of tactile human-robot interactions. Robot Auton Syst 58(10):1159–1176

Bae BC, Brunete A, Malik U, Dimara E, Jermsurawong J, Mavridis N (2012) Towards an empathizing and adaptive storyteller system. In: Eighth artificial intelligence and interactive digital entertainment conference, pp 63–65

Billah MM, Ahmed M, Farhana S (2008) Walking hexapod robot in disaster recovery: developing algorithm for terrain negotiation and navigation. Int J Mech Mechatron Eng (World Academy of Science, Engineering and Technology) 2(6):795–800

Breazeal C, Scassellati B (1999) A context-dependent attention system for a social robot. In: Proceedings of the 16th international joint conference on artificial intelligence. Morgan Kaufmann Publishers Inc., San Francisco, CA, USA, IJCAI '99, pp 1146 – 1153. http://dl.acm.org/citation.cfm?id=646307.687601

Camarillo DB, Krummel TM Jr JKS (2004) Robotic technology in surgery: past, present, and future. Am J Surg 188:2–15

CereProc (2019) Cerevoice. https://www.cereproc.com/text-to-speech

Chidambaram V, Chiang YH, Mutlu B (2012) Designing persuasive robots: how robots might persuade people using vocal and nonverbal cues. In: 7th ACM/IEEE International conference on human-robot interaction, pp 293–300

Chrungoo A, Manimaran SS, Ravindran B (2014) Activity recognition for natural human robot interaction. In: Social robotics. ICSR, 2014. Lecture notes in computer science, vol 8755. Springer, Cham, pp 84–94

Cirillo A, Cirillo P, Maria GD, Natale C, Pirozzi S (2017) A distributed tactile sensor for intuitive human-robot interfacing. J Sens 2017:14

Cooney M, Nishio S, Ishiguro H (2014) Importance of touch for conveying affection in a multimodal interaction with a small humanoid robot. Int J Humanoid Robot 12(1550002):1–22. http://orcid.org/10.1142/S0219843615500024

Eyben F, Wöllmer M, Schuller B (2010) Opensmile: the Munich versatile and fast open-source audio feature extractor. In: Proceedings of the 18th ACM international conference on multimedia, MM '10. ACM, New York, NY, USA, pp 1459–1462. https://doi.org/10.1145/1873951.1874246. http://doi.acm.org/10.1145/1873951.1874246

Fang Z, Yuan J, Magnenat Thalmann N (2018) Understanding human-object interaction in RGB-D videos for human robot interaction. In: Proceedings of the 35th computer graphics international (CGI 2018). ACM, pp 163–167

Feil-Seifer D, J Matatic M (2005) Defining socially assistive robotics. In: Proceedings of the 2005 IEEE 9th international conference on rehabilitation robotics workshops. IEEE, pp 465–468

Flandorfer P (2012) Population ageing and socially assistive robots for elderly persons: the importance of sociodemographic factors for user acceptance. Int J Popul Res. https://doi.org/10.1155/2012/829835

Fong T, Nourbakhsh I, Dautenhahn K (2003) A survey of socially interactive robots. Robot Auton Syst 42(3–4):143–166

Fritzsche M, Elkmann N, Schulenburg E (2011) Tactile sensing: a key technology for safe physical human robot interaction. In: 2011 6th ACM/IEEE international conference on human-robot interaction (HRI), pp 139–140. https://doi.org/10.1145/1957656.1957700

Ge S, Cabibihan J, Zhang Z, Li Y, Meng C, He H, Sazadeh M, Li Y, Yang J (2011) Design and development of nancy, a social robot. In: International conference on ubiquitous robots and ambient intelligence, pp 568–573

Goertzel B, Mossbridge J, Monroe E, Hanson D, Yu G (2017) Humanoid robots as agents of human consciousness expansion. CoRR abs/1709.07791. http://arxiv.org/abs/1709.07791, 1709.07791

GoogleCloudPlatform (2018) https://cloud.google.com/

Han J, Park IW, Park M (2015) Outreach education utilizing humanoid type agent robots. In: Proceedings of the 3rd International conference on human-agent interaction, HAI '15. ACM, New York, NY, USA, pp 221–222. http://doi.acm.org/10.1145/2814940.2814980

Hertenstein MJ, Holmes R, McCullough M, Keltner D (2009) The communication of emotion via touch. Emotion 9(4):566–573

Holthaus P, Pitsch K, Wachsmuth S (2011) How can I help? Spatial attention strategies for a receptionist robot. Int J Soc Robot 3(4):383–393

IshiguroLab (2018) Erica. https://eng.irl.sys.es.osaka-u.ac.jp/robot

Karreman D, Bradford GS, van Dijk B, Lohse M, Evers V (2013) What happens when a robot favors someone? How a tour guide robot uses gaze behavior to address multiple persons while storytelling about art. In: 8th ACM/IEEE International conference on human-robot interaction, pp 157–158

Keller I, Schmuck M, Lohan KS (2016) Towards a model for automatic action recognition for social robot companions. In: IEEE International symposium on robot and human interactive communication (RO-MAN), pp 85–90

Kim LH, Follmer S (2019) Swarmhaptics: haptic display with swarm robots. In: Proceedings of the 2019 CHI conference on human factors in computing systems, pp 1–13

Langer A, Feingold-Polak R, Mueller O, Kellmeyer P, Levy-Tzedek S (2019) Trust in socially assistive robots considerations for use in rehabilitation. Neurosci Biobehav Rev 104:231–239

Lee KM, Jung Y, Kim J, Kim SR (2006) Are physically embodied social agents better than disembodied social agents?: The effects of physical embodiment, tactile interaction, and people's loneliness in human-robot interaction. Int J Hum-Comput Stud 64(10):962–973. https://doi.org/10.1016/j.ijhcs.2006.05.002. http://www.sciencedirect.com/science/article/pii/S1071581906000784

Letourneau D, Michaud F, Valin JM, Proulx C (2003) Textual message read by a mobile robot. In: Proceedings of IEEE/RSJ international conference on intelligent robots and systems (IROS), pp 2724–2729

Library MU (2019) Pytesseract. https://github.com/UB-Mannheim/tesseract/wiki

Ma X, Yang X, Zhao S, Fu CW, Lan Z, Pu Y (2012) Using social media platforms for human-robot interaction in domestic environment. Int J Hum-Comput Interact 30. https://doi.org/10.1145/2350046.2350076

Mastrogiovanni F, Cannata G, Natale L, Metta G (2012) Advances in tactile sensing and touch based human robot interaction. In: 2012 7th ACM/IEEE International conference on human-robot interaction (HRI), p 489

Mavridis N (2015) A review of verbal and non-verbal human-robot interactive communication. Robot Auton Syst 63(1):22–35

Mavridis N, Petychakis M, Tsamakos A, Toulis P, Emami S, Kazmi W, Datta C, BenAbdelkader C, Tanoto A (2010) Facebots: steps towards enhanced long-term human-robot interaction by utilizing and publishing online social information. Paladyn, J Behav Robot 1(3):169–178

Mavridis N, AlDhaheri A, AlDhaheri L, Khanji M, AlDarmaki N (2011) Transforming IbnSina into an advanced multilingual interactive android robot. In: IEEE GCC conference and exhibition, pp 120–123

Mavridis N, Bourlai T, Ognibene D (2012) The human-robot cloud: situated collective intelligence on demand. In: 2012 IEEE international conference on cyber technology in automation, control, and intelligent systems (CYBER). IEEE, pp 360–365

Meghdari A, Alemi M, Khamooshi M, Amoozandeh A, Shariati A, Mozafari B (2016) Conceptual design of a social robot for pediatric hospitals. In: International conference on robotics and mechatronics, pp 566–571

Metta G, Sandini G, Vernon D, Natale L, Nori F (2008) The iCub humanoid robot:an open platform for research in embodied cognition. In: Proceedings of the 8th workshop on performance metrics for intelligent systems, pp 50–56

Michaud F, Letourneau D (2001) Mobile robot that can read symbols. In: Proceedings of IEEE international symposium on computational intelligence in robotics and automation, pp 338–343

Mishra N, Ramanathan M, Satapathy R, Cambria E, Magnenat-Thalmann N (2019) Can a humanoid robot be part of the organizational workforce? a user study leveraging sentiment analysis. In: 28th IEEE International Conference on Robot and Human Interactive Communication (RO-MAN), New Delhi, India, pp. 1–7. https://doi.org/10.1109/RO-MAN46459.2019.8956349

Murphy RR, Dreger KL, Newsome S, Rodocker J, Steimle E, Kimura T, Makabe K, Matsuno F, Tadokoro S, Kon K (2011) Use of remotely operated marine vehicles at Minamisanriku and Rikuzentakata Japan for disaster recovery. In: 2011 IEEE International symposium on safety, security, and rescue robotics, pp 19–25. https://doi.org/10.1109/SSRR.2011.6106798

Murphy RR, Tadokoro S, Kleiner A (2016) Springer handbook of robotics. Disaster robotics. Springer, Cham, pp 1577–1604

Mutlu B, Shiwa T, Kanda T, Ishiguro H, Hagita N (2009) Footing in human-robot conversations: how robots might shape participant roles using gaze cues. In: 4th ACM/IEEE International conference on human-robot interaction, pp 61–68

Nakauchi Y, Simmons R (2002) A social robot that stands in line. Auton Robots 12(3):313–324

Ogawa K, Nishio S, Koda K, Balistreri Giuseppe, Watanabe T, Ishiguro Hiroshi (2011) Exploring the natural reaction of young and aged person with telenoid in a real world. J Adv Comput Intell Intell Inform 15(5):592–597. http://orcid.org/10.20965/jaciii.2011.p0592

Oh JH, Hanson D, Kim WS, Han IY, Kim JY, Park IW (2006) Design of android type humanoid robot albert HUBO. In: IEEE/RSJ International conference on intelligent robots and systems, pp 1428–1433

Orejana JR, Bruce MacDonald HS, Aand Ahn, Peri K, Broadbent E (2015) Healthcare robots in homes of rural older adults. In: Tapus A, André E, Martin JC, Ferland F, Ammi M (eds) Social robotics. Springer International Publishing, Cham, pp 512–521

PALROBOTICS (2018) REEM-A: robotics research. https://en.wikipedia.org/wiki/REEMSpecifications

Pan Y, Zhao Q, Kamata S (2010) Document layout analysis and reading order determination for a reading robot. In: TENCON 2010 IEEE region 10 conference, pp 1607–1612

Ramanathan M, Yau WY, Teoh EK (2014) Human action recognition with video data: research and evaluation challenges. IEEE Trans Hum Mach Syst 44(5):650–663

Ramanathan M, Mishra N, Thalmann NM (2019) Nadine humanoid social robotics platform. In: Computer graphics international conference. Springer, pp 490–496

Ruhland K, Andrist S, Badler JB, Peters CE, Badler NI, Gleicher M, Mutlu B, McDonnell R (2014) Look me in the eyes: a survey of eye and gaze animation for virtual agents and artificial systems. In: Lefebvre S, Spagnuolo M (eds) Eurographics 2014—state of the art reports. The Eurographics Association. https://doi.org/10.2312/egst.20141036

Sabelli AM, Kanda T (2016) Robovie as a mascot: a qualitative study for long-term presence of robots in a shopping mall. Int J Soc Robot 8(2):211–221. https://doi.org/10.1007/s12369-015-0332-9

Sakagami Y, Watanabe R, Aoyama C, Matsunaga S, Higaki N, Fujimura K (2002) The intelligent ASIMO: system overview and integration. IEEE/RSJ International conference on intelligent robots and systems 3:2478–2483

Satapathy R, Guerreiro C, Chaturvedi I, Cambria E (2017) Phonetic-based microtext normalization for twitter sentiment analysis. In: 2017 IEEE International conference on data mining workshops (ICDMW). IEEE, pp 407–413

Shibata T (2012) Therapeutic Seal robot biofeedback medical device: qualitative and quantitative evaluations of robot therapy in dementia care. Proc IEEE (Invited Paper) 100(8):2527–2538

Sim DYY, Loo CK (2015) Extensive assessment and evaluation methodologies on assistive social robots for modelling human-robot interaction–a review. Inf Sci 301:305–344

Taheri A, Alemi M, Meghdari A, PourEtemad H, Basiri NM (2014) Social robots as assistants for autism therapy in Iran: research in progress. In: 2014 Second RSI/ISM international conference on robotics and mechatronics (ICRoM). IEEE, pp 760–766

Vieira AW, Nascimento ER, Oliveira GL, Liu Z, Campos MFM (2012) STOP: space-time occupancy patterns for 3d action recognition from depth map sequences. CIARP 2012: progress in pattern recognition, image analysis, computer vision, and applications, vol 7441. Lecture notes in computer science. Springer, Berlin, Heidelberg, pp 252–259

Waibel M, Beetz M, Civera J, d'Andrea R, Elfring J, Galvez-Lopez D, Häussermann K, Janssen R, Montiel J, Perzylo A et al (2011) Roboearth-a world wide web for robots. IEEE Robot Autom Mag (RAM) (Special Issue Towards a WWW for Robots) 18(2):69–82

Wikipedia (2018a) Nadine social robot. https://en.wikipedia.org/wiki/Nadine_Social_Robot

Wikipedia (2018b) Sophia (robot). https://en.wikipedia.org/wiki/Sophia_(robot)

Wikipedia (2018c) Topio. https://en.wikipedia.org/wiki/TOPIO

Zeller F, Smith DH, Duong JA, Mager A (2020) Social media in human-robot interaction. Int J Soc Robot 12:389–402

Zhang J, Zheng J, Magnenat Thalmann N (2015) PCMD: personality-characterized mood dynamics model toward personalized virtual characters. Comput Anim Virtual Worlds 26(3–4):237–245

Chapter 15
Exploring Potential and Acceptance of Socially Intelligent Robot

Nidhi Mishra, Evangelia Baka, and Nadia Magnenat Thalmann

Abstract Socially intelligent robots are dedicated mostly for social interaction with humans. They can assume two useful roles: a functional and an affective one. They aim to serve as an interface between humans and technology, and to increase their quality of life by providing companionship and assisting them in everyday tasks and routines. Although there is a growing attention for these robots in the literature, no comprehensive review has been yet performed to investigate the effectiveness and the usefulness of the aforementioned two roles. Therefore, we systematically reviewed and analyzed human interaction with the socially intelligent robot Nadine, under four different scenarios: interviewer, teacher, Customer guide, and companion. To support our research, we recorded EEG signals, body gestures, facial expressions, and psychometric data through a valid questionnaire. The ultimate purpose of this paper is to allow the understanding of human expectations and acceptance for socially intelligent robots.

15.1 Introduction

The idea of robots, as mechanical agent serving specific purposes, has started a very long time ago, described even in Greek mythology. Robots used to be giants, caged creatures, mainly found in automotive manufacturing lines. Over time, however, they have been evolving, obtaining an adaptable behavior and some human-like physical

N. Mishra (✉) · N. Magnenat Thalmann
Institute of Media Innovation, Nanyang Technological University, 50 Nanyang Drive, Singapore, Singapore
e-mail: nidhi.mishra@ntu.edu.sg

N. Magnenat Thalmann
e-mail: nadiathalmann@ntu.edu.sg

E. Baka
MIRALab, University of Geneva, Rte de Drize 7, 1227 Geneva, Switzerland
e-mail: ebaka@miralab.ch

© The Author(s), under exclusive license to Springer Nature Switzerland AG 2021
N. Magnenat Thalmann et al. (eds.), *Intelligent Scene Modeling and Human-Computer Interaction*, Human–Computer Interaction Series,
https://doi.org/10.1007/978-3-030-71002-6_15

features (Moravec 2020). In the past few years, it seems that they have started to be used in a social and even emotional context, introducing the concept of social robots. Robots with natural language features, able to participate in a conversation, appeared in the 1990s, with the example of MAIA (Antoniol et al. 1993) and RHINO (Burgard et al. 1998). In her seminal paper, Professor Breazeal, inventor of Kismet and Jibo, states that "Social robots have the ability to interact with people in an entertaining, engaging, or anthropomorphic manner" (Breazeal 2003; Breazeal and Velásquez 1998). The most noticeable quality in the interactions between a person and a social robot though is the emotion. In general, affection during human interaction has a vital role as it is important for learning processes, persuasion, and empathy. Affection can be expressed with several ways through verbal or non-verbal communication. However, it has been shown that putting robots in an anthropomorphic framework, by giving to them a personal name and even a story to follow, can affect human's behavior and reaction toward them (Edwards et al. 2019). So, what about the different roles a robot can follow? The purpose of the social robots in Human–Computer Interaction (HCI) is to cover or complement human needs in a more natural way and under different situations. People of different ages has different needs, and this is why the market is teeming with products trying to cover the various demands. For children, adults, elderly, robot can play a role of service, but the question is what degree of effectiveness. We should not forget that a robot cannot substitute a human, no matter its appearance but can approach the reactions and behavior of the latter. Motivated by the development of humanoid social robots and their placement into different areas, we come to the question of their acceptance and impact in our daily life. Most of the Human–Robot Interaction (HRI) studies examine one role of a given robot. This kind of study does not allow us to understand the most acceptable and consequently efficient role of a robot. To answer this question, in this paper, we want to discuss possible jobs a social robot can do and to what extent humans are willing to accept them under these roles. We use Nadine, a humanoid social robot, under four roles that can cover a broad enough range of service: interviewer, teacher, Customer guide, and companion. To evaluate our goal, we used a three-tier architecture containing EEG data, body movements and a questionnaire for personal and psychological factors.

15.2   State of the Art

Social robots have been tested in several roles serving various applications where verbal and non-verbal communication are needed, like assistance and companionship (Wada and Shibata 2007; Dautenhahn et al. 2006), receptionist (Makatchev et al. 2010), educational purposes (Li et al. 2016; Kanda et al. 2009), museum robots and tour guides (Yamazaki et al. 2012; Evers et al. 2014), or even involved in art, like musicians (Petersen et al. 2010) and dancers (Kosuge et al. 2003). In all the above, the main goal is the naturalness in the communication between the human and the machine, to facilitate each corresponding scenario. Social robotics is a continuously increasing field targeting the development of robots able to socio-emotionally interact

Table 15.1 Examples of social robots from several domains in a chronological order

Robot's name	Reference	Year	Type	Role
WABOT (Sugano and Kato 1987)	Sugano and Kato	1987	Humanoid	Piano Player
PARO (Shibata et al. 1997)	Shibata et al.	1997	Baby seal	Social reintegration of elderly people
Care-O-bo (Graf et al. 2004)	Graf et al.	2004	Non-humanoid	Home assistance for elderly people
RI-MAN (Odashima et al. 2006)	Odasima et al.	2006	Humanoid	On-site caregiver/lifting humans
ROBOTA (Billard et al. 2007)	Billard et al.	2007	Humanoid	Robot-assisted therapy for autistic children
IROMEC (Patrizia et al. 2009)	Marti et al.	2009	Non-humanoid	Children companion for knowledge enhancement
KASPAR (Dautenhahn et al. 2009)	Dautenhahn et al.	2009	Humanoid	Robot-assisted therapy for autistic children
SHIMON (Hoffman and Weinberg 2010)	Hoffman and Weinberg	2010	Humanoid	Playing of percussive instruments
JIBO (Breazeal and Faridi 2016)	Breazeal	2014	Non-humanoid	Personal assistant
SOPHIA (Weller 2017)	Hanson Robotics	2016	Humanoid	Social companion
Nadine (Mishra et al. 2019)	N. Mishra et al.	2019	Humanoid	Customer agent

and communicate with humans serving several domains like the ones mentioned before. Table 15.1 provides some examples of broadly used social robots over the years.

The question to all that is what people would like from a robot and among all what are the roles that a social robot can play and which one is the most preferable? Would a robot job interviewer, for example, be more efficient than a human?

15.2.1 Robot as Interviewer

Studies have highlighted that hiring biases are still apparent into companies and thus, a need of an efficient unbiased mechanical recruiter in crucial. The world's first robot designed to carry out unbiased job interviews, Tengai, is being tested by Swedish recruiters. She is placed on the table, at the eye level, in front of the candidate she is about to interview (Savage 2019). A similar robot is Matlda (Mat 2016), who has been programmed to conduct 25-min interviews in which she works through a roster of up to 76 questions. She records and analyzes the interviewee's responses, monitors facial expressions, and compares them to other successful employees within the hiring company. Nowadays, a lot of companies are using artificial intelligence to conduct interviews in English, trying to do the procedure more impersonal, and consequently eliminating any possible bias. HireVue (Money et al. 2007) has designed an artificial intelligence-enabled software; The interviewee uses their phone or laptop to answer a set of predetermined questions, and the AI analyzes their voice, body language, facial expressions and more to determine if the person is a right candidate for the job. Other examples are the companies AllyO (2016) and VCV.AI (2018) who are also working on bringing artificial intelligence to the hiring process.

15.2.2 Robots as Teacher

Another frequently used role is one of the teachers or the classroom companion. Robots and AI are or can be used at all levels of education from kindergarten (Fridin 2014), elementary schools (Fridin and Belokopytov 2014), high schools (Alemi et al. 2015) to universities (Rossi et al. 2015), executing several activities from administrative tasks, acting as a reminder about forthcoming due dates or answering mails (Miller 2016), to teacher (Ivanov 2016). Matilda (Munkeby et al. 2002) is an example of such kind of a robot, having facial and voice recognition, detecting emotions, dancing, and playing music, used recently as classroom companion for students with special needs. Robots need, at least in the foreseeable future, a human teacher to prepare the course materials. However, undoubtedly, they can serve as a motivation to students. In the U.S., large scale projects such as "The Robotics Alliance Project" (Schneider and Van Den Blink 2006) by NASA and "The Telepresence Robot Kit" (Do et al. 2013), or TeRK project (Nourbakhsh et al. 2006) have been undertaken to motivate students to be involved in "technological fields of study." Similarly, the "Center for Distributed Robotics" at the University of Minnesota has given opportunity to all its computer science students, at all levels, to experience robots, as the faculty believes that this approach can help students adhere to their engineering programs.

15.2.3 Robot as Customer Guide

Providing guidance to customers in a shopping mall is a suitable task for a social service robot. To be useful for customers though, the guidance needs to be intuitive and effective. Robots are predicted to have a profound impact on the service sector. The emergence of robots has attracted increasing interest from business scholars and practitioners alike. "Service robots lend a hand at China's banks and railway stations" (Lu et al. 2020), and "Will robots take your job?" (O'brien 2019) are a few of the increasing news headlines about the emergence of service robots. These headlines highlight that advances in robotics and Artificial Intelligence (AI) are gaining broad attention. Takayuki et al. (Kanda et al. 2009) explored possible robot tasks in daily life, developed a guide robot for a shopping mall and conducted a field trial with it. The robot was designed to interact naturally with customers and to affectively provide shopping information. The robot was semiautonomous, partially controlled by a human operator, to cope with the difficulty of speech recognition in a real environment and to handle unexpected situations. A field trial was conducted at a shopping mall for 25 d to observe how the robot performed this task and how people interacted with it. The robot interacted with approximately 100 groups of customers each day. The results revealed that 63 out of 235 people in fact went shopping based on the information provided by the robot. The experimental results suggest promising potential for robots working in shopping malls. In recent years, service firms increasingly have relied on Frontline Service frontline Robots (FSRs) that "exist primarily to interact with people" (Stock and Merkle 2017) and assist human users. Nestlé, for example, has placed hundreds of frontline social robots on shop floors to sell Nescafé in Japan.

15.2.4 Robot as Companion

Loneliness is a collective experience globally. The fight against social isolation and loneliness is an essential reason for social companion robots. While it's evident that a robotic companion cannot replace human interaction, a friendly and cute robotic creature is way better than no human care at all. Breazeal (2004) who developed Kismet one of the earliest social robot in the mid 1990s defined a sociable robot as one that "is able to communicate and interact with us, understand and even relate to us, in a personal way" (Breazeal and Scassellati 1999) She sees the pinnacle of achievement robots that "could befriend us, as we could them". BUDDY (Milliez 2018) is currently in development under the lead of Rodolphe Hasselvander, CEO and founder of Blue Frog Robotics in Paris, France. With human-like expressions, different feelings, and moods, BUDDY can carry on conversations with his human companions. Anyone can argue that BUDDY's programmed emotions aren't real, but no one can question the validity of the emotional response people have with their robot companions. The wide-eyed, flat-faced French robot has already been in high society having met and trolled French President Emmanuel Macron at last year's Vivatech. However, the creature is set to rather become the newest family member in every household. Its features allow it to protect the home, offer assistance in the kitchen, act as a personal assistant by reminding family members of important dates as well as a playmate for children. As an emotional robot, it promises to express various emotions throughout the day. It might cheerfully welcome you when you come home from work but might be grumpy if you do not spend much time with it. The tiny, wheel-powered robot is the Indian response to the robotic revolution started in the Western part of the world. It is the first companion robot developed by a Mumbai-based star-tup Emotix. Miko (2018) is aimed at children above the age of five years. Like the smart dinosaur of Cognitoys, it is also artificial intelligence-based growing and changing together with your kid. It can talk, respond, educate, and entertain. It understands the specific needs and emotions of your child and reacts accordingly. Nadine (Ramanathan et al. 2019) is leading in social robot and is world's most human-like robot. She is designed to give companionship to elderly and support them.

15.3   Research Questions

Robots have a lot of advantages, like providing a constant and correct work of the same always quality, working non-stop, do not discriminate. But undoubtedly, for the time being, they lack the human creativity and naturalness as well as the human personal approach. Thus, they are not always acceptable from humans and it is very interesting to investigate if this is general or can be altered based on the role a robot can have. The current research aims to address possible acceptance and limitations of the existing technology used in the broad area of HRI up to now. Although different kinds of robots have been used to contribute to several domains, like education, health, entertainment, both in virtual and physical environments, a robot that will make a human feel as comfortable and accepted as interacting with another human has not been reported yet. Towards this direction, we intend to answer the following research questions:

- What do participants think of a robot under four predefined roles (interviewer, teacher, customer guide, and companion?) and what is their preference?
- How do participants perceive robots in general?
- Does the attitude toward a robot can change after several interactions with it?

15.4   Materials and Methods

15.4.1   Nadine Social Robot

For our experiments, we have used Nadine, a realistic humanoid social robot with natural skin, hair, and appearance. Nadine's architecture (Ramanathan et al. 2019) consists of three layers, namely, perception, processing, and interaction. Nadine receives audio and visual stimuli from microphone, 3D cameras and web cameras to perceive user characteristics, and her environment, which are then sent to the processing layer. The processing layer is the core module of Nadine that receives all results from the perception layer about environment and user to act upon them. This layer includes various sub-modules such as dialogue processing (chatbot), affective system (emotions, personality, mood), Nadine's memory of previous encounters with users. Nadine can be easily personalized for different tasks by adding different chatbots and changing her memory. Nadine's memory, chatbot, emotional model, and gestures were modified for different roles.

15.4.2   Participants

40 participants (10 female, 30 male) from 21 to 65 years old and of several nationalities participated in our research. The experiment took place in the Institute for Media and Innovation (IMI) at the Nanyang Technological University (NTU) in Singapore. As we study the way of communication and interaction, we tried to include as many nationalities as possible to exclude any bias due to culture. We ensured that our participants had no previous experience with robots, or any advanced technology. A detailed consent form was signed before the onset of the procedure, followed by a detailed explanation of the experiment. Each participant received a small compensation for contributing and helping to our research.

15.4.3   Experimental Design

During the experiment, the participants were urged to interact with Nadine humanoid social robot which can be seen in Fig. 15.1 under the following four different scenarios:

- **Job Interviewer**, where participants had to answer several predefined questions, based on the procedure of a normal interview.
- **Customer guide**, hypothetically working in a shop of electronics, where the participants look for a new cell phone. Nadine was having a conversation with the participants regarding the possible features they would wish to have and at the end, she was proposing a cell phone model.
- **Teacher**, where Nadine was providing a short lecture on climate change. She was explaining the term of climate change and referring to the current situation, interacting with the participant by posing several relevant questions.
- **Companion**, where Nadine was following the flow of the subject that participants were choosing. They were able to interact freely in the predefined language (English). Non-native English speakers had the opportunity to speak with her in their own native language (French, German, Chinese, Hindi).

In the first three roles the scenario was predefined, and the thematic areas of the discussion were predefined and guided by the robot involved in the process, but the time of the interaction was up to the participants. In the companion mode, participants were the ones guiding the interaction, interacting freely. For evaluation of our results, we used a multi-modal approach recording:

- A Negative Attitude Towards Robot Scale (NARS) to assess users' overall attitude on robots.
- Psychometric measures through a validated questionnaire (Panas X) before and after the procedure, which will subjectively examine the emotional states of the participants.

Fig. 15.1 Example of a participant interacting with Nadine in the role of Customer guide. Nadine replies to participant's wish to buy a cell phone, proposing a model based on his requirements and budget

- Kinect to record the upper body skeleton movements.
- EEG recording to capture the brain activity.

The whole procedure took place in an isolated room where external noises were excluded, and the attention of participants could not be disturbed. The whole experimental process was video and audio recorded with the consent of the participants. The overall duration of the experiment for each participant was 45 min, including the time needed for the installation of the equipment. As the setup of the EEG was the most time-consuming, to avoid fatigue and boredom, we motivated the participants to sign the consent form and answer the first part of the questionnaire during this time.

15.4.4 NARS

To measure participant's attitudes toward robots in general, before their interactions with the Nadine social robot, we use a slightly adapted version of the NARS questionnaire (Syrdal et al. 2009).

15.4.5 Psychometric

To assess the psychometric factors in our experiment we used a reliable, validates questionnaire, including closed-ended Likert-scale questions. We examined humans' emotions, mood states, and the overall experience of the interactions. The mood states scale was based on the Positive and Negative Affect Schedule. The questionnaire was given to the participants before as well as after the experiment so that we could define any possible differences in their state or their expectations. Through the questionnaire, participants also noted their perception of friendliness and sociality of Nadine.

15.4.6 Body Movements

We used Kinect v2[1] by Microsoft to record the motion and body skeleton. Kinect is widely used in both industry and research communities (Shotton et al. 2011). It can capture both RGB and depth images of gestures. Kinect V2 facilitates us to detect and track the body joints. Since kinect V2 provides information of x, y, and z positions of 25 joints. The position of each joint is defined by the vector [x, y, z], where the basic unit is 1m and the origin of the coordinate system is Kinect v2 sensor itself. The orientation is also determined with three values expressed in degrees. The device does not return orientation values of head, hands, knees, and feet. We used the method proposed by Sapiński et al. (2019) in his paper Emotion Recognition from Skeletal Movements which is a different representation of affective movements, based on sequence of joints positions and orientations. The algorithm utilizes a sequential model of affective movement based on low-level features, which are positions and orientation of joints within the skeleton provided by Kinect v2. The method was used to classify action recognition, for seven affective states: neutral, sadness, surprise, fear, disgust, anger, and happiness.

15.4.7 EEG Recordings and Analysis

EEG signals were recorded and amplified using a NuAmps amplifier.[2] Given our research interest we examined some specific brain areas, so we used in total 23 channels. These channels were attached on a Quick cap according to the 10–20 system at the locations Fp, F, FC, T, CP, P, O. Curry 8 X was used for the data acquisition and the online processing with a sample 1000 Hz per channel. The analysis of the EEG data and the processing of the signal were carried in MATLAB. All data were carefully checked for artifacts, like eye blinks or head/body movements. Fast Fourier

---

[1]https://docs.depthkit.tv/docs/kinect-for-windows-v2.
[2]https://compumedicsneuroscan.com/applications/eeg/.

Fig. 15.2 The five Regions of Interest (ROIs) used for our experiment. 23 electrodes were selected according the needs of our research

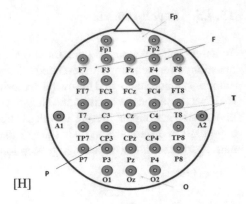

[H]

Transform was applied and then the power spectra were calculated. As shown in Fig. 15.2, we examined 5 ROIs including both hemispheres: Prefrontal (Fp), Frontal (F), Parietal (P), Temporal (T), and Occipital (O) for four brain states: theta (3–7 Hz), alpha (8–12), beta (13–30 Hz), and low gamma (30–42 Hz).

15.4.8 Statistics

Statistical analysis for the variables of EEG, Kinect data, and the questionnaire was conducted though SPSS. Repeated measures ANOVAs were used, and we followed up statistically significant results with Connover's post-hoc tests. The non-parametric Friedman test was used in case the data did not meet the sphericity requirement.

15.5 Results

Our goal is to study the effects HRI can have on human emotional states and behaviors and thus to assess the acceptance of humanoid robots, providing a first glance into this field of research.

15.5.1 NARS Data

The NARS data indicates the general attitude of the participants toward robots. The participants answered the questions on a Likert-type scale ranging from 1 (not at all) to 5 (extremely). The answers were coded, and averages were calculated. Three of the items were reverse coded to fit with the general direction of the answers (higher scores indicating more negative attitudes). From Table 15.2, it can be seen that the

Table 15.2 Average responses on the NARS questionnaire. Questions marked * are inverted

Question	Response
I would feel uneasy if I was given a job where I had to use robots	2.52
I would feel nervous operating a robot in front of other people	2.17
The word "robot" means nothing to me	2.39
I would hate the idea that robots or artificial intelligence were making judgements about things	2.52
I would feel very nervous just standing in front of a robot	1.91
I would feel paranoid talking with a robot	2.04
I would feel uneasy if robots really had emotions	2.48
Something bad might happen if robots developed into living beings	2.74
I feel that if I depend on robots too much, something bad might happen	2.48
I am concerned that robots would be a bad influence on children	2.22
I feel that in the future society will be dominated by robots	2.57
I would feel relaxed talking with robots*	2.04
If robots had emotions, I would be able to make friends with them*	1.96
I feel comforted being with robots that have emotions*	2.09
Total	2.3

average attitude toward robots is relatively neutral (2.3). The participants gave higher scores for questions which referred to the idea that robots could potentially develop into living beings, relying on robots, or them dominating people in the future. People also showed anxiety toward needing to use robots in their jobs. On the contrary, people expressed lower negative emotions when it came to standing in front of a robot or talking to one. They showed positive attitudes in regard to being relaxed while talking to robots or having emotional connections with them.

15.5.2 Psychometric Data

Our questionnaire gave us information about the participants' emotions during their interactions with Nadine, along with their preferences toward the four roles (job interviewer, teacher, companion, and customer guide). The role of Customer guide, as shown in Fig. 15.3 was found to be both the best supported role and the most preferred one.

Using the questionnaire, six emotions were investigated: three negative ones (nervous, shy, tired) and three positive ones (inspired, interested, confident). To test for the differences in questionnaire responses among the emotions and the roles of the robot, two independent-samples multiple ANOVAs were conducted, one for positive emotions and one for negative emotions. Emotions and roles were imputed as independent variables and the scores for each of the emotions was used as the dependent

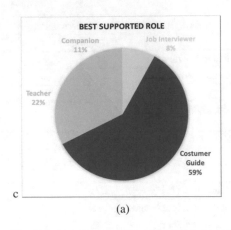
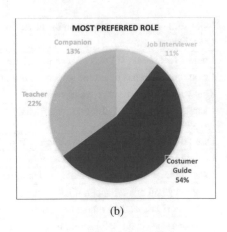

c

(a)   (b)

Fig. 15.3 Results from the questionnaire about the preference of the four roles. LEFT: the percentages for the best supported role. RIGHT: the percentages of the most preferred role

Table 15.3 Descriptive statistics for all the levels of positive emotions

	Interviewer		Teacher		Customer guide		Companion		Total	
Emotion	Mean	SD	Mean	SD	Mean	SD	Mean	SD	Mean	SD
Interested	3.78	0.89	3.22	1.25	3.62	0.95	3.43	1.17	3.51	1.08
Inspired	3.27	1.02	2.84	1.12	3.11	1.05	2.92	1.21	3.03	1.10
Confident	3.76	0.80	3.16	0.96	3.81	0.74	3.32	1.03	3.51	0.92
Total	3.60	0.93	3.07	1.12	3.51	0.96	3.23	1.15	3.35	1.06

variable. LSD post-hoc tests were computed to determine differences among different levels of variables. For the positive emotions, the ANOVA showed a significant main effect of both emotions (F (2, 432) = 10.789, $p < 0.01$) and roles (F (3, 432) = 6.463, $p < 0.01$). The interaction between the two factors was not significant (F (6, 432) = 0.232, $p = 0.945$). The descriptive statistics are presented in Table 15.3. As can also be seen from Table 15.3 and Fig. 15.4, the participants rated that they were interested and confident statistically significantly higher than that they were inspired ($p < 0.001$). There were no statistically significant differences between scores on inspired and interested ($p = 1$). This trend was the same for all roles. Furthermore, the interviewer and the customer guide roles were not statistically significantly different ($p = 0.513$), but the two had higher scores on positive emotions compared to both the teacher and the companion role ($p < 0.05$ for all differences). Lastly, there was no statistically significant difference between the teacher and the companion role ($p = 0.267$).

The multiple ANOVA for negative emotions indicated a significant main effect of both emotions (F (2, 432) = 3.82, $p = 0.023$) and role (F (3, 432) = 5.908, $p = 0.001$). There was no significant interaction between the factors (F (6, 432) = 0.39, $p = 0.885$). The descriptive statistics can be seen in Table 15.4. As can be seen from

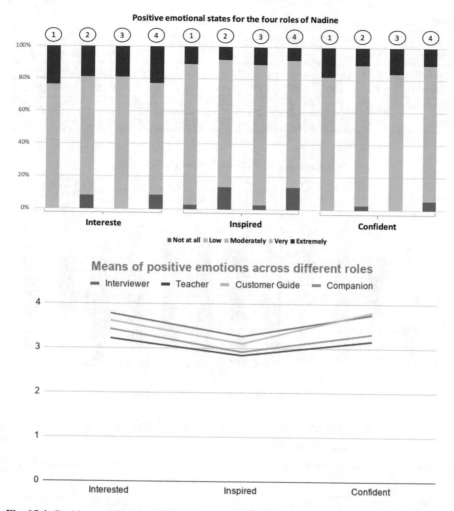

Fig. 15.4 Positive emotional states with their means for different roles

Table 15.4 and Fig. 15.5, there was no statistically significant difference between nervous and tired ($p = 0.797$), while both of them were higher than shy ($p < 0.05$ for both). These differences were the same across all roles. The role associated with the highest negative emotions was the interviewer, followed by the teacher. The difference between the two was not statistically significantly different ($p = 0.119$). However, the interviewer was statistically significantly higher than both customer guide and companion ($p < 0.05$ for both). The teacher role was not statistically significantly different from the companion role ($p = 0.075$), but was significantly higher than customer guide ($p = 0.032$). Lastly, customer guide and companion roles did not differ significantly ($p = 0.71$).

Table 15.4 Descriptive statistics for all the levels of negative emotions

	Interviewer		Teacher		Customer guide		Companion		Total	
Emotion	Mean	SD	Mean	SD	Mean	SD	Mean	SD	Mean	SD
Interested	2.08	0.92	1.86	1.11	1.57	1.01	1.54	0.80	1.76	0.99
Inspired	1.76	0.80	1.49	0.77	1.43	0.80	1.43	0.73	1.53	0.78
Confident	2.03	1.12	1.95	1.10	1.51	0.69	1.68	0.82	1.79	0.96
Total	1.95	0.96	1.77	1.02	1.50	0.84	1.55	0.78	1.69	0.92

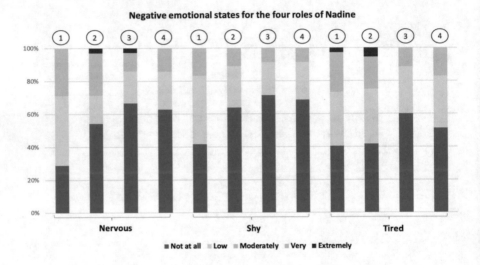

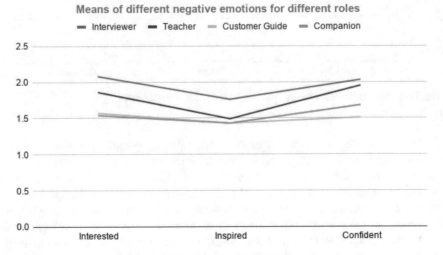

Fig. 15.5 Negative emotional states with their means for different roles

The participants felt moderately high levels of positive emotions. They felt interested and confident more than they felt inspired. The roles varied in the level of positive emotions: the interviewer role was the one which elicited the highest levels of positive emotions, followed by the customer guide role, the companion low, and lastly, the teacher role. On the other hand, the intensity of negative emotions was very low. Participants reported the lowest levels of feeling shy, and higher levels of feeling nervous and tired. In regard to these emotions, interviewer was the role with the highest levels of them, followed by teacher, and then companion and customer guide.

15.5.3 Kinect Data

In order to confirm the emotions reported by the participants, an objective measurement of emotion was recorded as well. As can be seen from Fig. 15.6, there were some differences among the roles in terms of different emotions. Sadness was the most prominent in the role of customer guide, followed closely by the role of interviewer. The role of companion had the lowest score for sadness. Similarly, companion had the highest rate of happiness. The second highest score for happiness was demonstrated with the customer guide role, and the lowest one was the teacher role. Surprise was also the most prominent in the companion and the customer guide roles and the least in the teacher role. The interviewer role evoked the most fear, and the customer guide evoked the least. Teacher and companion roles evoked medium amounts of fear. By far the highest score for anger was shown toward the teacher role, while the companion had the lowest amount of fear demonstrated. Finally, participants were most disgusted by the interviewer role and the least by the companion role.

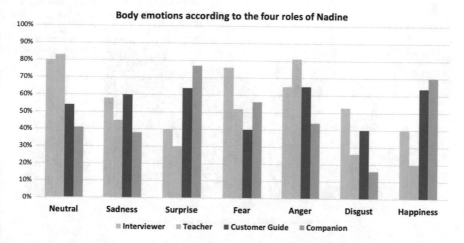

Fig. 15.6 Discreet emotions extracted from body skeleton movements through Kinect

15.5.4 EEG Data

The main purpose of using EEG in this experiment was to examine different patterns of neural electroconductivity that occur while interacting with Nadine when she is in different roles. This ought to provide us with the most objective measurement of the emotional states and attitudes we experience during interactions with robots. Based on this information, we can understand which one of the four roles enabled by contemporary technology brings the most positive emotions and usefulness to the user. As we mentioned, we have focused on five brain areas which are shown in Fig. 15.7. Thus, starting from the Prefrontal area, we noticed a theta rhythm for the role of the interviewer, whereas for the three other roles an alpha state was maintained. However, there was an increase in the frequency from one role to another (teacher, Customer guide, and companion accordingly). There was a statistically significant difference in the frequency of the theta state corresponding to the interviewer role (7.5 ± 1.2 Hz) in comparison to the other roles ($p < 0.01$). The other roles were characterized by an alpha state, with a statistically significant difference ($p < 0.05$) existing only between the teacher (9.7 ± 1.2 Hz) and the companion roles (11 ± 1.7 Hz).

In the frontal area, the results were somewhat different. The role of interviewer was marked by the existence of frontal theta oscillations (7.8 ± 1.1 Hz). This frequency was statistically significantly different ($p < 0.001$) from the other roles. Subsequently, the second role of the teacher was marked by an alpha rhythm (12 ± 2.5 Hz). The role of the teacher presented was significantly different from the companion role ($p <$

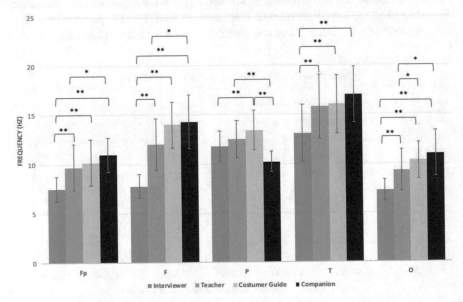

Fig. 15.7 The average frequencies in the five brain areas for the four roles of Nadine. Statistical significance is shown where existing (*for $p < 0.05$ and **for $p < 0.001$)

0.05), but not different from the customer guide role. The remaining two roles were marked by a beta state. Regarding the parietal area, an alpha rhythm was identified for the roles of the interviewer (11.8 ± 1.6 Hz) and the companion (10.2 ± 1 Hz). The role of the teacher (12.5 ± 1.8 Hz) and the Customer guide (13.4 ± 2 Hz) was represented by a beta state. The teacher role is uncertain, as it is on the limit between beta and alpha frequencies. In the temporal lobe, a general beta rhythm was found. The frequencies increased for each subsequent role. The role of interviewer, had a significantly lower frequency (13.1 ± 2.9 Hz) than the other roles ($p < 0.001$). The other three roles did not differ significantly from one another. Lastly, the occipital lobe was in the alpha rhythm during the interaction with all the roles, except for the role of the interviewer, where a theta state was found (7.3 ± 1.1 Hz). There was a gradual increase in frequencies from the first to the last role, with nearly all the differences being statistically significant ($p < 0.05$). The only exception was the difference between the last two roles (customer guide and companion) which can be seen from Fig. 15.8.

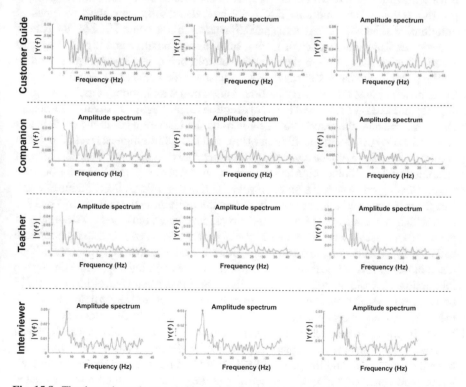

Fig. 15.8 The three channels recorded in occipital area showing the dominant brain state for each role in the power spectrum. Nadine's roles are shown in the order they were presented to the participants. In the first case (a), only a theta state was found (7.3 ± 1.1 Hz), whereas for the rest three roles, an alpha state with an increase of the frequency for each role was noticed. Case (d) concluded with an average value of 11 ± 2.3 Hz

15.6 Discussion and Future Work

In this study, participants interacted with the humanoid social robot Nadine in her four roles: interviewer, teacher, customer guide, and companion. The emotional reactions of the participants during these interactions were recorded. Three measures were used for this purpose: a questionnaire, a body-movement tracking device (Kinect), and EEG measurements. The participants also reported on their opinions about robots before the interaction. They expressed these opinions through the NARS questionnaire.

The NARS results indicate that the participants had relatively neutral opinions toward robots before the interaction. They were mostly worried about robots developing into living beings and dominating over people in the future. However, they expressed positive attitudes toward interacting with robots in a social or emotional manner.

The questionnaire helped us understand the emotions that the participants felt toward the different roles of Nadine. The results could be separated into two groups: positive and negative emotions If we combine the results from the two types of emotions, we can conclude that the participants were most emotional for the role of interviewer. This ambivalence of having both highest positive and highest negative emotions is probably due to the interviewer role being the first one presented to all the participants but also because an interview process has a stressful character by definition. Since this is their first time interacting with a robot, it makes sense to expect them to show the highest levels of emotions at the beginning of this experience. On the other hand, the teacher role seems to be the least enjoyable: the participants reported the lowest level of positive emotions and the second-highest level of negative emotions. Therefore, it seems that the participants did not enjoy this role. The roles of customer guide and companion had the same (lowest) levels of negative emotions, but the customer guide role had a higher level of positive emotions. So, it seems that this was the most enjoyed role, potentially due to the usefulness the participants can see in it, which is in concordance with previous studies which indicated a willingness of people to interact with robots in that context (Kanda et al. 2009). The companion role had the lowest scores on the positive emotions and the negative emotions alike. This result indicates that, while the participants experienced nothing unpleasant during the interaction, they did not experience positive emotions either. Hence, this role could be a neutral one. The teacher role was mainly unpleasant for the participants, which indicates that this role should be revised and improved. Lastly, the interviewer role is hard to interpret but remains the most interesting one. As we mentioned previously, it was the first one that the participants experienced, indicating that its results may stem from the excitement and the general feelings toward the robot in the beginning. To understand better such a role, interviews with the participants should be conducted in the future, so that the nuance of their emotions can be understood.

The interpretations based on the questionnaire can be put up against the Kinect data to order to confirm the emotions of the participants in regard to the different roles. First, the interviewer role showed high levels of fear, anger, and sadness among the participants. This is in line with the high negative emotions, which indicates that this role was unpleasant for the participants. They also showed relatively low levels of happiness and surprise, indicating that the positive emotions from the questionnaire can be attributed to excitement about the initial interaction with the robot and not the role it was in. The negative assessment of the teacher role based on the questionnaire was confirmed by the Kinect results. They indicated very low levels of happiness and surprise, along with very high levels of anger. Furthermore, the customer guide role was confirmed as eliciting high levels of positive emotions, such as happiness and surprise, along with, unexpectedly, high levels of anger. Finally, the role of companion actually showed the highest levels of positive emotions on the Kinect data, and an absence of negative emotions. Thus, it may be that the companion role elicited positive emotions, just not ones that could be detected by the questionnaire.

As a final demonstration of the participants' reactions during the interactions, EEG data was collected from five brain areas: prefrontal, frontal, parietal, temporal, and occipital.

For all the areas except for the parietal, a trend of the frequencies increasing throughout the experience was noticed, indicating an effect of familiarity. In the prefrontal area, the interviewer role elicited a theta rhythm, which has been linked to spatial working memory (Alekseichuk et al. 2016). Therefore, it may be that the participants engaged working memory during the interview phase because they needed to retrieve information in order to answer the questions. The alpha rhythm, present in the other roles, shows a strong engagement of the decision-making and behavior mechanisms.

The results were very different in regard to the frontal area. Frontal theta oscillations were detected for the role of interviewer (7.8 ± 1.1 Hz) which shows that the task was demanding (Cavanagh and Frank 2014) and apparently participants had to put a higher cognitive effort to get focused and interact with Nadine. Other studies have also noticed frontal theta oscillation during a first human–robot interaction (Urgen et al. 2013). Subsequently, for the second role of the teacher, alpha rhythm was detected and this rhythm can be associated with the participants' concentration. For the remaining two roles, a beta state was apparent, which means that participants were more relaxed, and they were putting less cognitive effort in their tasks. This makes sense, as the teacher role involves higher mental activities, while the roles of customer guide and companion represent less cognitively demanding interactions.

Regarding the parietal area, alpha rhythm was noticed for the roles of the interviewer and companion. This rhythm in the parietal cortex is linked with perception processes (Cavanagh and Frank 2014) and is in line with our previous research, where it was demonstrated that it is active only in human–robot interactions, and not in human–human interactions (Baka et al. 2019). This indicates that the participants were unintentionally focused to the stimuli they were looking at, which they were not familiar with. Alpha rhythm in the parietal cortex is also associated with emotional engagement and this explains the presence of this rhythm for the role of the companion, which was also seen as emotionally positive in the Kinect data. For the roles of the teacher and the customer guide a beta state was detected.

In the temporal lobe, a beta rhythm with an increase in the frequency in each role was detected. Temporal lobe is associated with auditory processing (Cavanagh and Frank 2014) and the beta rhythm shows that participants had no difficulties in following Nadine's speech. However, the role of interviewer showed the lowest value of the beta state. This means that the participants faced the biggest difficulty in deciphering robot's voice while being interviewed, which may be explained by the fact that this role was the first one, and participants had no prior robot experience. The more they interacted with the robot, the more familiar they became with it, in terms of audio processing.

Lastly, occipital lobe is the one related to the mechanisms of visual attention. In previous research, it has been proven that the human brain can understand the difference between a human and a robot, even if the robot shares the same physical appearance with the human (Baka et al. 2019). In that case, while looking at a humanoid robot, the occipital area of the brain is synchronized in an alpha state whereas while we interact with a human, beta state is dominant. This experiment verified this finding by detecting the alpha rhythm in all the roles except from the one of the interviewer, where a theta state was noticed, which is in line with the familiarity explanation that was previously described. The roles can be described in sum as follows:

- The interviewer role was the one that elicited the most intensive reactions, both in terms of emotions and neural activity. This is most likely due to it being the first role presented, with the participants being unfamiliar with Nadine. This can be also explained by the existence of the theta state in occipital area. Questionnaire revealed high levels of interest and inspiration. Aside from this, the role seemed to be dominantly unpleasant for the participants and required a lot of cognitive activity, as every normal job interview procedure. EEG results were in line with that, as they verified the emotional engagement with the existence of the alpha state in parietal lobe. Moreover, this one was the only role for which theta waves were dominant in prefrontal, frontal, and occipital areas. Participants voted that Nadine had the friendliest reactions under this role.
- The teacher role was the one with the most negative reactions. Kinect data and questionnaire revealed only negative emotions and tiredness. EEG data though showed the higher level of concentration as alpha waves in frontal area have appeared only for this role. The aforementioned suggests that this role should be significantly improved in the future.
- The customer guide role was the one that elicited the best emotional response, in terms of the most positive and the least negative emotions. It did not require heavy cognitive activity, questionnaire revealed high confidence level and participants showed no signs of stress as beta state was dominant in frontal area. Customer guide was voted by the participants as the most preferred and suitable role for Nadine.

- Lastly, the companion role had mixed results. It elicited positive emotions in the participants, but they were not captured with the questionnaire. Kinect data showed high levels of surprise and happiness. EEG verified the latter, as this role engaged the parietal lobe, associated with perception and emotional engagement more than the other roles. Moreover, beta state in frontal area confirms the absence of stress and anxiety.

15.7 Conclusion

This study had several limitations, which can serve as pointers for future research. The first one is that the roles were presented in the same order to all the participants, which lead to information about participants' legitimate reactions and their familiarity with Nadine being mixed. Future studies should develop a procedure in which the roles would be presented in random order or a fixed counter-balanced order. Interviewer role seems to be intimidating to start interacting for humans as humans in a position to answer the robot correctly which could have made impact on results.

Furthermore, the questionnaire employed in measuring emotions did not capture all potential emotions which may have occurred in the participants. Therefore, more extensive emotions questionnaire should be used in future research. Future studies may also want to implement interviews with participants in order to understand the nuances of the participants' interaction with the robot.

In conclusion, this study investigated the reactions of people in interaction with four roles of a social robot. The participants showed high levels of positive emotions and low levels of negative emotions in general. The customer guide was voted as the most preferred role, while the teacher was seen as the least enjoyable. Future studies are needed in order to understand these differences in greater detail.

Acknowledgements This research is supported by the National Research Foundation, Singapore under its International Research Centres in Singapore Funding Initiative. Any opinions, findings and conclusions or recommendations expressed in this material are those of the author(s) and do not reflect the views of National Research Foundation, Singapore.

References

(2016) Allyo. https://www.allyo.com/
(2016) Matlda. https://recruitingtimes.org/news/16065/robots-take-job-interview/
(2018) Miko robot. https://miko.ai/
(2018) Vcc.ai. https://vcv.ai/
Alekseichuk I, Turi Z, de Lara GA, Antal A, Paulus W (2016) Spatial working memory in humans depends on theta and high gamma synchronization in the prefrontal cortex. Curr Biol 26(12):1513–1521
Alemi M, Meghdari A, Ghazisaedy M (2015) The impact of social robotics on l2 learners' anxiety and attitude in english vocabulary acquisition. Int J Soc Robot 7(4):523–535

Antoniol G, Cattoni R, Cettolo M, Federico M (1993) Robust speech understanding for robot telecontrol. In: Proceedings of the 6th international conference on advanced robotics, pp 205–209

Baka E, Vishwanath A, Mishra N, Vleioras G, Thalmann NM (2019) "Am i talking to a human or a robot?": a preliminary study of human's perception in human-humanoid interaction and its effects in cognitive and emotional states. In: Computer graphics international conference. Springer, pp 240–252

Billard A, Robins B, Nadel J, Dautenhahn K (2007) Building robota, a mini-humanoid robot for the rehabilitation of children with autism. Assist Technol 19(1):37–49

Breazeal C (2003) Toward sociable robots. Robot Autonom Syst 42(3–4):167–175

Breazeal C, Faridi F (2016) Robot. US Patent App 29/546,668

Breazeal C, Scassellati B (1999) How to build robots that make friends and influence people. In: Proceedings 1999 IEEE/RSJ international conference on intelligent robots and systems. Human and environment friendly robots with high intelligence and emotional quotients (Cat. No. 99CH36289), vol 2. IEEE, pp 858–863

Breazeal C, Velásquez J (1998) Toward teaching a robot 'infant' using emotive communication acts. In: Proceedings of the 1998 simulated adaptive behavior workshop on socially situated intelligence. Citeseer, pp 25–40

Breazeal CL (2004) Designing sociable robots. MIT Press

Burgard W, Cremers AB, Fox D, Hähnel D, Lakemeyer G, Schulz D, Steiner W, Thrun S (1998) The interactive museum tour-guide robot. In: Aaai/iaai, pp 11–18

Cavanagh JF, Frank MJ (2014) Frontal theta as a mechanism for cognitive control. Trends Cognit Sci 18(8):414–421

Dautenhahn K, Walters M, Woods S, Koay KL, Nehaniv CL, Sisbot A, Alami R, Siméon T (2006) How may i serve you? a robot companion approaching a seated person in a helping context. In: Proceedings of the 1st ACM SIGCHI/SIGART conference on human-robot interaction, pp 172–179

Dautenhahn K, Nehaniv CL, Walters ML, Robins B, Kose-Bagci H, Assif N, Blow M, et al (2009) Kaspar–a minimally expressive humanoid robot for human–robot interaction research. Appl Bion Biomech 6(3, 4):369–397

Do HM, Mouser CJ, Gu Y, Sheng W, Honarvar S, Chen T (2013) An open platform telepresence robot with natural human interface. In: 2013 IEEE international conference on cyber technology in automation, control and intelligent systems. IEEE, pp 81–86

Edwards A, Edwards C, Westerman D, Spence PR (2019) Initial expectations, interactions, and beyond with social robots. Comput Human Behav 90:308–314

Evers V, Menezes N, Merino L, Gavrila D, Nabais F, Pantic M, Alvito P, Karreman D (2014) The development and real-world deployment of frog, the fun robotic outdoor guide. In: Proceedings of the 2014 ACM/IEEE international conference on human-robot interaction, p 100

Fridin M (2014) Storytelling by a kindergarten social assistive robot: a tool for constructive learning in preschool education. Comput Edu 70:53–64

Fridin M, Belokopytov M (2014) Robotics agent coacher for cp motor function (rac cp fun). Robotica 32(8):1265–1279

Graf B, Hans M, Schraft RD (2004) Care-o-bot ii-development of a next generation robotic home assistant. Autonom Robots 16(2):193–205

Hoffman G, Weinberg G (2010) Shimon: an interactive improvisational robotic marimba player. In: CHI'10 extended abstracts on human factors in computing systems, pp 3097–3102

Ivanov SH (2016) Will robots substitute teachers? In: 12th international conference "Modern science, business and education", pp 27–29

Kanda T, Shiomi M, Miyashita Z, Ishiguro H, Hagita N (2009) An affective guide robot in a shopping mall. In: Proceedings of the 4th ACM/IEEE international conference on human robot interaction, pp 173–180

Kosuge K, Hayashi T, Hirata Y, Tobiyama R (2003) Dance partner robot-ms dancer. In: Proceedings 2003 IEEE/RSJ international conference on intelligent robots and systems (IROS 2003) (Cat. No. 03CH37453), vol 4. IEEE, pp 3459–3464

Li J, Kizilcec R, Bailenson J, Ju W (2016) Social robots and virtual agents as lecturers for video instruction. Comput Human Behav 55:1222–1230

Lu VN, Wirtz J, Kunz WH, Paluch S, Gruber T, Martins A, Patterson PG (2020) Service robots, customers and service employees: what can we learn from the academic literature and where are the gaps? J Ser Theory Pract

Makatchev M, Fanaswala I, Abdulsalam A, Browning B, Ghazzawi W, Sakr M, Simmons R (2010) Dialogue patterns of an arabic robot receptionist. In: 2010 5th ACM/IEEE international conference on human-robot interaction (HRI). IEEE, pp 167–168

Milliez G (2018) Buddy: a companion robot for the whole family. In: Companion of the 2018 ACM/IEEE international conference on human-robot interaction, p 40

Mishra N, Ramanathan M, Satapathy R, Cambria E, Magnenat-Thalmann N (2019) Can a humanoid robot be part of the organizational workforce? a user study leveraging sentiment analysis. In: 2019 28th IEEE international conference on robot and human interactive communication (RO-MAN). IEEE, pp 1–7

Money R, Newman M, Hanson J (2007) On-line interview processing. US Patent App 11/400,547

Moravec HP (2020) H.p. (2020) robot. Encyclopedia britannica. https://www.britannica.com/technology/robot-technology

Munkeby SH, Jones D, Bugg G, Smith K (2002) Applications for the matilda robotic platform. In: Unmanned ground vehicle technology IV, vol 4715, pp 206–213. International Society for Optics and Photonics

Nourbakhsh I, Hamner E, Lauwers T, Bernstein D, Disalvo C (2006) A roadmap for technology literacy and a vehicle for getting there: educational robotics and the terk project. In: ROMAN 2006—the 15th IEEE international symposium on robot and human interactive communication. IEEE, pp 391–397

Odashima T, Onishi M, Tahara K, Takagi K, Asano F, Kato Y, Nakashima H, Kobayashi Y, Mukai T, Luo Z, et al. (2006) A soft human-interactive robot ri-man. In: 2006 IEEE/RSJ international conference on intelligent robots and systems. IEEE, p 1

O'brien M (2019) Will robots take your job? quarter of us workers at risk. AP News

Patrizia M, Claudio M, Leonardo G, Alessandro P (2009) A robotic toy for children with special needs: from requirements to design. In: 2009 IEEE international conference on rehabilitation robotics. IEEE, pp 918–923

Petersen K, Solis J, Takanishi A (2010) Musical-based interaction system for the waseda flutist robot. Autonom Robots 28(4):471–488

Ramanathan M, Mishra N, Thalmann NM (2019) Nadine humanoid social robotics platform. In: Computer graphics international conference. Springer, pp 490–496

Rossi P, Fedeli L, Biondi S, Magnoler P, Bramucci A, Lancioni C (2015) The use of video recorded classes to develop teacher professionalism: the experimentation of a curriculum. J e-Learn Know Soc 11(2)

Sapiński T, Kamińska D, Pelikant A, Anbarjafari G (2019) Emotion recognition from skeletal movements. Entropy 21(7):646

Savage M (2019) Meet tengai, the job interview robot who won't judge you. BBC Online 12

Schneider DR, Van Den Blink C (2006) An introduction to the nasa robotics alliance cadets program. National defense education and innovation initiative report

Shibata T, Yoshida M, Yamato J (1997) Artificial emotional creature for human-machine interaction. In: 1997 IEEE international conference on systems, man, and cybernetics. Computational cybernetics and simulation, vol 3. IEEE, pp 2269–2274

Shotton J, Fitzgibbon A, Cook M, Sharp T, Finocchio M, Moore R, Kipman A, Blake A (2011) Real-time human pose recognition in parts from single depth images. In: CVPR 2011. IEEE, pp 1297–1304

Stock RM, Merkle M (2017) A service robot acceptance model: user acceptance of humanoid robots during service encounters. In: 2017 IEEE international conference on pervasive computing and communications workshops (PerCom Workshops). IEEE, pp 339–344

Sugano S, Kato I (1987) Wabot-2: autonomous robot with dexterous finger-arm–finger-arm coordination control in keyboard performance. In: Proceedings of 1987 IEEE international conference on robotics and automation, vol 4. IEEE, pp 90–97

Syrdal DS, Dautenhahn K, Koay K, Walters M (2009) The negative attitudes towards robots scale and reactions to robot behaviour in a live human-robot interaction study

Urgen BA, Plank M, Ishiguro H, Poizner H, Saygin AP (2013) Eeg theta and mu oscillations during perception of human and robot actions. Front Neurorobot 7:19

Wada K, Shibata T (2007) Living with seal robots-its sociopsychological and physiological influences on the elderly at a care house. IEEE Trans Robot 23(5):972–980

Weller C (2017) Meet the first-ever robot citizen, a humanoid named sophia that once said it would destroy humans. Business Insider Nordic Haettu 30:2018

Yamazaki A, Yamazaki K, Ohyama T, Kobayashi Y, Kuno Y (2012) A techno-sociological solution for designing a museum guide robot: regarding choosing an appropriate visitor. In: 2012 7th ACM/IEEE international conference on human-robot interaction (HRI). IEEE, pp 309–316

Miller P (2016) Professor Pranksman fools his students with a TA powered by IBM's Watson. Available at: http://www.theverge.com/2016/5/6/11612520/ta-powered-by-ibm-watson (Accessed 18th May 2016)

Printed in the United States
by Baker & Taylor Publisher Services